LEARNING THEORIES FOR TEACHERS

Fifth Edition

LEARNING THEORIES FOR TEACHERS

Fifth Edition

Morris L. Bigge
California State University, Fresno

S. Samuel Shermis
Purdue University

HarperCollins*Publishers*

Executive Editor: Christopher Jennison

Full-Service Manager: Michael Weinstein

Production Coordinator: Cindy Funkhouser

Text Design: Merry Obrecht; Publication Services, Inc.

Cover Design: Publication Services, Inc.

Cover Illustration: Darrin Drda; Publication Services, Inc.

Production Manager: Priscilla Taguer

Compositor: Publication Services, Inc.

Printer and Binder: R. R. Donnelley & Sons Company

Cover Printer: The Lehigh Press, Inc.

Learning Theories for Teachers, Fifth Edition

Library of Congress Cataloging-in-Publication Data

Bigge, Morris L.
    Learning theories for teachers / Morris L. Bigge, S. Samuel
Shermis. —5th ed.
        p.   cm.
    Includes bibliographical references and index.
    ISBN 0-06-040674-7
    1. Learning. 2. Cognitive learning. I. Shermis, S. Samuel.
II. Title.
LB1060.B54 1991
370.15′23—dc20
                                                    91-30445
                                                    CIP

95 94   9 8 7 6 5 4

Contents

14/HOW ARE TEACHING-LEARNING THEORIES RELATED TO COMPUTER EDUCATION? 306

Index 323

Preface

This book is designed for use as a text in both graduate and undergraduate courses in *learning theory, educational psychology,* or *psychological foundations of education.* It should also prove useful as a supplementary text in other courses that emphasize the nature of contrasting psychologies of learning. The objective of the volume is to provide both prospective and in-service teachers, as well as other school personnel at all levels, with a comprehensive picture of modern learning theories in as readable a style as possible without oversimplifying the basic tenets, similarities, and differences of most of the important contemporary learning theories.

The text describes learning theories in such a way as to guide readers in critically constructing and evaluating their outlooks regarding the nature of the learning process and formulating their optimum roles in its promotion. Thus, it is written with the intent to contribute to a long-range sense of direction that will be conducive to more effective teaching.

We do not claim complete impartiality; our sympathy lies with the cognitive-interactionist theories of learning. Nevertheless, every effort has been made to provide a balanced treatment of learning theories. Consequently, the book should be equally usable by professors and students with various theoretical commitments. Actually, each theory is presented much as if we were adherents of that point of view. The volume contains occasional critical comments, but evaluations are usually weighted toward supporting the theory being presented. In most cases it is left much to the readers to discern the weaknesses of each theory in relation to contrasting ones.

Because a truly comparative approach to learning theory is necessarily semihistorical, this volume treats respective learning theories semihistorically as well as comparatively. The historical analysis is developed so as to help readers grasp and clarify points of confusion in modern education. Many contemporary educational principles and practices are rooted in frequently incompatible premises about the nature of humankind and its relationships with its physical-social environment. By recounting how psychological assumptions and theories arose and have evolved over time, the book helps readers see why the theories exist and the directions in which they point. Since some earlier theories of learning continue to influence today's teaching, they, as well as contemporary learning theories, are also considered.

Because psychological study centers on individuals, it is often necessary in its pursuance to use the generic third person pronouns. Yet, unfortunately, to date, no truly generic singular third person pronoun has been established. Since the use of *he, him,* and *his* for this purpose has been customarily and grammatically sanctioned, usage of these words seems to contribute to easy comprehension. Nevertheless, such usage definitely has its faults. In light of these facts, we have established the following ground rule: *In each sentence throughout the book, the first time a generic* he *is used it is to be followed by a diagonal slash and* she, *as follows:* he/she. *This indicates that the pronoun is used in a completely generic sense to mean* a person, *not a particular sex. In all other parts of the book as well, the pronouns* he, him, *and* his *are also intended to refer to a person in a generic sense. The reader should constantly bear this in mind as he/she reads the book.*

The general plan of the book is as follows: Chapter 1 lists the learning theories that are to be treated and introduces readers to various possible assumptions about the basic nature of humankind that underpin learning theories. Chapter 2 presents the more prominent representatives of learning theory originating before the twentieth century—mental discipline, natural unfoldment, and apperception—and develops their implications for current school practice. Chapter 3 introduces the two major contrasting twentieth-century "families" of learning theory—stimulus-response conditioning and cognitive interactionist theories. It also provides background by explaining how the families arose and how each relates to mechanistic and relativistic outlooks. Chapter 4 focuses on the specific explanation of learning that each contemporary family offers.

Chapters 5 through 9, written to give readers a "feel" for how psychologists think and work within their respective points of view, are more technical and specific than are Chapters 3 and 4. Chapter 5 describes the leading systematic, contemporary version of S-R conditioning theory or neobehaviorism: B. F. Skinner's *operant conditioning.* Professor Skinner presented his psychology as the great hope for improvement of current instructional techniques.

Many contemporary educators hold eclectic positions in regard to the nature of the learning process; they do not adhere to any one position. To represent this approach, in Chapter 6 we describe Jerome S. Bruner's cognitive-oriented eclectic learning theory. In Chapter 7 we develop Albert Bandura's systematic linear cognitive-interactionist social cognitive learning theory. Then in Chapters 8 and 9 we develop a contemporary, systematic cognitive field interactionist psychology as a leading current representative of the cognitive-interactionist family and apply its concepts to learning situations.

Chapter 10 describes the outlook in regard to *transfer of learning* that harmonizes with each learning theory. Its content grows directly from, and thereby constitutes a summary of, the content of earlier chapters. Chapters 11, 12, and 13 develop the relationships of the various learning theories to classroom practices. Chapter 11 centers upon the role of teachers in relation to the culture and their students, and the four levels of learning and teaching: autonomous development, memory, explanatory understanding, and exploratory understanding. It then treats the first two levels in some detail and develops the psychological meaning of the term *understanding*. Chapter 12 offers concrete directives for explanatory-understanding level teaching. A section of the chapter is devoted to Benjamin S. Bloom's and James H. Block's currently emphasized "mastery teaching."

Chapter 13 introduces the exploratory-understanding level of teaching and learning and its two basic investigative and reflective processes. It next reviews cognitive-interactionist psychology as presented in Chapter 7, on linear cognitive interaction, and Chapters 8 and 9, on cognitive-field interaction. Chapter 13 then shows how these psychologies underpin an exploratory-understanding level of teaching and learning. It next gives examples of both investigative and reflective teaching. It then develops the five aspects of reflective teaching and applies them to teaching the meaning of *race* and relates different evaluation procedures to the reflective level of teaching and learning.

Chapter 14 first describes how computers work and how their use may underpin different psychological approaches to teaching and learning through relating specific learning theories to computer education. The last section of the chapter specifically relates computer use to the exploratory-understanding level of teaching and learning.

There are so many people to whom we are indebted for their contributions that any attempt to name all of them would be futile. These include our former professors, especially the late Dr. T. L. Collier of Washburn University and the late Dr. Ernest E. Bayles of the University of Kansas, and former students, both graduate and undergraduate.

Dr. William B. Lieurance has contributed significantly to the explanation of reflective teaching in Chapter 13. Dr. June Lee Bigge, Professor Jeanette Bigge, and the late Dr. Maurice P. Hunt have made unique contributions to the development of this manuscript. Also, Lulla Shermis and Ruth Lehnert Bigge have greatly enhanced the quality of this book—Mrs. Shermis by reading and refining the meanings of expressions within the manuscript and by her indexing, and Mrs. Bigge by checking the grammatical accuracy and structure of sentences and by typing the additions to this fifth edition.

Although considerable assistance was received from all these individuals, we assume complete responsibility for the quality of the finished product.

Morris L. Bigge
S. Samuel Shermis

LEARNING THEORIES FOR TEACHERS

Fifth Edition

Chapter
1

Why Is Classroom Learning a Problem?

*L*asting changes in persons occur within the processes of maturation, learning, or a combination of the two.

Maturation is a developmental process within which a person from time to time manifests different traits whose "blueprints" have been carried in the person's cells from the time of conception. *Learning,* in contrast with maturation, is an enduring change in a living individual that is not heralded by genetic inheritance. It may be considered a change in insights, behavior, perception, or motivation, or a combination of these; learning always involves a systematic change in behavior or behavioral disposition that occurs as a consequence of experience in some specified situation.[1]

> Learning is basic to the development of athletic prowess, of tastes in food and dress, and of the appreciation of art and music. It contributes to ethnic prejudice, to drug addiction, to fear, and to pathological maladjustment. It produces the miser and the philanthropist, the bigot and the patriot. In short, it influences our lives at every turn, accounting in part for the best and worst of human beings and for the best and worst in each of us.[2]

Since teachers can do little to influence the maturational patterns of students except, perhaps, to accelerate or retard them to some degree, their most effectual area of endeavor always centers upon learning. Furthermore, because of humans' unique traits and capacities, learning is far more crucial to them than it is to the lower animals.

Human beings have some distinguishing characteristics that give a unique quality to a study of them. First, they talk and are *time-binding* individuals; *time binding* means that both a past and a future enter into their present perception of things. Second, they have a highly developed imaginative capacity. Also, they are cultural beings, building on their past in a peculiarly selective fashion. Then, people have a unique capacity for social interaction with their fellows, which enables them to transcend concrete situations and to live in a more or less imaginative realm. And most significantly, human beings, in their perceptual processes, may view themselves simultaneously as both subject and object, as knower and as known.

Whereas in the lower animals much behavior is instinctive, human children, benefiting from their high degree of plasticity, learn their many patterns of human behavior. The relatively long period of children's dependency upon adults, following their complete helplessness at birth, contributes to their acquisition of the culture of their group. Using their relatively high potential for intelligence and their capacity for communication through use of articulate speech and other symbols, members of each generation build upon the achievements—artifacts, ideas, customs, and traditions—of the preceding generation. A culture—social heritage—of a society is the result of many generations of cumulative learning.

People share with other mammals some primary organic drives, such as hunger, thirst, sex, and cravings for oxygen, warmth, and rest, and possibly a few primary aversions such as fear and rage. The first expression of these drives and aversions is primarily a maturational process, but in some way human beings seem to transcend these hereditary drives and aversions. Largely, this transcendence is centered in the human capacity to deal with a complex past, present, and future world so as to develop abstractions or generalizations that organize mazes of particulars into sensible patterns. Perhaps a desire to perceive, understand, imagine, and deal with ideas is just as much a part of people's basic nature as are the specific organic drives and aversions. Biologically, *Homo sapiens*—the human being—is a species of mammal characterized by superior knowing and discerning abilities.

Apparently, there is no group of human beings that has not, through learning, developed some devices for enriching its contacts with its surrounding world. In the development of these devices, people have attempted to derive satisfactions from understanding and manipulating their world as well as through merely touching, smelling, and tasting its various aspects. Moreover, contrasted with the capacities of less advanced animals, people's potential for becoming human lies largely in their capacity for extension of experience to a world of symbolism—to operate on an imaginative level of reality.

Animals seem to derive satisfaction from using whatever abilities they have. Accordingly, human beings derive satisfaction from using both their innate and acquired abilities. Thus, the very process of learning, both concrete and abstract, can become satisfying to them. In their social, aesthetic, economic, religious, and political life they show a tendency to explore. Not all people develop sophisticated ideological outlooks. But rarely if ever are there groups of people who subsist solely on a vegetative level with no imaginative or mentalistic endeavors. Even the most primitive cultures have developed some symbolistic folklore and ideology.

Not only have people wanted to learn, but often their curiosity has impelled them to try to learn *how* they learn. Since ancient times, at least some members of every civilized society have developed, and to some degree tested, ideas about the nature of the learning process. Thus, they have developed their respective learning theories.

WHAT IS A LEARNING THEORY?

A learning theory is a systematic, integrated outlook in regard to the nature of the process whereby people relate to their environments in such a way as to enhance their ability to use both themselves and their environments more effectively. Everyone who teaches or professes to teach has some sort of theory of learning. However, teachers may be able to describe their theories in explicit terms or they may not—in which case we usually can deduce from their actions the theories that they are not yet able to verbalize. Thus, the important question is not whether a teacher has a theory of learning but, rather, how tenable it is.

Quite often in our scientific age we erroneously think of theory as indefinite or indefensible conjecture that existed prior to the use of scientific method and evidence. Consequently, although we might not object to using the term in a description of the historical development of modern concepts of learning, we would expect the word *fact* rather than *theory* to be used in describing the current scene. After all, are we not now on solid enough ground for the term *theory* to be discarded? This, however, is not the case; theory definitely should not be abolished.

Any sharp distinction between theoretical, imaginative knowledge and the action that stems from such knowledge is faulty. Action, whether a part of teaching or any other activity in life, is either linked with theory or it is blind and purposeless. Consequently, any purposeful action is governed by theory. Learning theory is a distinct area within theoretical psychology.

Since the seventeenth century, many psychologists have concentrated upon developing systematic learning theories supported by experimentation. During this period more or less systematic theories of learning have emerged periodically to challenge existing theories. In recent years, much research of educational psychologists has centered upon problems relevant to cognitive, motivational, perceptual, memory, coding, and psycholinguistic processes within prevailing theories of learning. Now however, there is a growing interest in developing learning theories that are more comprehensive than earlier ones. After reviewing the current psychological scene, W. K. Estes recently wrote:

> I anticipate that the strongest current of opinion will swing back toward the main line of continuing sustained effort toward general theory, but perhaps with better perspective as to the ways in which this goal may be realized in psychology as compared to other sciences. For example, ... there is in fact more generality in cognitive theory than we ordinarily appreciate, commonality of ideas often being obscured by variations in labels.[3]

Typically, a new theory of learning is not translated into educational practice until 25 years or more have elapsed. Then, as a new theory eventually comes to affect educational policy and procedures, it usually does not replace its predecessors; it merely competes with them. Thus, as new theories have been introduced, they have been added to the old, and the educational scene has become more and more complex. Many teachers, from time to time, have adopted conflicting features from a variety of learning theories without ever realizing that they were basically contradictory in nature and could not be brought into harmony with each other.

WHY ARE THERE THEORIES OF LEARNING?

In most life situations, learning is not much of a problem. Most (lay) persons take it for granted that we learn from experience and let it go at that; they see little that is problematic about learning. Throughout human history, people have learned, in most cases without troubling themselves as to the nature of the process. Parents have taught children; master workers have taught apprentices. Both children and apprentices learned, and those who taught them felt little need for a grasp of learning theory. Teaching was done by "teachers" telling and showing students how, complimenting the learners when they did well, and scolding or punishing them when they did poorly. Teachers simply taught the way that they had been taught as children, youth, or apprentices.

When schools were developed as special environments to facilitate learning, teaching ceased to be so simple. The subjects taught in school were different from the matters learned as part of routine life in a tribe or society. Mastering school subjects, whether the three R's, foreign languages, geometry, history, or other study, appeared to children as an entirely different sort of learning task from those taken for granted in everyday life. Often their relevance to the problems of daily living seemed unclear. Hence, they struck a learner as quite different from the crafts and skills needed to carry on day-by-day social, economic, and political life.

Ever since education became formalized in schools, teachers have been aware that learning is school is frequently highly inefficient. For example, material to be learned may be presented to students innumerable times without noticeable results. Many students may appear uninterested; many may become rebellious and make serious trouble for teachers. Consequently, classrooms have often seemed like battlegrounds in which teachers and students made war against each other. Such a state of affairs may come to be taken for granted by teachers, students, and parents. Consequently, they may consider it "natural" that youngsters dislike school and try to resist school learning.

From the colonial period through the nineteenth century, most people in the United States probably made such placid assumptions concerning formal education. However, as soon as the professions of psychology and education developed, it was inevitable that professionals would begin asking questions. When teaching moved from the mother's knee to a formalized environment designed to promote learning, it was inescapable that some persons would begin speculating about whether schools were getting the best possible results. Then, professional psychologists and educators who critically analyzed school practices found that development of more or less systematic schools of thought in psychology offered a handy tool for crystallization of their thinking. Each of these schools of thought has contained, explicitly or implicitly, a theory of learning. In turn, a given theory of learning has implied a set of classroom practices. Thus, the way in which educators build curriculums, select materials, and choose instructional techniques depends, to a large degree, upon how they define "learning." Hence, a theory of learning may function as an analytical tool, being used by its exponents to judge the quality of a particular classroom situation.

Psychology is not a field of study characterized by a body of theory that is internally consistent and accepted by all psychologists. Rather, it is an area of knowledge characterized by the presence of several schools of thought. In some instances these may supplement one another, but at other times they are in open disagreement. Thus, we may find Psychologist X, who is both scholarly and sincere, opposed to many of the crucial ideas of Psychologist Y, who is equally scholarly and sincere. Such disagreement among psychologists may be disconcerting to students. But one of the challenges of psychological study lies in theoretical disagreement; only to the degree that students are willing to think for themselves can they emerge from their studies with something worthwhile. There is some consolation in the fact that similar disagreements also exist in the various sciences. Gaining an understanding and appreciation of the achievements of thinkers in any area is never easy. As stated by Taube, "After all, if the fox twists and turns, so must the hound."[4]

Everything teachers do is colored by the psychological theory they hold. Consequently, teachers who do not make use of a systematic body of theory in their day-by-day decisions are behaving blindly; little evidence of long-range rationale, purpose, or plan is observable in their teaching. Thus, teachers without a strong theoretical orientation inescapably make little more than busy-work assignments. True, many teachers operate in this way and use only a hodge-podge of methods without theoretical orientation. However, this muddled kind of teaching undoubtedly is responsible for many of the current adverse criticisms of public education.

Yet teachers need not base their thinking on tradition and folklore. Instead, they may be quite aware of the most important theories developed by educational psychologists, in which case their own psychological theory is likely to be quite sophisticated. The latter state of affairs is what professional psychologists interested in education of teachers are trying to induce. Teachers who are well grounded in scientific psychology—in contrast to "folklore psychology"—have a basis for making decisions that are much more likely to lead to effectual results in classrooms.

As a student, you may not have a broad background of either practical experience or "book knowledge" to bring to bear on the question of how children and youth learn. Nevertheless, even before reading further in this book, you should realize that there are some resources on which you can draw. All your life, you have been learning and continuing to do so, and you have been associating with others who were also learning, often from you. What seems to be the essential nature of the process called learning? What happens within, or to, you when you learn? Does the same thing happen to everyone? It probably would be helpful now to take paper and pen and write a one- or two-page essay on this subject. (You may not find this an easy assignment!) Repeat the assignment when you have mastered this book and see the difference in your two essays.

This book deliberately presents several competing theories of learning, providing different answers to many of the questions that might be raised, so that students will become increasingly sophisticated about the "schools of thought" that exist in psychology today and understand how differently each attacks respective problems. The comparative or systematic treatment herein employed requires, among other things, that students do considerable thinking for themselves.

HOW ARE LEARNING THEORIES EVALUATED?

Thinking for oneself is never easy. However, it may be easier to do a respectable job of critical thought if one is clearly aware of two competing kinds of criteria for judging the answers to questions, namely, *authoritarian* and *scientific*. Think about any statement that you consider to be true. Do you regard it as true merely because you read it somewhere or heard some teacher or other "authority" say it or because, when you examined all the available pertinent evidence, it seemed to have more factual support than any alternative statement? If you accept the statement "on faith" because someone told it to you, you have used an authoritarian criterion for judging truth. If you accept it because you have either pursued your own careful investigations of it or studied the investigations of others, you are operating within a more scientific framework.

Though we recognize the distinction between authoritarian and scientific approaches, the road to inquiry may still not be smooth. Often we are required to reach conclusions before we have had sufficient time either to conduct our own investigation or to study critically the investigations made by those who pose as authorities. In such cases we have no choice except to take someone else's word for it. Whose word do we take? In answering questions in psychology, we might turn to the writings of the most prominent psychologists. But, unfortunately, prominence does not guarantee validity. Less well-known persons may be more nearly right. Furthermore, in the field of psychology it is common for top-ranking authorities, who have spent lifetimes in research, to disagree. Such disagreement is, in part, the result of differing basic assumptions.

There are no final answers to questions concerning learning, and no theory can be found to be absolutely superior to all others. Nevertheless, teachers can develop learning theories of their own that, because of their internal *harmony* and data-based *adequacy*, they can support. Such theories may turn out to be somewhat replicas of those introduced in this book or, readers may benefit by contributions of several theories and derive one of their own. In either event, the quality of their teaching will be enhanced by their thinking through the question of the nature of the learning process that teachers want to promote in students.

Through study of theories of learning and their historical development, teachers should gain insight into the harmonies and conflicts that prevail in present educational theory. Through this insight, they should move toward developing adequate theories of their own. Before attempting to formulate their own learning theory, they would do well to examine carefully and critically the prevalent theories that have been developed by professionals in the area.

WHAT LEARNING THEORIES ARE REFLECTED IN SCHOOL PRACTICE?

In the remaining section of this chapter, we present an abbreviated sketch of the major lines along which learning theory has developed and provide an example of teaching nonreaders to read using each. Then, in Chapters 2 through 10, we develop each line of thought in considerable detail. At least ten different theories in regard to the basic nature of the learning process are either prevalent in today's schools or advocated by leading contemporary psychologists. Table 1.1 lists the ten major theories, groups some of them into families, and outlines the concepts involved. As students pursue the study of learning and teaching, they should find it helpful to refer to this table frequently.

What Leading Learning Theories Originated Before the Twentieth Century?

Column I of Table 1.1 lists ten learning theories. The first four, namely, the two *mental discipline* theories of the mind substance family, *natural unfoldment* or *self-actualization,* and *apperception* were developed prior to the twentieth century but continue to be highly influential in today's schools. Chapter 2 is devoted to an explanation and evaluation of these first four theories.

Mental discipline, of both kinds, means that learning consists of students' minds being disciplined or trained. In teaching nonreaders to read, teachers who are committed to mental discipline teach in such a way as to exercise the "muscles" of students' minds. These teachers would list words that they wanted students to be able to recognize, read, and spell, using flash cards in teaching them. They would drill their students extensively, test them daily, and have the low achievers return after school for further drill.

There would be "recitations," within which students would be drilled orally and take turns reading passages of their daily lessons. Those who did poorly would be scolded when they made mistakes, and some would be sent to their seats to "study." Students would be driven to stay with their lessons, thereby strengthening their perseverance and willpower. Strict discipline would be maintained in order to strengthen the faculty of attention as well as those of memory, will, and perseverance. The teacher would have little hesitation in using various kinds of physical and mental punishment, as the situation required.

Table 1.1 REPRESENTATIVE THEORIES OF LEARNING AND THEIR IMPLICATIONS
FOR EDUCATION

	Theory of Learning I	Psychological System or Outlook II	Conception of Humankind's Moral and Actional Nature III
Mental discipline theories of mind substance family	1. Theistic mental discipline	Faculty psychology	*Bad-active* mind substance continues active until curbed
	2. Humanistic mental discipline	Classical humanism	*Neutral-active* mind substance to be developed through exercise
	3. Natural unfoldment or self-actualization	Romantic naturalism or existential humanism	*Good-active* natural personality to unfold
	4. Apperception or Herbartianism	Structuralism	*Neutral-passive* mind composed of active mental states or ideas
S–R (stimulus-response) conditioning theories of behavioristic family	5. S–R bond	Connectionism	*Neutral-passive* organism with many possible S R connections
	6. Conditioning with no reinforcement	Classical conditioning	*Neutral-passive* biological organism with innate reflexes
	7. Conditioning through reinforcement	Instrumental conditioning	*Neutral-passive* biological organism with innate reflexes and drive stimuli
Interactionist theories of cognitive family	8. Goal insight	Gestalt psychology or configurationalism	*Neutral-interactive* individual in sequential relationships with environment
	9. Linear cognitive interaction	Social cognitive theory	*Neutral-interactive* purposive person in sequential relationship with environment
	10. Cognitive-field interaction	Field psychology or positive relativism	*Neutral-interactive* person in simultaneous mutual interaction with environment

Table 1.1 (*CONTINUED*)

Basis for Transfer of Learning IV	Emphasis in Teaching V	Key Persons VI	Contemporary Exponents VII
Exercised faculties automatic transfer	Exercise of faculties of the mind	St. Augustine J. Calvin J. Edwards	Many Hebraic-Christian fundamentalists
Cultivated mind or intellect	Training of intrinsic mental power	Plato Aristotle R. M. Hutchins	M. J. Adler Allan Bloom H. S. Broudy
Recapitulation of racial history, no transfer needed	Negative or permissive education centered on feelings	J. J. Rousseau F. Froebel Progressivists	P. Goodman J. Holt A. H. Maslow
Growing apperceptive mass	Addition of new mental states or ideas to a store of old ones	J. F. Herbert E. B. Titchener	Many teachers and administrators
Identical elements	Promotion of acquisition of desired S-R connections	E. L. Thorndike	A. I. Gates J. M. Stephens
Conditioned responses or reflexes	Promotion of Adhesion of desired responses to appropriate stimuli	J. B. Watson	E. R. Guthrie
Reinforced or conditioned responses plus stimulus and response induction	Environmental changes to increase the probability of desired responses	C. L. Hull K. W. Spense	B. F. Skinner
Transposition of tested generalized insights	Promotion of learning by aiding students in developing high-quality insights	E. E. Bayles B. H. Bode W. Kohler R. H. Wheeler	S. S. Shermis
Expectancies that result from reciprocal person-environment interaction	Development of observationally reinforcing components of modeled learning	E. C. Tolman	A. Bandura B. Weiner H. S. Bowers N. I. Feather
Continuity of life spaces, experience, or insights	Help students insightfully restructure their life spaces — contemporaneous situations	K. Lewin J. Dewey G. Allport A. Ames, Jr.	E. L. Deci M. L. Bigge J. S. Bruner D. Snygg

Natural unfoldment or *self-actualization*—the extreme opposite of mental discipline—is a procedure within which a child unfolds what either Nature or a Creator has enfolded within him. Teachers who adhere to this position would first wait for students to express a desire to learn to read before they would make any attempt to teach them. Then, the teachers would be much more concerned with the children's maturational development than with inculcation of any specific skills. Furthermore, they would make sure that each child's learning was a joyous experience.

Apperception is a process of new ideas associating themselves with old ones that already constitute a mind. Apperceptionists would teach students to read by starting with the alphabet and making sure that the students could recognize and say each letter. They then would tell the students how letters are put together to make words, how letters make sounds, how sounds are telescoped together, and how vowels and consonants work. In other words, the teachers would give them some rules. Next, they would talk to them about things that they already knew, such as dogs, cats, boys, and girls. Then they would show them *d o g* and explain that it stands for dog. They would be concerned primarily with making reading interesting and being sure that their students got the right ideas from their reading.

What Are the Leading Twentieth-Century Learning Theories?

Twentieth-century systematic learning theories may be classified into two broad families, namely, *S-R* (stimulus-response) conditioning theories of the behavioristic family and *interactionist* theories of the cognitive family. Throughout this book, the expression *interactionist theory* implies a *cognitive* process.

In Table 1.1, entries 5, 6, and 7—S-R bond, conditioning with no reinforcement, and conditioning through reinforcement—are encompassed by the generalized concepts S-R *conditioning theory* and *behaviorism,* which may be used interchangeably. Likewise, entries 8, 9, and 10—goal insight, linear cognitive interaction, and cognitive-field interaction—are representatives of the cognitive-interactionist family.[5]

For behaviorists or S-R conditioning theorists, learning is a change in observable behavior, which occurs through stimuli and responses becoming related according to mechanistic principles. Thus, it involves the formation of relations of some sort between series of stimuli and responses. Stimuli—the causes of learning—are environmental agents that act upon an organism so as either to cause it to respond or to increase the probability of a response of a certain kind. Responses—effects—are physical reactions of an organism to either external or internal stimulation.

For cognitive interactionists, learning is a process of gaining or changing insights, outlooks, expectations, or thought patterns. In thinking about the learning processes of students, these theorists prefer the terms *person* to *organism, psychological environment* to *physical* or *biological environment,* and *interaction* to either *action* or *reaction*. Such preference is not merely a whim; there is a conviction that the concepts *person, psychological environment* and *interaction* are highly advantageous for teachers in describing learning processes. They enable a teacher to see a person, the person's environment, and the interaction between the two all occurring at once; this is the meaning of *field*.

To summarize the difference between the two families very briefly, whereas S-R conditioning theorists interpret learning in terms of changes in strength of S-R connections, associations, habits, or behavioral tendencies; cognitive interactionists define learning in terms of reorganization of perceptual or cognitive fields so as to gain understandings. Consequently, whereas a behavioristic teacher desires to change the observable behaviors of students in a significant way, a cognitive-interactionist teacher aspires to help students change their understandings of significant problems and situations.

Behavioristic teachers, in teaching nonreaders to read, would first develop a list of words that they want to incorporate into the working vocabularies of their students. Prior to the introduction of specific letter-sound relationships, they would probably teach students to read whole words and to express their meanings. Within the S-R conditioning process, students are taught using either one, or a combination, of two procedures, namely, the *stimulus substitution* method of classical conditioning or the *response modification* method of instrumental conditioning.

When using stimulus substitution, the teachers, in any way possible, would get their students to say a specific word; then they would give them the appropriate stimulus, in the form of the written word, just prior to their saying that word. Consequently, in the future, upon being stimulated by that written word, students would be likely to say it.

In response modification, or reinforcement, students would be given a "reward"; that is, their behavior would be reinforced whenever they either completed a word properly or filled in the proper word in a blank space. There would be "feedback" from the reinforcing "reward," which would increase the probability that, on future occasions, students would accurately read or write the completed or filled-in words.

Cognitive-interactionist oriented teachers, in teaching nonreaders to read, would set out to help them develop an intelligent "feel" for sound-symbol relationships. Hence, they would help students get the ideas that surround the use of words. Accordingly, teachers would spend a greater proportion of teaching time conversing with their students in regard to significant verbal relationships. Specifically, they would help students grasp the relation between individual letters and verbal sounds, blend verbal sounds that are represented by letter groupings, and learn that there are many phonetically regular words but also some irregular ones. Students' verbal skills would be in the form of learned insights in regard to such matters as rhyming, telescoping sounds together, and sounding out words that are encountered visually.

In deciding upon their outlook on learning, teachers have at least three kinds of choices:

1. They may, in both theory and practice, adhere to one systematic position as much as possible.
2. They may eclectically, that is, selectively, borrow ideas from the various conflicting positions and arrange the borrowed ideas into a mosaic or patchwork that is available to be drawn upon as needed.
3. They may develop harmonized *emergent syntheses* from their study of the conflicting positions and their respective ideas.

An *emergent* outlook is something novel that appears in the course of the evolution of ideas. It is not an intermediate position, but a new outlook or concept. When an emergent outlook reflects the results of the interplay or conflicting ideas in arriving at something new, it is a *synthesis*. Whereas one forms an *eclectic compromise* by selecting aspects of opposing theories and taking a position somewhere among them so as to form a mosaic pattern, one achieves an *emergent synthesis* by selecting and modifying knowledge from incompatible positions, adding new thinking as needed, and developing a new position that is internally consistent and still more adequate than its precursors. Hence, an emergent synthesis in learning theory is a somewhat new systematic outlook that benefits from the ideas that have been incorporated in the prevailing psychologies of learning but does not form a compromise between those ideas.

Whereas mental discipline, apperception, natural unfoldment, behaviorism, and Gestalt psychology may be considered traditional systematic positions, cognitive-interactionist learning theory has been developed as an emergent synthesis that both benefits by, and develops from, the conflicting outlooks of these earlier positions.

Chapters 3 and 4 discuss the differences between the two families of twentieth-century scientific learning theories. Then Chapters 5 through 9 describe representative systematic and eclectic theories. Chapter 5 contains the description of a prominent systematic psychology of learning that represents the behavioristic family—B. F. Skinner's *operant conditioning* theory. Since many of today's educators adhere to some sort of eclectic position in regard to the learning process, a teacher should have some idea of the forms that eclecticisms may take. Hence, Chapter 6 presents a leading "eclectic" position— Jerome Bruner's cognitive-oriented eclectic learning theory.

Chapter 7 develops a *linear* cognitive-interactionist theory as developed by Albert Bandura, who thinks that the consequences of one's past behavior largely determine one's future behavior, but mostly because of their informative and incentive values. Then Chapters 8 and 9 present cognitive-field interactionism, developed by your authors, as a process of *simultaneous mutual interaction* of persons and their psychological environments.

Since each of Chapters 5 through 9 is devoted to the presentation of a specific position on learning, all statements, even when they are not attributed to either the position or an adherent, should be taken to represent the respective position that is being presented in a chapter.

WHAT CONCEPTS CHARACTERIZE THE RESPECTIVE LEARNING THEORIES?

In addition to listing the ten learning theories, Table 1.1 catalogs the concepts that characterize each theory, together with some people who represent each one. It is difficult to make a sharp distinction between "key persons" (column VI) and "contemporary exponents" (column VII). However, the criterion for selection of key persons has been that they have made a major contribution to the theory under consideration.

Each learning theory represents a more or less comprehensive psychological system or basic outlook, and each has its unique approach to learning. Accordingly, column II of Table 1.1 describes systematic psychologies or basic outlooks that are reflected in each theory of learning. We allude to these psychologies or outlooks from place to place throughout the book as we treat learning, teaching, and related problems.[6] Column V of Table 1.1 contains the pivotal teaching concept of each learning theory. We now briefly outline the content of column III, which is expanded throughout the remainder of the book.

How May Teachers Picture the Innate Moral and Actional Nature of Students?

A teacher's outlook in regard to the nature of the learning process is greatly influenced by that teacher's view of the nature and source of human motivation. Such motivation arises from some kind of relationship of people and their respective environments. But what is the nature of this relationship? What is the basic moral and actional nature of human beings as it expresses itself through each individual's dealings with his environment? This question may be rephrased as, "What would children and youths be like if each should be left entirely on his own?" This is the raw material with which teachers must work. Although teachers may not have thought out their answers to this question, the way they teach inevitably implies some position in regard to its answer. In fact, each theory of learning, especially as it is applied in schools, is closely linked to a conception of the basic innate moral and actional nature of human beings. Hence, when teachers seriously consider how they are going to teach children and youths, they inevitably formulate some assumptions about the essential moral and actional nature of students as human beings. This is the topic of column III in Table 1.1 and also of Table 1.2 and Figure 1.1.

Teachers' conceptions of people's basic innate moral and actional nature involves the fundamental way in which they view their students. This, in turn, has a major influence upon the way that they operate in classrooms and how their students learn, as well as upon the outcomes of the learning. There are at least five distinctly different ways in which teachers may view their students. They may think that students are (1) innately bad individuals in need of discipline;

Table 1.2 ASSUMPTIONS ABOUT PEOPLE'S BASIC MORAL
          AND ACTIONAL NATURE AND THE LEARNING
          THEORIES THEY IMPLY

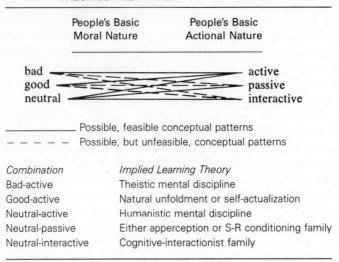

People's Basic
Moral Nature

People's Basic
Actional Nature

bad ——— active
good ——— passive
neutral ——— interactive

——————— Possible, feasible conceptual patterns
— — — — — Possible, but unfeasible, conceptual patterns

Combination	Implied Learning Theory
Bad-active	Theistic mental discipline
Good-active	Natural unfoldment or self-actualization
Neutral-active	Humanistic mental discipline
Neutral-passive	Either apperception or S-R conditioning family
Neutral-interactive	Cognitive-interactionist family

(2) neutral-active rational animals; (3) active, innately planned personalities that develop through unfoldment of their native instincts, needs, abilities, and talents; (4) passive/reactive minds or organisms whose development depends upon their being conditioned by outside forces; or (5) purposive persons who develop through their interaction with their respective psychological environments. The following three subsections are devoted to an explanation of the assumptions that a teacher may make in deciding to which of these alternatives to adhere.

It is essential to make clear that we are using the word *people* in a generic sense. It applies collectively to all members of the human species, and thus to all students at all levels of education and ability. Furthermore, as used here, *innate* and *basic* are synonymous adjectives; both mean "original" or "unlearned." Consideration of the basic nature of people would be quite simple were there but one answer. But, interestingly, there are several distinctly different and mutually opposed answers to this question, each enjoying a good deal of support. As students study this book, they should attempt to delineate their own positions in regard to this crucial problem.

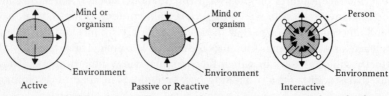

Figure 1.1 Models of mutually opposed assumptions in regard to the basic actional nature of people and their respective environmental relationships.

Each of the two aspects of the problem of people's basic nature has at least three possible alternatives. They may be stated as follows: In *basic moral nature* people are (1) innately *bad;* (2) innately *good;* or (3) innately *neutral,* that is, originally neither good nor bad. *Actionally,* in relationship to their environments, people are (1) innately *active;* (2) innately *passive* or *reactive;* or (3) basically *interactive.* Next, we review the nature of each set of alternatives and then describe their feasible combinations.

Three Alternate Assumptions Concerning People's Basic Moral Nature
If we assume people's moral nature to be innately bad, then we can expect nothing good from them. If left to themselves, their badness will naturally unfold; persons will show no traits other than bad ones. Conversely, if we assume that people are innately good, then unless they are corrupted by some outside force, everything that comes from them will be good. Assumed neutrality in people's basic moral nature simply means that by nature they are neither bad nor good but merely "potential," in a way that has no connection with innate badness or goodness. Notice that people's neutrality, as used here, refers only to the absence of innate goodness or badness; it in no sense means that students by nature are inactive.

Three Alternate Assumptions Concerning People's Actional Nature and Their Environmental Relationships   If, in actional nature, children and youth are taken to be *active,* then their underlying characteristics are inborn. Hence, their psychological natures come from within them. Environments only serve as locations for their natural unfoldment. Notice that persons merely moving physically are not necessarily being psychologically active. For persons to be psychologically active, their personal motive power must originate and be directed from within themselves. If persons are taken to be basically *passive* or *reactive,* their characteristics are largely a product of environmental influences. Thus, their natures are determined by their environments. This does not mean that people do not move about, but it does mean that they are nonpurposive and that their behavior is caused by forces from outside themselves.

If people are taken to be *interactive,* their psychological characteristics result from their making sense of their respective physical and social environments; their psychological natures arise from their personal-environmental relationships. Hence, one's psychological reality consists of that which one makes of what one gains through one's own unique experience. These three mutually opposed assumptions in regard to the nature of human beings and their environmental relationships may be illustrated by three models (Figure 1.1).

Five Alternate Combinations of Assumed Moral Natures with Assumed Actional Natures and Their Implied Environmental Relationships
When we consider the possible, feasible, combinations of assumptions concerning people's basic moral nature together with those concerning their actional relationship with their environment, we might reasonably assume the innate

natures of all students to be either bad-active, neutral-active, good-active, neutral-passive, or neutral-interactive (see Table 1.2).

Each of these assumptions in regard to the basic nature of students has definite implications for a theory of the learning process. If we assume students to be either bad-active or neutral-active, we will adhere to some form of mental discipline. This learning theory is described in the early part of Chapter 2 (pages 21–31). If we assume students are good-active, we will think of learning as natural unfoldment or self-actualization (see pages 31–32).

An assumption of neutral passivity may take the form of either mentalistic apperception or physicalistic stimulus-response conditioning theory. Apperception theory occupies the last section of Chapter 2 (pages 32–42). The different forms of S-R conditioning theory are discussed in Chapters 3 and 4. This theory is specifically represented by Skinner's operant conditioning theory, presented in Chapter 5.

The assumption that students are neutral-interactive is the pivotal thesis of cognitive-interactionist theories, which are described in Chapters 3 and 4 and specifically represented by linear cognitive interaction theory, described in Chapter 7, and cognitive-field interaction, treated in detail in Chapters 8 and 9.

The following quotations from Gordon W. Allport and Rollo May summarize the importance of our assumptions concerning people's basic nature.

> Theories of learning (like much else in psychology) rest on the investigator's conception of the nature of man. In other words, every learning theorist is a philosopher, though he may not know it. To put the matter more concretely, psychologists who investigate (and theorize about) learning start with some preconceived view of the nature of human motivation.[7]
>
> The critical battles between approaches to psychology . . . in our culture in the next decades, I propose, will be on the battleground of the image of man—that is to say, on the conceptions of man which underlie the empirical research.[8]

Next, we very briefly introduce the meanings of columns IV and V of Table 1.1.

What Is the Psychological Basis of Transfer of Learning to New Situations?

Transfer of learning, the subject of column IV of Table 1.1, is the relationship between a person's learning process and his ability to use what he/she has learned in future learning and life situations. Each learning theory has its correlative theory in regard to the nature of transfer and how it should be enhanced. Chapter 10 is devoted to the treatment of this subject. This, of course, is the key to the value of learning that occurs in schools. Schools should attempt to teach students in such a way that they not only accumulate many significant learnings applicable to life's situations but that they also develop a technique for acquiring new insights or understandings independently. These two goals of education constitute the realm of transfer.

What Are the Emphases in Teaching?

A book on learning theory, to be most meaningful to students, needs to treat, though in a theoretical manner, classroom application of psychological outlooks and principles. Such a treatment is the subject of Chapters 12, 13, and 14. Column V of Table 1.1 states the pivotal teaching concept of each learning theory. Although teaching theory, as such, is emphasized only in four chapters, readers will do well to consider it to some degree along with the subject matter of the chapters on learning.

By reading across each entry in Table 1.1, we can get a picture of ten different ways of looking at the problem of how students learn. For example, a person who embraces number 4, apperception, is committed to psychological *structuralism;* he/she assumes that students basically are of a *neutral-passive, mental* nature; his basis for transfer is the idea of *apperceptive mass;* in teaching, he emphasizes addition of new mental states or ideas to a store of old ones "housed" in the subconscious mind. The key historical persons in development of this outlook are J. F. Herbart and E. B. Titchener, and many teachers and administrators are, perhaps unknowingly, its contemporary exponents.

HOW IS PIAGET'S GENETIC EPISTEMOLOGY RELATED TO LEARNING THEORY?

Readers may wonder why a sizable section of this book is not devoted to presentation of the research and ideas of the eminent Swiss psychologist Jean Piaget (1896–1980). The reason is that Piaget was much more a developmental psychologist than a learning theorist. His studies of the nature of children of different ages can benefit teachers a great deal, providing they hold a tenable idea in regard to the nature of the learning process. For Piaget, the term *genetic* is synonymous with *developmental,* and *epistemology* is a theory of knowledge acquisition. Thus, his *genetic epistemology* is devoted to a study of the innate developmental stages of children as they relate to their acquisition of knowledge.

Piaget's studies are biologically oriented. Hence, he gives psychobiological factors preeminence and cultural learning factors only a secondary place in the explanation of human behavior. Accordingly, he wrote:

> There is no doubt that child psychology constitutes a kind of mental embryology not only as a description of the individual's stages of development but chiefly as the study of the very mechanisms of this development. Psychogenesis, moreover, represents an integral part of embryogenesis (which does not end at birth but on reaching the stage of equilibrium which is the adult state) and the intervention of social factors affects in no way the correctness of this statement, for organic embryogenesis is also partly a function of the milieu.[9]

For Piaget, the mental development of any child consists of a succession of three stages or periods: namely, sensorimotor, symbolic or preconcrete-operational, and concrete-operational. Each stage extends the preceding stage, reconstructs cognition on a new level, and comes to surpass the earlier stage. Then, during preadolescence and adolescence, the stage of *formal operations* emerges.

The key processes in the stages of child development are *assimilation* and *accommodation*. Assimilation consists of the filtering or modification of the input from the environment. In this process new knowledge meshes with the child's existing insights. Accommodation consists of the modification or change of the child's internal patterns of understanding to fit reality. In this process, existing internal insights are reconstructed so as to "accommodate" new data or information.

According to Piaget, during the sensorimotor stage (birth to 18 months or 2 years), a child lacks any symbolic function, therefore displaying only direct action on reality. During the symbolic or preconcrete-operational stage, which extends from 18 months to age 7 or 8, children are developing their abilities to represent things with symbols and to use differentiated signifiers of objects. Evidences of the development of these abilities are children's acquisition of language, their indications of dreams, their development of symbolic play, and their attempts at drawing and graphic representations.

On entering the stage of concrete operations (ages 7 or 8 to 12), children are learning to do in their heads what they had previously accomplished only through physical action. They are learning to think about things and thereby to deal with relations among classes of things. When well into this stage, children have become adept at doing thought problems and combining and dividing classes of concepts. These children internalize actions as related to objects, but they do not use verbally stated hypotheses. That ability appears during the stage of *formal operations* (ages 12 to 15),[10] when youths become able to think about their thoughts, construct ideals, reason realistically about the future, and reason about contrary-to-fact propositions. For example, they can think of "white" coal.[11]

HOW DO GAGNÉ'S *CONDITIONS OF LEARNING* CONSTITUTE MORE A METHOD OF INSTRUCTION THAN A THEORY OF LEARNING?

Sometimes Gagné's *Conditions of Learning* are taken to be an eclectic mechanistic theory of learning, but Gagné really outlines a plan for teaching and gives little attention to theories of learning. In his 1985 edition of *Conditions of Learning and Theory of Instruction,* Gagné states, "We shall not present a theory of learning but will draw some general concepts from previous theories."[12] Accordingly, Gagné's educational theory is centered, not upon any systematic theory of learning, but upon instruction through information processing. Gagné, Briggs, and Wagner, in their 1988 edition of *Principles of Instructional Design,*[13] continue to reflect this position.

In developing his information processing model of teaching, Gagné first lists five major categories of learning capabilities or educational outcomes. He next expands the meanings of the five categories through the use of eight conditions of learning or learning types. He then develops his nine principal instructional events.

Gagné's five major categories of learning capabilities or educational outcomes are intellectual skills, cognitive strategies, verbal information, motor skills, and attitudes.[14]

Gagné's eight *conditions of learning* or learning types are signal learning, stimulus-response learning, chaining, verbal association, discrimination learning, concept learning, rule learning, and mechanistic problem solving. He states that his describing eight varieties of learning implies "that there are eight corresponding kinds of changes in the nervous system which need to be identified and ultimately accounted for."[15] Also, from outside the organism, each variety seems clearly distinguishable from the others in terms of the conditions that must prevail for each to occur.

For Gagné, the nine principal instructional events are gaining attention, informing learners of the objective, stimulating recall of prior learning, presenting the stimulus, providing learning guidance, eliciting performance, providing feedback, and enriching retention and transfer.[16]

NOTES

1. W. K. Estes, *Handbook of Learning and Cognitive Processes, Volume I, Introduction to Concepts and Issues* (New York: Lawrence Erlbaum, 1975), p. 9.
2. Ernest R. Hilgard and Donald C. Marquis, *Conditioning and Learning*, 2d ed. (New York: Appleton-Century-Crofts, 1961), p. 10.
3. W. K. Estes, ed., *Handbook of Learning and Cognitive Processes, Volume VI, Linguistic Functions in Cognitive Theory*, Chapter 6, "On the Organization and Core Concepts of Learning Theory and Cognitive Psychology" (Hillsdale, NJ: Lawrence Erlbaum, 1978), p. 283.
4. Mortimer Taube, *Computers and Common Sense* (New York: Columbia University Press, 1961), p. 2.
5. W. K. Estes, *Handbook of Learning and Cognitive Processes, Volume I, Introduction to Concepts and Issues*, Chapter 1, "The State of the Field: General Problems and Issues of Theory and Metatheory," develops the history and current status of these theories.
6. The various systematic psychologies are described in Benjamin B. Wolman, *Contemporary Theories and Systems of Psychology* (New York: Harper & Row, 1960) and J. P. Chaplin and T. S. Krawiec, *Systems and Theories of Psychology*, 3d ed. (New York: Holt, Rinehart and Winston, 1974).
7. Gordon W. Allport, *Patterns and Growth in Personality* (New York: Holt, Rinehart and Winston, 1961), p. 84.
8. Rollo May, *Psychology and the Human Dilemma* (New York: Van Nostrand Reinhold, 1967), p. 90.
9. Jean Piaget, *Psychology and Epistemology* (New York: Grossman, 1971), p. 24.

10. See David Elkind, *Children and Adolescents: Interpretive Essays on Jean Piaget,* 2d ed. (New York: Oxford University Press, 1974), p. 23. Also, David Elkind, "Developmentally Appropriate Practice: Philosophical and Practical Implications," in *Phi Delta Kappan,* 71: (October 1989).
11. See Barry Gholson, *The Cognitive-Developmental Basis of Human Learning* (New York: Academic Press, 1980) for a current synthesis of Piaget's structural theory and information processing theory of developmental learning.
12. Robert M. Gagné, *The Conditions of Learning and Theory of Instruction,* 4th ed. (Fort Worth, TX: Holt, Rinehart and Winston, 1985), p. 2.
13. See Robert M. Gagné, Leslie J. Briggs, and Walter W. Wagner, *Principles of Instructional Design,* 3rd ed. (New York: Holt, Rinehart and Winston, 1988).
14. Gagné, *The Conditions of Learning,* 4th ed., pp. 68–69.
15. See Robert M. Gagné, *The Conditions of Learning,* 2nd ed. (New York: Holt, Rinehart and Winston, 1970), p. 62.
16. Gagné, *The Conditions of Learning,* 4th ed., pp. 246–255.

BIBLIOGRAPHY

The bibliography for Chapters 1 through 4 is at the end of Chapter 4.

Chapter
2

What Early Theories of Learning Are Reflected in Current School Practices?

*T*his chapter is devoted to three conceptions of the learning process that emerged prior to the twentieth century but continue to have great influence in today's schools: (1) *mental discipline*, (2) *natural unfoldment* or *self-actualization*, and (3) *apperception*. These three theories have one characteristic in common: All were developed as nonexperimental psychologies of learning. That is, their basic orientation is philosophical or speculative. The method used to develop these three conceptions of learning has been introspective and subjective. The philosopher-psychologists who evolved these theories tried to analyze their own thought processes and to describe in general terms what they thought they found. Since, according to mental-discipline theory, mental training is imparted by the *form* of studies as distinguished from their content, mental discipline is also called *formal discipline*. However, throughout this book we use *mental discipline* to denote this approach to learning.

WHAT IS MENTAL DISCIPLINE?

The central idea in mental discipline is that the mind, envisioned as a non-physical substance, lies dormant until it is exercised. Faculties of the mind such as memory, will, reason, and perseverance are the "muscles of the mind"; like physiological muscles, they are strengthened only through exercise, and subsequent to their adequate exercise they operate automatically. Thus, learning is a matter of strengthening, or disciplining, the faculties of the mind, which combine to produce intelligent behavior.

Adherents of mental discipline think that the primary value of history or any other disciplinary subject is the training effect it has on the minds of students. They are convinced that this effect will remain after the "learned" material has been forgotten. Furthermore, they consider the highest value of education to be its liberalizing effect. Education that is truly liberalizing prepares us not only to live in the world, but more important, to live with ourselves. James D. Koerner, a contemporary exponent of mental discipline, has written: "The purpose of [liberalizing] education is the harmonious development of the mind, the will, and the conscience of each individual so that he may use to the full of his intrinsic powers and shoulder the responsibilities of citizenship."[1]

According to the doctrine of mental discipline, a person is either a bad-active or neutral-active "rational animal," and education is a process of disciplining or training minds, which are the most essential aspects of persons. Proponents believe that in this disciplining process mental faculties are strengthened through exercise. Just as exercising an arm develops the biceps, exercise of mental faculties makes them more powerful. Choice of learning materials is of some importance but is always secondary to the nature of minds, which undergo the disciplinary process. Within mental discipline, persons are thought to be composed of two kinds of basic substances of realities, namely, rational minds and biological organisms. Thus, the concept "rational animal" is used in characterizing a human being. That which is disciplined or trained through education is *mind substance*.

What Is Mind Substance?

Mind substance is a self-dependent, immaterial essence or genuine being, which parallels the physical nature of human beings; it is just as real as matter, has a nature of its own, and operates in its own distinctive fashion. Furthermore, it usually is assigned the dominant position in a mind–body dualistic conception of humankind. Physical substance—rocks, buildings, plants, and animals—is characterized by extension in time and space; it has length, breadth, thickness, and mass. Mind substance, in contrast, is not extended; it has no length, breadth, thickness, or mass, yet it is as real as anything can be. In a sense, a human being is considered a mental and physical whole. However, body and mind are of such a nature as to have no common characteristic.

How did primitive people acquire the idea that they had substantive minds? We do not know, but it is plausible to suppose that dreaming was partially responsible. Picture hunters A and B lying down together after a hard day's hunting and a heavy feast. Hunter A has eaten too much and as a result is unable to sleep. Having been more moderate in his eating, hunter B sleeps all night, but his sleep includes an adventurous dream. Upon awakening in the morning, hunter B relates the experience of finding and stalking game during the night. Hunter A expresses disbelief and insists that hunter B has been on the ground beside him all night. But hunter B is equally insistent that he spent the night hunting and describes his dream so convincingly that both men decide that there must be *two* hunter B's. One, the physical person, slept on the ground throughout the night; the other, the mental person, must have come from within the first and carried on his escapades unhampered by bodily form. Thus, something like a modern concept of mind substance could have been born.

The mind substance concept has grown through the inventive genius of both primitive and civilized people, and it has become deeply embedded in present-day cultures. Consequently, quite often its existence is considered a self-evident truth; the familiar has come to be accepted as the self-evident.

A defensible mind substance theory must take mind out of space completely. As long as one attributes to mind some characteristics of matter, even though they are very thin and elusive, one implies that mind is of essentially the same nature as matter. Thus, to gain an understanding of a mind substance theory of learning, one must make a sharp distinction between mind and matter, and one must recognize that if a mind is nonspatial, it cannot be located in the brain or anywhere else, and that, to date, we have devised no way of determining experimentally the way in which spatial and nonspatial entities influence each other.

If one adheres to a mind substance theory, each student's substantive mind is assumed to be active in either an erroneous or inadequate fashion until it is either curbed or trained. Hence, one sees all learning as basically a process of developing or training minds. Accordingly, learning becomes a process of inner development within which various powers such as imagination, memory, will, and thought are cultivated. Education becomes a process of mental discipline.

What Forms May Mental Discipline Take?

The theory of mental discipline has at least two principal versions—*classical humanism* and *faculty psychology*. Each is an outgrowth of different cultural traditions. Classical humanism stems from ancient Greece. It operates on the assumption that the mind of a human being is an active agent in relation to its environment and that it is also morally neutral at birth.

Humanism is an outlook and way of life that is centered upon human interests and values. Classical humanism is only one of its forms. Two other quite different forms of humanism are existentialist humanism and scientific humanism. Existentialist humanism emphasizes the autonomous, active nature of human beings within which each person "does his own thing." This type of humanism includes a self-actualization psychology of learning (see page 31). *Scientific* humanists emphasize the enhancement of human welfare through the application of scientific processes to the solution of the prevailing social problems of human beings. This kind of humanism harmonizes best with cognitive–interactionist psychologies of learning.

"Faculty psychology" more often is associated with the *bad-active* principle of human nature than with the earlier Greek *neutral-active* principle. Because of differences in underlying assumptions concerning the basic nature of human beings, we find some difference between the kinds of education prescribed by classical humanists and that prescribed by faculty psychologists. However, all mental disciplinary approaches to learning have enough in common for them to be placed in a mind substance family (see Table 1.1).

Mental Discipline Within the Classical-Humanistic Tradition   Within the classical-humanistic tradition, a human mind is assumed to be of such nature that, with adequate cultivation, it can know the world as it really is. A person, being a rational animal, is free within limits to act as he chooses in the light of what he understands. Instead of being creatures of instinct, humankind enjoys a complex and delicate faculty of apprehension, whose basic aspect is *reason*. This capacity resides in every normal human individual and enables human beings to gain understanding of their needs and their environment, to direct their action in accordance with their understanding, and to communicate this understanding to other members of their group. Thus, the human mind is of such a nature that if it has been properly exercised and has an opportunity, it will educe truth, and thereby develops outward manifestations of its innate potential.

Within the classical-humanistic frame of reference, knowledge assumes the character of a fixed body of true principles, handed down as a heritage of humankind. These principles have been discovered by the great thinkers of human history and set down in the great books. Hence, classicists take the basic content of the school curriculum from philosophical and literary classics. To them, not only training the mind, but also studying the eternal truths contained in certain great books, is of primary importance.

Mental Discipline Implemented by Faculty Psychology   Although faculty psychology had been implicit in the classical tradition, it did not appear as an explicit, formalized psychological doctrine until the eighteenth century. Christian Wolff (1679–1754), a German philosopher, is credited with its development. His version was described in his *Rational Psychology*, published in 1734. Wolff's thesis was that the mind, although unitary, has different faculties that are distinct. The mind at times enters into particular activities in much the same way that the whole body at different times takes part in widely different acts. According to Wolff, the basic general faculties are knowing, feeling, and willing. The knowing faculty is divided into several others, which include perception, imagination, memory, and pure reason. The reasoning faculty is the ability to draw distinctions and form judgments.

The belief in a willing faculty is an outgrowth of the notion that human nature may be described in terms of the bad-active principle. If human nature is intrinsically evil, then a strongly developed will is necessary to harness inherent evil. *Will*, in the sense in which it is employed here, refers to ability to implement, or put into effective practice, a decision that has been made. A strongly developed will enables a person to "see a decision through" even though such action violates natural, that is, evil, impulses. Hence, if a person chooses to emancipate himself from his innate natural impulses, a well-developed will is necessary for success; he/she must make himself do what he does not want to do. Faculty psychologists have held that if a person pursues any type of unpleasant work long enough, his will will be strengthened.

Under faculty psychology, the task of a teacher is to find the kind of mental exercises that will train the various faculties most efficiently. Emphasis is not on acquiring knowledge but, rather, on strengthening faculties. A consistent faculty psychologist would not be especially interested in teaching "great truths" or the "heritage of the past" or any other type of subject except insofar as it is a good medium for exercising the faculties.

The special attention given by faculty psychology to development of the will has led to the notion that schoolwork is better for a child if it is somewhat distasteful. Consequently, when faculty psychology is a dominant influence in a school, teachers may deliberately keep their assignments both difficult and dull and use force if necessary to ensure that students complete them. Also, use of severe punishment, including ridicule and whipping, may be found in use in such a school.

How Did the Mental Discipline Theory of Learning Develop?

Mental discipline has roots extending into antiquity. Yet its manifestations continue to be quite evident in present-day school practices. In the fourth century B.C. Plato taught that mental training or discipline in mathematics and philosophy was a person's best preparation for participation in the conduct of public affairs. Once trained, by having his mind developed, a person was ready to solve problems of all kinds. Aristotle, who followed Plato, described at least five different faculties; the greatest, and the one unique to human beings, was reason. Faculties that humans had in common with lower animals were the vegetative, appetitive, sensory, and locomotive, but only human beings could reason.

Emergence of Classical Humanism   At the close of the Middle Ages, during the Renaissance, *classical humanism* emerged as an endeavor of people to gain more understanding of the universe and themselves. Classical humanists believed that human beings, rather than the Scriptures, were to be the starting point in satisfying humanity's urge toward individual development. To gain understanding of the ideal nature of human beings, humanistic scholars turned to the classics of ancient Greece and Rome. The resulting classical humanism of the Renaissance was developed on the assumption that a person was a neutral-active rational animal whose direction of growth was to be provided from within, not by yielding to the behest of every chance impulse, but by following principles that an individual formulated for guidance of his conduct. Thus, learning was regarded as a process of firm self-discipline, consisting of harmonious development of all of a person's inherent powers so that no one faculty was overdeveloped at the expense of others.

Within classical humanism, the Socratic method was popular as a teaching procedure. A teacher's function was to help students recognize what already was in their minds; environmental influence was considered of little consequence:

The Socratic method implies that the teacher has no knowledge, or at least professes to impart no information; instead, he seeks to draw the information from his students by means of skillfully directed questions. The method is predicated on the principle that knowledge is inborn but we cannot recall it without expert help.[2]

Nineteenth-Century Mental Discipline   The nineteenth century could be characterized as the century of mental discipline. Rooted in European traditions of idealistic and rationalistic philosophy, precepts of mental discipline had some currency in the early part of the century and gained great popularity in the middle and later decades. During this period, education was regarded as necessarily laborious. Schoolroom atmospheres were at least austere and sometimes harsh. Teachers usually were dictators, sometimes benevolent, but sometimes even spiteful. Children were expected to be respectful and obedient and to accept at face value whatever teachers told them. Curriculums were relatively fixed with an almost exclusive emphasis in elementary schools on the fundamental skill subjects and, in secondary schools, on such "disciplinary" subjects as Latin, history, and mathematics.

Reassertion of Classical Humanism in the Twentieth Century   Traditionally, classical humanists have been more interested in perfecting the minds of a few superior individuals than in elevating the intelligence of humankind as a whole. Accordingly, some twentieth-century classical humanists are attempting to repudiate the intellectual leadership of natural and social scientists in the affairs of life and to revert to the precepts of traditional philosophers as represented by Plato, Aristotle, and the medieval scholastics. Whereas scientists make great use of other symbols, classical humanistic literary intellectuals center their activity in words.

Some leading twentieth-century classical humanists are Mortimer J. Adler (1902-), Allan Bloom, Robert M. Hutchins (1899–1977), and Mark Van Doren.[3] Adler's *Paideia* principles include the following: "That the primary cause of genuine learning is the activity of the learner's own mind, sometimes with the help of a teacher functioning as a secondary and cooperative cause; [and] that the three kinds of teaching that should occur in our schools are didactic teaching of subject matter, coaching that produces the skills of learning and Socratic questioning in seminar discussions."[4] "But, of the three educational objectives—acquisition of knowledge, development of intellectual skills, and increase of understanding of basic ideas and issues—the third is by far the most important, and cannot be achieved without seminar discussions of truly great or almost great books."[5] In his *The Closing of the American Mind*, Bloom states, "Men may live more truly and fully in reading Plato and Shakespeare than at any other time, because then they are participating in essential being and forgetting their accidental lives."[6] For Bloom, Plato's *Republic* is "*the* book on education because it really explains to me what I experience as a man and a teacher."[7]

The two most influential groups in the United States who continue to favor a mental-disciplinary approach to education are some leaders in parochial education and those liberal arts professors who are under the influence of faculty psychology and the classical tradition. In addition to these there are many thousands of other persons, including some public school teachers, who gravitate toward a theory of mental discipline. The current introduction of "Renaissance schools" reflects this position, however, in a somewhat confused manner.

The Wedding of Classicism and Faculty Psychology   Faculty psychology, as developed by Wolff and his followers, was at first a challenge to classical humanism. Logically, faculty psychologists should consider one subject as good as another for exercising a particular faculty. Also, knowledge retained by a student was considered much less important than the disciplining effect of learning it. But these conclusions negate the classicist's insistence on the virtues of certain subjects and on learning and retaining the great truths that human experience has unveiled.

However, a rather easy compromise soon became apparent. If it could be established that the best subjects for training the faculties were the classics, then the classical curriculum could be defended. This argument gained strength, and by the late nineteenth century most secondary schools and colleges offered a curriculum limited mainly to the classical liberal arts. These subjects were regarded as valuable for a twofold reason: They were excellent tools for mind training, and they incorporated the great truths of human experience.

An Historical Example of Mental Discipline   A brief history of the teaching of Latin and Greek illustrates the development of mental discipline as a theory of learning. Throughout the Middle Ages, Latin served a practical purpose. It was the language of scholars throughout the Western world and the vehicle of instruction in schools. Thus, it was a living, growing, changing language that today we would call a "tool subject." During the Renaissance, Latin continued to be the language of scholarly communication, and both Latin and Greek were used in reading the classics, which contained those ideas considered the best that had been thought by humanity. To keep up with the thinking of his times, a scholar had to be able to read and use both Latin and Greek.

After the Renaissance, modern languages gradually came into more general use. English, German, and French rose to prominence and assumed the role previously played by Latin and Greek. By the end of the sixteenth century the communicative value of the classical languages was beginning to wane. Supporters of these languages, however, made a determined fight to preserve them. No longer needed for basic communication, Latin and Greek came to be heralded as the best subject matter for mental discipline. Throughout most of the nineteenth century the doctrine of the disciplinary value of these languages was generally accepted in American educational circles. Since, according to the classical humanists, disciplinary values were intangible and not susceptible to statistical treatment, evaluation of them was limited to analysis of opinions of recognized authorities on educational matters.

During the early years of the twentieth century, when the mechanistic learning theories that were opposed to mental discipline—apperception, connectionism, and behaviorism—were on the upsurge in educational circles, Greek practically dropped out of the educational picture and Latin suffered a great decline. However, by the middle of the twentieth century, a resurgence of the classical tradition was apparent. With it came its earlier associate, mental discipline, and the teaching of Latin began to be expanded again. Then, more recently, with the emphasis upon narrow vocationalism in schools, classical studies, including Latin, have dropped into the background once more.

How Has Mental Discipline Been Evaluated?

Mental discipline proponents generally have held that learning theory, curriculum construction, teaching methods, and educational practices cannot be evaluated scientifically. They are derived philosophically; hence, they can only be evaluated philosophically. However, by the early twentieth century an imposing array of psychologists and educators had become captivated by the potentiality of scientific processes, particularly objective and statistical procedures, as exemplified in fields such as physics and chemistry.

Whereas, on the one hand, mental disciplinarians insisted that science could not be applied in such a human enterprise as education, on the other hand, scientifically oriented educators and psychologists have insisted that science could and must be used in determining and evaluating educational processes.

When the classical-humanistic curriculum first took form, it represented the point of view of liberals of the time and reflected a desire for progress. Its adherents were sufficiently open-minded to permit changes. However, by the beginning of the twentieth century the classical curriculum had come under such sharp attack that its proponents were placed on the defensive. They pleaded for a return to a rigid Renaissance ideal, forgetting that the Renaissance ideal itself was an example of change and growth.

Almost to the end of the 1890s public high schools in the United States were loyal to the classical liberal tradition with its psychology of mental discipline. The famous Committee of Ten on Secondary School Studies upheld a doctrine of mental discipline throughout its 1893 report.

In the early 1900s Edward L. Thorndike (1874–1949) and Robert S. Woodworth (1869–1962), in a newer tradition of scientific psychology, performed experiments at Columbia University to test the validity of mental discipline as a psychology of learning. Their basic conclusion was that mental discipline is scientifically untenable. Their experiments showed that drill or training in performing certain tasks did not strengthen people's so-called faculties for performing such tasks. For example, students' development of neatness in one area of activity showed no or very little improvement of their neatness in other areas; students' arithmetic papers may be noticeably improved in neatness with no parallel improvement in neatness appearing in language and spelling papers.

Thorndike also noted that the results of his experimentation, if corroborated by similar experiments, would prove that the amount of general improvement, or mental discipline, that students achieve due to the study of any school subject is small and that the differences in improvement as a result of studying different subjects are also small. Thus, he concluded that the value of each subject must be decided largely by the special learnings that it provides; the languages, or any other liberal arts subjects, have no claims to preeminence as an educational medium. The order of influence, if any, of specific subjects upon the growth of intellect ranged from, first, arithmetic and bookkeeping to, last, biological sciences. The so-called disciplinary subjects appeared at all levels interwoven with nondisciplinary subjects. Thorndike reported in the *Journal of Educational Psychology*:

> If our inquiry had been carried out by a psychologist from Mars, who knew nothing of theories of mental discipline, and simply tried to answer the question, "What are the amounts of influence of sex, race, age, amounts of ability, and studies taken, upon the gain made during the year in power to think, or intellect, or whatever our stock intelligence tests measure?" he might even dismiss "studies taken" with the comment, "The differences are so small and the unreliabilities are relatively so large that this factor seems unimportant." The one causal factor which he would be sure was at work would be the intellect already existent. Those who have the most to begin with gain the most during the year. Whatever studies they take will seem to produce large gains in intellect.[8]

Thorndike was convinced that the principal reason that good thinkers seemed to have been made good thinkers by certain subjects that they had pursued is that good students tend to take the subjects that people generally identify with good thinking. Good students gain more than do poor students from the study of any subject. When good thinkers study Latin and Greek, these subjects seem to cultivate good thinking. However, "If the abler pupils should all study Physical Education and Dramatic Arts, these subjects would seem to make good thinkers."[9]

In 1914 Thorndike disposed of inborn faculties with two sentences:

> [There is] the opinion that attention, memory, reasoning, choice and the like are mystical powers given to man as his birthright which weigh the dice in favor of thinking or doing one thing rather than another.... This opinion is vanishing from the world of expert thought and no more need to be said about it than that it is false and would be useless to human welfare if true.[10]

In 1944 Alexander Wesman made a study following up Thorndike's earlier mental discipline studies. High school students were tested at the start and end of an academic year with a series of general intelligence and achievement tests. Gains on the tests during the year were observed for students taking differing course patterns to see whether some patterns of courses contributed more to gained intelligence than did others. Wesman's study revealed no superiority of any one school subject over any of the others studied; there was no superior addition to intelligence for any one of the achievement areas measured.[11]

A curriculum based on a classical-humanistic philosophy and the liberal arts may not seem very practical to most persons today. However, mental disciplinarians deliberately make a distinction between knowledge of immediate usefulness and practicality and essential matters grounded in eternal standards of truth, goodness, and beauty. Mental disciplinarians are convinced that knowledge of immediate practical value is of little importance. They hold that only the abstract principles of pure theory can free the human mind and promote people's distinctively human capacity for reason.

This emphasis is understandable. Most adherents of mental discipline are mind–body dualists who feel that mind is much the more important member of the partnership. Identification of education with development of minds tends to disparage other aspects of human activity. Thus, we are told that "Education, as a whole, can never be a 'science' in the strict sense of the term. It is part of the 'humanities.' "[12] Even in the face of James's, Thorndike's, and Woodworth's research in this area, many scholars continue to endow certain subjects, particularly the more abstract ones, with immensely superior transfer power.

Students who have mastered difficult subjects usually do have above–average proficiency in whatever areas of study and thinking they happen to pursue. Although it does not necessarily follow, it is easy to assign credit for this proficiency to the nature of the specific subjects that have been studied; it is often overlooked that people who elect or survive difficult subjects perhaps had more ability when they started them. This is an example of the *post hoc ergo propter hoc*—"after this, therefore on account of it"—fallacy; instructors and others may fallaciously reason that after taking certain courses, youth are good students; therefore, the courses made them into good students. We should recognize, however, that even though mental disciplinarians' reasoning may be fallacious in this regard, their procedure becomes a screening device, whether or not it is an educating one. A school may "maintain high standards" through teaching for mental discipline and grading so rigorously that a high percentage of students fail and drop out. By so doing, it can raise the average quality of its remaining students; but the increased quality of students, gained this way, is no indication of improved quality of instruction.

Today the concept of mental discipline is unpopular with most psychologists and professional educators. Experimental evidence indicates that memory as a general function is not improved by strenuous memorization of poetry. Likewise, reasoning in fields other than mathematics is not automatically improved by studying algebra and geometry. However, many scholars, parents, and other school patrons are convinced that Latin, science, and mathematics should be included in the school curriculum because they are "good for the students' minds."

In light of current psychological knowledge, it is difficult to justify school subjects purely in terms of improving students' minds through exercise. Evidently, there is transfer of learning, but not the general transfer implied in mental discipline. Methods of solving arithmetic problems can be transferred to the solution of problems in algebra. The learning of Latin may, and often does, facilitate the learning of English grammar. However, if experimental research is to be trusted, transfer is not automatic and is not a matter of disciplining minds.

WHAT IS LEARNING THROUGH UNFOLDMENT OR SELF-ACTUALIZATION?

We come now to the second major position to be treated in this chapter, often called "learning through unfoldment." This outlook on the nature of learning stems logically from the theory that people are naturally *good* and at the same time *active* in relation to their environments. All people are assumed to be free, autonomous, and forwardly active persons who are reaching out from themselves to make their worlds. Unless and until they are corrupted by some outside influences, every act that comes from them will be good. Each student is subjectively free, and his own personal choice and responsibility account for his life. He and she alone, is the architect and builder of that life.

Early development of this point of view usually is associated with Jean J. Rousseau (1712–1778). Later, the Swiss educational reformer Heinrich Pestalozzi (1746–1827) and the German philosopher, educator, and founder of the kindergarten movement Friedrich Froebel (1782–1852), to a large degree, used this outlook as a basis for their pedagogical thinking. The overall philosophical framework of the natural unfoldment position often has been labeled *romantic naturalism.*

A contemporary position that implies that human beings are good and active is *existentialist humanism.* This position contrasts with both classical humanism, within which people are considered neutral and active, and scientific humanism, within which they are considered neutral and interactive. Recent exponents of existentialist humanism include Abraham Maslow, Paul Goodman, and John Holt.[13]

Rousseau's position was that everything in nature is basically good. Since human hereditary nature is good, it need only be permitted to develop in a natural environment free from corruption. Rousseau qualified his interpretation of human nature as an active, self-directing agent by conceding that a bad social environment could make bad human beings; to him social institutions are not natural. Thus, his rejection of environmentalism was not complete. However, his emphasis was on natural, active self-determination.

Rousseau urged teachers to permit students to live close to nature so that they might indulge freely in their natural impulses, instincts, and feelings, He emphasized that in rural areas children need practically no schooling or tutoring. An example that he gave related to the learning of speech. A country boy, he said, ordinarily did not need instruction in speech. He called to his parents and playmates from considerable distances and thus practiced making himself heard; consequently, without tutoring, he developed an adequate power of speech. It was only the city boy, growing up in close quarters with no opportunity to exercise his voice in a natural way, who had need for speech instruction. Thus, Rousseau recommended that in teaching city boys, teachers should, insofar as possible, adopt the method through which country boys learn.

Within current existentialist humanism, the essence of a human being lies within that person's conscious self; each person alone is deemed sufficient for every situation. One's free-flowing emotional feelings, not one's intellectual thoughts, are taken to be the final authority for truth. Hence, a person arrives at decisions on all issues in accordance with the way that person feels and is completely confident of being right.

Since, according to the good-active definition of human nature, children grow up unfolding what nature has enfolded within them, devotees of this position tend to place great emphasis on the study of child growth and development and to minimize the study of learning. When they allude to learning, they seem to assume or imply that it, too, is little more than a process of growth and development in accordance with the genetic patterns of individuals.

Learning, in the traditional sense, generally is conceived to be some form of imposition of ideas or standards upon a person or organism. However, within existentialist humanism there is little need for this kind of learning. Instead, a student is expected to learn through the promptings of his own interests. Hence, there should be no coercion or prescription. A mind, in its growth process, may be considered analogous to an egg in the process of hatching. Its growth is a natural operation, which, without imposition from any outside source, carries its own momentum.

As an existentialist humanist views matters, his learning process runs counter to conventional orthodoxies and dogmas. Accordingly, his approach to learning contradicts most of the elements of conventional schools. Since existentialist humanists want their learning to center on their feelings, they express them freely, thereby living their way into learning.

Since existentialist humanists depreciate the value of learning 'as such they give a prominent place to the concept of *needs*, which they consider to be person-centered, as contrasted with needs being either environment- or situation-centered. As an organism or mind naturally unfolds through a series of stages, each stage is assumed to have its unique needs. Such child-centered needs have much in common with instincts; they are innate-determining tendencies or permanent trends of human nature that underlie behavior from birth to death under all circumstances in all kinds of societies.

WHAT IS APPERCEPTION?

The third major outlook toward learning that we describe—apperception—is far more complicated than either mental discipline or learning as unfoldment. *Apperception* is idea-centered learning. An idea is apperceived when it appears in consciousness and is assimilated to other conscious ideas. Thus, apperception is a process of new ideas associating themselves with old ones.

Adherents of both mental discipline and natural unfoldment either assume or imply the existence of an inborn human nature, some aspects of which are common to all people. Although, in their treatment of learning, supporters of both theories sharply differ from one another, they agree that the "furniture of minds" is innate. Whereas romantic naturalists in their emphasis upon natural unfoldment have expounded instinctive spontaneous development of persons, mental disciplinarians often agree that knowledge is inborn but insist that students need expert help to enable them to recall it.

Apperception, in contrast to both mental discipline and natural unfoldment, is a dynamic mental *associationism* based upon the fundamental premise that there are no innate ideas; everything a person knows comes to the person from outside himself. This means that mind is wholly a matter of content—a compound of elemental impressions bound together by association and formed when subject matter is presented from without and makes certain associations or connections with prior content of the mind.

An *associationism* is any general psychological concept within which it is assumed that the process of learning is one of combining irreducible elements and that, in recall, we connect ideas or actions simply because they were connected in our earlier experiences with them. There are two broad types of associationisms: (1) early mentalistic associationisms, such as apperception, which focus upon the association of ideas in a mind, and (2) more modern physicalistic stimulus-response associationisms, which focus upon formation of connections, either between cells in a brain and peripheral nervous system or between organic responses and environmental stimuli.

The method of studying human beings within a framework of associationism is analytic or reductionistic; learnings are reduced to their component structural parts. The basic elements that are associated may be mental, physical, or a combination of both. But in apperception, the associated elements are completely mental and constitute the *structures* of minds. Hence, whereas mental discipline implies that a mind is a *substance*, apperception implies that it is a *structure*.

How Did Apperception Develop?

The thinking that underlies modern associationism goes back to Aristotle, who in the fourth century B.C. observed that recollection of an item of knowledge was facilitated by a person's associating that item or idea with another when he/she learned it. Aristotle maintained that four kinds of connections or associations would aid or strengthen memory: contiguity of one idea with another, succession of ideas in a series, similarity of ideas, and contrast of ideas. Contiguity means "being together." If children are told about Eskimos and igloos at the same time, future mention of *Eskimo* will help them recall *igloo*. "A tiger is a big kitty" used the principle of similarity. If children learn that pleasure is the opposite of pain (contrast), mention of *pain* will aid them in thinking of *pleasure*.

In the seventeenth century John Locke (1632–1704) challenged the whole notion of innate faculties or ideas and with it the conception of learning as a development of innate potentialities or faculties. He replaced this notion with the idea that learning consists of persons gaining ideas in originally empty minds. Locke observed that he could find no common human nature at all. Realizing that he could find no ideas common to all people in any one society or to people in different societies, he developed his *tabula rasa* theory of the human mind. *Tabula rasa*, "blank tablet" means that there are no innate ideas. Locke was convinced that not only was a mind empty at birth but also any ideas that one holds must have come to one originally through one's senses.

Locke's theory that all of a person's ideas must come to him through his senses is called *empiricism*. Locke's empiricism was directly opposed to the earlier *rationalism* of Plato and Locke's immediate forerunner—René Descartes (1596–1650). Whereas these two scholars considered *reason* the source of knowledge, Locke insisted that knowledge was derived from *sense experience*. In his view, perception is synonymous with learning and is a product of sensory experience. Whereas Plato thought that individuals may, through mental training, apprehend ultimate reality consisting of ideas or forms, Locke thought that sensations impinging upon minds gave rise to ideas. Therefore, a mind has no direct contact with objects; only ideas of objects are perceived.

For Locke, ideas were the units of a mind, and *associations* consisted of combinations of ideas, which were either simple or complex. One of the operations of a mind was thought to be a compounding of complex ideas from simple ones. This notion of mental combination and analysis was a beginning of the "mental chemistry," which later characterized apperception.

To allow for associations within a mind, Locke recognized an "internal sense." He realized that if a mind were only a passive receptacle of sense impressions (which basically he thought it to be), the impressions would accumulate in a disorderly manner. Consequently, he gave mind a means for dealing with passive impressions once they were in. To mind, he attributed the ability to compare impressions, generalize them, and discriminate between them, meaning that it could associate ideas through contiguity, similarity, and contrast.

Locke's writings spearheaded a shift in the conception of education from mental discipline to habit formation. His *tabula rasa* theory implied that the original nature of human beings is neither morally good nor bad, nor actionally active. Instead, it is deemed morally neutral and actionally passive. Thus, a mind is the product of life experiences. Locke's thinking opened the way for psychologists to place their emphasis upon environmental nurture rather than upon hereditary nature. In school, this meant that teachers were to be the architects and builders of minds of children and youths; they were to develop a systematic instructional program centered in procedures designed to form proper habits in students. Teaching, then, became a matter of stimulating the senses as opposed to training the mental faculties.

Locke's work constituted a turning point in professional thinking about learning. Up to the seventeenth century most psychological thinking consisted of restatements and reinterpretations of the psychology of antiquity—mental discipline. This trend continued into the seventeenth and eighteenth centuries, but simultaneously, Locke spearheaded modern associationism—a new line of thought in regard to learning.

What Is Herbart's Apperception Theory of Learning?

Johann Friedrich Herbart (1776–1841) developed the first modern systematic psychology of learning to emerge from a *tabula rasa* theory of mind. Herbart was an eminent German philosopher-psychologist and a skilled teacher. In 1809 he succeeded Immanuel Kant in the world's most distinguished chair of philosophy at Königsberg, Germany, and held it until 1833. His speculative thinking developed from his dealing with problems of education. To him, morality was the supreme objective of education; he wanted to make children good. Thus, he developed a psychology to achieve this goal.

Whereas Locke and other early associationists had assumed that linkages or associations are passive in nature, Herbart's apperception theory replaced this passivity with *dynamic* ideas. However, in Herbart's apperception, *ideas*, not *persons*, are dynamic. Persons are passive *containers* within which laws of mental chemistry operate.

Herbart's influence on twentieth-century American education has been great. Although this theory was developed early in the nineteenth century, it did not reach the United States until the 1880s, when four young Americans— Charles DeGarmo, Frank McMurry, Charles A. McMurry, and Charles C. Van Liew—studied at the University of Jena and returned to the United States to spread Herbartian doctrine with religious fervor. "Like a tidal wave, interest in this elaborate system swept over American teachers and students of education during the nineties."[14]

From the early years of the twentieth century to the time its tenets were seriously challenged by behaviorism, Herbartianism dominated teacher education institutions in the United States. Thus, if one is to comprehend the psychological atmosphere of today's schools, it is essential that one understand the development, principles, and implications of the theory of apperception. Today, one seldom meets an avowed Herbartian; however, much of what occurs in our schools carries with it the implicit assumption that the neutral and passive minds of children are being filled. Although apperceptive teaching seldom is advocated as such in teacher education institutions, much actual teaching continues to follow a pattern much in harmony with the theory of apperception.

Herbart perpetuated a mind–body dualism that was prevalent in his time. This was a psychophysical parallelism within which the psychic aspect—mind— played the major role, particularly in the learning process. *Psychophysical parallelism* is a theory of mind and body according to which, for every variation in conscious or mental process, there is a concomitant, parallel neurological or body process. Yet there is no causal relation between body and mind; a person's mind does not affect his body, nor his body, his mind.

Through the use of the concepts *presentations*, *mental states*, *apperception*, and *apperceptive mass*, Herbart expanded the notion of a mind's neutral passivity into a systematic theory of learning and teaching. He thought that a mind had no innate natural faculties or talents whatsoever for receiving or producing ideas and that not even any remote dispositions toward perception, thought, willing, or action lay in it. He regarded a mind as nothing more than a battleground and storehouse of ideas. Ideas, he thought, had an active quality. They could lead a life of their own in a mind, which was completely passive. A mind was an aggregate, not of faculties, but of ideas or mental states. John Dewey (1859–1952) described the apperceptionists' view of mind in this way: "The 'furniture' of the mind *is* the mind. Mind is wholly a matter of 'contents.' "[15]

In his metaphysics Herbart posited for each person a unitary mind or soul that is part of ultimate reality and, consequently, exists prior to experience. Such a soul or mind (*Wesen*) really has no spatial or temporal nature. However, as with a mathematical point, in thinking about it we give it space and time dimensions.

> The soul has no innate natural talents nor faculties whatever, either for the purpose of receiving or for the purpose of producing. It is, therefore no *tabula rasa* in the sense that impressions foreign to itself may be made upon it; moreover . . . it is not a [mind] substance which includes in itself original activity. It has originally neither concepts, nor feeling, nor desires.[16]

The mind's being no *tabula rasa* means that it has its own unique receptivity.

Herbart's ambition was to build a science of human minds that would parallel the physical and biological sciences. He thought that the actual character of a mind consists of an arrangement of ideas, which are very much like the electrons of modern physics—they make up the object that contains them. Accordingly, a mind is an aggregate of contents resulting from a person's being presented certain ideas. Since Herbart thought of psychology as "mental chemistry," he felt that the chief role of psychology was to study the various blendings and amalgamations of ideas or mental states in minds. Discovery of the principles by which ideas combine and recombine like chemical elements was Herbart's object in psychological investigation.

Although Herbart felt that his psychology was scientific, probably most experimental psychologists today would not agree; he rejected experimentation and the use of physiological data, both of which have been cornerstones of twentieth-century behavioristic psychology. To him, observation and thought were the proper methods for psychological inquiry. Furthermore, the observation he had in mind was self-observation—introspection. By looking into his own mind, Herbart thought that its "chemistry" could be observed and described. He felt that it was proper that a science like physics was experimental, but that, equally appropriate, the "science" of psychology should be metaphysical and introspective.

How Does Apperception Work?

Herbart used the German term *Vorstellungen* to name the mental elements, which he deemed the constituent parts of a mind. *Vorstellungen* may be translated to mean presentations, mental states, or ideas. According to Herbartian psychologists, mental states constitute a nonspatial, mental reality that is experienced firsthand and stored in the subconscious mind. They have three forms—sense impressions, images or copies of previous sense impressions, and affective elements such as pleasure and pain. Such mental states furnish the total source of mental activity. The derived states, feeling and willing, are secondary factors that accompany mental states but are not a source or cause of mental activity. Thus, volitional willing has its roots in thought; right thinking produces right actions.

Mind is an aggregate of mental states, and a person's stock of mental states at any given time is his "apperceptive mass." Until a first presentation occurs, there is nothing whatever present in a mind; except for its inherent receptivity, it is completely passive. Mental states, the active structural parts of a mind, become associated to produce experience. Thus, new ideas are learned only as they are related to what is already in an apperceptive mass. Hence, it is the addition of new mental states to the old ones that produces the various types of mental processes. Furthermore, the particular combination of ideas that is predominant at any given time determines what will hold a person's attention at that time.

In Herbart's system of "mental chemistry," every mental state has an inherent quality, giving it an affinity for certain other mental states and an aversion for some others; respective ideas either attract or repel one another. Whereas the ideas of "book" and "school" would have an affinity and attract each other, the ideas of "book" and "fishing rod" probably would have a repugnancy and repel one another.

A Herbartian regards a mind as a battleground of contending ideas. Each idea in the mind of a person has once been in the center of the person's consciousness and strives to return, seeking self-preservation. Furthermore, it tries to enter into relations with other ideas. Having once held the center of consciousness and subsequently lost it, each idea, like a deposed king, keeps trying to occupy the throne once again. Compatible ideas may operate as teams, helping each other to remain in a conscious mind. But when two ideas are incompatible, one is likely to be submerged.

To Herbartians, all perception is apperception; it is a process of new ideas relating themselves to the store of old mental states. A mind is like an iceberg in that most of it is submerged below the level of consciousness. Memories stored in the subconscious enable one to interpret experience of the moment. Without a background of experience, any new sensation would mean almost nothing at all. In picturing a mind, Herbart introduced the idea of *threshold of consciousness*. Objects occupying consciousness are constantly changing. At any moment, several ideas may occupy the consciousness. However, one will be at the focus of attention, some will be sinking below the threshold, and others will be striving to rise into consciousness.

The subconscious aspect of mind–apperceptive mass—contains the store of perceptions and images that have been accumulated during all past experiences of an individual. Any of these ideas are ready to spring back into consciousness whenever a propitious opportunity occurs. The content of consciousness at any moment is the result of an interplay of many ideas. Apperception is a process not only of a person becoming consciously aware of an idea but also of the idea's assimilation into a totality of conscious ideas.

Within the apperceptive process Herbart saw the principles of frequency and association in operation. The principle of *frequency* means that the more often an idea or concept has risen into consciousness, the easier its return becomes. The principle of association holds that when a number of presentations or ideas associate, or form a mass, the combined powers of the mass determine the ideas that will enter consciousness.

Herbart recognized three levels or stages of learning: the stage of predominantly sense activity; followed by the stage of memory, characterized by exact reproductions of previously formed ideas; and the highest level, that of conceptual thinking or understanding. Understanding occurs when the common, or shared, attributes of a series of ideas make themselves seen. It involves generalization—deriving rules, principles, or laws from a group of specifics.

What Does Apperception Mean for Teaching?

According to apperception, right thinking will produce right action; volition or willing has its roots in thought. If a teacher builds up the right sequence of ideas, the right conduct follows. Hence, the real work of instruction is implantation not only of knowledge but also of inner volitions or will by means of presented ideas. Psychologically, students' mentalities are determined by the kind of ideas that are presented to them from without.

Since, in apperception, there is no substantive mind to be trained, it can no longer be said that learning is a matter of disciplining or training a mind; rather, learning is the formation of the apperceptive mass that constitutes a mind. Thus, the task of education is to cause present appropriate experiences to combine with an achieved background. The problem of education, then, is to select the right materials for forming the backgrounds or apperceptive masses of students. Teachers must start with the experiences that pupils already have had and then enlarge and enrich these experiences.

To Herbartians, the art of teaching consists of bringing to the attention of students those ideas that a teacher would like to have dominate their lives. Through controlling the experiences of students, an instructor builds up masses of ideas, which develop by assimilation of new ideas to them. Thus, by manipulating ideas the teacher constructs a student's "circle of thought." The goal is a comprehensive circle of thought closely connected or integrated in all its parts. A teacher is the architect and builder of the minds, and hence the characters, of students.

According to Herbart, at no time should a teacher enter into debate with his students on any matter. "Cases may arise when the impetuosity of the pupil challenges the teacher to a kind of combat. Rather than accept such a challenge, he will usually find it sufficient at first to reprove calmly, to look on quietly, to wait until fatigue sets in."[17]

What Are the Herbartian Five Steps in Learning?

Herbart and his followers were convinced that the learning process proceeds through an ordered series of steps that a teacher should understand and follow. Accordingly, effective teaching requires that regardless of obstacles, the proper succession of steps be pursued. Herbart's four steps, clearness, association, system, and method, were expanded to five by American Herbartians. Clearness became (1) preparation and (2) presentation; association became (3) comparison and abstraction; system became (4) generalization; and method became (5) application. Use of these steps came to be regarded as the general method to be followed in all teaching. The steps may be demonstrated by the following example, which involves a teacher teaching students the generalization that any object will float in liquid or in air if it weighs less than an equal volume of the liquid or air in which it is suspended.

1. *Preparation.* To bring relevant ideas into consciousness the teacher reminds students of certain experiences they have had with floating objects. The students will recall the floating of boats, balloons, bubbles, and the like.

2. *Presentation.* The teacher presents new facts about floating, perhaps through means of demonstrations. For example the teacher might demonstrate how oil floats on water or how a steel ball will float on mercury.

3. *Comparison and Abstraction.* If the teacher has performed the first two steps properly, students will see that the new facts have similarities with those already known. Hence, in the students' consciousness, the new and old ideas associate; they are welded together because of their natural affinity for each other. At this point, students should also see the nature of the common elements that give the two sets of facts their mutual attractiveness. Sorting out this common element is what is meant by abstraction.

4. *Generalization.* In this step, students attempt to name the common elements of the two sets of facts as a principle or generalization. They arrive at the principle of flotation which was the stated objective of this instruction.

5. *Application.* The newly learned principle is then used to explain further facts or solve problems relating to flotation. This is done through assigned tasks or problems. The teacher might ask students to explain why boats can be made successfully from steel, or give them a problem that requires them to determine whether a certain object would float in a certain medium. For example, the teacher might ask, "Given a freight barge of specified weight and displacement, how much weight could be placed in it without causing it to sink?"

What Is the Herbartian Doctrine of Interest?

The importance of student interest held a prominent place in the theory of apperception. Present-day policy of "making subject matter interesting" probably has strong roots in apperception. Whereas followers of faculty psychology saw little or no point in student interest (some even saw it as a deterrent to developing willpower), Herbartians gave it a central place in their system. But since the Herbartian doctrine of interest implied that students were neutral and passive, the fact that students were interested did not mean that they necessarily were either involved or perplexed; it merely meant that they were receptive to certain kinds of ideas.

Because formation of mind, to Herbartians, is wholly a matter of presenting the proper educational materials, the task of a teacher is to select the proper subject matter and to arrange its presentation on the basis of the current store of ideas in the student's mind. If the new material involves ideas with a natural affinity for those already present, the student will feel interest.

Interest means "the natural bent or inclination of the mind to find satisfaction in a subject when it is properly presented."[18] Thus, it is an active power residing in the *contents* of the mind, which depends upon the nature of the apperceptive mass and determines what ideas are to receive attention. A person thinks, feels, and wills in accordance with his dominant mental states. To develop a variety of interests, one must acquire a large apperceptive mass. Herbart listed six classes of interests under two major categories—those awakened by the phenomena of nature apart from people and those involving the direct study of human affairs. He then assumed an affinity between the historical development of humankind and the stages of mental development of children. He was convinced that the history and great literature of the world, when properly selected and arranged, would make a strong appeal to the interests and understanding of children at their successive periods of growth.

How Does Apperception Influence Today's Schools?

Since it was the approach to teaching that was stressed most in a great many of our teacher education institutions from about 1900 to 1920, and then much later was used simultaneously with conflicting theories of learning and teaching, apperception remains quite influential even today.

One area in which Herbartian influence frequently is still seen is that of lesson plans. In the Herbartian system actual teaching was always preceded by the teacher's construction of a formal lesson plan, built around the "five steps." Teachers followed these plans on the assumption that the thinking of students could be made to conform to the formal steps. Today, many professors of education continue to insist that there is a fixed order of steps for teaching and learning; they require their students to write lesson plans in which the material to be taught is arranged according to definite steps, and in supervising student teachers they insist that the prepared lesson plans be followed.

Herbartianism has its weaknesses; nevertheless, it has made some important contributions to the development of education. Its attack upon the doctrine of mental discipline and faculty psychology has been of great significance. In a more positive vein, it has emphasized a psychological approach to teaching and learning that implies a need for sound methods of teaching based upon knowledge of people and their mental functions. Hence, it has directed attention to a need for adequate teachers and enriched curriculums, and preparation of teachers has been made an important business. Also, it has made student "interest" a significant idea and has emphasized the importance of a background of experience in the process of perception.

Herbart, in developing a scientific though not experimental psychology, pointed the way for the latter experimental scientific movement in psychology named *structuralism*. Structuralism was developed in the nineteenth century by Wundt in Germany and Titchener in the United States. Its subject matter is the content of consciousness, which is studied only by introspection. Structuralism however was highly important in that it helped pave the way for modern psychologies that have focused on mental processes and at the same time have been experimental in the best scientific sense.

Although apperceptionist psychology was built on fundamentally different premises from the natural unfoldment theory of followers of Rousseau, it was equally incompatible with mental discipline. Hence, apperception, like Rousseauean permissiveness, can be considered a counterinfluence to mental discipline. However, the formal, rigid approach of apperceptionists, coupled with what seemed to be emphasis upon rote learning, made their teaching appear on the surface to be much like the kind of education practiced by the mental disciplinarians. The teacher remained central and dominant in the educational process. Herbartianism seems to commit teachers to a program of indoctrination. Its approach to teaching requires teachers to determine precisely what their pupils are to be taught. Each lesson plan includes the answers as well as the questions. Students arrive at these answers through a largely mechanical process completely dominated by the teacher. Apperceptive education is conceived as a process similar to filling a storage container. Since students depend completely upon the teacher, who provides all of the leadership in learning, critical thinking is discouraged and students tend to be docile. Facts are acquired for test purposes, then rapidly forgotten; their transfer value tends to be very low. Furthermore, problem-centered teaching is largely disregarded. If learning is the mechanical process that Herbart and Herbartians describe, then how does reflective, creative thinking enter the educational scene?

Within Herbartianism, a teacher might teach for explanatory understanding but not for exploratory understanding (see pages 259–260). In commenting upon Herbartianism, John Dewey felt constrained to say, "It takes . . . everything educational into account save its essence—vital energy seeking opportunity for effective exercise."[19] Since Herbartian theory at no time suggests that a person is psychologically interactive with his environment, it inescapably gives students little or no chance for active participation and constructive thinking.

Another criticism of Herbartianism is theoretical, but nevertheless vitally important. Explanations of the apperceptive process seem to contain no adequate treatment of how the first ideas enter a mind so that apperception—perception upon perception—can take effect. How does the first idea tie up with an old one?

We should recognize, however, that, regardless of their shortcomings, apperceptionists have told us much about experience that otherwise might escape our attention. They have realized that when a person has a new experience there is a "reception committee" of background ideas that helps him interpret it. Furthermore, apperceptionists have noted that experiences, in some way, abide after they have been undergone and that they have considerable influence in determining the nature of subsequent experiences.

NOTES

1. James D. Koerner, ed., *The Case for Basic Education* (Boston: Little, Brown, 1959), p. v.
2. George F. Kneller, *Existentialism and Education* (New York: Philosophical Library, 1958), p. 134.
3. See Mortimer J. Adler, *The Paideia Proposal* (New York: Macmillan, 1982).
4. Mortimer J. Adler, *Reforming Education*, (New York: Macmillan, 1988), p. 310.
5. Ibid. p. xxxi.
6. Allan Bloom, *The Closing of the American Mind* (New York: Simon & Schuster, 1987), p. 380.
7. Ibid, p. 381.
8. Edward L. Thorndike, "Mental Discipline in High School Studies," *Journal of Educational Psychology* 15, no. 2 (February 1924):95.
9. Ibid., pp. 96–98.
10. Edward L. Thorndike, *Educational Psychology* (New York: Teachers College Press, 1914), p. 73.
11. Alexander Wesman, "A Study of Transfer of Training from High School Subjects to Intelligence," *Teachers College Record* (October 1944): 391–393.
12. Robert Ulich, *Professional Education as a Humane Study* (New York: Macmillan, 1956), pp. 112–113.
13. See Abraham Wandersman, Paul J. Poppen, and David F. Ricks, eds., *Humanism and Behaviorism: Dialogue and Growth* (Oxford: Pergamon, 1976) for a contrast of current existentialist humanism and behaviorism.
14. Frederick Eby and C. F. Arrowood, *The Development of Modern Education* (Englewood Cliffs, NJ: Prentice Hall, 1934), p. 786.
15. John Dewey, *Democracy and Education* (New York: Macmillan, 1916), p. 84.
16. Johann Friedrich Herbart, *A Text-Book in Psychology*, trans. Margaret K. Smith (New York: Appleton-Century-Crofts, 1891), p. 120.
17. Johann Friedrich Herbart, *Outlines of Educational Doctrine* (New York: Macmillan, 1904), p. 165.
18. Charles A. McMurry, *The Elements of General Method* (New York: Macmillan, 1903), p. 85.
19. Dewey, *Democracy and Education*, p. 84.

BIBLIOGRAPHY

The bibliography for Chapters 1 through 4 is at the end of Chapter 4.

Chapter
3

What Are the Two Major Families of Contemporary Learning Theory?

*T*he two most prominent families of contemporary learning theory are the *stimulus-response conditioning* theories of the *neobehavioristic* family and the *interactionist* theories of the *cognitive* family. These have been in the process of development throughout the twentieth century and have roots that extend back into even earlier periods. In a sense, both families have been protests against the inadequacies and inconsistencies of earlier psychological systems. Their immediate forerunners are mental discipline and apperception.

For assistance in interpreting the content of this chapter, refer to Table 1.1 on pages 8 and 9. Items 5, 6, and 7 of the Table deal with stimulus-response conditioning theories of the neobehavioristic family. Items 8, 9, and 10 refer to interactionist theories of the cognitive family.

Although the two psychological approaches contrast in most respects, they also have an area of commonality; both are scientific approaches to the study of human beings, and both assume people's basic moral proclivity to be neutral— neither innately bad nor innately good. Their great difference centers upon the behavioristic assumption that human beings are *passive* or *reactive* and the cognitive-interactionist assumption that they are *interactive* in relationship with their environments. In this and the succeeding chapter we explain in some detail the basic differences between the two families of learning theories by showing the respective presuppositions, assumptions, or commitments of adherents of each approach in regard to some specific issues.

Students should realize that within each of the two families of psychological theory there is considerable diversity. For example, in the neobehavioristic family, followers of K. W. Spence and B. F. Skinner are in disagreement on many points. Likewise, in the cognitive-interactionist family, followers of Kurt Lewin differ considerably in outlook from followers of Kurt Koffka, and proponents of cognitive-field theory differ significantly with both. Whereas contemporary representatives of the cognitive-interactionist family consider persons to be neutral-interactive, early Gestaltists, because of their roots in German idealism, often implied that persons were neutral-active. Thus, the situation in psychology is somewhat like that in politics; many persons gravitate toward one or the other of our two political parties, but despite some common interests, both the Democrats and the Republicans exhibit wide ranges of views. In the final analysis, however, neobehaviorists have certain key ideas in common, just as cognitive interactionists do. Hence, it is proper to consider each family as a definite grouping that can be discussed in terms of the ideas common to its members.

If students are aware that despite variance within each family the two families differ sharply from one another, they will better understand the ensuing chapters on learning. The two families provide answers to fundamental issues in psychology that are often quite incompatible. Thus, in dealing with the following questions, a person oriented toward neobehaviorism is likely to give a significantly different answer from that given by a cognitive interactionist: What is intelligence? What happens when we remember and when we forget? What is perception? What is motivation? What is thinking? What is the role of practice in learning? How does learning transfer to other situations?

Before students adopt the orientation of one family of psychology or the other, they should recognize that objections may be made to any position one takes in psychology and to any currently available theory of learning. However, although the evidence is not clear enough to warrant dogmatic assertions about learning, one may emerge from a careful study with the knowledge that the ideas central to one family of psychological theory may be more tenable and have fewer disadvantages than the ideas central to the other.

Although all modern psychologists, irrespective of their orientation, generally accept the methods and results of experimentation, there is wide divergence in interpretation of experimental results and equally wide divergence on how a given interpretation should be applied to the solution of a concrete learning problem. These differences appear to stem from disagreement over the fundamental nature of human beings and their relationship to their environment and the nature of motivation and perception. Despite disclaimers by some psychologists, it also appears advisable to attach a number of issues in psychology to related issues in philosophy. A psychologist's philosophical leaning may not only determine the kinds of experiments he/she conducts but also may influence the conclusions he/she draws from the evidence that is secured through experimentation.

This chapter develops the historical and philosophical roots and the philosophical thinking of each of the two families. Then Chapter 4 focuses on the two families' meanings of learning and thinking.

WHAT ARE THE HISTORICAL AND IDEOLOGICAL ROOTS OF CURRENT NEOBEHAVIORISMS?

During the 1920s and 1930s, teachers' colleges moved away from the promotion of Herbartianism as such. But this does not mean that Herbartian ideas were completely abandoned in schools. They were then, and are today, accepted and practiced by many teachers. However, before the twentieth century had been under way very long, a new form of associationism had become popular. This was a nonmentalistic, physiological associationism. Its chief exponents during the first third of the century were John B. Watson (1878–1958) and Edward L. Thorndike. Watson's psychology was known as behaviorism. Thorndike's was called connectionism, but it too, in the broadest sense of the term, was "behavioristic."

Although the psychological systems of Thorndike and Watson no longer are advocated in their original forms, many contemporary psychologists have orientations sufficiently similar to theirs to be termed *neobehaviorists*.[1] Some leading contemporary neobehaviorists or *S-R conditioning theorists* are Robert Glasser, Donald O. Hebb, Neal E. Miller, O. Hobart Mowrer, Burrhus F. Skinner, and J. M. Stephens. In its broadest sense the term *behaviorism* encompasses all S-R conditioning theories; these include S-R bond or connectionism, behaviorism, and neobehaviorism. Thus, throughout this book we use the expressions *behaviorism* and *S-R conditioning theory* interchangeably.

Current behavioristic psychologies have had four principal roots— Herbartian and Wundtian introspectionism, physiological psychology, Thorndikean connectionism, and Watsonian early behaviorism.

How Did Introspectionism Lead into Behaviorism?

As we observed in Chapter 2, early associations, led by Locke and Herbart, were primarily interested in mental structures. Hence, their concern was with the association or connection of ideas in minds. This contrasts with modern behavioristic associationism, which is rooted in the behavior of organisms. However, nineteenth-century Herbartianism led into twentieth-century Wundtian structuralism, which was the prevalent psychological position just prior to the rise of behaviorism, and early behaviorism, like structuralism, was atomistic and reductionistic—a whole consisted of the sum of its parts.

Wilhelm Wundt (1832–1920) was trained in medicine. He turned from medicine to physiology and physiology to psychology. In 1879 he established the first psychological laboratory of modern history. His method was introspection; he and his students observed the workings of their own respective minds. Students from various parts of the world went to Wundt's laboratory at Leipzig to study introspection. But many became psychological heretics, turning to study of observable behavior of other persons and animals.

What Did Physiological Psychology Contribute to Connectionism and Behaviorism?

Nineteenth-century forerunners of modern experimental psychology tended to be philosophical dualists; they considered people to consist of minds and bodies, each genuinely real. There was considerable speculation in regard to the nature of the relationship of minds and bodies but seldom a denial of the reality of either. In the transition period between apperception and neobehaviorism, much vacillation took place between emphasis upon the workings of biological organisms and the functions of either substantive or structural minds.

Late in the nineteenth century, interest in bodily functioning became apparent among many psychologists. This group of "physiological psychologists" thought that psychology could become a true science only if it switched its focus to bodily processes. In a century that placed ever increasing emphasis upon experimental science, introspection more and more appeared as a highly unreliable procedure. One could reflect upon the workings of one's own mind, but what did this prove? Scientists were ceasing to be concerned with any kind of evidence that was not "publicly verifiable," that is, subject to public observation and tests. Thus, they began to focus their attention on objects or events that could be observed with the "five senses," could be studied in the same manner by any number of trained investigators, and would lead to uniform conclusions.

To a growing number of psychologists, the only logical alternative to the method of introspection was to focus on observable forms of behavior. Such behavior included not only bodily movement, as seen by an observer watching a subject, but also the internal physical processes that were related to overt bodily behavior. Why epinephrine is secreted and how long it takes one to react to a pinprick are equally challenging questions to a physiological psychologist. Both can be measured objectively, described in terms of definite mechanical sequences or quantities, and reported statistically. Before the twentieth century was very far along, a large number of psychologists had come to feel that psychology, in time, could be made as "scientific" as physics.

Early in the nineteenth century, psychologists such as Pierre Florens (1794–1867) proposed that conclusions drawn from animal experimentation should be equally applicable to humankind. This notion gained wide acceptance and greatly simplified the work of experimental psychologists: After all, it is much cheaper and more convenient to experiment with rats than with human beings.

Some of the most notable animal learning experiments of the late nineteenth and early twentieth centuries were conducted by thee Russian physiologist and pharmacologist, Ivan Petrovich Pavlov (1849–1936). Pavlov wrote about the "psychical processes" that appeared in animals during his study of secretions of their digestive juices. In his study he placed food before a hungry dog and simultaneously sounded a bell or tuning fork. He found that if this procedure was repeated enough times, the sound alone would cause the dog to salivate. Pavlov's work was extremely influential, especially among the behaviorists in the United States.

What Was Thorndike's Connectionism?

Edward L. Thorndike, whose behavioristic psychology was called *connectionism*, was an "eclectic" in the sense that he retained in his thinking certain elements of Herbartian "idea associationism," and, at the same time, was strongly influenced by the new physiological psychology (see Chapter 6 for an example of eclecticism). Consequently, he assumed that there were both physical and mental events or units and that learning was a process of linking the two in various combinations. A mental unit was something sensed or perceived; a physical unit was a stimulus or a response. Specifically, he saw learning as a process of connecting a mental with a physical unit, a physical with a mental unit, a mental with a mental unit, or a physical with a physical unit.

Thorndike's animal experiments, making use of chicks, dogs, and cats, were more comprehensive than Pavlov's and, over the long run, more influential in the United States. Thorndike's famous "laws of learning" were derived mainly from his interpretation of how hungry cats behave when placed in a cage from which they cannot escape—until they learn how to do so. Since Thorndike was a dominant figure in the psychology of learning for almost half a century, we describe his ideas in some detail.

Thorndike's theory of learning, connectionism, is also called *S-R bond* theory. It implies that, through conditioning, specific responses come to be linked with specific stimuli. These links, bonds, or connections are products of biological, that is, synaptic, changes in a nervous system. Thorndike thought that the principal way in which S-R connections are formed is through random trial and error (or selecting and connecting). Because of Thorndike's influence the term *trial-and-error* became popularized and found its way into the vocabularies of many American educators.

In a typical trial-and-error experiment, Thorndike would place a hungry cat in a cage that could be opened from inside only by pulling a loop or striking a latch or button. He also would place some food that the cat relished outside the cage. The cat would claw, bite, and scurry wildly about until it accidentally touched the release and was freed. The experiment would be repeated and the animal would behave the same except that over the course of a number of successive "trials" the total time required by the cat to get out of the cage and to the food would decrease. Eventually, the cat would learn to escape immediately without random activity. Thorndike inferred from the timed behavior of his cats that learning was a process of "stamping in" connections in the nervous system. Thus, it had nothing to do with insight or "catching on."

Thorndike formulated a number of "laws" of learning and classified them as either primary or secondary. He expressed his primary laws by the terms *readiness, exercise,* and *effect.* His secondary or subordinate laws were identified by the expressions *multiple response, set* or *attitude, prepotency of elements, response by analogy*, and *associative shifting*.[2] We describe here only his three primary laws:

1. *The Law of Readiness*. Thorndike termed the neuron (or neurons) and the synapse (or synapses) involved in establishment of a specific bond or connection a *conduction unit*. He assumed that because of the structure of a nervous system, in a given situation certain conduction units are more predisposed to conduct than others. He also thought that "*for a conduction unit ready to conduct to do so is satisfying,* and *for it not to do so is annoying.*"[3]

2. *The Law of Exercise or Repetition*. According to this law, the more times a stimulus-induced response is repeated, the longer it will be retained. As Thorndike put it, "Other things being equal, *exercise strengthens the bond between situation and response.*"[4]

3. *The Law of Effect*. The law of effect stated the famous pleasure-pain principle so frequently associated with Thorndike's name. A response is strengthened if it is followed by pleasure and weakened if followed by displeasure. In Thorndike's words,

> [To] a modifiable connection being made . . . between an S and an R and being accompanied or followed by a satisfying state of affairs man responds, other things being equal, by an increase in the strength of that connection. To a connection similar, save that an *annoying* state of affairs goes with or follows it, man responds, other things being equal, by a decrease in the strength of the connection.[5]

> By a satisfying state of affairs [positive reinforcer] is meant one that the animal does nothing to avoid, often doing such things as attain and preserve it. By a discomforting or annoying state of affairs is meant one which the animal commonly avoids and abandons.[6]

In his later writings Thorndike disavowed his law of exercise or repetition and one-half—the annoyance aspect—of his law of effect. But he seemed not to have had the courage of his convictions. Through implication, he continued to emphasize repetition in learning. His law of effect shifted its emphasis to pleasure, but the pain aspect was not completely discarded.

Students will readily see that Thorndike's laws of learning are closely related and may operate together. For example, if an organism is ready to respond, then response is pleasurable and this fact in itself will tend to fix the response. Also, the laws appear to be exceedingly mechanical. Furthermore, they seem to leave no room for any sort of thought or insight and do not appear to require the assumption of any kind of purposiveness of humankind or lower animals.

The psychological concept of *purposiveness* has no direct relationship to the problem of cosmic or teleological purpose. Within a purposive as contrasted with a mechanistic psychology, one assumes that each animal or person, whatever its developmental level, is seeking some end or purpose and that one can predict its behavior most accurately when one anticipates what it is trying to accomplish.

What Was Watson's Behaviorism?

John B. Watson, much more strongly than Thorndike, felt the need to base psychology exclusively on the concepts of physics and chemistry. To him, mind and all kinds of mentalistic concepts were not only unsusceptible to scientific inquiry but also irrelevant to the real task of psychology. Watson drew heavily upon Pavlov's work and became convinced that learning was as Pavlov described it, namely, a process of building conditioned reflexes through the substitution of one stimulus for another.[7]

Watson's followers and other "pure behaviorists" came to reject certain of Thorndike's ideas, because it seemed impossible to exclude mind and mind-related concepts from them. The pure behaviorists were also bothered by Thorndike's concepts of satisfaction and annoyance. To behaviorists these seemed to be mentalistic concepts, which should be repudiated in a truly scientific psychology. Thus, they confined their study to only those aspects of animal life that are sufficiently overt to make possible highly objective observation and measurement of them.

Although Watsonians rejected some of Thorndike's ideas, they saw great promise in one of his secondary laws, *associative shifting*. According to this law, any response that is possible can be linked with any prior stimulus. An animal's "purposes or thoughts" have nothing to do with such learnings. We may illustrate this law by using an example involving the training of an animal. Suppose we wish to train a dog to sit up at the verbal command "Up." It is only necessary to induce the dog to sit up repeatedly by dangling a piece of meat or other food above him immediately after the verbal command "Up" is issued. Once this procedure has been repeated enough times, the dog should respond properly—without error—whenever the command is given. In this example, as long as the same "adequate stimulus" is used throughout the experiment, it would not matter if the command were replaced by any other accompanying stimulus to which a dog is sensitive—a light, a bell, snapping the fingers, whistling. Furthermore, by using the same basic procedure, one should be able to teach a dog to perform any other act of which it is capable—standing on its rear legs, rolling over, playing dead, and so on. This principle of learning, fundamental to behaviorism, is that of *stimulus substitution*.

Watsonian behaviorists have defined a living organism as a self-maintaining mechanism. They have assumed that the essence of a human machine is a system of receptors (sense organs), conductors (neurons), switching organs (brain and spinal cord), and effectors (muscles) attached to levers (bones)—plus, of course, fueling and controlling organs such as the stomach and glands. When an organism is defined in such mechanistic terms, mentalistic concepts can be entirely eliminated. Not only can they be dropped out of the picture but they actually begin to seem rather fanciful. Can one imagine a machine "having tender sentiments" or "soaring on the imagination"? Thus, among behaviorists, there developed an attitude toward the earlier mentalistic psychologists similar to that of a modern physician toward a primitive witch doctor.

The position of a Watsonian behaviorist can be illustrated amusingly in a morning conversation. Ordinarily, a conventional greeting would go as follows: "Good morning, how are you?" "I'm fine, and yourself?" "Just fine." But such greeting implies introspection. Each person is "looking into himself" in order to decide what kind of shape he/she is in. Presumably (according to a behaviorist), this is scientifically impossible; instead the two persons would need to inspect each other. The proper salutation of a behaviorist would be, "Good morning, you appear to be fine; how am I?"

Who Are the Neobehaviorists?

A large number of contemporary psychologists assume that life can be explained in essentially mechanistic terms, but they have adopted positions somewhat different from those of the Watsonian behaviorists. We refer to these contemporary S-R conditioning theorists as *neobehaviorists*.

Contemporary S-R conditioning theorists continue to assume that life can be explained in essentially mechanistic terms, but they place less emphasis on the operation of the brain and nervous system than did their predecessors. Watson himself had felt that the precise nature of neural mechanisms was largely irrelevant to an understanding of learning; but Watson's followers, like Thorndike, exhibited a strong interest in neural physiology and the physical mechanics of S-R linkages.

Neobehaviorists differ from the original behaviorists in another respect. In their experimentation they have tended to focus attention more on response modification than on stimulus substitution. Response modification refers to the fate of responses that are made—whether they will be strengthened, weakened, or changed by subsequent events.

Another interesting feature of neobehaviorism is its advocates' attempt to explain behavior that appears to be purposive. The apparent purposiveness of organisms has always bothered psychologists who are behavioristically oriented, because they have felt that it is difficult to recognize purposiveness without slipping into a mind-body dualism and its accompanying mysticism. However, because what seems purposive must be explained in some way, neobehaviorists have tended to develop mechanical explanations for apparent purposiveness. Thus, apparent purposiveness either is regarded as a product of a pattern of stimulation in which certain stimuli are more potent than the rest and thus lead an organism in one way rather than another or is interpreted as "drive reduction," that is, as a relieving reaction to the stimulation induced by organic drives such as hunger or sex. Thus, neobehaviorists continue to be careful to explain apparent purposiveness in a way that does not require the assumption of conscious behavior or intelligent experience.

Contemporary neobehaviorists also differ from early behaviorists in that their approach is more "holistic." Early behaviorism was "atomistic" in the sense that it focused on the "elements" of a situation. Attempts were made to identify specific stimuli and to describe the behavior of an organism as a product of numerous discrete and isolatable reactions. Today, S-R conditioning theorists are more likely to talk in terms of "stimulus situations," complex configurations of stimulation, and "molar behavior"—the coordinated behavior of a whole act of an organism.

Well-known contemporary neobehaviorists and their followers are greatly interested in the psychology of learning. However, at one extreme Spence thought that, in its present stage of development, psychology has little to offer schools, and at the other extreme Skinner represented his psychology as the means of immediately placing education on an efficient basis.

WHAT ARE THE ORIGINS OF COGNITIVE-INTERACTIONIST PSYCHOLOGY?

The second major family of contemporary learning theories—cognitive-interactionist psychology—originated in Germany during the early part of the twentieth century. Leaders in its early development were the Gestalt psychologists Max Wertheimer (1880–1943), Wolfgang Köhler (1887–1967), and Kurt Koffka (1886–1941). All three migrated to the United States, where they devoted their professional lives to development and refinement of the Gestalt position.

Gestalt is a German noun for which there is no equivalent English word, so the term was carried over into English psychological literature. The nearest English translation of *Gestalt* is an organized "configuration" or "pattern," including all that the pattern is composed of. Thus, we refer to related theories that either represented or grew out of Gestalt psychology as interactional or configurational psychology. As configurational psychology has evolved, other names such as *organismic, field phenomenological,* and *cognitive-field psychology* have developed from it. Cognitive-interactionist psychology was introduced into the United States in the middle 1920s. It has gathered a large number of exponents and now can be considered the leading rival of the behaviorisms. However, a great many psychologists are *eclectic* in the sense that they borrow elements from both schools of thought but do not identify with either.

Gestalt psychology was formally outlined by Wertheimer in 1912. Its central idea is that an organized whole is greater than the sum of its parts. For example, a triangle is greater than the sum of the three line segments that form it. This is because of its Gestalt.

The notion that a thing cannot be understood by studying its constituent parts but only by studying it as a totality is probably very old. Gardner Murphy suggests that it can be found in the literature of pre-Socratic Greece.[8] Various Greek writers proposed that the universe could best be understood through "laws of arrangement" or "principles of order," rather than through study of its basic building blocks, the elements. In contrast, other Greek writers were "atomists," who sought the key to understanding through a study of individual elements. Just as the former might be called the originators of the Gestalt idea, so the latter might be called the originators of the atomistic idea that characterized early behaviorism.

The nineteenth-century forerunners of Wertheimer include Ernst Mach (1838–1916) and Christian Von Ehrensfels (1859–1932). Although Mach held that the worlds of physics and psychology are essentially the same, he also argued that psychology must take into account those sensations that do not correspond to the physical reality before the viewer. These "nonphysical" sensations are sensations of *relationship*. For example, a person may see three dots on a sheet of paper and think of them as the points of a triangle. There is nothing in the individual dots to suggest this; it is their configuration that prompts the relationship.

In the 1890s, following Mach, Von Ehrenfels pursued the same ideas. He stated that, in all perception, qualities appear that represent more than the physical items sensed. A perceiver tends to confer on the physical objects of a perception a form, configuration, or meaning; he/she tries to organize or integrate what he sees. A school of thought began to form along the lines explored by these two men, and a new term came into use—*Gestaltqualität*, which means approximately "the quality conferred by a pattern."

Wertheimer and his followers formulated a series of "laws" of perception and identified them by the concepts *Prägnanz, similarity, proximity, closure, good continuation,* and *membership character.* According to the *basic law of Prägnanz,* if a perceptual field is disorganized when a person first experiences it, he/she imposes order on that field in a predictable way that follows the other five laws. *Similarity* means that similar items (dots, for instance) tend to form groups in perception. *Proximity* means that perceptual groups are favored according to the nearness of their respective parts.

Closure means that closed areas are more stable than unclosed ones. Draw a 340° arc and ask a viewer what you have drawn; the viewer very likely will say "a circle." This is an example of closure. Since to achieve closure is satisfying to one, closure might be considered a dynamic alternative to Thorndike's mechanistic law of effect. *Good continuation* is closely related to closure. It means that, in perception, one tends to continue straight lines as straight lines and curves as curves.

According to the law of *membership character,* a single part of a whole does not have fixed characteristics; instead, its characteristics are gotten from the context in which it appears. As Gardner Murphy puts it, "the Gestaltist insists that the attributes or aspects of the component parts, insofar as they can be defined, are defined by their relations to the system as a whole in which they are functioning."[9] For example, a patch of color in a painting derives its quality from its context—the surrounding picture pattern—more than from anything inherent in itself.

The Gestalt "laws" imply that in perception, one's organization of a field tends to be as simple and clear as the existing conditions allow. Hence, a person, in experiencing his world, imposes an organization that is characterized by stability, simplicity, regularity, and symmetry. A viewer groups individual items in a field so they will have a pattern; he/she relates similar items as are required for completeness; and, if present patterns are meaningful, he tries to maintain them into the future. Imposing a "good" Gestalt, as happens when the foregoing events occur, is a psychological task. It does not necessarily involve any change in the physical environment. Rather, it represents a change in how a viewer "sees" or perceives his physical environment.

Two of Wertheimer's German colleagues, Wolfgang Köhler and Kurt Koffka, were primarily responsible for publicizing Gestalt psychology and establishing it in the United States. Köhler is famous, among other things, for his celebrated study of the learning process in chimpanzees (*The Mentality of Apes*, 1925). He set out to test Thorndike's hypothesis that learning is a matter of random trial and error in which correct responses are gradually stamped in. Köhler observed that in addition to the fact that they exhibited learning that might appear accidental, his apes also displayed a type of learning that appeared insightful. Hence, Köhler concluded that Thorndike's laws of learning were inadequate. Koffka's book *Growth of Mind* (1924) contained a detailed criticism of trial-and-error learning as conceived by Thorndike. Koffka's book not only criticized Thorndike but also the major ideas of behaviorism.

Kurt Lewin took the spirit of Gestalt theory, added to it some new concepts, and coined a new terminology. He developed a *field* psychology that he also called *topological and vector psychology*. Lewin spent his later years in the United States, where he acquired a considerable following. Lewin's psychological theory has contributed much to current cognitive-field theory, which is developed in Chapters 8 and 9.

During the development of the Gestalt-field family, its adherents have made two significant changes in their position concerning the presumed moral and actional nature of human beings. The original German Gestaltists— Köhler, Koffka, and Wertheimer—thought that people were neutral-active beings whose activities conformed to a set of psychological laws of organization. But the American Gestaltists, such as Raymond H. Wheeler and Ernest E. Bayles, considered people to be neutral-interactive, purposive individuals whose interaction consisted of *sequential* relationships with their environments. Then, cognitive-field theorists adopted the Lewinian position and built their thinking around neutral-interactive persons perceptually in *simultaneous mutual interaction* with their psychological environments. For that reason, this family has come to be known as *cognitive-interactionist*.

It is in the process of developing an *emergent synthesis* from the two horns of the active-passive or subjective-objective dilemma that cognitive-field learning theory has emerged (see page 12 for an explanation of the meaning of an emergent synthesis). Within this psychology, learning is neither equated with unfoldment and sheer expression of inner urges nor is it a conditioning process that comes from the environment impinging upon a biological organism from without. Instead, cognitive-field psychologists find the clue to the meaning of learning in the aspects of a situation within which a person and his psychological environment come together in a psychological field or life space.

As a result of experimentation conducted by cognitive interactionists, behaviorists generally are coming to recognize that the earlier atomistic stimulus-response idea, based as it was on the principle of simple reflex arcs, does not explain human behavior or learning adequately. Thus, there is a tendency among contemporary S-R conditioning theorists to speak of "molar behavior" or behavior of the whole organism in contrast to piecemeal or "molecular" behavior. Accordingly, such psychologists characteristically refer to "total responses to patterns of stimulation." However, since these psychologists continue to think in terms of mechanically related stimuli and responses, they are still within the basic pattern of S-R conditioning theory.

WHAT IS THE PHILOSOPHICAL THINKING BEHIND THE TWO PSYCHOLOGICAL FAMILIES?

The purpose of this section is to explore some of the philosophical implications of the two families of psychology. When a contrast is drawn between their underlying philosophical premises, differences between the two families are made much clearer. Although many psychologists have tried during the past century to divorce psychology from philosophy, it is doubtful that this is possible. There is no science so "pure" that it lacks philosophical implications. Even physicists find it helpful to make assumptions about the basic nature of their materials and processes; hence, they too become involved in philosophical formulations.

Since any psychological system rests upon some particular conception of basic human nature, psychology is deeply involved with philosophy from the very start. The issue among contemporary psychologists is whether a human being is an active creature of instincts and needs (as exemplified in the self-actualization of existentialist humanism), an essentially *passive* or *reactive* organism that is the product of a unique stimulus-response history in a determining environment (as implied in S-R conditioning theory) or a *purposive person* who is interacting with his psychological environment (as currently implied in contemporary cognitive-interactionist psychology). Each of the two latter positions harmonizes with an allied philosophical outlook: S-R conditioning theory with earlier *scientific realism* or contemporary *logical empiricism,* and cognitive-field theory with earlier *pragmatism* or contemporary *positive relativism,* also called *cognitive-field experimentalism.*

How Does Logical Empiricism Underpin S-R Conditioning Theory?

Scientific realists have been convinced that the physical world that is experienced by human beings is real and essentially what it appears to be when observed through the senses. Furthermore, even if there were no human beings around to observe it, the physical world would exist in the same state. Reality, like existence, is independent of a thing being known. Scientific realists have assumed that the physical world is governed by natural laws, which operate inexorably and without change. Further, they have assumed that a basic principle of the universe is sequential cause and effect; every event is determined by events that have gone before it. Thus, the universe is a vast mechanism governed by natural laws, which are essentially mechanical in nature.

Contemporary logical empiricists—the current representatives of scientific realism—think that we should abandon dogmatic, other-worldly, supernaturalistic, and tender-minded ways of thinking and replace them with critical, worldly, naturalistic, and empirical fact-minded outlooks and procedures. Logical empiricists are likely to assume that there is a kind of hierarchy of the sciences, some being much more objective and reliable than others. They place at the top of the hierarchy physics and chemistry, aided by mathematics. These sciences are regarded as models that other sciences should emulate. For logical empiricists, just as the art of agriculture is based upon biological and chemical scientific knowledge, so education should be based upon the pure sciences of biology and psychology. To a consistent logical empiricist, nothing should be asserted to be real or meaningful unless, through observation, it can be subjected to objective study, using only publicly verifiable data. If anything exists, it exists in some amount; if it exists in some amount, it can be measured.

Let us trace how this overall point of view has been extended to psychology. Early in human history, people commonly believed in animism, that is, that all objects, including even rocks, have minds or spirits. Since primitive people had not other way of explaining most types of natural events, animism provided at least some basis for understanding their surroundings. However, as people learned more about natural causation, animism declined in popularity. In other words, when human beings came to understand something about gravity, a person no longer needed to attribute a mind and will to a rock to know why it fell on his head.

As time went on, mechanical explanations began to be applied to all sorts of physical events involving nonliving objects. Increasingly, the nonliving parts of the universe were believed to consist of atoms in motion, each inert by itself but subject to the push and pull of lawful forces external to itself.

Since living objects, especially human beings, seemed, on the surface at least, to be willful and unpredictable, they did not appear to conform to the mechanical concepts that applied to the world of nature. Thus, some kind of vitalistic mind-force was attributed to them. The belief in a nonmaterial mind-force as applied to human beings led to a distinctive conception of learning as a process of disciplining or training minds. This gave us the classical humanistic tradition in education. Although actual teaching under the classical mind-training approach may appear to be highly mechanical, the conception of human nature that underlies it definitely is nonmechanistic in that it assumes the existence of a mind substance, which is capable both of free will and of spontaneous "uncaused" behavior.

Apperception, the first modern associationism, was a mechanistic, though mental, psychology. Although in developing his learning theory Herbart perpetuated the idea that human beings have a mystical aspect, his mechanistic psychology opened the way for rejection of vitalism and accompanying mentalistic concepts, which are inconsistent with a "realistic" interpretation of the universe. Consequently, as the associationistic psychologies developed, psychologists found themselves in increasing sympathy with the tenets of scientific realistic philosophy.

Realistic, mechanistic psychology, then, has been an outgrowth of the attempt of S-R conditioning theorists to make psychology as "scientific" as physics. Thus, S-R conditioning theorists have equated stimulus and response in psychology with cause and effect in physics.

The issue between mechanistic and nonmechanistic psychology is nowhere stated more clearly than by the neobehaviorist Donald O. Hebb (1904–1985). Hebb said flatly that psychology's only hope of remaining scientific was to assume that a person is basically a mechanism. Thus, as far as the basic outlook of a psychologist is concerned, there were for Hebb only two alternatives—mechanism and vitalism.

He wrote that observable behavior is the factual basis of psychology and that we do not include in the definition of psychology anything that is not at least potentially observable. He then stated,

> *Psychology* is . . . the study of the more complex forms of integration or organization in behavior . . . this includes also the study of processes such as learning, emotion or perception that are involved in organizing the behavior. "Integration" or "organization" refers to the pattern or combination of different segments of behavior in relation to each other and to external events impinging on the organism.[10]

Furthermore, with respect to the type of study that psychologists can undertake, Hebb wrote, "All one can know about another's feeling and awareness is an inference from what he *does*—from his muscular contractions and glandular secretion."[11]

To a psychologist such as Hebb, cognitive-interactionist psychology would appear to be little more than "confusionism." The philosophical orientation of a behavioristic psychologist is usually so thoroughly mechanistic that any other outlook seems untenable. It was in their evaluation of this behavioristic position that David L. Horton and Thomas W. Turnage wrote in 1976, "In many ways the most damaging aspect of the behavioristic concept was the assumption that man is a passive receiver of inputs to which he responds in automatic and stereotyped ways."[12]

Logical empiricists and their behavioristic psychological counterparts continue to think in terms of stimuli being causes and responses being effects and of there being a time lapse between physical stimuli and organic responses. To quote Hebb further, "Temporarily integrated behavior, extended over a period of time, is treated as a series of reactions to a series of stimulations. . . . Stimulus followed directly by response is the archetype of behavior."[13] Accordingly, logical empiricists, in harmony with behaviorists, treat human beings as basically extremely well-designed, clever machines, who learn through accumulating memories in an additive process. Human responses are a chance affair and a human being is a biological organism with a history of conditioned behavior. For logical empiricists, words such as *foresight, purpose,* and *desire* are literary terms, not scientific ones.

In their approach to education, logical empiricists, and likewise behaviorists, are very much environmental determinists in the sense that they assume that the surrounding environment should, and inescapably will, largely control the behavior and learning of students. Thus, teaching practices advocated by behavioristic psychologists are closely in tune with the logical empiricist-realistic outlook. Such psychologists tend to recommend that subject matter be selected by qualified adults prior to the teaching act, that it reflect facts and skills useful in contemporary society, and that it be conditioned into students. There is an implicit assumption that if a given item of subject matter impinges upon a student, there will be a definite and predictable effect. Only secondary, if any, mention is made of such concepts as student goals or problem solving.

How Does Positive Relativism Underpin Cognitive-Interactionist Psychology?

Positive relativism has emerged during the past 70 or 80 years and is, in a sense, a reaction against the absolutistic ways that have characterized many facets of human thinking throughout history; thus, it contrasts sharply with logical empiricism. Logical empiricists, earlier called scientific realists, assume the existence of an ultimate reality, which consists of fixed natural laws, and define truth as that which corresponds to natural law and consequently is unchanging. In contrast with logical empiricists, positive relativists neither assert nor deny an absolute existent reality. Rather, they define psychological reality as that which we "make of" what we gain from our environment. They then deal with reality, so defined, in achieving truth and designing behavior. Thus, whereas for a logical empiricist reality is the same as an objective existence, for a positive relativist reality is psychological and thereby different from any objective existence; it is what people gain through their five-plus senses.

The *positive* aspect of positive relativism denotes that such a relativism, to quote Webster's is, "logically affirmative" and "capable of being constructively applied," as in "positive proposals for the betterment of society."[14] The philosophy being affirmative implies that its proponents assert the availability of truth and reality and thereby affirm the feasibility of a body of constructive knowledge. Its capability of being constructively applied signifies that it is structured so as to direct its adherents toward promotion of further development, improvement, and advancement of themselves and society. Hence, a person is being positively relativistic in his thinking and action when he/she harbors no absolutes and simultaneously attempts to strengthen or improve matters or to develop something better to take their place.

A position kindred to positive relativism is "irrealist relativism." Its adherents, represented by Professor Nelson Goodman of Harvard, hold an attitude of unconcern with absolutistic issues such as those involving the differences between realism and idealism or between rationalism and empiricism. They hold that there is "no unique, ready-made absolute reality apart from and independent of versions and visions."[15] The forms and the laws pertinent to our worlds do not lie there ready-made to be discovered, but are imposed by our contrived world-versions in the sciences, the arts, our perceptions, and our everyday practices.

Irrealistic relativists further think that there are many right world-versions, some of them irreconcilable with others. "A version is not so much made right by a world as a world is made by a right version."[16] To quote Goodman again, "Never mind mind, essence is not essential, and matter doesn't matter."[17]

A central idea of relativism is that anything derives its qualities from its relationships to other things. For example, a fairly tall girl, seen in the company of taller girls, may appear to be short. This principle is one with which everyone is familiar. Relativistic philosophy only extends, explores, and develops its numerous implications and ramifications.

It might appear that if relativism were a valid concept, a person could never make a definitive statement about anything, except to say that it "is closer than something else," "is to the left of something else," "is darker than something else," or "is smaller than something else." However, this is not an insurmountable problem. In order to view a thing relativistically, one simply determines a convenient vantage point for reference. One can say that one's automobile has 200 horsepower, and be quite confident in such an assertion. The unit of measure, 1 horsepower, is an arbitrary standard humanly contrived and susceptible to future change, yet it has definite usefulness as a point of reference. Such relatively fixed points of reference are *relatively absolute*. The word *absolute*, so used, is an adjective; it means no more than that the point of reference is one of relative fixity or stability.

If one assumes that objects have to be dealt with relationally, rather than as things-in-themselves, then a distinctive method of defining truth or knowledge and an equally distinctive method of arriving at truth are required. Relativists question the notion that human beings are able to find and use final or absolute truth. Consequently, they have little interest in "eternal verities." Nevertheless, they are deeply concerned with truths, relativistically defined. Relativists regard knowledge as insights developed and held by human beings using human methods.

The development of the notion that knowledge is a matter of human interpretation, and not a literal description of what exists external to people, reflects a shift from an absolutistic to a relativistic view of science. A scientific law (including a principle of psychology) is a statement that seems true to all or most of those who are competent to study the matter. The relativistic test of truth is *anticipatory accuracy*, not correspondence to ultimate reality. Thus, in a sense, a scientific law is a generalization about which there is considerable agreement among those scientifically competent in its area; it is in a way a matter of consensus. Its test, however, is not the consensus but its predictive accuracy. Relativists assume that no scientific law is "sacred"; any law may change, and indeed, over the course of time most will. A significant aspect of the thinking of relativists is their expectancy of change.

Positive relativists do not mean that truth has no objective standard and that it always varies from person to person, group to group, and time to time.

In fact, they recognize that, fortunately, many truths have been so adequately tested that we may safely treat them as if they were certainties. However, their definition of certainty is "something in which I have tremendous faith."[18]

But what grounds does a relativist have for judging anything true? To quote Bayles, an insight is considered true "if, and only if, the deduced behavior pattern, when tested experientially or experimentally, produces the results which were anticipated.[19] Thus, an insight is true if it proves to be quite accurate—if what one supposes will follow from its application actually does follow. Therefore, for a relativist, truth is not based upon eternal and universal principles. Rather, it is of human origin and humanity will change it as need be. But this does not mean that truth is unimportant or ephemeral. It does mean that truth tends to evolve as human experience evolves.

Both logical empiricists and positive relativists assume that the most valid method of inquiry is scientific in nature; it is based on testable evidence. But they define "scientific method" in quite different ways and, as the foregoing discussion has indicated, they seek different ends from it. To a relativist, scientific method is not merely a sequence of steps such as a physicist supposedly uses. Instead, it is any form of intellectual pursuit that is based upon testable evidence and is productive in relation to the goals of the thinker. To be sure, there are some measuring sticks or criteria of scientific truth; these criteria may be encompassed under the headings of *pertinency, adequacy,* and *harmony* in light of obtainable data. A conclusion, to be properly scientific, must be based upon adequate pertinent data, it must reflect consideration of all pertinent data, and it must harmonize all the data, that is, make the data add up. If a single pertinent fact seems to be contradictory, if it remains unexplained, then the conclusion is not to be trusted.

Positive relativists construe science much more broadly than do logical empiricists. They assume that the scientific approach can be applied in a wide range of situations. They do not think in terms of a hierarchy of sciences, with physics, chemistry, and mathematics at the top. They are also more flexible with respect to the kinds of data that will be considered. In psychological research, logical empiricists are likely to admit only data of observable physical objects or substances. Conversely, positive relativists in psychology will consider all the data of human experience, including what might seem to be introspective. Thus, in the formation of hypotheses to be tested, they may go beyond the information that is at hand.

Current positive-relativistic cognitive-interactionist psychology essentially is an emergent synthesis, but not a compromise, that has developed from an ideological conflict between the psychological tenets of existentialist humanistic self-actualization and those of logical-empiricist behaviorism (see page 12 for an explanation of the concept *emergent synthesis*).

To existentialist humanists, learning is largely equated with unfoldment and is a product of inner urges. Logical-empiricist psychologists, at the other extreme, have considered all human development to be a product of biological maturation and learning and have assumed that learning is a conditioning process that occurs through the environment's impinging upon an individual from without.

In bridging the two positions, positive relativists assume that a child or youth is what he/she is because of the psychological interaction between himself and his culture. With the emphasis upon interaction, the responsibility for development rests neither with the person alone nor with the environment alone. Instead, it is in a person and his environment coming together in a psychological field that cognitive-field psychologists find their clue to psychological development and learning. Since the number of possible culture patterns is infinite, the possibilities for variety in human development likewise become infinite. Thus, within its biological limits, human nature might become anything.

HOW DO THE TWO FAMILIES DEFINE REALITY?

Historically, the term *reality* has connoted a transcendental, independent, and absolute existence. Accordingly, behaviorists have tended to treat reality and existence as identical concepts. Thus, for them, the term *reality* refers to physical objects and processes, which exist or are "there" in their own right. The chair on which the reader is sitting may be said to exist, and to a behaviorist the chair is a good example of reality (not one's impression of the chair, but the chair itself). The chair exists in its own right; the way one perceives it is not relevant to its reality.

Cognitive interactionists make a distinction between reality and existence. Without denying independent existence of objects, or even of other people's ideas, they think that each person sizes up or interprets his supposed world in such a way that it will form a meaningful pattern for him, and this interpretation is the reality on which he/she designs actions. Thus, a person's knowledge of things is always limited by the impossibility of one's ever getting completely "outside oneself." Consequently, any perception of a physical-social world will be colored to some degree by the purposes and experiences of the observer as well as by the procedures used in observing the perceived object. To a positive relativist, reality consists of the *interpretations* that a person makes of himself and of his surroundings as he/she interacts with them. If reality is to be regarded as interpretations or meanings, rather than as preexistent physical objects as such, it is obvious that reality will be in a constant state of flux. None of these statements, however, should be taken to mean that a person literally makes his world; rather, in any field—science, social relations, morality, even religion—each individual makes, not *the* world, but *his notion* of the world.

To understand fully the way cognitive interactionists differ from behaviorists in their meaning of reality, one must explore the differences between exponents of the respective outlooks in their definitions of *environment, perception*, and *experience*. We have already suggested some of these differences; now we dig more deeply.

How Is Environment Defined by the Two Groups of Psychologists?

S-R conditioning theorists maintain that a person's psychological and physical environments are identical; his environment consists of all his physical and social surroundings. Because environment is defined in objective, physical terms, presumably anyone can see, hear, smell, feel, or taste the environment of anyone else.

In contrast, cognitive interactionists think of a person's environment as being psychological; it consists of what one makes of what is around one—that portion of a life space or perceptual field that surrounds a person or self. A psychological environment includes impressions of parts of the physical environment but not necessarily all of it. It also extends beyond its physical environment. Sometimes a person's psychological environment includes largely memories or anticipations; in this case the person is scarcely aware of the physical world currently around him. Hence, he/she is operating on a highly imaginative level. (See Chapter 9, page 204, for a distinction between imaginative and concrete levels of reality.)

Since each person's perceptual environment is unique, obviously two persons may appear to be in the same location in space and time (or as nearly so as possible) and yet have very different psychological environments. Furthermore, the behaviors of two equally intelligent persons who are confronted with the same "objective facts" may differ drastically because each is different in his purposes and experiential background. Whenever a person has a new experience, he/she changes his environment and will never again be able to recapture the old environment in its identical form. The cognitive-interactionist conception of environment helps explain why in a particular family one son may become a minister and another turn to crime; their interpretations of their world differ radically, even though to an outsider their social and physical environments would appear quite similar.

How Do the Two Groups Define Perception?

Behaviorists define perception in such a way as to make it analogous with taking photographs. The sense organs in literal fashion "read" a person's social and physical surroundings and record this "reading" in the nervous system. After sensing something, a person may derive a meaning for it. But note that, according to behaviorists, sensation comes prior to meaning and the two processes, sensing and finding meaning, are regarded as separate. A behaviorist assumes that sensation may be indiscriminate, in that a person tends to "take in" all aspects of the physical world to which his sense organs are sensitive. Such a psychologist defines perception, then, as a two-step process (sensing and deriving meaning) that focuses on particular objects of the environment only insofar as chance and previous conditioning directs.

A cognitive interactionist, on the other hand, does not separate a person's sensation of an object from the process of gaining its meaning. In a cognitive interactionist's view, a person will rarely sense an object unless it has relevance to some purpose of the person. It is this relevance to purpose, this instrumental quality, of an object that constitutes its meaning, and unless a person sees some meaning in an object he/she will pay little or no attention to it. Thus, a cognitive interactionist sees perception as a unitary process in which sensation hinges on meaning and meaning on sensation. Perception, then, is highly selective and always related to a person's purposes at the time of perception. In his goal-seeking behavior, a person actively seeks out those aspects of his environment that will either help or hinder, and usually it is to these that a person is primarily sensitive.

To a cognitive interactionist, the meaning of a sensation or perception is always related to the total situation. Relationships, not a summation of individual elements, determine the quality of any perceptual event. Any psychological event is a result of the interaction of many factors; hence, perception always involves a problem of organization. A thing is perceived as a relationship within a psychological field, which includes the thing, the viewer, and a complex psychological background that incorporates the viewer's purposes and results of previous experience. Considering these notions, it is obvious that, to a cognitive interactionist, the senses do not directly mirror physical objects in one's geographical environment. Hence, the camera analogy, which fits the behavioristic idea of perception, seems gross oversimplification.

Here is one example of perceptual interaction. Parents and siblings usually constitute important aspects of a child's psychological environment. When a second child arrives in a family, the first child sizes up—perceives—the situation. Whether the first child feels rejected depends, not upon the physical stimuli as such received from the parents and the sibling, but upon what the first child makes of the relationship of the parents and the second child. The important question is not "Do the parents actually favor child number two?" but rather, "Does child number one "see" child number two as favored over child number one?" In this situation the parents and the other child are key aspects of each child's and parent's psychological environment. The way child number one perceives the situation has important bearing upon the environments of child number two and the parents. Each person in a situation interacts with the others.

Cognitive interactionists make a sharp distinction between interaction of physical objects in a physical environment and the subject of psychology— interaction of psychological realities in a psychological environment. A person interacts by relating himself, as he/she understands himself, to his interpretation of what is around him. Of course, while interacting, one may move one's body and manipulate objects in one's physical environment in ways conspicuous to observers. But psychological interaction and physical reaction are two different processes. A person can interact within a psychological field while being seated in an armchair in front of a fireplace.

Any idea can be ridden too hard, and the reader has probably already thought of cases in which cognitive interaction does not seem to fit. For example, a person who is not aware of danger may be shot in the back. It seems fairly clear that in such a case the person has been a passive victim of a feature of the environment that was active in relation too that person. However, all this example suggests is that there are situations in which a person has no control over what happens to him. Cognitive interactionists do not deny this; instead, they operate on the not inconsistent assumption that a person seeks to manipulate purposefully, *whenever possible*, all those aspects of the environment that at the time mean anything to him. The person may or may not be successful, but his life space will be different as a result of the attempt.

What Is the Meaning of Experience?

Behaviorists tend to think of *experience* as a literary term, not a scientific one. Some behaviorists do employ the term in explaining their learning theories, but they give it only minor importance. Other behaviorists, led by B. F. Skinner, espouse *radical behaviorism*, which means that they have little or no place in their learning theory for such concepts as experience, awareness, or consciousness.

A behaviorist may concede that thought appears to occur, but is likely to insist that if human beings are to be studied with true scientific objectivity, most kinds of mentalistic concepts must be ruled out of bounds. Skinner expresses this notion clearly:

> the private event [that is, thought or consciousness] is at best no more than a link in a causal chain, and it is usually not even that. We may think before we act in the sense that we may behave covertly before we behave overtly, but our action is not an "expression" of the covert response [that is, thought] or the consequence of it. The two are attributable to the same variables.[20]

When behaviorists do use the term *experience*, they interpret it mechanistically. Accordingly, to them, it means the conditioning process by which a human organism either learns new responses or changes old ones as the result of stimuli impinging on its sensory organs. If a child touches a hot stove and if a link is formed between the sight of a stove and a withdrawal response, then it might be said that the child has had an experience. No thought needs to have occurred and no insights need to have been developed.

Cognitive interactionists give their conception of *experience* a major place in their learning theories, but they define experience in terms of persons purposively interacting with their respective psychological environments and realizing the consequences of so doing. Hence they regard experience as rooted in insightful behavior. From this point of view, experience is a psychological event that involves a person acting purposefully with anticipation of the probable or possible consequences of such action. Thus, experience is interaction of a person and his perceived environment. This is what Dewey meant when he said, "An experience is always what it is because of a transaction taking place between an individual and what, *at the time*, constitutes his environment."[21] He further stated that "To 'learn from experience' is to make a backward and forward connection between what we do to things and what we enjoy or suffer from things in consequence."[22] Experience includes an active and passive element, combined in a peculiar fashion:

On the active hand, experience is *trying....* On the passive, it is *undergoing*. When we experience something, we act upon it, we do something with it; then we suffer or undergo the consequences. We do something to the thing and then it does something to us in return; such is the peculiar combination. The connection of these two phases of experience measures the fruitfulness or value of the experience. Mere activity does not constitute experience.[23]

Every experience both extracts something from experiences that have gone before and modifies in some way experiences that follow. Furthermore, to some degree every experience influences the conditions under which future experiences may be had. Thus, in the case of a reasonably normal person, successive perceptual fields or life spaces tend to be similar to, though not identical with, one another.

WHAT DOES MOTIVATION MEAN FOR EACH FAMILY?

Motivation refers to the "mainsprings" or instigative forces of behavior; people do what they do because of motivation. As in the case of concepts treated previously in this chapter, S-R conditioning theorists and cognitive interactionists hold contrasting and seemingly incompatible ideas about the nature of motivation. These differences arise from the contrasting conceptions of basic human nature held by the two schools of thought. If one views human beings mechanistically, as most behaviorists do, one will prefer a theory of motivation compatible with this outlook. Conversely, if one views human beings as purposeful, reflective, and creative individuals, as most cognitive interactionists do, one will have quite a different theory of motivation.

What Is Motivation to Adherents of S-R Conditioning?

As we have seen, adherents of S-R conditioning tend to regard a human being as a behaving intricate machine. Machines operate with induced regularity, according to fixed principles. Even a machine as complicated as a computer does not operate purposefully as we generally use the term. A computer does not know what to do until it has been programmed by a human being. Even computers that can correct their own errors and do other seemingly fantastic tasks still behave as they do because some person has designed and regulated them. In a sense, a machine has no more purpose than a falling rock; it acts, but it has no thought-out goal. Many S-R conditioning theorists attribute this same quality to the nature of human beings.

To a behavioristic psychologist, all motivation arises either directly from one's organic drives or basic emotions or from a tendency to respond that has been established by prior conditioning of the drives and emotions. Motivation means that an organism is either deprived of something toward which there is an appetitional need or confronted with a discomforting stimulus. Organic drives, such as hunger, thirst, and sexual need, and the emotions—fear, anger, and "love"—produce behaviors that are both predictable and irresistible. The drives and emotions are "built into" the organism, and it can do little to resist them. Conditioning produces a series of learned behaviors that spring into action whenever relevant stimuli appear. These conditioned responses and operants operate more or less automatically; a person makes them because he/she must. Thus, through conditioning, the machinelike body has been regulated to behave in a predictable manner. To a behaviorist, then, all behavior is either stimulus-directed or stimulus-determined. Whether the stimulus comes from within the organism or without, motivation is defined as the urge to act that results from prior stimulation.

There are certain obvious aspects of the behavior of people or lower animals that do not appear to be adequately explained by the mechanical concepts of S-R conditioning theory. One of these is *attention*. At any given time a person pays attention to one thing rather than to another. At this moment the reader of this book is "attending" to this page rather than to a television program or a poker game. Thus, the fact of attention may seem to demonstrate that human behavior is governed by purpose. However, though S-R conditioning theorists concede that a person may often respond selectively to one or a small group of stimuli at a time, they believe that what appear to be selective responses can be explained according to behavioristic principles and that the existence of purpose need not be assumed. According to an adherent of S-R conditioning, an organism selects one response rather than another because of the particular combination of its genetic inheritance, its prior conditioning, and the present physiological drives and stimuli that are operating at the moment of perception. To an S-R conditioning theorist, to introduce purpose as an explanation of motivation is to risk introducing some kind of metaphysical guiding force and to make impossible a truly scientific approach to the study of behavior.

A behaviorist's theory of motivation has important implications for education. According to this viewpoint, children do not have to "want" to learn history in order to learn it. They only have to be persuaded to study it, to repeat the verbal responses that we associate with a knowledge of history. Anyone can learn anything, within the limits of the organism's capability, if put through the pattern of activity necessary for conditioning to take place. Thus, behaviorists talk little about matters such as "psychological involvement" or "helping students see the point of learning." Instead, they engage students in behavior and assume that behavior with appropriate conditioning automatically produces learning. Teachers carefully plan which learnings (responses) they want students to develop. They then induce these responses and condition them with stimuli.

What Is Motivation to Cognitive Interactionists?

Present-day cognitive interactionists tend to avoid the use of behavioristic concepts such as *drive*, *effect*, and *reinforcement* on the one hand and mentalistic concepts such as *vitalism* and *consciousness* on the other. For them, some key concepts in dealing with motivation are *goal*, *expectancy*, *intention*, and *purpose*. Within this frame of reference, behavior is a function of a total situation— a person interacting within a field of psychological forces. A person's psychological field includes purposes and goals, interpretation of relevant physical objects and events, and memories and anticipations.[24] Accordingly, motivation cannot be described as merely an impulse to act triggered by a stimulus. Rather, it emerges from a dynamic psychological situation, characterized by a person's desire to do something.

A cognitive interactionist regards motivation as a product of disequilibrium within a psychological situation, which includes goals and often barriers to the achievement of these goals. A goal may be either positive or negative—something one wants either to achieve or to avoid. When a barrier, that is, any obstacle to the direct and immediate achievement of a goal, appears, a person feels tension and he/she tries to relieve that tension either by surmounting or by circumventing the barrier. The tendency to release tension by proceeding toward a goal, including the overcoming of whatever barriers are in the way, is motivation.

The particular form that motivation takes and its intensity are functions of a field of psychological forces in which no distinction can be made between "inner" and "outer." That is, one cannot identify a category of forces that stems exclusively from physiological drives and another category that stems from the outside environment. Hence, cognitive interactionists object to the manner in which behaviorists attribute motivation to independently acting organic drives and stimuli.

Whereas S-R conditioning theorists make much of pleasure and pain, or satisfaction and annoyance, as instigators of behavior, cognitive interactionists are more likely to talk about *success* and *failure* as motivators, the former truly being the "reward" for completing an act. Success and failure are not merely achievements as such but represent the relationship between a person's ambitions and his achievements. If he/she has a certain level of aspiration and is able to achieve this level, he feels good about it. If he/she attains success at one level of aspiration, he is likely to raise the level and to continue doing so as long as he is able to perform successfully.[25]

Teachers who espouse a cognitive-interactionist concept of motivation are likely to approach teaching in fundamentally different ways from teachers who operate within a behavioristic framework. Such teachers are deeply concerned with the problem of personal involvement, that is, in helping students see a need to learn. Hence, the personal goals of students are always observed. This does not mean that the teachers cater to students' every whim. Often they try to help them rethink their goals and discard those that are trivial and whimsical. Much of the time the teachers attempt to arrange the teaching-learning situation so that students will adopt goals quite new to them. They are convinced that, unless a child or youth realizes a need to learn something, the child or youth either will not learn it at all or will learn it only in a transitory and functionally useless way.

NOTES

1. *Neo* is a word element meaning "new," "recent," or "modified." When used as a prefix, it refers to a school of thought that is derived from an earlier school

of thought but refined in various ways. See T. W. Wann, ed., *Behaviorism and Phenomenology* (Chicago: University of Chicago Press, 1965), pp. 7–21.

2. See Gordon H. Bower and Ernest H. Hilgard, *Theories of Learning*, 5th ed. (Englewood Cliffs, NJ: Prentice Hall, 1981), for descriptions of the subordinate laws.

3. Edward L. Thorndike, *Educational Psychology*, vol. 1 (New York: Teachers College Press, 1913), p. 127 (italics in original).

4. Edward L. Thorndike, *Education* (New York: Macmillan, 1912), p. 95 (italics in original).

5. Thorndike, *Educational Psychology*, p. 172.

6. Edward L. Thorndike, *Animal Intelligence* (New York: Macmillan, 1911), p. 245.

7. See Julian Janes, *The Origin of Consciousness in the Breakdown of the Bicameral Mind* (Boston: Houghton Mifflin, 1982), pp. 14–15.

8. Gardner Murphy, *Historical Introduction to Modern Psychology* (New York: Harcourt Brace Jovanovich, 1949), p. 284.

9. Ibid., p. 288.

10. Donald O. Hebb, *A Textbook of Psychology* (Philadelphia: Saunders, 1958), pp. 15–16.

11. Donald O. Hebb, *The Organization of Behavior: A Neuro-Psychological Theory* (New York: Wiley, 1949), p. xiii.

12. David L. Horton and Thomas W. Turnage, *Human Learning* (Englewood Cliffs, NJ: Prentice Hall, 1976), p. 444.

13. Donald O. Hebb, *A Textbook of Psychology*, p. 46.

14. From *Webster's Third New International Dictionary*, copyright ©1961 by G. & C. Merriam Company, publishers of the Merriam-Webster dictionaries, p. 1770, definition 4a (1) of *positive*. By permission.

15. Nelson Goodman, *Of Mind and Other Matters*, (Cambridge, MA: Harvard University Press, 1984), p. 127.

16. Ibid., p. 127.

17. Ibid., p. 43.

18. Hugh Skilling, "An Operational View," *American Scientist* 52, no. 4 (December 1964):390A.

19. Ernest E. Bayles, *Democratic Educational Theory* (New York: Harper & Row, 1960), p. 113.

20. Reprinted with permission of Macmillan Publishing Co., Inc. from B. F. Skinner, *Science and Human Behavior* (New York: Macmillan, 1953), p. 279. Copyright ©1953, Macmillan Publishing Co., Inc.

21. John Dewey, *Experience and Education* (New York: Macmillan, 1938), p. 41 (our italics).

22. John Dewey, *Democracy and Education* (New York: Macmillan, 1916), p. 164.

23. Ibid., p. 163.

24. See Richard de Charms, *Enhancing Motivation* (New York: Irvington, 1976), p. 8.

25. See Bernard Weiner, ed., *Achievement Motivation and Attribution Theory* (Morristown, NJ: General Learning Corporation, 1974), Chapter 1.

BIBLIOGRAPHY

The bibliography for Chapters 1 through 4 is at the end of Chapter 4.

Chapter
4

How Do the Two Families of Contemporary Learning Theory Describe the Learning Process?

*T*his chapter continues the analysis begun in Chapter 3 but centers on some of the more technical aspects of the learning theories developed by S-R conditioning and cognitive interaction theorists. Some repetition of ideas stated in Chapter 3 is inevitable, but the focus is quite different. In Chapter 3 we opened discussion of the two major contemporary versions of the nature of learning. We now treat them in some detail. As already noted, whereas contemporary S-R conditioning theorists—the neobehaviorists—conceive of learning as *conditioning* or *reinforcement* of behaviors, cognitive interactionists think of it as *development of generalized insights*—understandings—which provide a potential guide for behavior.

Do animals, including human beings, learn simply by being conditioned step by step under the tutelage of a teacher or experimenter, or do both lower animals and people learn by surveying their situation and grasping insightful relationships? Let us set up a hypothetical experiment and speculate on how animals will behave. Our subjects are rats in an elevated maze (see Figure 4.1). The alleys are formed of strips of wood without sidewalls. They are raised high enough from the floor so that the rats will not jump off. The gate in the maze is made so that the weight of a rat will cause it to lower and permit the rat to run through.

In order to accustom the rats to the maze and to develop in them preferential tendencies with reference to the three possible pathways to food, we give them some preliminary training, depriving them of food for 24 hours, then

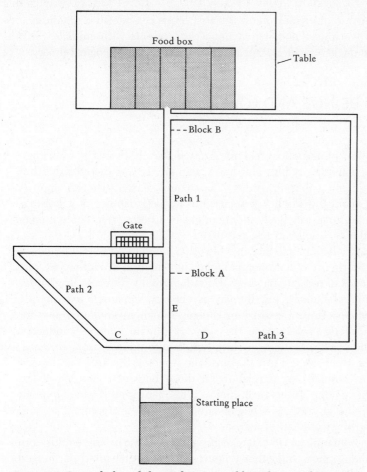

Figure 4.1 Ground plan of elevated maze used by Tolman and Honzik.

Source: From E. C. Tolman and C. H. Honzik, "'Insight' in Rats," University of California Publication in *Psychology* 4, no. 14 (1930) p. 223. By permission of University of California Press.

placing them in the starting box and permitting them to find their way to the food box. They are given ten such trials per day and soon learn (after trying the various paths) to take the shortest, path 1, to the food. We then block path 1 at point A. When this is done, the rats will turn back to the choice point (fork in the road) and almost always (about 93 percent of the time) take path 2.

Now, what will the rats do when for the first time the block is placed in the common section of paths 1 and 2 (at point B)? They will return toward the starting place on path 1 and turn at the intersection of the three paths. But will they take path 2 or 3? Have they sized up the situation and "seen" that the block is on path 2 as well as path 1? If so, they will take path 3. On the other hand, if the rats are operating mechanistically, they will take the second shortest path to the food, path 2, at least half the time.

We will return to our experiment. But first let us consider the significance for humanity of learning theory based upon experiments with animals. Such experiments occupy a very important place in modern psychological theory.

DO HUMAN BEINGS AND LOWER ANIMALS LEARN ALIKE?

Until modern times philosophers took for granted that there was an unbridgeable gulf between human beings and lower animals. It was thought that human beings possessed a unique quality: They could reason, whereas animals could not. This quality was believed to arise from the existence of a substantive mind—a mind-force, relatively independent of a body, which only human beings, among the earth's creatures, possessed.

Chapter 2 describes the manner in which this belief in body-mind dualism led to a distinctive theory of learning and teaching—mental discipline. As long as people were considered rational animals fundamentally different from other forms of life, animal biology and human psychology remained two sharply separated disciplines. Until a century or so ago, human psychology relied for its source of knowledge solely upon the study of human beings—conducted through inspiration, introspection, and intuition, tempered by reason. However, in past centuries, there were a few persons who rejected the idea that human beings and lower animals are unrelated. Of these Rousseau was one of the earliest and most striking. In his book *Émile* (1762), Rousseau strongly implied that a human being at birth is a healthy little animal—a creature like, and continuous with, other animals of nature.

During the Romantic period (late eighteenth and early nineteenth centuries), many philosophers and literary figures believed that mind permeated the entire universe, including all living things. Furthermore, this universal mind substance was believed to be unitary—everywhere the same. People possessed more of it than did lower animals, but the difference between the human and animal minds was considered one of degree rather than of kind. Of course, not all scholars accepted this view. The psychologist Wundt, for example, was convinced that consciousness—a product of mind—was unique to human beings. It was the work of Charles Darwin (1809–1882) and other evolutionists of the nineteenth century that most definitely gave humankind a place in the animal kingdom. Darwin noticed particularly the close similarity of the bodily structure and functions of persons and the lower animals. In his *Descent of Man* he also presented much evidence of the existence of psychological, as well as physical, continuity throughout the animal kingdom. Hence, he wrote, "There is no fundamental difference between man and the higher animals in their mental faculties."[1] But in a later section he qualified this opinion by writing, "There can be no doubt that the difference between the mind of the lowest man and that of the highest animal is immense."[2] However, despite this qualification, Darwin appears to have maintained consistently that in their fundamental aspects people and the lower animals exhibit a commonality of both physical and mental characteristics.

Antagonists of the theory of evolution defied Darwin to explain why, if there is a continuity between people and lower animals, human beings can reason, whereas lower animals seem to be governed by instinct rather than by reason. Darwin countered with the explanation that much human action, too, is to be interpreted as instinctive in origin and that animals, on their level, also exhibit a capacity for reason.

During the latter part of the nineteenth century the idea that there is a continuity among animal species, and that behavioral tendencies, including learning, are broadly similar throughout the animal world, rapidly gained in popularity among biologists and psychologists. As we note in Chapter 3, Pierre Flourens proposed in the nineteenth century that conclusions drawn from animal experimentation should be equally applicable to human beings. Pavlov also made this assumption, as did his American contemporaries, Thorndike and Watson.

In addition to the advantage of economy and convenience in using lower animals rather than humans in a psychological laboratory, experiments that our mores would prevent being tried on people can obviously be performed on animals. Furthermore, many persons have thought that it is easier to isolate simple units of behavior in lower animals than in human beings; although in humans the units may be substantially the same, they are often combined in a manner too complex for ready study. Thus, it has been thought that one might learn more about types of behavior that are fundamental to the animal kingdom by studying the lower animals rather than by studying people. Consequently, animal experimentation has become extremely popular among psychologists. Now, if people and lower animals do learn alike, do people learn like lower animals, or do lower animals learn like people?

Do People Learn Like Lower Animals?

Use of results of animal experimentation by behaviorists has been governed by the assumptions that the learning process is essentially the same throughout the animal kingdom and that what we discover about learning in lower animals is transferable to human situations. Behaviorists generally have thought that human behavior, including learning, is a purposeless, mechanical, chancelike process. In their mechanical trial-and-error processes, people learn like the lower animals do. So, learning in both lower animals and human beings is a matter of forming mechanical relationships between an organism and its environment through either chance or design.

Since psychological laws of learning, as well as of other behavior, are subsumed under, and agree with, physiochemical laws concerning living organisms, there is no place in behavioristic theory for insight when it is defined as a perception of relationships.

Behaviorists do sometimes use the term *insight*, but they mean something quite different from what cognitive interactionists do. When used by behaviorists, the term describes a special and rare kind of learning. To use Woodworth's definition, insight is "some penetration into the absolutely true nature of things."[3] But to Woodworth and other behaviorists, the ordinary form that learning takes is S-R conditioning. In fact, the most systematic behaviorists deny that there can be two entirely different kinds of learning; therefore they prefer to describe *all* learning as conditioning. Since insight obviously implies something very different from conditioning, many behaviorists do not use the term at all. To them it connotes something intuitive and mystical that cannot be described operationally. In contrast, cognitive interactionists seldom use the term *conditioning*; instead they regard *development of generalized insights or understandings* as the most descriptive phrase available to describe the manner in which learning actually takes place.

In Chapter 3, pages 46 to 49, we describe briefly the general nature of the animal experimentation undertaken by behaviorists. These psychologists have hoped to formulate laws of human learning by observing overt behavior of laboratory animals placed in various kinds of situations such as puzzle boxes and mazes. By the early 1920s the manner in which behaviorists conducted their experiments came under the fire of cognitive interactionists, whose criticism is developed in the following section.

Do Lower Animals Learn Like People?

Whereas behaviorists have assumed that people learn like lower animals, and more specifically like their own experimental animals in their own type of experiments, cognitive interactionists have given the question a reverse twist: Do lower animals learn like people? Of course, if there is a continuity between humans and the lower animals, both ideas should make equal sense and both should be answerable in the affirmative. But cognitive interactionists have had something else in mind. Although not denying the likelihood of a fundamental similarity in the behavior of people and lower animals, they have been interested in raising questions about the whole approach of the behaviorists.

One of the sharpest criticisms that cognitive interactionists can make of the behavioristic conception of learning is directed against the tendency of the latter to deny purpose a central role in learning. They note that behaviorists usually placed their animals in situations entirely foreign to them and often allowed them only a bare minimum of freedom. Consequently, there was no place for their animals to begin a solution and little opportunity for them really to try various alternatives. Since the locks, levers, and mechanical devices that were used were above the animals' level of comprehension, for them to achieve the correct procedure it was necessary that they stumble upon the key by chance. Because lower animals are less discerning of the kind of relationships that seem important to people than are human beings, animals appear, in a humanly contrived "problem," to make completely random movements. Thus, on the surface, the nature of the discovery of the relationship between the release mechanism and an animal's escaping from a puzzle box appeared to be completely mechanical. Having set the stage against animals displaying genuinely purposive, problem-solving activity, even if they are capable of such, behaviorists have concluded that learning is a mechanical trial-and-error process.

To cognitive interactionists the tension that motivates an animal to learn is tension *toward a goal* or *away from an aversion*. Thus, to some degree learning always involves purpose. Furthermore, purposiveness in learning is not restricted to humanity. Abundant experimental evidence indicates that learning is purposive, even among animals quite low on the phylogenetic scale.

An animal behaving purposively does not make random motions—even though on the surface it may appear to do so. Instead, it tries everything at its command, but if the problem is too difficult, its trial moves will appear random to an observer. If one eye of a slug or a honeybee is blinded, the animal at first place appears to go through meaningless motions. However, more careful observation reveals that it is demonstrating something other than mere random responses. It assumes a posture that orients its body toward the light source; thus, it flexes its legs on one side and extends them on the other as if it wanted to move in relationship to the light.

Cognitive interactionists have further criticized experimentation of behaviorists on the ground that it has been so arranged that even if animal learning were insightful, the development of insight would not be noticed. The real nature of any psychological process can be concealed by having the experimenter design experiments in line with adverse predetermined conclusions, and this is what critics have insisted that behaviorists have been inclined to do. In an attempt to refute the contention of behaviorists that learning is mechanical—a mere matter of forming connections through trial and error or chance—cognitive interactionists have designed entirely different types of animal experiments. Their experiments involved creation of problematic situations that animals might conceivably resolve through development of insight. Such situations were geared in difficulty to the presumed potential intelligence of the animals being studied.

Let us now return to the three-path experiment described at the beginning of the chapter. This actually is a classic experiment performed by Tolman and Honzik at the University of California. When the rats turned back out of path 1, they did not take path 2 but path 3—the longest path, but the only one now open to the food box. *Of the 15 rats, 14 behaved in this way.* This indicates that the rats "sized up" the situation—they had developed insight. Using path 3 was a relatively new and creative solution of what, to the rats, was a real problem.[4]

Köhler's famous experiments with chimpanzees further illustrate the cognitive interactionist approach to animal experimentation. Köhler spent four years on the island of Tenerife working with chimpanzees. A typical experiment involved suspending food (usually bananas) from the ceiling of a cage and then providing a chimpanzee with a tool or tools with which to knock down or reach for the fruit. The tool might be a pole of adequate length, a pole in sections that could be joined, or boxes that could be stacked and climbed. Köhler's chimpanzees, rather than gradually acquiring right responses and eliminating wrong ones, seemed at some point in a problem to develop insight into it—to grasp, often rather suddenly, the relationship involved. The chimpanzees seemed to get the idea of "tool use" and to apply it in new situations calling for tool use.[5]

Köhler also experimented with "stupid" chickens and found considerable evidence that even chickens can sense relationships and that it is relationships to which they respond rather than to specific stimuli. He taught chickens to expect food only from the darker of two papers placed side by side. For the lighter paper he then substituted one even darker than the original dark one. In 70 percent of the trials the chickens switched their preference from the originally preferred dark paper to the paper that was still darker, suggesting that they had achieved an insight: "If I go to the darker of two surfaces, I will get food." The chickens had "generalized," that is, sensed the relationship of darker to lighter *as a general principle* in "food getting."[6]

Two American Gestalt psychologists, Raymond H. Wheeler and Francis T. Perkins, performed a great deal of animal experimentation in the 1920s and 1930s. Among their most frequently cited experiments was one with goldfish in which the fish received food after responding properly to a configuration of lighting. The fish learned to pick the light of brightest, medium, or dimmest intensity, even though the experimenters kept varying the absolute intensity and the serial arrangement of lights. Wheeler and Perkins also reported numerous other studies made by themselves and others in which animals ordinarily regarded as not very intelligent learned to respond to relationships in an apparently intelligent way.[7]

The question arises, "How far down the phylogenetic scale can an investigator go and still observe animals behaving as if they could perceive a relationship?" To perceive a relationship one must get the feel of how a thing works. At first thought it would seem that to do this an animal must have a certain minimum of sensory and neural equipment—perhaps a brain, even if it is only rudimentary. However, one well-known American biologist, H. S. Jennings (1868–1947) concluded differently. Jennings spent much time observing the behavior of protozoa, such as euglenae, paramecia, and amoebae. He found that the actions of protozoa are not only highly variable but also readily modified and decided that their behavior could not be explained merely in terms of simple physiochemical reactions. Jennings though that insofar as their observable behavior was revealing, it was as reasonable to infer the presence of purposive behavior among protozoa as among human beings.[8]

Adolf Portmann, a contemporary biologist, has supported Jennings's earlier thinking in this regard. He states, "Biological research today must concentrate, therefore, on how things appear to animals, not what they actually are—which is a great change from the days a few decades back when biologists were supposed to reduce everything to physio-chemical laws."[9]

What are we to conclude from all this? One possible conclusion is that an animal experimenter, depending upon his orientation, is likely to arrange his experiment so that animal behavior appears to be either chancelike and mechanical or insightful. A famous philosopher, Bertrand Russell, noted that psychologists could demonstrate two fundamentally different types of response in their animal experiments, depending entirely upon how they arranged the experimental situation. Russell commented humorously: "Animals studied by Americans rush about frantically, with an incredible display of hustle and pep, and at last achieve the desired result by chance. Animals observed by Germans sit still and think, and at last evolve the solution out of their inner consciousness."[10] However, the state of affairs with regard to experimentation with lower animals is probably not so indecisive as Russell's comment would lead one to think. Once a student orients himself, in either a behavioristic or a cognitive-interactionist direction, he/she benefits by the broadest possible knowledge of all available experimental, as well as other, evidence.

Behaviorists have clearly shown that animals can be put in experimental situations where they demonstrate overt behavior that seems trial and error, chancelike, blind, and mechanical. Furthermore, there seems to be little question but that human experimental subjects can be put in situations causing them to appear to demonstrate the same kind of behavior. The only requirement for such an experiment seems to be that the problem presented the learner be one with which his previous experience has in no way equipped him to cope.

On the other hand, cognitive interactionists have demonstrated that, whether one is dealing with the lower animals or human beings, situations can be arranged in which learning shows an "Aha!" quality. That is, an experimental subject, in learning something, seems to "catch the point" or to get the feel of a confronting situation. If people and the lower animals do seem to learn insightfully in situations that permit it, then serious doubt is cast upon the validity of the notion that learning is purposeless, mechanical, and chancelike.

Cognitive interactionists insist that to describe learning throughout the animal kingdom, we do well to begin with human examples. As we examine the purposive behavior of ourselves or others, learning often, perhaps always, appears to be a matter of *seeing through things*, of *gaining understanding*. If we start with the assumption that lower animals learn in the same way, we devise experiments that enable them to reveal such learning.

This does not mean that if we are studying, say, a dog, we dare anthropomorphize him—attribute to him human characteristics; it does mean that we must guard against mechanizing him—making a machine of him. The way to study a dog is to "dogize" him, just as in studying a child we should "childize" him. In short, we must consider each lower animal as well as each human being on its own level. If we always keep this in mind, we can probably make some generalized statements about learning that will hold true with respect to most or even all forms of animal life.

IS LEARNING STIMULUS-RESPONSE CONDITIONING?

Within neobehaviorism, learning is considered nonpurposive habit formation. Habits are formed through conditioning, which either attaches desired responses to specific stimuli or increases the probability of desired responses. A stimulus triggers an action or response, which can take only one form because of the nature of the stimulus, the condition of the organism, and the "laws of learning" involved. Explanation for what organisms, including people, do is sought in their genetic endowment, the environmental circumstances that surround them, the stimuli that impinge on them, and the actions, including verbalizations, that they emit. These actions or behaviors are either respondents or operants. A *respondent* is behavior that is elicited by a stimulus. An *operant* is behavior that is controlled by its consequences, that is, the stimulus that follows it.

Thus, in the eyes of neobehaviorists, learning is a more or less permanent change of behavior that occurs as a result of conditioning. Accordingly, the learning process consists of impressions of new reaction patterns on pliable, passive organisms. Since learning arises, in some way, from the impingement of environment on organisms, the key concepts of neobehaviorists are *stimuli*, which consist of excitement provided by an environment, and *responses*, which consist of reactions made by an organism. Consequently, the problem of the nature of the learning process is centered in a study of the relationships of processions of stimuli and responses and what occurs between them. Because the focus is always on behavior, in practical application neobehavioristically oriented teachers strive to change behaviors of their students in the desired direction by providing the right stimuli at the proper time. Teachers who adopt this approach to learning decide specifically what behaviors they want their students, when finished products, to manifest, and then proceed to stimulate them in such a way as to evoke and fix those behaviors.

A child or youth is something to be molded in the proper fashion. Learning primarily is a process within which both verbal and nonverbal behaviors are changed. Such behaviors are inculcated by adults telling, showing, directing, guiding, arranging, manipulating, rewarding, punishing, and, at times, coercing the activities of children and youth. Accordingly, teaching is a matter of adults setting behavioristic environmental conditions—stimuli—to ensure that the students accomplish educational goals.

What Are the Two Forms of Stimulus-Response Conditioning?

Conditioning is the formation of some sort of stimulus-response sequential relation that results in an enduring change in either the pattern of behavior or the likelihood of a response of an organism. It takes either one or a combination of two forms, called classical and instrumental conditioning. *Classical conditioning* is conditioning that occurs without reinforcement. It is a process of *stimulus substitution*, which is based upon the *adhesive principle*. The adhesive principle means that a response is attached to a stimulus through the stimulus's occurring just prior to the response so that future recurrence of the stimulus will evoke or cause the response.

Instrumental conditioning, also called *reinforcement* or *operant* conditioning, is a process of response change or modification that is based upon the feedback principle. The *feedback principle* means that the reduction or satisfaction of an organic need or drive stimulus increases the probability of occurrence of future responses of the kind that the organism emitted immediately prior to being fed, watered, satisfied sexually, or otherwise satiated; there is feedback from the satisfaction of some deprivation to reinforcement of the type of behavior that preceded it.

A *need*, as used here, is an objective, biological requirement of an organism, which must be met if the organism is to survive and grow. Examples of needs are an organism's requirement for food or escape from pain. A *drive stimulus* is an aroused state of an organism. It is closely related to the need that sets the organism into action, and it may be defined as a strong, persistent stimulus that demands an adjustive response. Whenever an organism is deprived of satisfaction of a need, drive stimuli occur. In Table 4.1, under classical conditioning, S_1 is the originally adequate, unconditioned stimulus, S_2 is the conditioned stimulus, and R is the conditioned response; under instrumental conditioning, S is the reinforcing stimulus and R is the reinforced response.

Classical Conditioning   Classical conditioning is usually associated with such incidents as Pavlov teaching a dog to salivate at the ringing of a bell; thus, it is *stimulus substitution*. In Pavlov's conditioning experiment, the sound of a bell occurred prior to, or simultaneously with, the dog's salivation, which was caused by the presence of food. Then in the future, the dog salivated at the ringing of the bell, even when the food was not present.

In classical conditioning a new stimulus is presented along with an already adequate stimulus—such as the smell of food—and just prior to the response that is evoked by that stimulus. Thus, an organism learns to respond to a new stimulus in the same, or similar, way it responds to the old, unconditioned stimulus—one already adequate to evoke the response. The new stimulus

Table 4.1   TWO BASIC FORMS OF STIMULUS-RESPONSE CONDITIONING

	Classical Conditioning	Instrumental Conditioning
Order of stimulus and response	S-R Conditioning	R-S Conditioning
Nature of the process	Stimulus substitution	Response modification
Psychological principle involved	Contiguity (no reinforcement)	Reinforcement
	Adhesive principle	Feedback principle
The basic paradigm	S_1 ⟶ ⟶ R S_2 - - - ⟶	R←S

becomes the conditioned one, and the response that follows both stimuli becomes the conditioned response. A *conditioned response*, then, is one that is associated with, or evoked by, a new—conditioned—stimulus. In Pavlov's experiment the sound of the bell became the new, conditioned stimulus that evoked the old, unconditioned response—salivation. Then, salivation became a conditioned response.

Classical conditioned learning is revealed in the behavior of an organism by the increasing capacity of a previously neutral stimulus, with successive training trials, to evoke a response that was originally evoked by some other stimulus. A *neutral stimulus* is one whose first occurrence does nothing toward either evoking or reinforcing the response that is under study.

Instrumental Conditioning or Reinforcement   Just as classical conditioning theory derives from the early work of Pavlov, instrumental conditioning theory has emerged from the foundation built by Thorndike. Instrumental conditioning or reinforcement is *response modification* or *change*. An animal first makes a response, then receives a "reward"; the response is instrumental in bringing about its reinforcement. There is a *feedback* from the reinforcing stimulus that follows the response that the organism is learning; a dog is fed after it "speaks" and, thereby, the likelihood that it will "speak" in the future is increased.

Neobehaviorists who emphasize the importance of reinforcement in learning assume that some psychological conclusions are fairly well established:

1. Patterns of action develop through an organism's responses to repeated stimuli accompanied by "fumble and success" type of trial-and-error learning under conditions of positive or negative reinforcement.
2. Reinforcement occurs through satisfaction of either basic biological needs like hunger or sex or secondary needs such as a need for security, recognition, or aesthetic gratification.
3. Educational encouragement must take the form of positive and negative reinforcers.

A positive reinforcer is a stimulus whose *presence* strengthens a behavior; a negative reinforcer is a stimulus whose *withdrawal* strengthens a behavior. Note that negative reinforcement psychologically is different from punishment. Reinforcement also may be either *primary* or *secondary*.

Primary Reinforcement   Primary reinforcement strengthens a certain behavior through the satisfaction of a basic biological need or drive. Secondary reinforcement is sometimes called high-order reinforcement. The reinforcers in secondary or high-order reinforcement have acquired their power of reinforcement indirectly through learning; poker chips, for which a chimpanzee will work, and money, for which a person will do almost anything, are secondary reinforcers.

The drive-reduction sequence of primary reinforcement proceeds as follows:

1. Deprivation of satisfaction of a basic requirement, such as that for food, produces a state of need in an organism.
2. The need expresses itself as a tension state or drive stimulus, which energizes the organism into action (a food-deprived animal shows the restless activity whose manifestation is called the hunger drive).
3. The activity achieves satisfaction of the need and relieves the tension state.
4. The form of the activity that immediately preceded the satisfaction of the need or reduction of the drive is reinforced.

Secondary Reinforcement   Secondary reinforcement is reinforcement that is brought about by occurrence of an originally neutral stimulus along with a reinforcing stimulus. When a neutral stimulus such as a sound or light is repeatedly paired with food in the presence of a food-deprived (hungry) animal, the formerly neutral stimulus becomes a secondary, conditioned reinforcer. Thus, secondary reinforcement is higher-order reinforcement; it results when originally neutral stimuli become associated with primary reinforcing stimuli and thereby become effective in reducing needs. In this way, neutral stimuli acquire the power of acting as reinforcing agents; a chimpanzee learns to accept the poker chips that accompany food as a "reward" just as readily as he accepts food. Consequently, future actions of the chimpanzee are reinforced by his receiving poker chips immediately after he performs them; this is secondary reinforcement.

Extinction   In addition to the two kinds of positive conditioning—*classical* and *instrumental*—there is also a negative conditioning process—*extinction*. Through classical and instrumental conditioning, an organism *gains* responses or habits; through extinction it *loses* them. Extinction is the process whereby an organism gradually loses a response or habit through its repeating the response a number of times while no reinforcing stimulus accompanies it. Any habits gained through either classical or instrumental conditioning may be lost through extinction. (See Chapter 5, page 109 for a more extensive description of extinction.)

How May We Group S-R Conditioning Theories?

Nearly all S-R conditioning theorists are alike in their emphasis upon a mechanical treatment of stimuli and responses.[11] Most agree that at no time is purposiveness to be attributed to human behavior. But they differ rather sharply in their interpretations of the significant stimulus-response sequential relationships that occur in learning procedures.

On the basis of their positions in regard to the specific nature of learning, we may divide behaviorists into three groups. One group has made classical conditioning, through temporal contiguity of prior stimuli and their caused responses, the heart of the learning process and has held that reinforcement is not necessary for conditioning to occur. A second group has been committed to reinforcement theories within which significant—reinforcing—stimuli follow responses. The third group, the *two-factor theorists*, contend that there are two basically different learning processes: conditioning independent of reinforcement and conditioning governed by principles of reinforcement. (See Table 1.1, items 5, 6, and 7, for representatives of these positions.)

Currently, most behavioristic-oriented teachers represent either the second—reinforcement—group or a behavioristic-centered eclectic psychology. In Chapter 5 we describe B. F. Skinner's philosophically consistent, logical-empiricistic *operant conditioning*, the leading representative of the reinforcement group.

IS LEARNING DEVELOPMENT OF INSIGHT?

This section of the chapter centers upon the tenets of Gestalt psychology and the goal-insight theory of learning, as developed by Ernest E. Bayles (1897–).[12] Dr. Bayles' thinking serves as a background and forerunner for understanding current cognitive-interactionist learning theories. Gestalt psychologists have viewed human beings as interactive, purposive individuals acting in sequential relationships with their environments in keeping with prevailing psychological laws of organization.

The key concept of Gestalt psychologists in describing learning is *insight*. A generalized insight is an understanding. Gestaltists regard learning as a process of developing new insights or changing old ones. Insights occur when an individual, in pursuing his purposes, sees new ways of utilizing elements of his environment, including his own bodily structure. The noun *learnings* denote the new insights or meanings that are acquired.

Gestalt theorists attack three weaknesses in the theory that learning is conditioning: (1) the attempt of behaviorists to explain complex interrelated organizations in terms of simpler elements, that is, to insist that learning consists of an accumulation of individual conditioned responses or operants, each relatively simple in itself but eventuating in a complicated pattern of habits; (2) behaviorists' tendency to attribute learning to reduction of basic organic drives; and (3) behaviorists' tendency to ignore the apparent purposiveness of much behavior. Thus, "The chief trouble with behaviorism . . . is that it leaves out so much behavior."[13]

Gestalt psychologists view learning as a purposive, explorative, imaginative, and creative enterprise. This conception breaks completely with the idea that learning consists of either linking one thing to another according to certain principles of association or building behaviors in a deterministic, mechanistic fashion. Instead, the learning process is identified with nonmechanical development or change of insights.

The Gestalt definition of insight is a sense of, or feeling for, pattern or relationships. To state it differently, insight is the "sensed way through," or "solution" of, a problematic situation. Insights often first appear as vague "hunches." We might say that an insight is a kind of intelligent "feel" we get about a situation that permits us to continue to strive actively to serve our purposes. When are insights verbalized? Perhaps at once; perhaps never. We probably know many things that we never manage to put into words. This is a problem on which animal experimentation sheds some light. Animals below human beings cannot talk; they can communicate but not by placing sounds together in coherent subject-predicate sentences. Yet the evidence indicates that when they are confronted with what to them are problems, they insightfully learn.[14]

Gestalt psychologists do not use the term *insights* in a way to imply that they are necessarily true. Granted, the term sometimes is used this way by others. But the relativistic orientation of Gestalt theorists necessarily leads them to think of insights as trial answers or hypotheses that either may or may not help a person toward his goal. Hence, they may or they may not be true. Truth, relativistically defined, is that quality of a tested insight that enables its possessor to design behavior that is successful in achievement of whatever it is designed to achieve.

Insights, then, are to be considered not literal descriptions of objective physical-social situations but, rather, as interpretations of one's self and one's perceived environment on the basis of which pertinent action may be designed. Although insights are not physicalistic descriptions of objects or processes in the environment, they necessarily do take account of the physical environment. Their usability depends in part upon how well this is done. Insights may misinterpret a physical environment so badly that they are useless as rules of action, in which case they are to be regarded as false.

It is important to understand that insights are always a learner's own. It is true, of course, that they may become his own through adoption. An insight is usable to a learner only if he/she can "fit it in," that is, understand its significance—for him. A teacher cannot give an insight to a student as we serve a person food on a platter. He/she may acquaint students with his insights, but they do not become insights for students until students see their meaning for themselves and adopt them as their own.

One objection frequently raised against the Gestaltist tendency to construe all learning as insightful is that some learning tasks are performed successfully without apparent development of insight—for example, when a child memorizes the multiplication tables. Gestalt psychologists concede that some learning appears highly mechanical, but they are convinced that it is not so mechanical as it may appear. Accordingly, they contend that even though children may repeat the multiplication tables until they appear to have memorized them by rote, what they actually have done is to get the feel of some pattern that is present in the tables. The pattern may lie in the relationship of the numbers or perhaps merely in the order in which the student placed the numbers to "memorize" them.

One's use of the term *insights* does not imply that, for a person to learn something, he/she must understand *all* aspects of its use. Any degree of "feel for a pattern" is sufficient to constitute insightful learning. For example, in learning to extract the square root of a number, one might develop an insight as to why the method works, or the insight gained might be much more superficial; it might merely be a "feel" for the method—the pattern of steps—with no real understanding of the basic algebraic formula $(x + y)^2 = x^2 + 2xy + y^2$.

What Are Some Examples of Insightful Learning?

Before a military rifleman can become a sharpshooter, he must get a "feel" for his rifle. Often, a Tennessee squirrel hunter was slow in learning to be an army rifleman. He had an excellent feel for his squirrel gun, but a squirrel gun was not an army rifle. In his army training he had to change old insights as well as develop new ones. On his squirrel gun, his sights were fixed immovably to the barrel. To hit a squirrel, he had to take wind and distance into consideration and move the rifle away from a line on the target (windward and upward) to give "Tennessee windage" and "Kentucky elevation." He had developed truthful insights to the point that he could behave intelligently without thinking; he could aim his gun and pull the trigger while giving very little attention to what he was doing.

Since his army rifle had movable sights, which prior to aiming the rifle were to be adjusted to allow for windage and elevation, a soldier was supposed to set his sights and then line them directly on his target. Under pressure of target practice, the soldier used his new insights to adjust his sights correctly, but when he began to fire, he gave his rifle Tennessee windage and Kentucky elevation and missed the target completely. He had used two sets of incompatible insights. He could learn to shoot his army rifle accurately only by getting a complete feel for his army rifle and by leaving most of his squirrel-gun aiming insights out of the picture.

What is the answer to $\sqrt{(\text{dog})^2} = ?$ How did you know it was "dog"? Had you ever before worked with square root and "dog" at the same time? If you knew the answer was "dog," you had an insight into the problem. Perhaps you have never put the insight into words, but you knew that when x is equal to or greater than zero, $\sqrt{x^2} = x$ and $\sqrt{4^2} = 4$. Your insight, when verbalized, would run something like, "The square root of anything squared is that thing." Conversely, you may have "learned"—memorized—"The square root of a quantity squared is that quantity" and still not know the answer to $\sqrt{(\text{dog})^2} = ?$.

Teaching for development of insights has definite implication for methods of teaching and learning spelling. Groups or families of words might be studied in such a way that students develop a feeling for a certain spelling pattern. Once a pattern is discovered, other words can be sought that conform to it. *Cat*, *fat*, and *bat* are "at" words. Now, what about *hat*, *mat*, *pat*, *rat*, and *sat*? As students, working cooperatively with their teacher, find other word families, they will soon encounter words that apparently should, but do not, fit a given family—they find some limitations to an insight. They then seek other words with the same divergence from the "rule" and make a family of them. Or, in case there is only one divergent word, they think of it as an exception. As the insights into patterns of spelling are put into words, a class can formulate rules; but rules will now be generalized verbalizations of the student's insight as contrasted with meaningless statements memorized at the beginning of study.

How Is Insight Related to Understanding and Generalization?

Often, when an insight is first "caught," it applies to a single case. Even so, a person is likely to assume that the insight may work in similar situations. Suppose, for example, that after studying a particular situation, we hypothesize, "Mary became a shoplifter because she felt unwanted by her parents." The natural next step is to think, "Boys and girls who feel unwanted at home tend to become thieves." Of course, this generalization is only suggested. It is not warranted by evidence from a single case. Before generalizations become reliable, that is, before they become understandings, it is usually necessary that they rest on a number of specific insights, all suggesting the same conclusion. In short, dependable generalizations—understandings—usually are products of considerable experience. Furthermore, they are prone to change in the course of experience, evolving continuously in the direction of greater usefulness as tools of thought.

An *understanding* of a thing or process is its generalized meaning; that is, it is a tested generalized insight. Thus, it entails one's ability to use an object, fact, process, or idea in several or even many somewhat different situations. It is one's understandings that enable one to behave intelligently—with foresight of consequences. A tested generalization or understanding is assumed to be valid in any future situation similar to the situations in which it was tested. Tested generalizations have the character of rules, principles, or laws. Such generalizations are frequently if-then statements: If we take a given action, then the probability is high that a given consequence will follow.

We emphasize that tested generalizations should be regarded as probabilities, not absolute answers. Although, to behave with foresight, we must assume that our generalizations have predictive value, the predictions are always, to some degree, based upon probability. Yet many insights have been so adequately tested that we may safely treat them as if they were certainties. Certainties, so construed, are insights in which we have tremendous faith but still not absolute commitment.

HOW IS OBSERVABLE BEHAVIOR CHANGE RELATED TO LEARNING?

Cognitive-interactionist theories contrast sharply with S-R conditioning theories in regard to the manner in which adherents of the two respective positions use observable behavior of persons as psychological data. Behaviorists use observable behavior, and only observable behavior, as data. Consequently, they restrict learning objectives to those expressible in terms of observable behaviors. In contrast, cognitive interactionists also study observable behaviors, but they infer from them the changing personalities, environments, and insights of the persons being studied. Thus, whereas for behaviorists one's physical behavior is also one's psychological behavior, for cognitive interactionists psychological behavior is something quite different from mere physical movement.

For behaviorists, *"behavior*, as a technical psychological term, may be defined as the publicly observable activity of muscles or glands of external secretion as manifested, for example, in movements of parts of the body or the appearance of tears, sweat, saliva, and so forth."[15] But when cognitive interactionists use the term *behavior*, they give it quite a different meaning. For them, it is any change in a person, the person's perceived environment, or the relation between the two that is subject to psychological principles. *Psychological*, as used here, means involving purpose and intelligence. Hence, psychological behavior is not the same as physical movement. Such behavior is not directly observable but must be inferred from the observable actions and demeanors of persons.

Cognitive interactionists think that behaviorists err in making the observable results of learning synonymous with the learning itself. For them, a change of observable behavior may be *evidence that learning has occurred or is occurring*, but such behavioral change is not the learning. Thus, a change in biological behavior does not necessarily mean that learning has occurred. A person who is in a dark alley and is struck from behind and knocked down may gain from this experience a healthy respect for dark alleys, but the change in behavior—falling down—is not equivalent to any change in insight that may have occurred. Furthermore, a person may use insights that he/she has gained through an earlier experience as the basis for a change in his present behavior.

Many changes in the behavior of school children probably do not reflect their teacher's desired changes in student insights. Judy may start saying "please" and "thank you" without an insightful grasp of the implications of doing so, or she may labor hours every night over homework without having her work produce any change of mind about matters implicit in the homework itself. (Of course, the assignment may cause changes in her attitude toward teachers and school.)

Learning and change in observable behavior often occur side by side and seem to be interrelated. Consequently, behaviorists contend that any change of behavior is learning and, conversely, that any learning is a change of behavior. Thus, the current practice among many educators of defining learning as "change in behavior" usually reflects a behavioristic psychology. But cognitive interactionists maintain that not only may a change in observable behavior occur without learning, but learning may also occur without any *observable* related changes in behavior. This is true in innumerable situations. There may be an insight but no opportunity or occasion for a change in behavior, as when one decides it would be nice to give more to charity but does not have the money to do so. Also, when new insights compete with older ones that have a strong hold on a person, the new insights may fail to change the person's behavior. For example, one may decide that racial discrimination is bad but continue to practice it.

Because of their emphasis on behavioral change, many people with a behavioristic orientation think that doing something a number of times will necessarily affect one's future behavior. Thus, if one smokes a pack of cigarettes a day for several weeks, one supposes oneself to have become a habitual smoker.

Cognitive interactionists deny that this is the case. Doing a thing either once or many times will affect subsequent behavior only to the degree in which doing it gives the doer a feeling for the act or insight into the consequences of its performance. It is the perceptual process, not the action as such, that is crucial.

The emphasis of behaviorists on changing behavior has often led to school practices designed to produce a desired kind of behavior and to methods of evaluation that measure overt behavior and little else. Teachers, or other school authorities, decide which specific behaviors they want students to display. They then stimulate the students in such a way as to evoke the desired behaviors. The success of the process is judged by how dependably the behavior can be invoked in the future (usually on tests). Cognitive interactionists protest this approach to education. They emphasize changes in experience rather than in behavior, with experience defined as an interactive event within which a person, through acting and seeing what happens, comes to see and feel the consequences of a given course of action. They grant that when a person learns something, his observable behavior usually changes, but they further note that it does not follow that, for learning to take place, a change in observable behavior must occur at the same time, or that from a change in overt behavior we can always accurately infer the full nature of the insight related to it.

For cognitive interactionists, learning is a persistent change in knowledge, skills, attitudes, values, or commitments. It may, or it may not, be reflected in changes in overt behavior. One does not "learn by doing" except insofar as one's doing contributes to a change in one's insights. For learning to result, the doing must be accompanied by the doer's realization of the consequences of the act. Thus, learning occurs through, and results from, experience, and "mere activity does not constitute experience."[16] For an activity to be included in experience, it must be interrelated with a realization of the consequences that accompany it.

HOW DO ADHERENTS OF THE TWO LEARNING FAMILIES DESCRIBE THE THINKING PROCESS?

In its broadest meaning, the term *thinking* may embrace simple association or recall, reverie, fantasy, dreams, autism, and animism as well as creative ideational activity. However, in the more restricted sense in which we use the term herein, it is a directed, goal-oriented activity of an individual; in other words, it is a creative, problem-solving process.

Thinking, then, is goal-related problem solving. It is an attempt to work through a situation in order to find the means to achieve an end. For the purpose of analysis, we may distinguish two levels of problem solving, but any line drawn between them is necessarily arbitrary. One level may be termed *simple problem solving*, which does not involve weighty decisions. Examples of problems on this level are expressed in the following questions: Shall I wear a red or green tie today? Shall I drive or walk to work? Shall I spend the evening reading a book or watching a motion picture? During the solution of problems of this kind, our tension level remains relatively low, and we usually solve these problems without lengthy deliberation. Once we have made a decision, we are unlikely to worry about it later.

The other level of thinking may be termed *complex problem solving*. This level of problem solving usually requires much effort and time and is accompanied by relatively high tension. The distinguishing characteristic of this level is that each problem presents the persons involved with something new. Although many elements of the problem may be familiar, some are unfamiliar. Consequently, each act of complex problem solving requires some degree of originality or creativity. Examples of such problems are suggested by questions like: Shall I encourage my son to go to college? Shall I seek a divorce? Shall I change my registration from Democrat to Republican? Of course, not all complex problem solving involves such weighty questions. Deciding which insecticide to use or which service station to patronize might also require complex problem solving procedures.

How Is Thinking Associated with Learning?

Since our principal tools of thought—concepts—are learned, people generally associate learning and thinking quite closely. Furthermore, one objective of education upon which persons of various shades of opinion seem to agree is that "students should be taught to think." However, when people attempt to define thinking and to specify the proper procedure for its promotion, the apparent agreement soon fades away. Let us now take the question, "Should students be taught to think as part of their activity in school?"

Readers will recall that prior to the advent of scientific approaches to psychological study in the eighteenth century, the main thrust of psychology, back into antiquity, was mental discipline with its accompanying mind-substance theory. Mental disciplinarians have thought that thinking was the operation of a trained faculty of a substantive mind. This trained faculty has been called *rational power* or *reason*. Hence, students' learning to think consists of exercising this faculty of their mind. Accordingly, there are two kinds of subject matter—one, like geometry, that trains minds and one, like geography, that merely gives students information.

Both behaviorists and cognitive interactionists construe thinking within a scientific frame of reference, though in their respective manners. Hence, both take strong exceptions to a mental-disciplinary conception of thinking but differ sharply in their scientific conceptions and explanations of the thinking process. In the next sections we outline in some detail the psychological meaning of thinking within the two scientific approaches.

Within Behaviorism, What Is Thinking?

For most behaviorists, an "idea" or "thought" consists of a symbolic movement that constitutes an intermediate step between overt stimuli and responses. *Symbols* are events that represent something beyond themselves. They may be either substitute stimuli or substitute responses. Whenever an organism is responding in a certain way and the stimulus that originally was adequate to evoke the response is absent, it is responding to a symbolic stimulus. A symbolic response is an incipient or partial movement that takes the place of a completely expressed pattern of behavior. It may take the form of a shrug of the shoulders, a facial expression, a nod of the head, or a change in posture. In thinking, symbolic movements may be so slight that the individual may be aware of only a "thought" divorced from any movement. Nevertheless, when one thinks some slight muscular or neural action occurs.

A person's thinking, then, is his responding symbolically to symbolic stimuli. Thought is not some mysterious mentalistic process that is the cause of behavior but the behavior itself. Thus, thinking is symbolic or incipient trial-and-error behavior that culminates in learning. Like all other instances of an organism's behavior, it is a function or result of a set of antecedent or preceding conditions.

In thinking, an organism makes symbolic, miniature responses that sample the feedbacks that would occur if the action represented symbolically or incipiently were really carried out. Thus, to S-R conditioning theorists, thought consists of very small preparatory responses. These can be observed in the incipient or miniature trial-and-error movements of a rat at a "choice point" in a maze. Here, small movements, this way and that, often precede the rat's actually moving down a pathway. In human beings, this process is more subtle and elaborated but no different in kind from that of rats and other lower animals.

In its broadest sense, thinking behavior is both verbal and nonverbal and both overt and covert. However, any nonverbal or covert aspects are considered to function much like the observable ones; they too are segments of stimulus-response sequences. Accordingly, behaviorists assume that once natural laws governing the relationship of observable stimuli and responses are identified and established, internal processes likewise can be described in terms of stimulus-response sequences that conform to the same laws. Thus, ideational thought, a variable that intervenes between observable stimuli and responses, likewise consist of stimuli and responses, though covert ones.

Although B. F. Skinner and some other contemporary neobehaviorists have considered the study of any private, internal events irrelevant to a functional analysis of behavior, many others follow John B. Watson's earlier leadership in considering thinking basically to be implicit speech—talking to oneself. Thus, they associate thought very closely with language, which is a rich collection of symbols. So considered, thought basically is laryngeal activity supported by oral and nasal functions. However, it is closely aligned with gestures, frowns, shrugs, and grimaces, which stand for more overt actions or behaviors.

In the thinking process, words, other symbols, and incipient movements become *cues* for behavior. Cues are stimuli of faint intensity that evoke or guide an organism's movements. Any uniqueness people may have involves their "better" use of cues. Thus, three principal factors make human thinking processes "higher" than those of other animals:

1. People have greater capacity to respond selectively to more subtle aspects of the environment as cues.
2. They are also able to make a greater variety of distinctive responses that constitute cues for their actions; they are more able to stimulate themselves.
3. They can emit a greater number of cue responses simultaneously. Thus, they can elicit many more of their own future responses based upon patterns of cues that represent, or result from, several different earlier patterns of stimulation.[17]

How Does Cognitive-Interactionist Psychology Treat Thinking?

Cognitive interactionists consider thinking to be an exploratory learning process consisting of both investigative and reflective learning. (See Page 271.) *Investigative* learning consists of students' selecting problems for inquiry, then pursuing their inquiries as far as feasible. *Reflective* learning consists of problem raising and problem solution. Teacher and students combine both fact-gathering and deductive processes in such way as to construct, elaborate, and test hypotheses. Reflective thinking and scientific processes have much in common; but the term *reflective* is better suited to describing student thinking than is *scientific*.

For many persons, science implies white-gowned technicians, microscopes and telescopes, chemical tables, and cyclotrons. Furthermore, it suggests precise measurement, use of mathematics, a large amount of rather esoteric wizardry, and neglect of moral values. However, *scientific* in its broadest sense covers not only a special kind of gadgetry and techniques but also a unique outlook, attitude, and method of inquiry.

Reflective thinking refers to the essential but nongadgetlike features of scientific method with which we may approach all problems, whether they are physical, social, or psychological. John Dewey gave us a classic definition of reflective thinking when he characterized it as the "active, persistent, and careful consideration of any belief or supposed form of knowledge in the light of the grounds that support it and the further conclusions to which it tends."[18]

Five rather definite aspects are present in each complete act of reflection. However, no one should suppose that a person goes through them in the consecutive, orderly fashion in which they may be listed. Any or even all of the aspects may develop concurrently. Moreover, reflection normally is characterized by confusion, hesitation, back-tracking, and "going around in circles." In many cases it appears to a thinker that he/she will never reach a solution at all. And once reached, a conclusion often must be abandoned and the process started all over again. Reflection is seldom easy; at best it is exhilarating and exciting, and at worst it is painfully hard work beset with many frustrating moments.

The principal aspects of reflective thinking are:

1. *Recognition and definition of a problem.* This occurs when one becomes aware either of conflicting goals or of a goal having an intervening obstacle to

its achievement. Often a problem consists of a newly sensed discrepancy in known data.

2. *Formulation of hypotheses.* Hypotheses are possible answers in the form of invented generalizations that, to be used most successfully, must be verified by human experience. In a relativistic sense, all scientific generalizations are hypotheses in which greater or lesser degrees of assurance can be placed. They range from hunches, based on minimum data, to laws, which reflect a very high degree of factual verification.

3. *Elaboration of logical implications of hypotheses.* This process includes deducing the implications or consequences of both the hypotheses whose observations already have been made, so that the hypotheses may be checked against present knowledge, and the hypotheses whose observations have not yet been made, so that the hypotheses may be tested through experiments yet to be designed.

4. *Testing of hypotheses.* This involves attempts to verify the implications or consequences that were deduced under the third aspect in terms of both the data of previous experience—*scrutiny-explanation*—and data procured in experimental tests—*prediction-verification.*

5. *Drawing conclusions.* This consists of either accepting, modifying, or rejecting the hypotheses, or concluding that as of now the available pertinent evidence does not warrant taking any stand at all. (See Chapter 13 for the development of reflective teaching based upon reflective thinking.)

NOTES

1. Charles Darwin, *The Descent of Man* (New York: Appleton-Century-Crofts, 1920), p. 66.
2. Ibid., p. 125.
3. R. S. Woodworth, *Psychology* (New York: Holt, Rinehart and Winston, 1940), pp. 299–300.
4. E. C. Tolman and C. H. Honzik, " 'Insight' in Rats," University of California Publication in *Psychology* 4, no. 14 (1930):215–232.
5. Wolfgang Köhler, *The Mentality of Apes* (New York: Vintage Books, 1959).
6. See Henry E. Garrett, *Great Experiments in Psychology* (New York: Appleton-Century-Crofts, 1941), pp. 216–219.
7. Raymond H. Wheeler and Francis T. Perkins, *Principles of Mental Development* (New York: Crowell, 1932).
8. H. S. Jennings, *Behavior of the Lower Organisms* (New York: Columbia University Press, 1923), p. 335.
9. Adolf Portmann, *New Paths in Biology* (New York: Harper & Row, 1964), pp. 91–92.
10. Bertrand Russell, *Philosophy* (New York: Norton, 1927). The Germans referred to obviously are the Gestaltists.
11. See B. F. Skinner, *About Behaviorism*, New York: Knoff, 1974.
12. See Ernest E. Bayles, *Democratic Educational Theory*, New York: Harper, 1960.
13. Rollo May, *Psychology and the Human Dilemma* (New York: Van Nostrand Reinhold, 1967), p. 190.
14. See Wolfgang Köhler, *The Mentality of Apes.*

15. Donald O. Hebb, *A Textbook of Psychology*, 3d ed. (Philadelphia: Saunders, 1972), p. 15.
16. John Dewey, *Democracy and Education* (New York: Macmillan, 1916), p. 163.
17. See Sigmund Koch, ed., *Psychology: A Study of a Science*, vol. 2, *General Systematic Formulations, Learning, and Special Processes* (New York: McGraw-Hill, 1959), p. 247.
18. John Dewey, *How We Think* (Lexington, MA: Raytheon/Heath, 1933), p. 9.

BIBLIOGRAPHY, CHAPTERS 1 THROUGH 4

Adler, Mortimer J. *The Paideia Proposal*. New York: Macmillan, 1982. Develops a classical-humanist approach to education based upon the "great books."

Adler, Mortimer J. *Learning For the Lifelong Pursuit of Wisdom*. New York: Macmillan, 1986. An expansion and clarification of classical-humanistic education.

Adler, Mortimer J. *Reforming Education*. New York: Macmillan, 1988. A restatement of Adler's classical-humanist position accompanied by excerpts from his previous works.

Allport, Gordon W. *Patterns and Growth of Personality*. New York: Holt, Rinehart and Winston, 1961. Emphasizes the importance of assumptions in regard to the nature of humankind.

Bayles, Ernest E. *Democratic Educational Theory*. New York: Harpers, 1960. Develops democratic, reflective education. Assumes students to be neutral and interactive.

Berkson, William and John Wettersten. *Learning From Error*. LaSalle, IL: Open Court, 1984. A critique of historically developed learning theories.

Bloom, Allan. *The Closing of the American Mind*. New York: Simon and Schuster, 1987. A sharply critical appraisal of current educational procedures. Recommends that schools return to classical education.

Bolles, Robert C. *Theory of Motivation*, 2d ed. New York: Harper & Row, 1975. A behaviorist raises questions concerning the usefulness of behaviorism. Summarizes much pertinent research.

Bower, Gordon H. and Ernest E. Hilgard. *Theories of Learning*. Englewood Cliffs, NJ: Prentice Hall, 1981. An encyclopedic systematic, critical presentation of the most prominent learning theories current among contemporary psychologists.

Bower, Gordon H. *Psychology of Learning and Motivation*. Vol. 22, *Advances in Research and Theory*. New York: Academic Press, 1988. Covers recent research on learning and motivation.

Brief, Jean-Claude. *Beyond Piaget: A Philosophical Psychology*. New York: Teachers College Press, 1983. An extension of Piaget's theory of development.

Bruner, J. S. et al. *Contemporary Approaches to Cognition, A symposium held at the University of Colorado*. Cambridge, MA: Harvard University Press, 1957. For the advanced student. Includes a range of positions, all of which focus on psychological, rather than on behavioral facts.

Cantril, Hadley, and Charles H. Bumstead. *Reflections on the Human Venture*. New York: New York University Press, 1960. Treatment of major issues in psychology from a relativistic view. Draws evidence largely from insights of novelists, poets, and playwrights. Excellent quotations. A profound book, likely to become a classic.

Cattell, Raymond B., and Ralph M. Dreger, eds. *Handbook of Modern Personality Theory*, New York: Hemisphere, 1977. Chapters 15, 16, and 18 cogently relate learning theories to personality theories.

Chaplin, James P., and T. S. Krawiec. *Systems and Theories of Psychology*, 3d ed. New York: Holt, Rinehart and Winston, 1974. A treatment of the evolution of psychological thought, which is traced from classical scholars to the major contemporary theories. Shows the continuity of thought from philosophy and physiology to psychology. Contains a good list of biographical sketches of contributors to psychological thought. Chapters 6–10 are especially pertinent to learning.

Coen, David. *J. B. Watson: The Founder of Behaviorism, A Biography*, London: Routledge & Kegan Paul, 1979. A positive appraisal of Watson's contributions to psychological science as applied especially to education and advertising.

de Charms, Richard. *Enhancing Motivation*. New York: Irvington, 1976. Theory and procedure of a school motivation project. Distinguishes "origins" and "pawns"—origins accept "personal causation" for their school experiences, whereas pawns do not—they are merely pushed around.

Dewey, John. *Democracy and Education*. New York: Macmillan, 1916 (also in paperback, 1961 ed.). Incisive, enlightening statements concerning natural unfoldment, apperception, and mental (formal) discipline. Pages 130–138 are devoted to Rousseauean natural development; 65–68, to Froebelian unfoldment; 70–79, to mental discipline; and 81–84, to Herbartian apperception.

Elkind, David. "Developmentally Appropriate Practice: Philosophical and Practical Implications." *Phi Delta Kappan* 71, no. 2 (October, 1989): 113–117. Champions Piagetian developmental educational psychology as an alternative to psychometric educational psychology. "A teacher training program that is truly developmentally appropriate would have its students major in child development" (p. 116).

Estes, W. K. *Handbook of Learning and Cognitive Processes, Volume I, Introduction to Concepts and Issues*. New York: Lawrence Erlbaum, 1975. Good introduction to issues in learning theory.

Gagné, Robert M. *The Conditions of Learning*, 2nd ed., New York: Holt Rinehart and Winston, 1970. Develops eight conditions of learning, eight phases of an act of learning and teaching procedures.

Gagné, Robert M. *The Conditions of Learning and Theory of Instruction*, 4th ed., 1985. Develops five categories of learning, eight conditions of learning, and nine principal instructional events.

Gagné, Robert M., Leslie J. Briggs, and Walter W. Wagner. *Principles of Instructional Design*, 3rd ed., New York: Holt, Rinehart and Winston, 1988. Develops a theory of instruction loosely drawing some concepts from theories of learning.

Gall, Meredith D. and Beatrice A. Ward. *Critical Issues in Educational Psychology*, Boston: Little, Brown, 1974. An excellent book of readings to supplement this volume. Chapters represent the various psychological issues as represented by leading figures in learning theory.

Geiger, George Raymond. *John Dewey in Perspective*, New York: Oxford University Press, 1958. By an astute student of Dewey and the "relativistic" position that

Dewey helped develop. This book is somewhat easier reading than most of Dewey's works, yet it gives an accurate picture of Dewey's thoughts.

Gholson, Barry. *The Cognitive-Developmental Basis of Human Learning*, New York: Academic Press, 1980. A current synthesis of Piaget's structural theory and information-processing theory of developmental learning.

Hebb, Donald O. *A Textbook of Psychology*, 3d ed., Philadelphia: Saunders, 1972. A textbook in general psychology that treats psychology as a biological, not a social, science. Mechanisms of behavior in learning, perception, and emotion are discussed in a thoroughly behavioristic manner. Learning is considered a neural change that continues to exist after the learning act.

Herbart, Johann Friedrich, *Outlines of Educational Doctrine*, New York: Macmillan, 1904. The best source in English for Herbart's views on education. It gives Herbart's psychological orientation, then follows with practical advice for instruction.

Hilgard, Ernest R., ed. *Theories of Learning and Instruction*. The National Society for the Study of Education, Chicago: University of Chicago Press, 1964. A modern symposium on learning theory. Professional problems in developing psychological methodologies and educational technologies. Integrating psychologies of learning with technologies of instruction.

Hill, Winifred F. *Learning: A Survey of Psychological Interpretations*, 4th ed. New York: Harper & Row, 1984.

Horton, David L. and Thomas W. Turnage. *Human Learning*. Englewood Cliffs, NJ: Prentice Hall, 1976. Comprehensive review of phenomena and theories of human learning, memory, and language. Chapter 13, "Review and Overview," is highly pertinent to contemporary learning theories. These psychologists do not "consider S-R theory as a promising candidate for the future," because of its usual neglect of perceptual memory, organization in memory, speech perception, and language learning.

Hulse, Stewart H. et al. *The Psychology of Learning*, 4th ed. New York: McGraw-Hill, 1975. A scholarly but difficult presentation of neobehavioristic theory of learning. Includes an extensive list of references on learning.

Irwin, Francis W. *Intentional Behavior and Motivation*. Philadelphia: Lippincott, 1971. A cognitive-behavioral approach to human motivation within a logical-empiricistic frame of reference. Key concepts—situation, act, and outcome—are defined behavioristically and as occurring serially. Emphasizes expectancies and intentions at the expense of effect, drive, and reinforcement on one hand and vitalism, mentalism, and consciousness on the other.

Janes, Julian. *The Origin of Consciousness in the Breakdown of the Bicameral Mind*. Boston: Houghton Mifflin, 1982. A good book to stimulate thought concerning the current educational scene.

Klein, Stephen B. and Robert R. Mowrer, eds. *Contemporary Learning Theories: Pavlovian Conditioning and the Status of Traditional Learning Theory*. Hillsdale, NJ: Lawrence Erlbaum Associates, 1989. The ideas of sixteen psychologists on Pavlovian conditioning and the status and modifications of *traditional* learning theory. Brief descriptions of traditional learning theories.

Klein, Stephen B. and Robert R. Mowrer, eds. *Contemporary Learning Theories: Instrumental Conditioning Theory and the Impact of Biological Constraints on Learning*. Hillsdale, NJ: Lawrence Erlbaum, 1989. A contrast between traditional and contemporary learning theory. The views of seventeen psychologists on instrumental conditioning and biological constraints on learning. Ideas and research of contemporary learning theorists.

Kneller, George F., *Movement of Thought in Modern Education*, New York: John Wiley and Sons, 1984. A philosophical approach to the historical development of educational thought.

Köhler, Wolfgang. *The Mentality of Apes*. New York: Vintage Books, 1959. Especially Chapter 7. An extensive report of Köhler's experiments with animal learning during World War I, at Tenerife.

Lindzey, Gardner, and Elliot Aronson, eds. *The Handbook of Social Psychology*, 2d ed. Vol. 1, *Historical Introduction and Systematic Positions*. Reading, MA: Addison-Wesley, 1968. Contains excellent presentations of seven systematic psychological approaches that have definite implications for learning as well as for social psychology. Stimulus-response, mathematical, cognitive psychoanalytic, field, role, and organization positions are presented.

Logan, Frank A. *Fundamentals of Learning and Motivation*. 2d ed. Dubuque, IA: Brown, 1976. Presents various constructs of behavioristic psychology. Includes a glossary of terms.

May, Rollo. *Psychology and the Human Dilemma*. New York: Van Nostrand Reinhold, 1967. A psychiatrist's presentation of views that harmonize with Gestalt-field learning theory.

Phye, Gary D. and Thomas Andre, eds. *Cognitive Classroom Learning*. Orlando, FL: Academic Press, 1986. Develops cognitive instructional psychology as an alternate to behavioral psychology.

Piaget, Jean. *Psychology and Epistemology*. New York: Grossman, 1971. Presents the psychological and philosophical theory on which Piaget's conclusions are based. Develops his meaning of genetic epistemology.

Rousseau, Jean Jacques. *Émile*, trans. Barbara Foxley. New York: Dutton, 1911, in the Everyman's Library. A complete translation of Rousseau's *Émile*. It is Rousseau's account of rearing and educating a fictitious boy born to eighteenth-century city dwellers.

Salakian, William S. *An Introduction to the Psychology of Learning*, 2nd ed. Itasca, IL: Peacock Publishers, 1984. A good source book for the historical development of learning theories and their application.

Skinner, B. F. *About Behaviorism*. New York: Knopf, 1974. Professor Skinner explains what behaviorism is all about.

Skinner, B. F. *Recent Issues in the Analysis of Behavior*. Columbus, OH: Merrill Publishing Company, 1989. Aimed at all behavior analysts. Skinner appraises what he has attempted and what he has accomplished.

Snelbecker, Glenn E. *Learning Theory, Instructional Theory, and Psychoeducational Design*. New York: McGraw-Hill, 1974. Develops historical and contemporary psychological learning theories along with related instructional theories and "psychoeducational" innovations. Good background reading.

Thorndike, Edward L. *Selected Writings from a Connectionist's Psychology*. New York: Appleton-Century-Crofts, 1949. A collection of Thorndike's papers to give students a firsthand knowledge of connectionist psychology. His autobiography gives the reader a picture of how educational psychology has developed.

Tolman, E. C., and C. H. Honzik. " 'Insight' in Rats." University of California Publication in *Psychology* 4, No. 14 (1930): 215–232. This study was unique in that behaviorists tested rats for insight and found it.

Wandersman, Abraham, Paul J. Poppen, and David F. Ricks, eds. *Humanism and Behaviorism: Dialogue and Growth.* Oxford: Pergamon, 1976. Contrasts existentialist humanism and behaviorism and explores development of a synthesis of the two positions. In part III Walter Mischel develops an alternative to either extreme—a "cognitive social learning" view.

Watson, John B., and William McDougall. *The Battle of Behaviorism.* New York: Norton, 1929. A debate between McDougall, the eminent psychologist of instinct theory, and Watson, the upsurging behaviorist. The sharp conflict between mentalist and physicalistic psychology becomes clear.

Weiner, Bernard. *Theories of Motivation from Mechanism to Cognition.* Chicago: Markham, 1972. Develops theories of motivation that parallel theories of learning. Distinguishes sharply between "mechanistic" and "humanistic" psychology.

Chapter
5

How Does Skinner's Operant Conditioning Work?

B. F. Skinner (1904–1990) was a professor of psychology at Harvard University for many years. His work centered upon psychological research on learning processes. He thought of himself as a radical behaviorist. In 1989 he wrote, "When I am asked what I regard as my most important contribution, I always say, 'the original experimental analysis of operant behavior and its subsequent extension to more and more complex cases.' "[1] He noted that human behavior is the product of three kinds of selection—natural selection within ethology, operant conditioning within behavioral analysis, and cultural evolution of social contingencies of reinforcement within cultures. His research has centered upon operant conditioning within behavioral analysis.[2]

Professor Skinner considered the purpose of psychology to be predicting and controlling the behavior of individual organisms. He insisted upon limiting scientific psychological study to the observable behavior of organisms; his only data being those acquired by sensory observation. Since such terms as *willpower, sensation, image, drive* or *instinct* imply nonphysical events, he opposed their use by psychologists or teachers in any connection with their thinking *scientifically* about people. For Skinner, a member of the human species "begins as an organism and becomes a person or self as he acquires a repertoire of behavior.... There is no place in the scientific position for a self as a true originator or initiator of action."[3] Behavior is "the movement of an organism or of its parts in a frame of reference provided by the organism itself or by various external objects or fields of force."[4]

Skinner's psychology is a strictly behavioral-engineering type of science that is devoid of theory in any usual sense. He has insisted that psychology is a science of overt behavior and only overt behavior. Accordingly, he defined learning as a change in either the form or the probability of responses. In most cases this change is brought about by operant conditioning.

Operant conditioning is the learning process whereby a response is made more probable or more frequent: An *operant* is strengthened—reinforced. (Reinforcement is explained in Chapter 4, page 78.) An operant is a set of acts—behavioral atoms—that constitutes an organism's doing something—raising its head, pushing a lever, saying "horse." It is so called because behavior operates upon the environment and generates consequences. In the process of operant conditioning, operant responses are modified or changed. Reinforcement means that the probability of the repetition of certain classes of responses is increased.

Skinner thought that nearly all human behavior is a product of either biological natural selection or psychological operant reinforcement. He noted that in everyday life, in various fields including education, people constantly change the probabilities of responses of others by arranging reinforcing consequences. Furthermore, through being operantly reinforced, people learn to keep their balance, walk, talk, play games, and handle tools and instruments; they perform a set of motions, reinforcement occurs, and the likelihood of repeating the motions is increased. Thus, operant reinforcement improves the efficiency of behavior.

Whenever something reinforces a particular form of behavior, the chances are better that that behavior will be repeated. The task of psychologists is to gain more understanding of conditions under which reinforcement works best, thereby opening the way for cultural control through social engineering. To the many "natural" reinforcers of behavior, a host of artificial reinforcers may be added.

> Any list of values is a list of reinforcers—conditioned or otherwise. We are so constituted that under certain circumstances food, water, sexual contact, and so on, will make any behavior which produces them more likely to occur again. Other things may acquire this power.... An organism can be reinforced by—can be made to "choose"—almost any given state of affairs.[5]

"People behave in ways which, as we say, conform to ethical, governmental, or religious patterns because they are reinforced for doing so."[6] An organism can be reinforced by (that is, it can be made to "choose") almost any given state of affairs. Literature, art, and entertainment are contrived reinforcers. Whether a person buys a book, a ticket to a performance, or a work of art depends upon whether it is reinforcing to him, and it is usually reinforcing to him if he had been reinforced when he previously purchased such an article. Skinner found *operant conditioning* highly effective in training lower animals and was confident that it promises equal success when used with children and youth. In operant conditioning, teachers are considered architects and builders of students' behavior. Learning objectives are divided into a large number of very small tasks and reinforced one by one. Operants—sets of acts—are reinforced or strengthened so as to increase the probability of their recurrence in the future. In this process it is of prime importance that teachers employ properly timed and spaced schedules of reinforcement.

When Skinner said that behavior is controlled by the environment, he meant two quite different environmental functions. The environment shapes and maintains repertoires of behavior, but it also serves as the occasion upon which behavior occurs. "An operant is a class of responses, not an instance, but it also is a probability."[7]

HOW DID SKINNER USE ANIMALS IN STUDY OF OPERANT REINFORCEMENT?

"Two major claims have been made for Skinner's radical behaviorism: first that it has generated an effective science of behavior based on experimental work with non-human animals; second, that this science can be used to predict, control, and interpret the everyday behavior of our own species."[8] Professor Skinner and his associates experienced remarkable success in training animals. In one college class period, by presenting food to a hungry pigeon at the right time, Skinner implanted in the bird three or four well-defined responses such as turning around, pacing the floor in a figure-eight pattern, stretching the neck, and stamping the foot.

Skinner's basic thesis was that, since an organism tends in the future to do what it was doing at the time of reinforcement, one can, by rewarding each step of the way, lead it to do very much what the experimenter wishes it to do. Using this thesis as a basis for his procedure, he taught rats to use a marble to obtain food from a vending machine, pigeons to play a modified game of tennis, and dogs to operate the pedal of a refuse can so as to retrieve a bone.

Skinner focused his early study on lower animals because their behavior is simpler, conditions surrounding them may be controlled better, basic processes are revealed more readily and can be recorded over longer periods of time, and observations are not complicated by social relations between subjects and the psychologist. However, he later conducted research on learning using human beings of various ages and abilities.

The "Skinner box" is a simple box that contains a rat, a lever, and a device for delivering a pellet of food each time the rat presses the lever. Recording devices are set outside the box so that the experimenter can go home at night and see in the morning what the rat has been doing. There also are Skinner boxes for the study of pigeons and other animals. A rat or pigeon learns rapidly in a Skinner box, because in the box there is little else for it to do. Skinner wrote "The barest possible statement of the process is this: We make a given consequence contingent [dependent] upon certain physical properties of behavior (the upward movement of the head), and the behavior is then observed to increase in frequency."[9]

A pigeon's behavior can be reinforced in such a way that neck stretching will become habitual. The pigeon is placed in a cage so that the experimenter can sight across its head at a scale pinned on the far wall of the cage. The height at which the head is normally held is established on the scale; then some line, which is reached only infrequently, is selected. The experimenter, keeping an eye on the scale, quickly opens the food tray whenever the bird's head rises above the established line. As a result, learning occurs.

> We observe an immediate change in the frequency with which the head crosses the line. We also observe, and this is of some importance theoretically, that higher lines are now being crossed. We may advance almost immediately to a higher line in determining when food is to be presented. In a minute or two, the bird's posture has changed so that the top of the head seldom falls below the line which we first chose.[10]

By training two pigeons separately to do their parts in a total performance, Skinner constructed a social scene within which competition was exemplified by two pigeons playing a modified game of Ping-Pong. He accomplished the training through operant reinforcement. First, the pigeons were reinforced when they merely pushed the ball. Then, when the ball got by one pigeon, the other was reinforced. He has also trained pigeons to coordinate their behavior in dancing in a cooperative manner that rivals the skills of human dancers.

Reinforcement procedures may vary according to intervals of time and the number of responses between reinforcements. A schedule of reinforcement is a pattern of "rewarding" behavior based upon a fixed time interval and a fixed number of responses between "rewards." In a laboratory Skinner and Ferster had obtained performances appropriate to each of nine different ratio-interval schedules.[11] Skinner thought that this achievement made more plausible the extension of laboratory results to daily human life. To him, learning, in the everyday life of people, was more complicated but nevertheless of the same basic nature as a lower animal learning through operant conditioning.

In operant conditioning experiments, the species of organism studied has made surprisingly little difference. "Comparable results have been obtained with pigeons, rats, dogs, monkeys, human children, and psychotic subjects. In spite of great phylogenetic differences, all these organisms show amazingly similar properties of the learning process.[12]

WHAT PSYCHOLOGICAL THEORY UNDERLIES SKINNER'S TEACHING PROCEDURES?

Throughout his study and writings, Professor Skinner adhered rigorously to a basic conviction that psychologists should restrict their study to the correlations between stimuli and responses and not meddle with any "make-believe" psychology that constructs intervening physiological or mental links between stimuli and responses. "We can predict and control behavior without knowing anything about what is happening inside."[13] He considered only past events to be relevant to prediction of behavior. Accordingly, he stated, "Behavior is shaped and maintained by its consequences [what follows it], but only by consequences that lie in the past. We do what we do because of what *has* happened, not what *will* happen."[14] "Even if we could discover a spider's felt intention or sense of purpose, we could not offer it as a cause of the behavior."[15] Thus, any mentalistic description of behavior offers no real explanation of it. Instead, it only impedes its more effective analysis. Skinner, like both Thorndike and Watson before him, assumed that human beings are neutral and passive and that all behavior can be described in sequential mechanistic terms. In his study of human beings and lower animals, he was constantly mechanistic and elementistic; to him, psychology was the science of behavior.

What Is the Meaning of the "Science of Behavior"?

Skinner saw a great and crucial future for a science of behavior. In his view, since a science of behavior is concerned with demonstrating the consequences of cultural practices, the presence of such a science will be an essential mark of the culture or cultures that will survive in the future. The culture most likely to survive is the one in which the methods of science are most effectively applied to the problems of human behavior.[16] Consequently, throughout his work he strove constantly to be scientific to the nth degree. He saw science as "more than a set of attitudes. It is a search for order, for uniformities, for lawful relations among the events in nature. It begins, as we all begin, by observing single episodes, but it quickly passes on to the general rule, to scientific law."[17]

A Scientific-Realistic Definition of Science   Skinner worked on the basic assumption that there is order in nature, including human behavior, and that it is the function of science to discover the order; this is the commitment of a scientific-realistic, as opposed to a positive-relativistic, scientist. Within Skinner's scientific-realistic outlook, science is concerned with the discovery of preexistent laws, which govern the world about us. Knowledge of these laws enhances predictability, and thereby control, of the variables that cause events to occur. This is as true in psychology as in physics or chemistry. Thus, human beings, through discovery of laws and organization of them into systems, enable themselves to deal effectively with aspects of the naturalistic world. "Science is in large part a direct analysis of reinforcing systems found in nature; it is concerned with facilitating the behavior which is reinforced by them."[18]

Human Behavior, a Subject of Science   According to Skinner, it is not to be assumed that human behavior has any peculiar properties that require a unique method or special kind of knowledge. "The experimental analysis of behavior is a rigorous, extensive, and rapidly advancing branch of biology."[19] Thus, the variables of psychology, like the variables of any other science, must be described in physical terms. In Skinner's psychology the *dependent variable* in a situation is the behavior of an individual organism. The *independent variable* consists of external conditions of which the behavior is a function. This means that behavior operates upon the environment to generate consequences. Notice that in this process neither the person nor the environment but it—behavior—behaves; behavior is a phenomenon of nature. Just as wind blows, behavior behaves.

The laws of the science of psychology are as definite as those of any other science. "It is decidedly not true that a horse may be led to water but cannot be made to drink."[20] Through applying the laws of psychology and arranging a history of severe deprivation, one can make absolutely sure that drinking will occur; likewise, a desired behavior can be caused in a human being.

Skinner's goal in psychology was to achieve the degree of prediction and control in regard to human behavior that had been achieved by the physical sciences. The scientist of behavior evaluates probability of behavior and explores conditions that determine it. Through gathering data in regard to the frequencies of responses that have already occurred, one is able to make accurate statements about the likelihood of occurrence of a single future response of the same kind; frequency of response indicates probability of response.

> We are concerned, then, with the causes of human behavior. We want to know why men behave as they do. Any condition or event which can be shown to have an effect upon behavior must be taken into account. By discovering and analyzing these causes, we can predict behavior; to the extent that we can manipulate them, we can control behavior.[21]

In keeping with his physicalistic commitment (a physicalist is one who holds human thoughts and actions to be determined by physical laws), Professor Skinner stated, "I do not see any distinction between predicting what an individual is going to do and predicting what, let us say, a sailboat is going to do."[22] "Operant conditioning shapes behavior as the sculptor shapes a lump of clay."[23]

How Is the Science of Behavior Related to Determinism?

Skinner's psychology implies a strictly naturalistic determinism. He noted that a scientific conception of human behavior dictates one practice and a philosophy of personal freedom another and that a scientific conception of human behavior entails the acceptance of an assumption of determinism. Determinism means that behavior is caused and that the behavior that appears is the only kind that could have appeared. Skinner emphasized that the same type of determinism that is commonly accepted as applying to machines applies equally to human beings. Accordingly, he stated, "Man is a machine, but he is a very complex one. At present he is far beyond the powers of men to construct—except, of course, in the usual biological way."[24]

As machines have become more lifelike, living organisms have been found to be more like machines. Today, many machines are deliberately designed to operate in ways that resemble "human behavior." "Man has, in short, created the machine in his own image."[25] Since mechanical calculators now solve equations either too difficult or too time-consuming even for mathematicians to conquer, human beings have lost much of their uniqueness.

Determinism carries with it the implication that environment determines an individual even when the individual alters his own environment.

It does not matter that the individual may take it upon himself to control the variables of which his own behavior is a function or, in a broad sense, to engage in the design of his own culture. He does this only because he is the product of a culture which generates self-control or cultural design as a mode of behavior.[26]

All human behavior, including the behavior of machines which man builds to behave in his place, is ultimately to be accounted for in terms of the phylogenic contingencies of survival which have produced man as a species and the ontogenic contingencies of reinforcement which have produced him as an individual.[27]

"As accidental traits, arising from mutations, are selected by their contribution to survival, so accidental variations in behavior are selected by their reinforcing consequences."[28] "The scientist, like any organism, is the product of a unique history."[29] Science is of major importance in human affairs but even scientists and science are not free. Science, too, is a part of a naturally determined course of events, and it cannot interfere with that course.[30]

HOW IS OPERANT CONDITIONING NONPHYSIOLOGICAL AND NONPHENOMENOLOGICAL?

Skinner's system of operant conditioning has no place for study of either physiological or phenomenological psychology. *Physiological psychology* is devoted to study of physiological, neurological, and biological functions within an organism. *Phenomenological psychology* centers upon what events mean to the persons involved. In a sense it is similar to physiological psychology in that it, too, is centered upon what takes place within a person. However, it differs sharply from physiological psychology in that major emphasis is placed upon the process of conscious experiencing. Because Skinner rejected the use of the intervening variables that, in both physiological and phenomenological psychology, occur between stimuli and responses and represent the organism ("O" in S-O-R psychology), his friends sometimes speak of him dealing with the "empty organism."

How Is Operant Conditioning a Nonphysiological Psychology?

Skinner was convinced that the practice of looking inside an organism for an explanation of behavior has tended to obscure the variables that lie outside the organism and are immediately available for scientific analysis. These variables outside the organism are in its environmental history and its immediate environment. Psychologists' study of them permits behavior to be explained scientifically just as behavior of nonliving objects is explained scientifically by physicists. These independent variables are of many sorts, and their relation to behavior often is subtle and complex; nevertheless, according to Skinner, it is only through analyzing them that we may hope to reach an adequate account of behavior.

Since statements about operations of the nervous system are not expressed in the same terms and cannot be confirmed by the same method of observation as the facts for which they are supposed to account, they are theories. Thus, Skinner felt that they could make little contribution to a scientific psychology. In the present stage of science an adequate neurological explanation of behavior is impossible. However, this fact in no way implies that a scientific psychology of learning cannot be established separate from any neurological theory.

How Is Operant Conditioning a Nonphenomenological Psychology?

Statements about mental events, like neurological statements, are also theoretical. Thus, Skinner belittled attempts of psychologists to infer what a physical situation means to an organism or to distinguish between the physical world and the psychological world of experience. He constantly emphasized that events affecting an organism must be capable of being described in the language of physical science. Accordingly, he stated, "I regard myself as an organism responding to its environment."[31] To him, the "free inner man," who is held responsible for the behavior of the external biological organism, is only a pre-scientific substitute for the external causes of behavior, which are susceptible to scientific analysis. Hence, there is no place in scientific psychology for study of the intra-personal experiences of people as such. Accordingly, he writes, "What we have learned from the experimental analysis of behavior suggests that the environment performs the functions previously assigned to feelings and introspectively observed inner states of the organism."[32]

Skinner regarded the practice of some scientists who indicate that they are describing only half the universe and that there is another half—a world of self, mind, or consciousness—as a part of the cultural heritage from which science has emerged but which now stands in the way of a unified scientific account of nature. Even in discussing the higher human function, thinking, Skinner saw little need for the concept *self*. He recognized that behavior is a function of the environment, that environment presumably means any event in the universe capable of affecting the organism, and that a very small part of this universe is private—enclosed within the organism's own skin. Thus, some independent variables, for example, an aching tooth, may be related to behavior in a unique way. However, he sees no reason to suppose that the stimulating effect of an inflamed tooth is essentially different from that of a hot stove. "The alternative to the use of the concept [self] is simply to deal with demonstrated covariations in the strength of responses."[33]

Private Events   Skinner thought that students of a science of behavior should face the problem of privacy but that they should do so without abandoning the basic position of "radical behaviorism." Radical behaviorists think that "an adequate science of behavior must consider events taking place within the skin of the organism, not as physiological mediators of behavior, but as part of behavior itself."[34]

Private stimuli are either interoceptive or proprioceptive ones. *Interoceptive* stimuli are those received by nerve endings in the internal organs, for example, the stimuli provided by hunger pangs or a full bladder. *Proprioceptive* stimuli are received through afferent nerve endings in the muscles of the body, for example, the stimuli provided by lame or sore muscles.

Any personal feelings, at their best, are accompaniments, not causes, of behavior. Furthermore, covert responses are not the causes of related overt ones; both are the products of common independent variables. Consequently, the conditions that one feels, not one's feelings as such, are the important factors in a study of behavior. Radical behaviorism "does not *reduce* feelings to bodily states; it simply argues that bodily states are and always have been what are felt. It does not *reduce* thought processes to behavior; it simply analyzes the behavior previously explained by the invention of thought processes."[35] "No matter how defective a behavior account may be, we must remember that mentalistic explanations explain nothing."[36]

In Skinner's system there is no place for the statement that behavior is under the control of an incentive or goal. A scientific psychology, as Skinner defines it, replaces statements that might use such words as *incentive*, *goal*, or *purpose* with statements about conditioning. A person may feel a purpose, but such a feel has no casual effect. "A person is not an originating agent; he is a locus, a point at which many genetic and environmental conditions come together in a joint effect."[37]

Instead of saying that a person behaves because of the consequences that are to follow behavior, we simply state that the person behaves in a particular manner because of the consequences that have followed similar behavior in the past. When one is "looking for something" one is emitting responses that in the past produced something as a consequence. When one says, "I am looking for my glasses," what one really means is " 'I have lost my glasses,' 'I shall stop what I am doing when I find my glasses,' or 'When I have done this in the past, I have found my glasses.' "[38]

Professor Skinner used the analogy that astronomers may speak figuratively of the sun rising and setting, but they do not do so when they are performing the role of scientists. Likewise, psychologists and teachers properly may use such literary descriptions of human activity as that the person *expected, hoped, observed, felt, knew, remembered, feared, was hungry*, or *was anxious*. But as behavioral scientists they should report only observed facts such as the *organism was reinforced when it pushed the lever*, the *intake of food was so much*, or *aversive stimuli or preaversive stimuli were present*.[39]

Since the terms *pleasant* and *satisfying* do not refer to any physical property of reinforcing events, and physical sciences use neither of these terms nor their equivalents, they, too, should be deleted from the language of a science of psychology. Furthermore, because behavior is always the behavior of an individual, a science of behavior that concerns only the behavior of groups is not likely to be of help in understanding particular cases. Thus, "A 'social force' is no more useful in manipulating behavior than an inner state of hunger, anxiety, or skepticism."[40]

WHAT IS THE NATURE OF OPERANT CONDITIONING OR REINFORCEMENT?

Operant conditioning is a learning process whereby a given response is made either more probable or more frequent by the occurrence of a reinforcing stimulus immediately following the response. In the pigeon experiment, reported on page 98, the process of operant conditioning is the change in frequency with which the head is lifted to a given height, the *reinforcer* is food, and the *reinforcement* is food presentation after the response is emitted. The *operant* is the behavior upon which the reinforcement is contingent—the height to which the head must be raised.

In operant conditioning the important stimulus is the one immediately following the response, not the one preceding it. Any emitted response that leads to reinforcement is thereby strengthened. However, it is not the specific response that is strengthened but, rather, the general tendency to make the response. Hence, carefully stated, an operant is a class of responses of which a specific response is an instance or member. A rat presses a lever and gets food. Consequently, the rat will be more likely to press the lever again. What is changed is the future probability of responses in the same class. The operant as a class of behavior, rather than the response as a particular instance, is reinforced. It is not correct to say than an operant reinforcer strengthened the response that preceded it; the response has already occurred and cannot be changed. What has been changed is that the probability that that class of responses will occur in the future has been increased. Since each reinforcement builds up a reserve of responses, a pigeon may continue to raise its head or a rat to press the lever several, or even many, times after food has ceased to appear.

The *law of operant conditioning* is that if the occurrence of an operant is followed by presentation of a reinforcing stimulus, the strength—probability— is increased. What is strengthened is not a stimulus-response connection; the operant requires no specific eliciting stimulus. Insofar as the organism is concerned, the only important property of the operant contingency is time; the reinforcer follows the response. The process of operant conditioning may be described adequately without any mention of a stimulus that acts before the response is made. In reinforcing a pigeon's neck stretching, one must only wait for neck stretching to occur. It is not necessary for the experimenter to elicit it. "The statement that the bird 'learns that it will get food by stretching its neck' is an inaccurate report of what has happened."[41] A cognitive-field interactionist explanation of how the bird learns, of course, would be just this.

An operant-reinforcement approach to teaching a ninth grader that biological man is *Homo sapiens* would be to show the student *man* along with several other more complicated words, one of which is *Homo sapiens*. If the student chooses "non sequitur," or any expression other than *Homo sapiens*, nothing happens. If he/she chooses "Homo sapiens," the teacher says "wonderful." This is reinforcement, and they proceed to a new "problem."

What Is a Contingency of Reinforcement?

Skinner's units of learning are "contingencies of reinforcement." A *contingency of reinforcement* is a sequence within which a response is followed by a reinforcing stimulus. The ordered interrelations between three terms or variables compose such a contingency. These variables are (1) a discriminative stimulus (S^D); (2) the behavior or response itself (R); and (3) the reinforcing stimulus (S^{rein}). So, Skinner's paradigm of reinforcement is ($S^D - R - S^{rein}$). A discriminative stimulus (S^D) occurs prior to the response (R) being reinforced. It is any stimulus or pattern of stimuli that arises from the nature of the space within which the organism is placed, the apparatus used to sense occurrences of the response, or any special stimulating devices that may be used. Thus, it sets, or discriminates, the conditions under which a behavior occurs. The reinforcing stimulus (S^{rein}) follows the discriminative stimulus and the response and renders consequences to the organism.

A hen that plays a piano at a fair, when a person places a dime in the appropriate slot, is an example of applied operant conditioning. The cage, the piano, the feed trough, and the lighted bulb in the corner of the cage constitute the S^D—discriminative stimulus—playing the piano is the operant that is being reinforced, and pellets being eaten constitute the S^{rein}—reinforcing stimulus. Pellets have been given her only after she had played the piano when the light was on. At no other time has she received a pellet. Thus, when the dime drops the light is turned on, the hen strikes the keys the required number of times, then a pellet is dropped and the hen eats the pellet.

Operant reinforcement, then, not only strengthens a given response; it also may bring the response under the control of a discriminative stimulus. But the discriminative or controlling stimulus does not elicit the response; it merely sets the occasion upon which the response is more likely to occur.[42] Therefore, when a response occurs and is reinforced, the probability that it will occur again in the presence of similar stimuli is increased.

In a contingency, the occurrence of an operant—response—is *followed* by presentation of a reinforcing stimulus, and the strength—probability—of recurrence of the operant is increased. The three-term contingency of operant reinforcement can be observed when a child is taught to read; a given response is reinforced with "right" or "wrong" according to how the student responds to the appropriate visual stimulus—a word or sentence.

The key to successful teaching or training is to analyze the effect of reinforcement and to design techniques that manipulate the process with considerable precision so as to set up specific reinforcing contingencies. In this way the behavior of an individual organism may be brought under precise control. Implicit in operant behaviorism is the conviction that "When all relevant variables have been arranged, an organism will or will not respond. If it does not, it cannot. If it can, it will."[43]

How Does Operant Differ from Respondent or Reflexive Conditioning?

Skinner acknowledged two kinds of learning—operant and respondent or reflexive. But he placed far greater emphasis upon operant learning. *Respondent* or reflexive behavior is behavior that is elicited by a stimulus; *operant* behavior is behavior that is controlled by its consequences, that is, what follows it.

Reflexive learning involves such situations as are described in the Pavlovian dog studies. Essentially, it is a process of stimulus substitution. An organism already responds reflexively to a natural or unconditioned stimulus. Then a new stimulus is presented along with the original stimulus and the organism comes to respond to the new stimulus in the same way it formerly did to the original one. In reflexive or respondent conditioning the key stimulus is the one that precedes the response. Whereas reflexive learning is an S-R process, operant learning is an R-S one. In operant learning the most significant stimulus is that which immediately follows the response. Recall that, for Skinner, any modification of the environment constituted a stimulus. (See Table 4.1, page 77.)

WHAT ARE THE PROCESSES OF OPERANT REINFORCEMENT AND EXTINCTION?

In operant conditioning an operant is strengthened through its *reinforcement* or weakened through its *extinction*. The psychologist's task is simply to account for probability of responses in terms of a history of reinforcement and extinction. The effect of reinforcement is always to increase the probability of response. Extinction is the reverse of reinforcement. When a reinforcing stimulus no longer occurs following a response, the response becomes less and less frequent; this is operant extinction. Conditioning builds up a predisposition to respond, which extinction exhausts. We discuss extinction on page 109, but first, we describe the kinds of reinforcers and types of reinforcement.

What Are the Two Kinds of Reinforcers?

Any stimulus whose presentation or removal increases the probability of a response is a reinforcer. Consequently, there are two kinds of reinforcers or reinforcing events—positive and negative. A positive reinforcer is any stimulus whose *presentation* strengthens the behavior upon which it is made contingent; a negative reinforcer is any stimulus whose *withdrawal* strengthens that behavior. Since in both cases responses are strengthened, reinforcement is taking place. A positive reinforcement consists of presenting a stimulus, of adding something—food, water, or a teacher's smile—to an organism's environment. A negative reinforcement consists of removing something—a loud noise, and electric shock, or a teacher's frown—from the situation. In both of these cases the probability that the response will recur is increased.

Although in lay usage both positive and negative reinforcers are "rewards," Skinner warned against defining a positive reinforcer as pleasant or satisfying and a negative reinforcer as annoying. "It would be as difficult to show that the reinforcing power of an aversion stimulus is due to its unpleasantness as to show that the reinforcing power of a positive reinforcer is due to its pleasantness."[44] When a person reports that an event is pleasant, this simply means that the event is of such kind that it reinforces him. Physical science uses no such terms as "pleasant" and "unpleasant" or their equivalents. The terms in no way refer to physical properties of reinforcing agents.

Is Punishment Reinforcement?

Skinner thought that *punishment* is a basically different process from reinforcement. Whereas reinforcement involves presentation of a positive stimulus or removal of a negative one, punishment consists of presentation of a negative stimulus or removal of a positive one. Again, whereas reinforcement is defined in terms of strengthening of a response, punishment is a process that weakens a response. Stated succinctly, when a stimulus is involved in *strengthening* a response, there is reinforcement; when a stimulus is either presented or withdrawn in an attempt to *weaken* a response, there is punishment. Whereas reinforcement can be used to good advantage in controlling organisms, in the long run punishment works to the disadvantage of both the punished organism and the punishing agency. Its results are neither predictable nor dependable. Extinction—permitting a behavior to die out by not reinforcing it—and not punishment is the appropriate process for breaking habits.

What Are the Types of Operant Reinforcement?

There are two rather distinct types of operant reinforcement—stimulus discrimination and response differentiation. Nearly all human learning can be classified under these two. However, the process of respondent or reflexive conditioning should not be completely ignored. Through operant reinforcement, a relatively complete new unit of behavior may be learned or an existing unit of behavior may be refined. In general, reinforcement that leads to behavior acquirement is a process of discrimination of stimuli, whereas behavior refinement or skill development is a process of differentiation of responses.

Discrimination of Stimuli   Operant stimulus discrimination is the establishment of a certain type of behavior that occurs as the result of a given stimulus either preceding or accompanying that behavior and the behavior then being reinforced. If an operant behavior is reinforced by S^{rein} when a discriminative stimulus S^D is present but is not reinforced when that S^D is not present, the tendency for the organism to respond with that operant behavior when the S^D is present gradually becomes strengthened, and the tendency for it to respond in like manner when not that S^D but some other stimuli are present is gradually extinguished. As stated before, S^{rein} symbolizes the reinforcing stimulus, which follows the operant response (R), and S^D indicates the discriminative stimulus, which is the stimulus that either precedes or accompanies the operant response or behavior (R).

Through the use of a discriminative stimulus followed by reinforcement, such as giving a pigeon pellets when it stretches its neck while a light is on, it can be made to be more likely to respond by stretching its neck at times when the light is on. Imitative behavior is an example of the result of discriminative operant reinforcement. Such behavior does not arise because of any inherent reflexive or mentalistic mechanism but develops in the history of an individual as a result of discriminative reinforcements. The visual stimulation of someone waving a hand is the occasion upon which waving a hand probably received reinforcement. The reinforcement, not the stimulation from the other person waving his hand, is the cause of future hand waving in similar situations. Because objects in shop windows into which other people are looking are likely to reinforce looking into such windows, when a person sees other people looking into a shop window he/she too is likely to look. Thus, "Attention is a controlling *relation*—the relation between a response and a discriminative stimulus. When someone is paying attention he is under special control of a stimulus."[45]

Operant discrimination of a stimulus causes an organism readily to respond in a given manner when the occasion is appropriate for it to do so. In an elementary schoolroom a teacher says "yellow"; a girl points to yellow on a color chart; she then is reinforced for doing so, but only on those occasions when the teacher has first said "yellow." In this way the girl is conditioned to point to yellow only after the teacher, or someone similar to the teacher, has said "yellow."

Rules, laws, and maxims constitute a special category of discriminative stimuli. As well as specifying the occasions upon which a behavior will occur, they also often describe the behavior itself and its reinforcing consequences. Thus, each rule, law, or maxim is effective as the first part of a set of contingencies of reinforcement.[46] Whereas behavior that is reinforced is under the control of succeeding stimuli, rules, laws, and maxims are under the control of prior ones.

Differentiation of Responses   Skills are improved through differentiating reinforcements of varying responses. Many differentiating reinforcements may be supplied automatically by mechanical exigencies of the environment of an organism. To throw a ball skillfully, a person must release it at the proper moment; instances in which release comes before or after the proper moment are not reinforced. However, in more complex skill learning, reinforcement must be supplied by a teacher, teaching machine, or computer. In this process any reinforcement that develops skill must be immediate. "By reinforcing a series of successive approximations, we bring a rare response to a very high probability in a short time."[47]

Through the procedure of operant conditioning, within which differentiation of responses is reinforced, a hungry pigeon that is well adapted to the experimental situation and the food tray can usually be brought to respond by pecking a specific spot in two or three minutes. To get the pigeon to peck a specific spot as quickly as possible, one first gives the bird food when it turns slightly in the direction of the spot. This increases the frequency of turning toward the spot. Reinforcement is then withheld until the bird makes a slight movement toward the spot. Then positions that are successively closer to the spot are reinforced. Then reinforcement is given only when the head is moved slightly forward, and finally only when the beak actually makes contact with the spot.

What Is Extinction?

Extinction is a process whereby a learned behavior or response becomes less and less frequent or completely disappears, as the result of its ceasing to receive reinforcement on repetition. Whereas the mere passage of time after reinforcement has surprisingly little effect upon loss of an act or habit, extinction is an effective way of removing an operant from the habit repertoire of an organism. When unaccompanied by extinction, forgetting takes place very slowly if at all. Note the key difference there: Whereas mere forgetting is the losing of a habit through the passage of time, extinction requires that the response be emitted without reinforcement.

Operant extinction takes place much more slowly than operant reinforcement does. However, as an organism responds less and less, a gradual process of extinction may be detected. Since behavior during extinction is a result of the conditioning that preceded it, extinction occurs quickly when only a few incidents of a given response have been reinforced and is greatly protracted when there has been a long history of reinforcement.

The extinction process includes the interesting phenomenon of spontaneous recovery. Even after prolonged extinction, an organism, at the beginning of another session of an activity in which it had been trained but now is no longer being reinforced, often will respond at a higher rate for at least a few moments.

Sometimes an extinction curve is disturbed by an emotional effect. Failure of a response to be reinforced not only leads to operant extinction but also may be accompanied by a reaction commonly called frustration or rage. A pigeon that has failed to receive reinforcement flaps its wings and engages in other emotional behavior. An auto mechanic, who is in the habit of having bolts unscrew when he/she turns his wrench, vents his spleen when one breaks off instead. However, after exercising his vocabulary, he/she turns back to the next bolt. Likewise, a pigeon or rat will turn again to the operating key of the box when the emotional response has subsided. Extinction curves often show cyclic oscillation as the emotional response builds up, disappears, and builds up again.

The resistance to extinction generated by intermittent reinforcement of a response is much greater than that achieved by the same number of reinforcements being given for consecutive responses. If we only occasionally reinforce a child's good behavior, the behavior survives much longer after reinforcement is discontinued than if we had reinforced every instance up to the same total number of reinforcements. Since intermittent reinforcement generates longer extinction curves than continuous reinforcement does, there is no simple relation between the number of reinforcements and the number of unreinforced responses necessary for extinction.

HOW MAY OPERANT CONDITIONING BE APPLIED TO SCHOOLROOM PRACTICES?

Michael Wessells summarizes Skinner's psychological goals in ten points:[48]

1. Regard observable behavior as the proper subject matter of psychology.
2. Aim to predict and control behavior through its functional analysis.
3. Search for general laws of learning by analyzing relatively simple responses under well-controlled conditions.
4. Proceed inductively, avoiding hypothesis construction and testing.
5. Avoid any use of statistics or averaging of data.
6. Focus study upon accessible, manipulable variables.
7. Look to environment for the causes of behavior; avoid loosely defined theoretical constructs, staying close to observable data.
8. Reject any mentalistic inner causes or explanations.
9. When necessary, translate everyday explanations into behavioral statements.
10. Regard private events as physical, lawful ones and treat subjective events as collateral ones.

For Professor Skinner, "Teaching is the arrangement of contingencies of reinforcement which expedite learning."[49] He thought that the most effective control of human learning requires instrumental aid. He was appalled at the present inefficient practices in schools and recommended a procedure whereby they can be corrected. He was convinced that when teachers have taught successfully, regardless of whether they have thought in mental disciplinary, apperceptive, or behavioristic terms, they actually have arranged effective contingencies of reinforcement. But Skinner also thought that teachers are more likely to do this well if they understand what it is that they are doing.

For Skinner, the primary function of teachers is to transmit a culture to children and youth. Such transmission consists of natural selection plus operant conditioning. Education is a procedure of processing, storing, and retrieving information, "showing and telling are ways of 'priming' behavior, of getting people to behave in a given way for the first time so that the behavior can be reinforced."[50] But we do not learn by imitating. Instead, consequences must follow for behavior to be learned. "Educators have turned to discovery and creativity in an effort to interest their students, but good contingencies of reinforcement do that in a much more profitable way."[51]

Skinner recognized that the first task of teachers is to shape proper responses, to get children to pronounce and write responses properly. But he saw their principal task as bringing proper behavior under many sorts of stimulus control. Teaching spelling, for Skinner, was mainly a process of shaping complex forms of behavior. In other subjects the same process should be used to bring responses under the control of appropriate stimuli. To achieve this task, Skinner recommended the use of *programmed instruction*.

Programmed instruction is a system of teaching and learning within which preestablished subject matter is broken down into small, discrete steps and carefully organized into a logical sequence in which it can be learned readily by the students. Each step builds deliberately upon the preceding one. A learner can progress through the sequence of steps at his own rate: he/she is nearly always right and is reinforced immediately after each step. Reinforcement consists of the learner either being given the correct response immediately after he/she registers it or being permitted to proceed to the next step only after he has registered that response. Programmed instruction may be accomplished either with or without the use of teaching machines or computers. (Teaching machines are described on page 115 and computers on pages 306–309.)

Skinner stated "The computer is the ideal teaching machine.... Computers can teach best...by leading the student through carefully prepared instructional programs. They can prime and prompt behavior and reinforce it immediately."[52]

Skinner's linear programming presents a series of frames to a student. A *frame* constitutes a contingency of reinforcement. It consists of a discriminative stimulus in the form of a question. The student's answer is the response, and the student making the "right" response in the form of the "right" answer is the reinforcing stimulus. The following is an example of a frame: "A warmblooded animal that suckles its young is called a _____."

Succeeding frames develop new learning in such small increments that students get the "right" answer on more than 90 percent of the frames. It is assumed that a student's making a right response and immediately learning that it is right is in itself a reinforcer. Consequently, the student is more likely to repeat that response or answer in a future similar situation. Also, he/she will move on to the next frame. Thus, a pellet is to a rat what a piece of candy is to a small child and what making the "right" response is to an older student.

What Are the Shortcomings of Current Educational Practice?

Skinner believed that it is in bringing correct responses under stimulus control that the greatest inefficiency of current teaching procedures occurs. "In education we design and redesign our curricula in a desperate attempt to provide a liberal education while steadfastly refusing to employ available engineering techniques which would efficiently build the interests and instill the knowledge which are the goals of education."[53] Consequently, he notes the following current weaknesses in educational practices:

1. Behavior is dominated by aversion (escape) stimulation.
2. Too great a lapse of time exists between behavior and its reinforcement.
3. A skillful program of reinforcement that moves forward through a series of progressive approximations to the final complex desired behavior is lacking.
4. Reinforcement of desired behavior occurs much too infrequently.

Behavior Dominated by Aversion Stimulation   Although the type of threatened displeasure or pain has been changed in the past 50 years, behavior in the lower grades is still dominated by aversive stimulation—children are trying to escape or keep away from something. Fifty years ago children read numbers, copied numbers, and memorized tables to escape the birch rod or cane; that is, as far as they were concerned, they did these things to avoid or escape punishment. Today, students behave the way they do primarily to escape the threat of a series of minor distasteful events—the teacher's displeasure, criticism or ridicule by their classmates, a poor showing in competition, low marks, or a trip to the principal's office. When children are dominated by this atmosphere, getting the right answer is in itself a rather insignificant event. Thus, the emphasis in teaching and learning is not centered where it should be—in operant conditioning.

Excessive Time Lapse Between Behavior and Reinforcement   Unless explicit mediating behavior has been set up, the lapse of only a few seconds between a response and its reinforcement destroys most of the effect. A grade on a test taken near the end of the week is too far away from the behaviors the students emitted—sent out—in studying the subject matter earlier in the week. Reinforcing stimuli should follow the desired responses immediately.

Through use of the generalized reinforcer—approval—schools and society reinforce acquisition of the type of behavior learned in school. This is done by awarding grades, promotions, keys, diplomas, degrees, and medals. Skinner noted that these reinforcers do reinforce students' going to school and gaining a diploma or degree; their shortcoming is that they seldom if ever reinforce the subject matter elements themselves.

Absence of a Program of Serial Reinforcement   A carefully planned program of teaching should move forward step by step by reinforcing a series of progressive approximations to the final behavior that is desired. To bring a human organism into possession of mathematical, or any other systematic, behavior most efficiently, a long series of reinforcement contingencies is necessary. Since teachers have only so much time, they cannot deal with students' responses one at a time; it is usually necessary for them to reinforce the desired behavior only in blocks of responses.

Infrequency of Reinforcement   Perhaps the most serious criticism of current classroom procedures is the relative infrequency of reinforcement of the desired acts of students. It is just not humanly possible for one teacher to provide an adequate number of reinforcement contingencies for a class of 30 or 40 children. Skinner estimated that although adequate efficient mathematical behavior at the level of the first four grades requires somewhere between 25,000 and 50,000 reinforcement contingencies, a teacher at best could provide only a few thousand. Thus, even our best schools may be criticized for their inefficiency in teaching drill subjects such as arithmetic. Skinner believed that advances recently made in techniques for control of the learning process suggest that classroom practices should be thoroughly revised.

What Are the Relevant Considerations in Conditioning (Teaching) a Child?

In order to plan a procedure for inculcating certain desired behavior in a child some specific questions need to be answered.

1. What behavior is to be established?
2. What reinforcers are available?
3. What responses are available?
4. How can reinforcements be most efficiently scheduled?

Behavior to Be Established   To teach efficiently, the first job of a teacher who is an adherent of operant conditioning is to determine carefully just what he/she plans to teach at a specific time; the teacher is the architect and builder of behaviors who must decide what he wants to teach, then teach it. The objectives are specific and are defined in terms of desired behaviors. Thus, operant behaviorism requires a teacher-centered classroom.

Reinforcers Available   What does a school have in its possession that will reinforce a child? Since the sheer control of nature in itself is reinforcing, the material to be learned may provide considerable automatic reinforcement. Children play for hours with mechanical toys, paints, and puzzles. These feed back significant changes in the environment and are reasonably free of aversive stimulation. Automatic reinforcement from manipulation of the environment is probably rather mild. However, in teaching, the net amount of reinforcement in each contingency is of little significance. When properly and carefully used, a series of very slight reinforcements may be tremendously effective in controlling behavior.

In addition to automatic reinforcement arising from manipulation of the environment, some other reinforcers are available and often used. A child behaves in a certain way and the behavior is reinforced by its immediate consequences. Reinforcement may follow from a child's excelling others. However, when children are competitively "rewarded," the reinforcement of one child is, of necessity, aversive—"punishing"—to others. The good will and affection of the teacher also may be reinforcing. A positive "reward" or "consequence" (stimulus) strengthens the behavior that is part of the contingency including that stimulus; it has nothing to do with satisfying organismic purpose.

Responses Available   In planning a program of progressive approximations that will lead to the desired final form of behavior, a teacher must have at hand an inventory of the responses that are available throughout the conditioning process.

Most Efficient Scheduling of Reinforcements   To schedule reinforcements efficiently means to make them contingent upon the desired behavior. Here two considerations are involved: (1) gradual elaboration of extremely complex patterns of behavior into small units or stages and (2) maintenance of the behavior in strength at each stage.

> The whole process of becoming competent in any field must be divided into a very large number of very small steps, and reinforcement must be contingent upon the accomplishment of each step.... By making each successive step as small as possible, the frequency of reinforcement can be raised to a maximum, while the possibly aversive consequences of being wrong are reduced to a minimum.[54]

According to operant conditioning,

> learning a subject like fundamentals of electricity is largely a matter of learning (or giving) a large number of correct responses to logically related sequences of questions that constitute the subject.... Once a subject has been carefully divided ("programmed") into a series of many small bits of information ("steps") a student has only to learn by repetition and reward ("rapid and frequent reinforcement") the correct answer to a series of questions about the small bits of information.[55]

This is the purpose of programmed instruction.

Skinner contended that the necessary requirements for adequate reinforcement are not excessive, but they probably are incompatible with current realities of present-day classrooms. Experimental studies of learning have indicated that in order to arrange the contingencies of reinforcement that are most efficient in controlling learning in an organism, mechanical and electrical devices must be used. As mere reinforcing mechanisms, teachers are out of date—and would be so even if each teacher devoted all his time to a single child. Only through mechanical devices can the necessarily large number of contingencies be provided. "We have every reason to expect, therefore, that the most effective control of human learning will require instrumental aid."[56]

How Do Teaching Machines Work?

In Skinner's view, education must become more efficient to a degree that cannot be accomplished merely by our building more schools and preparing more teachers; adequate systems of labor-saving capital equipment, that is, teaching machines, must be developed. He is critical, too, of traditional education, which makes students more and more the passive receivers of instruction. Teaching machines, he feels, encourage students to take an "active" role in the instructional process—they must develop the answers before they are reinforced.

Requirements of an Appropriate Teaching Machine   Skinner thought that in light of modern psychological knowledge, an appropriate teaching machine has two basic requirements: First, a student must compose each response rather than select it from a set of alternatives. Second, in acquiring complex behavior, a student must pass through a carefully designed sequence of steps; each step must be so small that it always can be taken, yet in taking it the student must move somewhat closer to fully competent behavior, and the machine must operate so as to make sure that steps are taken in a carefully prescribed order.[57]

Operation of a Teaching Machine   Let's see how Skinner described a teaching device.

> The device consists of a box about the size of a small record player. On the top surface is a glazed window through which a question or problem printed on a paper tape may be seen. The child answers the question by moving one or more sliders upon which the digits 0 through 9 are printed. The answer appears in square holes punched in the paper upon which the question is printed. When the answer has been set, the child turns a knob. The operation is as simple as adjusting a television set. If the answer is right, the knob turns freely and can be made to ring a bell or provide some other conditioned reinforcement. If the answer is wrong, the knob will not turn. A counter may be added to tally wrong answers. The knob must then be reversed slightly and a second attempt at a right answer made. (Unlike the flash card, the device reports a wrong answer without giving the right answer.) When the answer is right, a further turn of the knob engages a clutch which moves the next problem into place in the window. This movement cannot be completed, however, until the sliders have been returned to zero.[58]

What Are the Advantages of the Use of Mechanical Teaching Devices?

Skinner claimed a long list of advantages available through use of mechanical teaching devices [computers and teaching machines] in present-day classrooms.[59]

1. Reinforcement for the right answer is immediate.
2. Provided traces of earlier aversive control can be erased, mere manipulation of the device probably will be reinforcing enough to keep an average student at work for a suitable period each day.
3. All at one time, a teacher may supervise an entire class at work on such devices; yet each student may complete as many problems as possible in the class period and progress at his own rate.
4. Any person who is forced to leave school for a period may return at any time and continue from where he/she left off.
5. Each person may advance at his own rate, and when one gets too far ahead of the class, one may be assigned to other tasks.
6. Through carefully designing materials, teachers may arrange problems in a serial order in the direction of an immensely complex repertoire.

7. Since the machines record the number of mistakes, tapes can be modified to enhance their effectiveness.
8. Knowing just what each student has done, a teacher can apply necessary supplementary reinforcement at the greatest vantage point.

In building a case for teaching machines or computers, Skinner stated, "The effect upon each student is surprisingly like that of a private tutor."[60] He then elaborated the nature of this similarity with the following points:

1. There is a constant interchange between programs and students; thus, the machine induces sustained activity.
2. The machine insists that a given point be thoroughly understood before the student moves on.
3. It presents that material for which the student is ready.
4. Partly through its constructed program and partly through its techniques of prompting or hinting, the machine helps the student to come up with the right answer.
5. Like a private tutor, it reinforces the student for every correct response.

Is Thinking a Lawful Operant-Behavioral Process?

Skinner recognized that "it is quite possible that the behavior of a man thinking is the most subtle and complex phenomenon ever submitted to scientific analysis."[61] But he also emphasized that thinking or originality is not absence of lawfulness, and it should never be considered a spontaneous process. As long as thinking is identified with spontaneity or lawlessness, it is a hopeless task to attempt systematically to influence a child's thinking in any way. Thinking, like the rest of the behavior of an organism, is a lawful process. Thus, verbal behavior, in terms of which human thinking eventually must be defined, should be treated in its own right as a substantial goal of education. In inculcating this behavior, learning devices can teach verbal thinking—that is, establish the large and important repertoire of verbal relationships encountered in science and logic.

Skinner believed it of critical importance for us to realize that, in radical behaviorism, thought is not some mysterious process that is the cause of behavior but the behavior itself. A human being thinking is a human being behaving, and human thought is operant, not reflexive, behavior. "Shakespeare's thought was his behavior *with respect to his extremely complex environment.*"[62] "In the broadest possible sense, the thought of Julius Caesar was simply the sum total of his responses to the complex world in which he lived."[63]

Skinner has observed that study of what traditionally has been called the human mind is more appropriately a study of concepts and methods that have emerged from an analysis of behavior. Thinking behavior is verbal or nonverbal, overt or covert. It is primarily the verbal behavior of humanity that has survived in recorded form, but from this and other records we can know something about human nonverbal behavior. When we say that Caesar thought Brutus could be trusted, we do not necessarily mean that he ever said as much. Rather, he behaved verbally and otherwise as if Brutus could be trusted. The rest of Caesar's behavior, his nonverbal plans and achievements, were also part of his thoughts.

Although, in earlier behavioristic analyses, thinking was identified with subaudible talking, Skinner felt that nothing is gained by doing so. There are difficulties in assuming that covert behavior is always executed by the muscular apparatus responsible for the overt form. Furthermore, the data that give rise to the notion of covert speech can be treated, as such, with a high degree of rigor. Rather than identifying thinking with talking, a better case can be made for identifying it with a special kind of behaving, that which automatically affects behavior and is reinforcing because it does.

"It is important that the student should learn without being taught, solve problems by himself, explore the unknown, make decisions, and behave in original ways, and these activities should, if possible, be taught."[64] But we should not attempt to teach thinking while teaching subject matter. "If thinking can be analyzed and taught separately, the already-known can be transmitted with maximal efficiency."[65] "It is as important to define the terminal behavior in teaching thinking as in teaching knowledge."[66]

Thinking is more productive when verbal responses lead to specific consequences and are reinforced because they do so. Just as an artist paints what reinforces him visually, a speaker or writer says that which is reinforced by hearing it or writes that which is reinforced by reading it. However, in any case the solution to a problem is simply a response that alters the situation so that another strong response can be emitted. "Reinforcing contingencies shape the behavior of the individual, and novel contingencies generate novel forms of behavior."[67]

The key to effective teaching of thinking, as well as of any other behavior, is immediate feedback. To teach thinking, we should "analyze the behavior called 'thinking' and produce it according to specifications. A program specifically concerned with such behavior could be composed of material already available in logic, mathematics, scientific method, and psychology."[68]

How Does Reinforcement Theory Relate to the Accountability Movement?

The current accountability movement in education consists of teachers or schools listing their specific goals and objectives in advance and then being held accountable for their achievements. One of the chief purposes claimed for the accountability movement is to reorganize curriculums so that their results can be measured in a rather precise way and the effectiveness of teachers judged by the amount of training exhibited by their students. Although usually not stated by proponents of accountability, the psychological assumptions of this movement are those of mechanistic psychology, particularly of reinforcement.[69]

To install a program of accountability in a school, one states precise, detailed objectives for every course, putting them in terms of some outcome that can be quantified. In practice, this leads to what are called *behavioral objectives*—objectives stated as overt behaviors to be demonstrated by pupils. An overt behavior might be something spoken or written on paper; a mark made on a test paper; the bodily skill required for an athletic task; or the completion of a shop or home economics project. Any behavior that cannot be measured with precision is excluded from the goals of the program. Such "behaviors" as meditating, reflecting, imagining, and reasoning are clearly not suited to an accountability program, because they do not produce measurable overt behaviors or, if they do, it may be long after the students have completed the school year during which the teacher was accountable for visible training.

Once behavioral objectives are formulated, teachers deploy a content selected to be directly pertinent to the behaviors as stated. Both objectives and content are often accumulated around three categories of objectives: cognitive (intellectual), affective (emotional), and psychomotor (bodily skills). To measure behavioral outcomes, teachers either develop their own short-answer tests or use standardized achievement tests. Testing is frequent, because the behavioral objectives to be achieved by students are typically both small and narrow in scope, so that they can be achieved in a week or two of concentrated drill.

Training under an accountability program has either of two names—performance-based education (PBE) or competency-based education (CBE). Common curriculum and instruction procedures may be identified under both labels, or there may be a significant difference in application of the two concepts. *Performance* implies the exclusive use of objectives that can be stated strictly in terms of overt performance. *Competency* can be defined broadly enough to include objectives that refer to thought processes, such as understandings, provided they can be measured objectively.

According to the mandates of PBE or CBE, teachers have the primary responsibility for inducing in students the behaviors specified in the behavioral objectives. Objectives, presumably, will reflect strongly what adults want trained into students. Usually, the only provision for individual differences among students is that some are allowed more time than others to acquire a given behavior. Presumably, in a given subject, all teachers will attempt to teach the same things about a subject, since they are all controlled by the same objectives.

NOTES

1. See B. F. Skinner, "Controversy?" in Sohan Modgil and Celia Modgil, eds., New York: Falmer Press, 1987, p. 11.
2. B. F. Skinner, *Recent Issues in the Analysis of Behavior* (Columbus, OH: Merrill Publishing Company), 1989, p. 27.
3. B. F. Skinner, *About Behaviorism* (New York: Knopf, 1974), p. 225.
4. B. F. Skinner, *The Behavior of Organisms* (New York: Appleton-Century-Crofts, 1938), p. 6.
5. B. F. Skinner, *Cumulative Record*, 3d ed. (New York: Appleton-Century-Crofts, 1972), p. 35. (This and other excerpts from *Cumulative Record* are reprinted by permission of Appleton-Century-Crofts.)
6. Skinner, *Cumulative Record*, p. 34.

7. B. F. Skinner, *Recent Issues in the Analysis of Behavior*, p. 36.
8. Modgil and Modgil, eds., *B. F. Skinner, Consensus and Controversy*, p. 342.
9. B. F. Skinner, *Science and Human Behavior* (New York: Macmillan, 1953), p. 64. (This and other excerpts from *Science and Human Behavior* are reprinted by permission of The Macmillan Company.)
10. Ibid., pp. 63–64.
11. See C. B. Ferster and B. F. Skinner, *Schedules of Reinforcement* (New York: Appleton-Century-Crofts, 1957).
12. See B. F. Skinner, *The Technology of Teaching* (New York: Appleton-Century-Crofts, 1968), p. 14.
13. Skinner, *Recent Issues in the Analysis of Behavior*, p. 130.
14. Ibid., p. 15.
15. B. F. Skinner, *Contingencies of Reinforcement* (New York: Appleton-Century-Crofts, 1969), p. 194.
16. Skinner, *Science and Human Behavior*, p. 446.
17. Ibid., p. 13.
18. Skinner, *Contingencies of Reinforcement*, p. 143.
19. Skinner, *About Behaviorism*, p. 231.
20. Skinner, *Science and Human Behavior*, p. 32.
21. Ibid., p. 23.
22. B. F. Skinner, *Cumulative Record* (New York: Appleton-Century-Crofts, 1961), p. 201.
23. Skinner, *Science and Human Behavior*, p. 91.
24. Skinner, *Contingencies of Reinforcement*, p. 294.
25. Skinner, *Science and Human Behavior*, p. 46.
26. Ibid., p. 448.
27. Skinner, *Contingencies of Reinforcement*, p. 297.
28. Skinner, *About Behaviorism*, p. 114.
29. Skinner, *Cumulative Record*, 1972, p. 123.
30. Skinner, *Science and Human Behavior*, p. 446.
31. Richard I. Evans, *B. F. Skinner: The Man and His Ideas* (New York: Dutton, 1968), p. 65.
32. Skinner, *About Behaviorism*, p. 248.
33. Skinner, *Science and Human Behavior*, p. 258.
34. Skinner, *Contingencies of Reinforcement*, p. 228.
35. Skinner, *About Behaviorism*, p. 241.
36. Ibid., p. 224.
37. Ibid., p. 168.
38. Skinner, *Science and Human Behavior*, p. 90.
39. Skinner, *Contingencies of Reinforcement*, pp. 236–240.
40. Skinner, *Science and Human Behavior*, p. 36.
41. Ibid., p. 64.
42. Skinner, *Contingencies of Reinforcement*, p. 23.
43. Skinner, *Science and Human Behavior*, p. 112.
44. Skinner, *Science and Human Behavior*, p. 173.
45. Ibid., p. 123.
46. Skinner, *Contingencies of Reinforcement*, pp. 160–170.
47. Skinner, *Science and Human Behavior*, p. 92.
48. Michael Wessells, "The Limits of Skinner's Philosophy of Science and Psychology," in Modgil and Modgil, eds., *B. F. Skinner, Consensus and Controversy*, pp. 113–122.

49. Skinner, *Contingencies of Reinforcement*, p. 15.
50. Skinner, *Recent Issues In the Analysis of Behavior*, p. 99.
51. Ibid, p. 103.
52. Skinner, *Recent Issues In the Analysis of Behavior*, p. 94.
53. Skinner, *Cumulative Record*, p. 300.
54. Skinner, *The Technology of Teaching*, p. 21.
55. Reprinted from H. T. Fitzgerald, "Teaching Machines: A Demurrer," *The School Review* 70 (Autumn 1962): 248–249. By permission of the University of Chicago Press. ©1962 by The University of Chicago.
56. Skinner, *The Technology of Teaching*, p. 22.
57. Ibid., pp. 33–34.
58. B. F. Skinner, *Cumulative Record*, p. 154.
59. Skinner, *The Technology of Teaching*, p. 24.
60. B. F. Skinner, "Teaching Machines," *Science* 128 (October 24, 1958):971.
61. Skinner, *The Technology of Teaching*, p. 140.
62. B. F. Skinner, *Verbal Behavior* (New York: Appleton-Century-Crofts, 1957), p. 450.
63. Ibid., pp. 451–452.
64. Skinner, *The Technology of Teaching*, p. 116.
65. Ibid., p. 116.
66. Ibid., p. 117.
67. Skinner, *Verbal Behavior*, p. 255.
68. Skinner, *The Technology of Teaching*, p. 52.
69. See Robert M. Gagné, Leslie J. Briggs, and Walter W. Wagner, *Principles of Instructional Design*, 3d. ed. (New York: Holt, Rinehart and Winston, 1988.)

BIBLIOGRAPHY, CHAPTER 5

Evans, Richard I. *B. F. Skinner: The Man and His Ideas*. New York: Dutton, 1968. A transcription of a taped interview with Professor Skinner, wherein his position is set forth sharply and highly understandably. Recommended order of reading is Chapters 3, 2, 1, 4, and 5.

Ferster, C. B., and B. F. Skinner. *Schedules of Reinforcement*. New York: Appleton-Century-Crofts, 1957. A report of scientific study of various reinforcement schedules.

Fitzgerald, T. T. "Teaching Machines: A Demurrer." *The School Review* 70 (Autumn 1962):247–256. A well-written, sobering critique of machine teaching written by a director of education and training for an automotive plant. He considers mechanical reinforcement theory "an intrinsically undemocratic—worse, an antiintellectual— theory of learning" and concludes with the statement, "Teaching machines only teach (condition) machines."

Gage, N. L. *The Scientific Basis of the Art of Teaching*. New York: Teachers College Press, 1978. Page 43 speaks of the "Roman-Candle" history of teaching machines.

Gagné, Robert M., Leslie J. Briggs, and Walter W. Wagner. *Principles of Instructional Design*. New York: Holt Rinehart and Winston, 1988. Develops instructional procedures centered upon reinforcement theories of learning and educational accountability as developed by Skinner and Gagné.

Galanter, Eugene. *Automatic Teaching: The State of the Art*. New York: Wiley, 1959. A collection of papers, including one by B. F. Skinner, that treats the experimentation, analysis, and programming related to machine teaching. Chapter 15, "Teaching Machines and Psychological Theory," by Howard H. Kindler, is an excellent critique on the teaching-machine movement.

Hilgard, Ernest R., and Gordon H. Bower. *Theories of Learning*, 4th ed. Englewood Cliffs, NJ: Prentice Hall, 1975. Chapter 7, "Skinner's Operant Conditioning," is a descriptive interpretation of Skinner's operant conditioning theory of learning.

Holland, James G., and B. F. Skinner. *The Analysis of Behavior.* New York: McGraw-Hill, 1961. A programmed textbook for an introductory course in psychology to be used as a substitute for a teaching machine. A student is to learn the basic terms and principles of behavioristic conditioning; he writes the correct answer to a question, then is reinforced by finding it on the next page.

Lumsdaine, A. A. "Educational Technology, Programmed Learning, and Instructional Science," in Ernest R. Hilgard, ed., *Theories of Learning and Instruction*, National Society for the Study of Education. Chicago: University of Chicago Press, 1964. A comprehensive treatment of applications of programming to instructional procedures.

Machan, Tibor R. *The Pseudo-Science of B. F. Skinner.* New Rochelle, N.Y.: Arlington House, 1974. A caustic review and critique of Skinner's major works. Emphasizes importance of human freedom and dignity.

Modgil, Sohan and Modgil, Celia, eds. *B. F. Skinner, Consensus and Controversy.* New York: Falmer Press, 1987. Critical evaluations of B. F. Skinner's psychology by 28 psychologists. Authors are both positive and negative in their critiques, which are written as essays in honor of Professor Skinner.

Pryor, Karen. "Behavior Modification: The Porpoise Caper." *Psychology Today* 3, no. 7 (December 1969):46–49, 64. Porpoises, in having their behaviors modified, seem to get the idea in regard to the "payoff" and behave beyond the expectations of their trainers, that is, to show creative behavior. "Some of Malia's spontaneous stunts were so unusual that the trainers couldn't imagine achieving them with the shaping system."

Skinner, B. F. *The Behavior of Organisms.* New York: Appleton-Century-Crofts, 1938. Skinner's early systematic statement of operant behavior and conditioning.

Skinner, B. F. *Walden Two.* New York: Macmillan, 1948. A novel proposing and describing a community within which maximum use is made of conditioning to control human welfare. It deals with the educational and social implications of behaviorism.

Skinner, B. F. *Science and Human Behavior.* New York: Macmillan, 1953. An application of "realistic" scientific method to a study of human behavior centered around operant conditioning. Scientific analysis is extended to the behavior of people in groups and the operation of controlling agencies such as government and religion. Its final section analyzes education as a process of control of human behavior.

Skinner, B. F. *Verbal Behavior.* New York: Appleton-Century-Crofts, 1957. An explanation of how verbal behavior, including thinking, takes its place in the larger field of human behavior; it, too, is learned through operant conditioning. Ways of manipulating verbal behavior of individuals are tested.

Skinner, B. F. "Teaching Machines." *Science* 128 (October 24, 1958): 969–977. Professor Skinner's strongest presentation of the use for teaching machines.

Skinner B. F. "A Case History in Scientific Method," in Sigmund Koch, *Psychology: A Study of Science, 2, General Systematic Formulations, Learning, and Special*

Processes. New York: McGraw-Hill, 1959. Skinner's own personal history illustrating his philosophy of science and psychology of behavior. He relates how he was operant conditioned to perform in certain ways as he studied the conditioning of animals. The chapter is interesting reading. See pages 359–379.

Skinner, B. F. *The Technology of Teaching.* New York: Appleton-Century-Crofts, 1968. An expansion of the concept that teaching consists of arranging contingencies of reinforcement. Provides psychological rationale for making teaching a process of changing the behaviors of organisms.

Skinner, B. F. *Contingencies of Reinforcement.* New York: Appleton-Century-Crofts, 1969. Professor Skinner's theoretical analysis of his psychological system and its comparison with other systems.

Skinner, B. F. "The Machine That Is Man." *Psychology Today* 2 (April 1969):22–25, 60–64. Disposes of "inner man" by replacing him with genetic and environmental variables. "In pigeon and Indian alike, adventitious reinforcements generate ritualistic behavior."

Skinner, B. F. *Beyond Freedom and Dignity.* New York: Knopf, 1971. A presentation of Skinner's psychology for general consumption. Denies existence of either autonomous or cognitive man. An attack on the concepts of human freedom and dignity.

Skinner, B. F. *Cumulative Record*, 3d ed. New York: Appleton-Century-Crofts, 1972. A series of Skinner's papers that reflect the implications of his position. Chapters on "The Science of Learning and the Art of Teaching" and "Teaching Machines" are particularly pertinent to our discussion in this chapter.

Skinner, B. F. *About Behaviorism.* New York: Knopf, 1974. Skinner's statement of the philosophy of the science of human behavior. His controversion of psychological positions that conflict with behaviorism. Lists and criticizes 20 statements commonly made about behaviorism. Behavioristically describes knowing and thinking processes.

Skinner, B. F. "Whatever Happened to Psychology As The Science of Behavior?" *American Psychologist* 42, no. 8 (1987) 1–7. Summarizes early behaviorism, radical behaviorism, and their obstacles—humanistic psychology, psychotherapy, and cognitive psychology.

Skinner, B. F., *Recent Issues in the Analysis of Behavior*, Columbus, OH: Merrill Publishing Company, 1989. A collection of Skinner's most recent papers, written primarily for other psychologists; centered on theoretical and professional issues.

Chapter
6

How Does Bruner's Cognitive Psychology Treat Learning and Teaching?

*J*erome S. Bruner (1915-) may be identified as a cognitive learning and developmental psychologist. His approach to psychology is eclectic, but in a highly sophisticated sense. He has spearheaded voluminous research into human perception, motivation, learning, thinking, and narrative theory and practice. In his study of human beings he thinks of them as information processors, thinkers, and creators.

Professor Bruner was born in New York City. He received his bachelor's degree from Duke in 1937 and his Ph.D. from Harvard in 1941. In 1952 he became a professor of psychology at Harvard. He helped establish the research center for cognitive studies at Harvard in 1960 and served as its director for a number of years. He also has been on the psychology staffs of Princeton and Cambridge and in 1973 was named Watts Professor of Experimental Psychology at Oxford University. Recently, he has been a member of the Graduate Faculty of the New School for Social Research. Bruner's research and thought has been greatly influenced by the works of the eminent Swiss "genetic epistemologist," Jean Piaget. However, he does not accept Piaget's idea of innate stages of human psychological development.

Bruner's eclecticism extends beyond contributions of various systematic psychologies to integrate knowledge from biology, anthropology, linguistics, philosophy, and sociology. Kernels of his thinking may be traced back to Charles Sanders Peirce, William James, John Dewey, the Gestalt psychologists, the organismic biologists, Kurt Lewin, Edward C. Tolman, Gordon Allport, various social anthropologists, and other progenitors of contemporary cognitive psychology. Bruner, throughout his writing, acknowledges contributions of many thinkers, going back for decades, that have helped shape his thinking.

Accordingly, his major contribution lies in two directions. First, he has collected a wealth of empirical research and contributed a great deal of his own that provide an impressive underpinning for his thoughts and conclusions. Second, he has stated his ideas in a way that has been fresh enough to capture the attention of educators everywhere, and he has set in motion innovations for which there may have been plausible theoretical bases for some time but which had never really gotten off the ground.

Although Professor Bruner seems not to have developed a systematic learning theory as such, a generalized theory about, and outlook concerning, learning is implicit in his various works. His principal concern has been with the means whereby people actively select, retain, and transform information, and this is the essence of learning. Accordingly, he has centered his interests on the problem of what people do with information that they receive and how they go beyond discrete information to achieve generalized insights or understandings that give them competence. He considers the *explanation* of many psychological phenomena as currently a hopeless task. Hence, he sees his role as primarily that of a *describer* of psychological concepts and operations.

HOW DOES BRUNER VIEW HUMAN MOTIVATION?

Bruner's research has led him to think that "subjects do not mechanically associate specific responses with specific stimuli but, rather, tend to infer principles or rules underlying the patterns which allow them to transfer their learning to different problems."[1] For him, an individual is best viewed as neither a mystical active self nor a passive recipient of information. Accordingly, he has steered a middle emergent course between mystical vitalism and behavioristic environmental determinism.

Bruner rejects any kind of transcendental vitalistic "purposivism" by saying that it has nothing to offer but "cheap solutions."[2] However, there is little question that his psychology is immanently purposive in the sense that he sees learning as being goal-directed. Accordingly, he makes such statements as "Anticipatory categorizing, then, provides 'lead time' for adjusting one's response to objects with which one must cope,"[3] and "It is this future-oriented aspect of categorizing behavior in all organisms that impresses us most."[4] But he is reluctant to hypothesize about what lies behind human purposing. After discussing various historical researches and assertions that have been made on the subject, he concludes that, on the basis of earlier theories, not much advantage is served by trying to go beyond such statements as "The person strives to reduce the complexity of his environment," or "There is a drive to group things in terms of instrumental relevance...."[5]

Bruner shows some sympathy for postulating a primary need, other than the "animal drives," which might be called "curiosity" and which keeps an organism active even in the absence of organic tensional states. He points out that our cognitive activity is not dominated at all times by concerns for such things as food and sex. After all, we should explain in some way why a person may want to learn to play chess. He thinks that over and beyond the mastery of a body of knowledge, learning should *"create a better or happier or more courageous or more sensitive or more honest man."*[6] Thus, curricula should be constructed in terms of the instrumental assistance that knowledge imparts to the exercise of values. But one's possession of certain bodies of knowledge does not, in itself, predispose one to either evil or magnanimity. There are both knowledgeable and innocent sinners and both knowledgeable and innocent saints. Knowledge, then, should serve the learning of values by giving students a sense of the alternative ways in which one can succeed or fail in the expression of values.

Bruner thinks that there is a kind of "golden mean" in student motivation, somewhere between apathy and wild excitement, for which a teacher should strive. In answer to his own query as to what the optimum level of aroused attention is, he says, "Frenzied activity fostered by the competitive project may leave no pause for reflection, for evaluation, for generalization, while excessive orderliness, with each student waiting passively for his turn, produces boredom and ultimate apathy."[7]

Two central unifying themes recur in Bruner's writing. The first is that the acquisition of knowledge, whatever its form, is an active process. The second is that a person actively constructs his knowledge by relating incoming information to a previously acquired psychological frame of reference. This frame of reference is a "system of representation" or "internal model" that gives meaning and organization to the regularities in experience and permits an individual to go beyond the information given him. Therefore, each person should be regarded as an active participant in the knowledge getting process, who selects and transforms information, constructs hypotheses, and alters those hypotheses in light of inconsistent or discrepant evidence. (Note that Bruner uses the concept *active* to convey very much the same notion that cognitive-field interactionists use the concept *interactive* to convey.)

Bruner has been convinced that any discipline can be presented to any fairly normal child, regardless of age, in an intellectually respectable fashion. In the 1970's many nationally organized and funded curriculum projects were based on this conviction. For instance, both MACOS (Man: a Course of Study), developed by Bruner, and a sociology inquiry series developed by the American Sociology Association, consisting of units from anthropology and sociology, were used by many schools in the United States. Here, anthropologists' description of the Netsilik Eskimos were used to demonstrate not only how the Netsilik culture was organized and structured but also how anthropologists inquired into a culture.

For Bruner, people are *transactional selves*; accordingly, "It can never be the case that there is a 'self' independent of one's cultural-historical existence."[8] A self is a construction that is the result of action and symbolization. "The 'reality' of most of us is constituted roughly into two spheres: that of nature and that of human affairs."[9] The former is more likely to be structured in a paradigmatic mode of logic and science, the latter in the mode of story and narrative. The former is centered around compelling, natural ideas of causation. The latter is centered upon the drama of human intentions and their vicissitudes. Bruner notes that one cannot teach even mathematics of physics without transmitting a stance toward nature and the use of the mind. "The language of education, if it is to be an invitation to reflection and culture creating, cannot be the so-called uncontaminated language of fact and 'objectivity.' "[10] Language not only transmits; it also creates or constitutes knowledge or reality.

Bruner's charge against psychologists, in general, is that they have tended to disregard the puzzling problem of the relationship of knowledge as detached information and knowledge as a guide to purposeful action or performance. He sees a selective intention or self-imposed direction characterizing people's knowledge and its use. But he notes that the "apparent mentalism" implied by such an observation tends to repel many psychologists; it seems to leave organisms "wrapt in thought." Nevertheless, he thinks that psychologists, and teachers as well, should zero in on what it is that keeps learners involved in the activity of learning so as to achieve competence beyond bare necessity and immediate payoff.

Bruner is mildly critical of the mainstream of educational psychology in that its representatives have often given inadequate attention to which versions of subject matter are appropriate for various childhood periods. They have assumed that the particular version of what is taught does not matter very much; one thing is much like another, and all learning may be reduced to a pattern of molecular stimulus-response connections. The only real problem for many educational psychologists, as they have viewed matters, has been a quantitative one of providing children and youth with more experiences. Hence, their eyes have often been closed in regard to the pedagogical problem of how to represent knowledge, how to sequence it, and how to embody it in forms that are appropriate to the various ages of learners.

HOW IS LEARNING A COGNITIVE PROCESS?

Bruner sees learning as involving three "almost simultaneous processes":

1. Acquisition of new information
2. Transformation of knowledge
3. Check of the pertinence and adequacy of knowledge

New information may either be a refinement of previous knowledge or be of such nature that it runs counter to a person's previous information. For example, a person may learn the details of the circulatory system after he/she already knows vaguely that blood circulates; or, after thinking of energy as being wasted, he may learn of the energy conservation theorem in physics. In *transformation* of knowledge, one manipulates knowledge to make it fit new tasks. Transformation, then, entails the way we deal with information to go beyond it by means of either extrapolation or interpolation or by converting it into another form. We *check* the pertinence and adequacy of knowledge or information by evaluating whether the way we manipulate it is adequate to the task at hand; such an evaluation often involves judgments of knowledge's plausibility.

Bruner labels his view of learning or cognitive growth as "instrumental conceptualism." This view is centered on two tenets concerning the nature of the knowing process:

1. One's knowledge of the world is based on one's constructed models of reality.
2. Such models are first adopted from one's culture, then adapted to one's individual use.

A person's perception of an event, then, is essentially a constructive process within which the person infers a hypothesis by relating his sense data to his model of the world and then checks his hypothesis against additional properties of the event. Thus, a perceiver is viewed not as a passive, reactive organism but, rather, as a person who actively selects information, forms perceptual hypotheses, and on occasion distorts the environmental input in the interest of reducing surprise and attaining valued goals. The act of perception, then, is one of categorization that is based upon a person making an *inferential leap* from observed cues to identification of a class of objects.

A person's maturing intellectual or cognitive growth is characterized by the increasing independence of his responses from the immediate nature of the stimuli that are involved. Such growth depends upon the person's internalizing events into a "storage system" that corresponds to aspects of the environment. It involves the person's increasing capacity to say to himself and others, by means of words and symbols, what he/she either has done or will do. Through growth, a person gains his freedom from stimulus control through mediating processes . . . that transform the stimulus prior to response.

For Bruner,

> mental growth is not a gradual accretion, either of associations or of stimulus-response connections or of means-end readiness or of anything else. It appears to be much more like a staircase with rather sharp risers, more a matter of spurts and rests. The spurts ahead in growth seem to be touched off when certain capacities begin to develop.[11]

Here we see Professor Bruner's writing about there being something like "steps" in human development and learning. But he differs sharply with Piaget in that he emphasizes that

> these steps or spurts or whatever you may choose to call them are *not* very clearly linked to age: some environments can slow the sequence down or bring it to a halt, others move it along faster. In the main, one can characterize these constrained sequences as a series of prerequisites. It is not until the child can hold in mind two features of a display at once, for example, that he can deal with their relationship, as in a ratio.[12]

Thus, Bruner's phases of human development are not saltatory stages proceeding by leaps, as developed earlier by Rousseau and later described by Piaget.

Rather, human development and learning are a matter of an individual getting his perceptual field organized around his own person as a center, then imposing other, less egocentric axes upon that field.

Almost any mature person seems to have proceeded through the elaboration of three systems of skills that correspond to the three major tool systems to which he/she must link himself for a full expression of his capacities. These three systems of skills are Bruner's three *modes of representation*. Bruner identifies these modes of representation of reality as *enactive*, *iconic*, and *symbolic* modes. They usually appear in the life of a child in that order, and each depends upon the previous one for its development. Yet all three of them extend more or less intact throughout an individual's life, and they are partially translatable into one another. *Representations* consist of systems of rules or generalizations by means of which an individual, in a manageable way, conserves the recurrent features of the environment. In cognitive-field terminology, representations are generalized insights—understandings. A person's representations collectively constitute that person's model of reality.

The *enactive* mode of representation is highly manipulative in character. It consists of knowing some aspect of reality without the use of imagery or words. Hence, in it one represents past events through making appropriate motor responses. This mode is marked by an individual's single-track attention. "Knowing" consists primarily in knowing how to do something: a set of actions that are appropriate for achieving a certain result. For example, a child enactively knows how to ride a bike or tie a knot.

Iconic representation is based upon internal imagery. Knowledge is represented by a set of summary images or graphics that *stand for* a concept but do not fully *define* it. For example, a diagrammatic triangle stands for the concept of triangularity. Iconic representation depends upon visual or other sensory organization along with the use of summarizing images that are representative of greater "chunks" of the environment. Iconic representation, then, is mainly governed by principles of perceptual organization and by techniques for making economical transformations in perceptual organization. These techniques for transformation include filling in, completing, and extrapolating knowledge from available sensory experience. The high point in a child's iconic representation is usually between the ages five and seven, when a child depends most upon personal sensory images.

As a person approaches adolescence, language becomes increasingly important as a medium of thought. Then, the individual achieves a transition from the use of iconic representations, based upon sensory imagery, to the use of symbolic representation, based upon an abstract, arbitrary, and more flexible system of thought. Language is the archetype of symbolic representation. It enables individuals to deal with what might or what might not, as well as with what does, exist in experience. Hence, it is the principal tool of reflective thinking. The symbolic mode of representation is evidenced by a person's ability to consider propositions rather than objects, to give concepts a hierarchical structure, and to consider alternative possibilities in a "combinatorial fashion."[13]

Bruner uses the study of a balance beam to illustrate the distinction between the three modes of representation:

> A quite young child can plainly act on the basis of the "principles" of a balance beam, and indicates that he can do so by being able to handle himself on a see-saw. He knows that to get his side to go down farther he has to move out farther from the center. A somewhat older child can represent the balance beam to himself either by a model on which rings can be hung and balanced or by a drawing. The "image" of the balance beam can be varyingly refined, with fewer and fewer irrelevant details present, as in the typical diagrams in an introductory textbook in physics. Finally, a balance beam can be [symbolically] described in ordinary English, without diagrammatic aids, or it can be even better described mathematically by reference to Newton's Law of Moments in inertial physics.[14]

A person grows up through the process of internalizing the ways of acting, imaging, and symbolizing that exist in his culture. The way in which the person develops his powers through the use of the three modes of representation depends upon three conditions:

1. The supply of amplifiers, such as skills, images, and conceptions that his culture has in stock
2. The nature of the life that is led by the individual
3. The extent to which the person is incited to explore the sources of concordance or discordance among the three modes of knowing, namely, action, image, and symbol.[15]

A person's intellect is not strictly his own; rather, to some degree, it is communal in the sense that its unlocking and empowering process depends greatly upon the success of the person's culture in developing means of enhancing that process. Thus, the range of people's intellects should not be estimated separately from the means a culture provides for empowering their minds. For Professor Bruner, the term *mind* means the process within which a person actively constructs knowledge by relating incoming information to a previously acquired psychological frame of reference or model of reality. The use of amplifiers of mind—skills, images, and conceptions—requires a commonly shared human capacity, but each society fashions and perfects this capacity to its own needs. But, Bruner warns, there is "a respect in which a lack of means for understanding one matter places out of reach other matters that are crucial to man's condition whatever his culture."[16]

HOW DO MODELS OF THE WORLD CONTRIBUTE TO LEARNING?

Bruner makes much of the structured *models* of the world with which a culture equips its members. Such models enable persons to predict, interpolate, and extrapolate further knowledge. For Bruner, to interpolate is to alter a position through application of new knowledge; to extrapolate is to go beyond the information that is given. He states that "Our knowledge of the world is not merely a mirroring or reflection of order and structure 'out there' but consists rather of a construct or model that can, so to speak, be spun a bit ahead of things to predict how the world *will* be or *might* be."[17] Instead of being "driven" in some mechanistic fashion,

> The child first learns the rudiments of achieving his intentions and reaching his goals. En route he acquires and stores information relevant to his purposes. In time there is a puzzling process by which such purposefully organized knowledge is converted into a more generalized form so that it can be used for many ends. It then becomes "knowledge" in the most general sense—transcending functional fixedness and egocentric limitations.[18]

Models, in essence, *are expectancies*. Through his construction of models, a person does not simply deal with the information before him; he goes far beyond the information given him. "Almost by definition, the exercise of intellect, involving as it must the use of shortcuts and of leaps from partial evidence, always courts the possibility of error."[19] Hence, a person learns about the world in a way that enables him to make predictions of what comes next by matching what is presently experienced to an acquired model and reading much from the model.

The existence of models of the world reflects our general tendency to categorize. We organize experience to represent not only particulars but also classes of events of which the particulars are examples. "The eighteenth-century assumption that knowledge grows by a gradual accretion of associations built up by contact with events that are contiguous in time, space, or quality does not fit the facts of mental life."[20] Language, pictorial and diagrammatic conventions, theories, myths, and modes of reckoning and ordering all are examples of people's models of the world through which they carry on vicarious actions by means of various technological devices.

HOW DOES BRUNER CENTER LEARNING UPON CONCEPTUALIZATION OR CATEGORIZATION?

For Bruner, learning is the act of connecting things that are akin and combining them into structures that give them significance. Remembering is not merely one's re-citation of fixed, lifeless traces, but more a matter of achieving imaginative reconstructions. Bruner opposes the notion of people being passive receptors in perception, concept attainment, and reasoning. He thinks that in each case the acquisition of knowledge depends upon an active process of construction. Learning at its best is thinking, and thinking is the process whereby one makes sense of a hodgepodge of perceived facts through the process called either *conceptualization* or *categorization*. Hence, his goal of research is "to describe and, in a small measure, to explain what happens when an intelligent human being seeks to sort the environment into significant classes of events so that he may end by treating discriminably different things as equivalents."[21]

Bruner notes that human beings have a fantastic capacity to discriminate objects or processes in their environment. He then observes that for one to make any sense of one's environment one must be able to select, from and almost infinite number of discriminable objects and events, those that appear to have something in common and to treat these events as either a single category or a manageable number of categories. Accordingly, individuals categorize all discriminable colors into one concept, *color*, or into a few concepts, such as the "primary colors" or "the colors most fashionable in clothing this season." Similarly, they categorize people by social class, common personality traits, religious affiliation, nationality, size, or age.

How Do Strategies Aid Categorization?

Running through all of Bruner's works is the theme that a thinker rarely can describe the actual process by which he attains his thought-goals. However, he/she may be able to describe it in fragmentary and often misleading ways, or he may not be able to describe any part of it. In the latter instance answers seem to emerge in a flash—what is commonly labeled "Aha learning." Inability of a thinker to verbalize the process by which he/she has learned does not mean that nothing describable has occurred. There may have been a lengthy series of acts of weighing evidence and making decisions that the thinker performed on an unverbalized level.

Regardless of whether thought processes are formal and susceptible to verbalization or largely indescribable, any sequence of decisions purposefully undertaken to attain a goal is labeled by Bruner a *strategy*. Accordingly, a strategy is *any sequence of decision requiring mental events that is goal-oriented*. It is through the use of strategies that conceptualization occurs. The selection of a strategy has its own goal, namely, an evaluation that weighs three dynamic factors against one another. These factors are the informational situation, the cognitive strain, and the risk. We consider each factor in turn.

1. *Informational situation.* Everyone begins a thought task with a certain amount of information in his possession, but the task at hand may require a great deal more. The person decides just how much more information should be gathered in relation to the strain and risk elements involved. Hence, if the total situation warrants, much time may be spent in data gathering. A classical example of meticulous and extended data gathering prior to making a conclusion is to be found in the work of Charles Darwin. Apparently, he was reasonably sure he could stand the strain, but the risk of announcing an indefensible conclusion was so great that much of a lifetime was spent in data gathering. On the other hand, under very different conditions a person may spend little or no time gathering data, because either the strain is too great or possible failure is too inconsequential.

2. *Cognitive strain.* Thinking may be a most arduous activity. It not only may take time, but it may also require numerous frustrating attempts to grasp that which is just beyond a person's reach. Furthermore, a thinker's uncertainty about the reliability of his thought may produce states of high anxiety. Nevertheless, virtually everyone who is living on a higher than vegetablelike mental level will frequently set for himself very difficult intellectual goals—often more difficult than he/she can achieve.

3. *Risk*. When failure portends highly unpleasant consequences, a person tends to put more effort into data processing and is willing to endure more cognitive strain than if the consequences of failure are negligible. Also, individuals vary greatly in the amount of risk they are willing to assume.

The time-consuming work of an individual devising and improving strategies appears to center in his selection of information or instances that will "fit" a category. This involves learning to identify the cues that will distinguish relevant information from the irrelevant. The more accurately and rapidly a person can identify cues, the faster that person can sort instances into categories.

What Are Two Types of Categories?

Bruner's two basic types of categories are those of *identity* and *equivalence*. An identity category if formed by putting into one intellectual class a number of different variations of the same object. The moon goes through a series of phases ranging from a barely visible crescent to a full orb, yet we classify each phase of the moon as "moon." An equivalence category is one in which different kinds of objects are considered quite similar to one another and so are placed in the same class. Equivalence categories take three forms: affective, functional, and formal. However, the forms are not mutually exclusive. Bruner states, "It is obvious that there are close relationships between affective, functional, and formal categories and that they are often convertible one into the other."[22]

1. *Affective equivalence categories*. If certain objects or processes in the environment evoke the same affective (emotional or feeling) response in a person, he/she tends to classify them together. For example, one might have a category that one labels "the most terrifying experiences I have ever had," within which he/she includes having certain nightmares, being lost in a wilderness, facing surgery with only a small chance of survival, and hallucinating the devil.

2. *Functional equivalence categories*. A functional category arises when objects that are seen as having the same function are placed in the same category. "Fruit" is a functional category, even though it contains such diverse objects as breadfruit, tomatoes, apples, and pomegranates.

3. *Formal equivalence categories*. Formal categories arise when a person deliberately specifies the intrinsic properties that an object must have for him to place it in a given category. Formal categorization centers on the use of both verbal and mathematical symbols. It may involve highly abstract concepts, for example, "force" as it is defined in physics.

WHAT IS THE PURPOSE OF EDUCATION?

Professor Bruner reminds us that schooling is a particularly important instrument of the culture by means of which intellectual skills are amplified. Hence, the major emphasis in education should be placed upon student skills in handling things, seeing and imagining objects, and performing symbolic operations, particularly as they relate to the technologies that make them so powerful in their human, that is, cultural expression.

Most learning in most settings is a sharing of the culture. "Social realities are not bricks that we trip over or bruise ourselves on when we kick at them, but the meanings that we achieve by the sharing of human cognitions."[23] Meanings, then, are that which we can agree upon or accept as a working premise.

A culture, as it is interpreted by its members, is constantly being re-created. "Education is (or should be) one of the principal forums for performing this function—though it is often timid in doing so."[24] Joint culture re-creation is an appropriate objective of schooling and a step in one's becoming a member of an adult society within which one lives out one's life. It is this forum aspect, the capacity of a culture to refine and modify itself, that gives its participants an active role rather than the role of passive spectators. It follows, from this view of culture as a forum, that induction into a culture through education, if it is to prepare the young for life as lived, should also partake of the spirit of a forum, within which there is negotiation and re-creation of meaning. This contrasts with *transmission* of knowledge and values by those who know more to those who know less or know it less expertly.

Bruner's cross-cultural studies of cognition lead him to say that "intelligence is to a great extent the internalization of 'tools' provided by a given culture. Thus, 'culture-free' means 'intelligence-free.'"[25] Cultural variations yield variations in modes of thought. Hence, the nature of the specific culture of students plays a central role in influencing the course of their cognitive growth.

How, then, is the power and substance of a culture to be changed into an instructional form? First of all, bodies of theory must be translated into structures that permit children and youth to achieve closer and closer approximations to the most powerful representation of a theory, beginning with a highly intuitive and enactive representation and then, as the child grasps that, moving on to a more precise and powerful statement of the theory. Within this process, one of the most crucial ways in which a culture provides aid in intellectual growth is through a dialogue between the more experienced teachers and the less experienced students providing a means for the internalization of dialogue in thought.

Bruner emphasizes that "*How* one *talks* comes eventually to be how one *represents* what one talks about."[26] If one fails to develop a sense of reflective intervention with the knowledge that one encounters, one will be operating from the outside in; knowledge will control one. But, if one develops a sense of reflective intervention, one will select and control knowledge as needed. If one develops a sense of self premised upon one's ability to penetrate knowledge for one's own use and if one can share and negotiate the results of such penetration, one becomes a member of a culture-creating community. "Much of the process of education consists of being able to distance oneself in some way from what one knows by being able to reflect on one's own knowledge."[27]

Bruner notes that the prevailing practices of today's schools often foster weakened self-images in students, and he thinks that the one most pervasive aspect that prevents humankind from reaching its full potential is a lack of confidence not only in its own capacities but also in the ability to develop them further. Hence, schools, first of all, should encourage students to discover the value and amendability of their own guesses, to discover the utility of first-order approximations in their approaching a problem, and to realize the activating effect of their trying out hypotheses even when they, at first sight, may seem to be wrong ones.

The second major aim of education should be the development of students' confidence in the solvability of problems by the use of "mind" in the sense of relating present conditions and future results or consequences. To achieve this confidence, students need to develop *understandings*, backed by a sense of how one both achieves and transforms knowledge; for example, "in teaching history we [should] give the student a working sense of the methods and conjectures by which the historian operates...."[28]

The third aim is to foster student self-propulsion, to lead students to operate on their own in regard to various subject matters. Students should be permitted to deal directly with the materials to be mastered so as to locate the form of the problem. Confrontation with materials and practice in being problem-finders and problem-solvers permits students to become partners in determining when they are right and when they are wrong as well as when, and to what degree, materials are relevant or irrelevant.

A fourth aim should be to develop "economy in the use of mind."[29] Teachers should promote in learners a drive to look for relevance and structure. Such a drive gives students a greater tendency to suspend superficial first impressions and to look beneath the surface for less obvious but more powerful matters, that is, to be reflective.

A fifth goal of education is development of intellectual honesty. Such honesty consists of students' eager willingness to use the apparatus and materials of a discipline to check and correct their solutions, ideas, and notions. Students can and should be brought to an appreciation of the forms of intellectual honesty that may be achieved in the various disciplines. Education should also contribute to students' willingness and ability to participate in community living, and they should teach the underlying values of the American creed. But Bruner deplores overemphasis upon students' merely getting along well with their fellows.

Bruner summarizes his discussion of goals of formal education by stating that he has emphasized "the training of our students in the use of mind... with confidence, energy, honesty, and technique. It is in these processes that we place our confidence, not in any particular outcome."[30] "What is learned is competence, not particular performances."[31] To accomplish this goal, a teacher should be a day-to-day working model with whom students *interact*, not merely one to *imitate*. In his interactions with students a teacher imparts attitudes toward the subject at hand as well as toward learning itself.

A learned discipline may be conceived as a *way of thinking* about certain phenomena, and there is nothing more central to a discipline than its way of thinking. Hence, a school should provide students early opportunities to learn the ways of thinking, that is, to solve problems, to conjecture, and to evaluate ideas much as these processes are carried on at the heart of a discipline. In teaching ways of thinking, both personal and social relevance should be emphasized, but social relevance should not be sacrificed to mere personal excitement. Relevance consists of means-end relationships through which we bring knowledge and conviction together.

WHAT IS BRUNER'S THEORY OF INSTRUCTION?

Professor Bruner states that a theory of instruction should take into account (1) the nature of persons as knowers, (2) the nature of knowledge, and (3) the nature of the knowledge getting process. He thinks that

> Man is not a naked ape but a culture-clothed human being, hopelessly ineffective without the prosthesis provided by culture. The very nature of his characteristics as a species provides a guide to appropriate pedagogy, and the nature of his nervous system and its constraints provides a basis for devising reasonable if not inevitable principles for designing a testable pedagogy.[32]

As to the nature of knowledge, Bruner emphasizes that educators should cease striking an exclusive posture of neutrality and objectivity. Accordingly, he states, "Knowledge, we know now as never before, is power. This does not mean that there are not canons of truth or that the idea of proof is not a precious one. Rather, let knowledge as it appears in our schooling be put into the context of action and commitment."[33] Hence, we should provide students with opportunities to learn skills in problem solving by giving them a chance to develop these skills on problems that, for them, have an inherent passion, for example, racism, crime in the street, pollution, war and aggression, or problems involving marriage and the family.

Education should concentrate more on the unknown and the speculative, using what is known as a basis for extrapolation. It particularly should concentrate on subjects that have a visible growing edge but whose problems have no clearly known solutions, for example, the life sciences and the human sciences. However, adequate study in these areas entails study in the arts, literature, philosophy, science, mathematics, and logic.

In regard to the knowledge getting process, the critical question is as follows: "How do you teach something to a child, arrange a child's environment, if you will, in such a way that he can learn something with some assurance that he will use the material that he has learned appropriately in a variety of situations?"[34] This includes a student's development of an approach to learning that enables him not only to learn the material that is presented in a school setting but also to learn it in such a way that he/she will use the information in the solution of problems.

For Bruner, a theory of instruction should cover five major aspects:

1. The optimal experiences to predispose learners to learn
2. A structuring of knowledge for optimal comprehension

3. Specification of optimal sequences of presentation of materials to be learned
4. The role of success and failure and the nature of reward and punishment
5. Procedures for stimulating thought in a school setting

We complete the chapter by briefly considering each of these in turn.

What Optimal Experiences Predispose Learners to Learn?

Bruner sees a need for some rather specific changes in teaching practices as they relate to the process of converting external masses of knowledge that are embodied in the culture into rules for our thinking about the world and ourselves. His suggested changes highlight the role of students' intention and goal-directedness in learning and the conversion of students' skills into the management of their own intellectual enterprises.[35]

"Learning and problem solving require the *exploration of alternatives*."[36] Instruction that is geared to promote this function should minimize the risk involved in exploration; it should maximize the informativeness of error; and it should seek to weaken the effects of previously established constraints on exploration and curiosity that students' families and cultures may have imposed upon them.[37] Teachers should share the process of education with learners. "The reward of mastering something is the mastery, not the assurance that some day you will make more money or have more prestige."[38] Students should be in on where they are trying to go, what they are trying to get hold of, and how much pertinent progress they are making. As one learns, one also learns how to learn. Once a situation is mastered, a person alters the way in which he/she approaches new situations in search of information. Within a more effective approach to learning, a student not only learns the material at hand, but he/she also learns it in such a way that he can use the gained information in solving problems.

Teachers who are not blind to the interdependent nature of knowledge will, in their teaching procedures, develop something approximating the give and take of a seminar in which discussion is the vehicle of instruction.[39] But teachers cannot have "reciprocity" as it is promoted by seminars and at the same time "demand that everybody learn the same thing or be 'completely' well rounded in the same way all the time."[40]

How May Knowledge Be Structured for Optimum Comprehension?

Bruner suggests that the ultimate aim of teaching any subject or group of related subjects is "general understanding of the structure of a subject matter."[41] "Grasping the structure of a subject is understanding it in a way that permits many other things to be related to it meaningfully."[42] Furthermore, knowledge has a *hierarchical* structure, which may be expressed in each of the three modes of representation through the *coding* or structuring system that one develops.

The task of teachers is to give students a grasp of the structure of knowledge in such a way that they can discern knowledge that is significant from information that is less so. Since "everything cannot be taught about anything,"[43] if teaching is to be accomplished at all, students must, in some way, achieve a generalized set of basic ideas or principles. These constitute a structure of knowledge that is optimal for comprehension.

The value of a knowledge structure depends upon its power for simplifying information, generating new propositions, and increasing the manipulability of a body of knowledge. The inventive task of teachers and curriculum makers, then, is to translate propositions to levels that are appropriate to the mentalities of the persons who are being asked to master them. Hence, knowledgeable experience should be *coded* in such a way that it is usable by students in both present and future learning and living situations.

Bruner defines a *coding system* as "a set of contingently related, nonspecific categories"[44] that makes up one's pattern of enactive, iconic, and symbolic representations. Therefore, one's coding system constitutes the structure of one's knowledge. It is a person's manner of grouping and relating information concerning his world. It is a hypothetical construct that is not directly observed but is inferred from the nature of observable antecedent and consequent events and is subject to constant change and reorganization.

It is one's coding system that enables one to go beyond the information given, that is, to develop inventive behavior or to be creative. Bruner proposes that when one goes beyond the information given, one does so by virtue of one's ability to place available empirical facts into a more generic coding system. The person then deduces additional information from his coding system, based on either learned contingent probabilities or learned principles of relating materials.

For Professor Bruner, much of what has been called *transfer of learning* can be fruitfully considered a case of a person applying learned coding systems to new events. Positive transfer represents a case where an appropriate coding system is applied to a new array of events. Negative transfer characterizes a case either of a person misapplying a coding system to new events or of the absence of a coding system that may be applied.[45]

The problem of improving instruction "concerns the best coding system in terms of which to present various subject matters so as to guarantee maximum ability to generalize."[46] Bruner provides an example of a technique that teachers may use to discover whether children are learning proper codes in school. It is as follows:

> We provide training in addition, then we move on to numbers that the child has not yet added, then we move to abstract symbols like $a + a + a$ and see whether $3a$ emerges as the answer. Then we test further to see whether the child has grasped the idea of repeated addition, which we fool him by calling multiplication. We devise techniques of instruction along the way to aid the child in building a

generic code to use for all sorts of quantities. If we fail to do this, we say that the child has learned in rote fashion or that, in Wertheimer's moralistic way of putting it, we have given the child "mechanical" rather than "insightful" ways of solving the problem. The distinction is not between mechanical and insightful, really, but whether or not the child has grasped and can use the generic code we have set out to teach him.[47]

It appears, then, that Bruner views the process of coding as one within which concepts are combined into generalizations or knowledge structures. Furthermore, generalizations permit both "backward and forward" predictions of which particularized statements are most likely to be either true or false. Accordingly, he states "a good theory—a good formal or probabilistic coding system . . . should permit us to go beyond the present data both retrospectively and prospectively."[48] A formal code either takes the form of, or is subsumed under, some principle of logic; a probabilistic or informal code is a generalization that is acquired inductively, perhaps even intuitively.

Bruner cites a significant coding experiment conducted by Miller, Postman, and himself. They arranged some fifth-grade children into two groups—those who fell in the lowest quartile on a standard spelling achievement test and those who fell in the highest quartile. In short, they identified a group of poor spellers and a group of good spellers. They first confronted these students with a set of pseudowords (i.e., letter combinations that were not real words) that only slightly resembled English words. Both groups identified the words as English to about the same degree. But when both groups were presented with a group of pseudowords that resembled English very closely in letter patterning (and which, as Bruner says, "but for the grace of God, might have been in the dictionary") the good spellers were much more likely than the poor to identify the words as English.

Bruner suggests that the good spellers had learned to code the English language with respect to typical letter patterning. He concludes, "The difference between the two groups is in what they had been learning while learning to spell English words. One group had been learning words more by rote, the others had been learning a general coding system based on the transitional probabilities that characterize letter sequences in English."[49]

Successful coding produces a situation within which new instances can be recognized with no further learning and the memory of instances already encountered no longer depends upon sheer retention. Knowing a code, a student can reconstruct the fact that all positive instances that are encountered are characterized by certain critical attributes.[50] It is obvious, therefore, that the more extensively a subject can be encompassed by systematic coding, the easier the subject is to be understood and utilized.

As code is built upon code or generalization is built upon generalization, a learner increasingly achieves a grasp of a subject. That is, he/she sees an ever-increasing number of concepts and generalizations as related. The more generalized a coding system is, the more useful it is to a learner in that it relieves him of any need to learn and try to remember a great mass of isolated facts.

What Are Optimal Sequences of Presentation of Materials to Be Learned?

An important task of an instructor is to convert knowledge into forms that fit growing minds or intellects. Materials to be taught should be tailored, sequenced, and put in forms appropriate to respective learners' existing modes of representation. Bruner states repeatedly that "Any idea or problem or body of knowledge can be presented in a form simple enough so that any particular learner can understand it in a recognizable form."[51] Thus, "Any subject, in short, can be taught to anybody at any age in some form that is honest and useful. The burden of proof is upon those who teach, as well as upon those who learn. It is meaningless to say that the calculus cannot be taught in the first grade. There are useful things about calculus that can be [taught] and with profit to later learning."[52] The task of schools, then, is to convert knowledge into structures that are within the grasp of learners of various ages and to arrange the structures in an optimum sequence of materials to be learned.

"Where an individual is starting to learn a body of knowledge completely from the beginning, *the task of instruction involves some optimal orchestration of the three systems of representing that knowledge.*"[53] In general, since the course of development in children runs from enactive representation through iconic representation to symbolic representation, it may well be that that sequence is the best starting technique with children. However, we may, to some degree, translate each of the systems of representation into the others. Furthermore, each may be pursued without its interfering with the others. For example, "a great shortstop can superbly perform his fielding of a curving grounder in a manner that is quite independent of his knowledge of the differential equations that describe the path of the ball through space."[54]

Since a child's mastery of complex skills depends upon his prior acquisition of some elementary ones, early training in elementary intellectual skills is critical for later learning. Furthermore, "There likely are critical periods in the use of certain linguistic forms or in the development of certain forms of imagery—critical periods after which learning becomes increasingly difficult to achieve."[55] However, this phenomenon arises more from the sequences of instruction that have been followed than from any innate predisposing factors in learning.

Bruner states that we should not think in terms of *an* optimal sequence for presenting *a* body of knowledge. Rather, we should recognize that

> Optimal sequences of learning cannot be specified independently of the criteria by which final learning is to be judged. Such criteria may include (1) speed of learning, (2) resistance to forgetting, (3) transferability of what has been learned to new instances, (4) form of representation in terms of which what has been learned is to be expressed, (5) economy of what has been learned in terms of cognitive strain imposed, and/or (6) effective power of what has been learned in terms of its ability to generate new hypotheses and combinations.[56]

Achieving one of the criteria does not necessarily bring a person closer to achieving others; for example, speed of learning is sometimes antithetical to transfer or to economy. Thus, our strategies should have as their objective the particular form of representation that is appropriate to the persons and the subject matters that are involved. One would not teach the practical geometry of a carpenter's work by the same means one would employ in teaching highly symbolic geometry. There are optimizing strategies for achieving both a particular form of representation and a type of learning. Furthermore, certain strategies will increase the likelihood both that the knowledge that is gained will be converted into economical conceptual structures and that the learner will recognize the transferability of the learned material to new similar situations.[57]

The road, then, to a teacher's successful structuring of a subject matter is the development of a *spiral curriculum*. Such a curriculum begins with rudiments that children already have learned and builds upon them by adding more complex and subtle categories and codes; teaching, as it moves upward, constantly circles back to build upon previous understandings. Such "a curriculum ought to be built around the great issues, principles, and values that a society deems worthy of the continual concern of its members."[58] For example, "If the understanding of number, measure, and probability is judged crucial in the pursuit of science, then instruction in these subjects should begin as intellectually honestly and as early as possible in a manner consistent with the child's forms of thought."[59] Then, let the topics be developed and redeveloped in later grades. In this way, when students take a tenth-grade course in biology, they will not need to approach the subject cold. A teacher should teach "readiness"; not simply wait for it to develop.

How Are Success and Failure and Reward and Punishment Involved in Learning?

Professor Bruner recognizes a role for reinforcement in learning, particularly in younger children, but he recommends "a considerable de-emphasis of 'extrinsic' rewards and punishments as factors in school learning."[60] He thinks that external reinforcement may start a particular act going and may lead to its repetition, but it does not nourish the long course of learning by which students build serviceable models of the world. When behavior becomes more long-range and competence-oriented, it comes under the control of cognitive structures and operates more from the inside out. He sums up his position as follows:

> I am proposing that to the degree that competence or mastery motives come to control behavior, the role of reinforcement or extrinsic pleasure wanes in shaping behavior. The child comes to manipulate his environment more actively and achieves his gratification from coping with problems. Symbolic modes of representing and transforming the environment arise and the importance of stimulus-response-reward sequences declines.[61]

Bruner, then, recognizes the role of both extrinsic and intrinsic rewards in teachers promoting learning, but he thinks that intrinsic rewards are the more important of the two. He sees a need to emphasize intrinsic motives and rewards in the form of (1) the satisfaction that is gained from quickened awareness and understanding, (2) the challenge to exercise one's full mental powers, (3) a developing interest and involvement, (4) the satisfaction gained from one's identity with others, (5) the pleasure received from one's cognitive or intellectual mastery, (6) one's sense of competence and accomplishment, and (7) the development of "reciprocity," which involves a deep human need to respond to others and to operate jointly with them to achieve an objective.

Bruner distinguishes between two terminal alternative states that follow one's attempt to know something or master some task—*success and failure* and *reward and punishment*. Success and failure are inherent to the task at hand; thus, they constitute intrinsic motivation. Reward and punishment usually are controlled by one's parents or teacher; thus they constitute extrinsic motivation. Hence, "the use of reward and punishment seriously affects the informative utility of successful and unsuccessful attempts at problem solving."[62] One reason for this is that an action followed by strong external reward will tend to increase the likelihood of the same kind of behavior, and this result *may* or *may not* be desirable. If the learning is an achievement of a transitional state en route to more powerful learning, repetition of the behavior is not desirable. A second reason is that a behavioral error followed by an external punishment is more likely to disrupt a behavior than to provide a basis for its correction.

What Procedures Stimulate Thought in a School Setting?

The several modes of a person acquiring knowledge, including the perception of events, the attainment of a concept, the solution of a problem, the discovery of a scientific theory, and the mastery of a skill, all appear to be viewed by Bruner as examples of a problem solving process. The process basically consists of two major steps: (1) an intuitive leap from available sense data to a tentative hypothesis by relating incoming information to an internally stored model of the world based upon past experience and (2) a confirmation check, in which the tentative hypothesis is tested against further sense data. If the two match, the hypothesis is maintained; if they mismatch, the hypothesis is altered in a way that acknowledges the discrepant evidence. The sense data that are used may be called cues, clues, instances, or experimental results. The *hypothesis* may be called a category rule, principle, or theory. The *internal model* may be called a generic coding system, a system of representation, a cognitive structure, or a paradigm.

When Bruner uses the concept of *intuitive leaps*, he is referring to unverbalized thought processes, sometimes very rapid, sometimes long and drawn out, that lead to an insight that can be verbalized and treated as a hypothesis. He reiterates the value of this process, reciting various major breakthroughs in human thought that have occurred this way. Furthermore, he advocates that teachers encourage students to play hunches and propose bold and even improbable ideas.

"If information is to be used effectively, it must be translated into the learner's way of attempting to solve a problem."[63] Instruction, then, according to Bruner, should have its object "to make the learner or problem solver self-sufficient."[64] But Bruner does not restrict discovery to the act of finding out something that before was unknown to humankind. Rather, discovery includes "all forms of obtaining knowledge for oneself by the use of one's own mind. . . ."[65] Discovery, "whether by a schoolboy going it on his own or by a scientist cultivating the growing edge of his field, is in its essence a matter of rearranging or transforming evidence in such a way that one is enabled to go beyond the evidence so reassembled to additional new insights."[66]

A child, left to himself, will go about discovering things for himself, but certain forms of home and school atmospheres lead some children to be greater "discoverers" than others. Teachers should aim to give students a firm grasp of their subjects in such a way as to promote students' being autonomous and self-propelled thinkers who will proceed to learn on their own when their formal schooling is ended.

There is a striking difference in the acts and outlooks of persons who see the tasks before them as being problems to be solved rather than behaviors to be manifested. Although many persons by school age have come to expect quite arbitrary and meaningless demands to be made upon them by adults, they still, through encouragement and instruction, can quite quickly be led to participate in finding and solving significant problems. But problem solving, when developed, should be intrinsic, not extrinsic.

Extrinsic problem solving consists of students expending "extraordinary time and effort figuring out what it is that the teacher wants—and usually coming to the conclusion that she or he wants tidiness or remembering or doing things at a certain time in a certain way."[67]

Within *intrinsic problem solving*, one does not simply personalize knowledge by linking it to the familiar. Rather, one makes a familiar object or situation an instance of a more general case. Through problem solving, one goes about exploring a situation. This process is opened by an individual acquiring a representation or model of reality with which the individual interacts and thereby participates in an "inventive" process. The next step in the growth of one's problem solving process consists of sensing a problem, that is, recognizing that there is a difference between where one is now in relation to a given task and where one wants to be.[68]

Bruner notes that "it is often necessary in initiating learning and problem solving in young children (and in older ones as well) to resort to an initial regimen of praise and reward for each successful act."[69] But he also emphasizes that *"Optimum phasing requires a gradual process of giving the rewarding function back to the task and the learner."*[70] Hence there is an educational danger in creating a learner's dependence upon a reward and a rewarder to keep his learning going.

For a learner to perform the rewarding function on himself, in place of any external reward, he/she must have a continuously available knowledge of results. "Knowledge of results should come at that point in a problem solving episode when the person is comparing the results of his tryout with some criterion of what he seeks to achieve."[71]

NOTES

1. Jerome S. Bruner and Jeremy M. Anglin, *Beyond the Information Given: Studies in the Psychology of Knowing* (New York: Norton, 1973), p. xv.
2. Jerome S. Bruner, Jacqueline J. Goodnow, and George A. Austin, *A Study of Thinking* (New York: Wiley, 1956), pp. 245–246.
3. Ibid., p. 14.
4. Ibid., p. 14.
5. Ibid., pp. 14–15.
6. Jerome S. Bruner, ed., *Learning About Learning: A Conference Report*, U. S. Department of Health, Education, and Welfare, Cooperative Research Monograph No. 15, 1966, p. 203.
7. Jerome S. Bruner, *The Process of Education* (Cambridge, MA: Harvard University Press, 1960), p. 72.
8. Jerome S. Bruner, *Actual Minds, Possible Worlds* (Cambridge, MA: Harvard University Press, 1986), p. 67.
9. Ibid., p. 88.
10. Ibid., p. 129.
11. Jerome S. Bruner, *Toward a Theory of Instruction* (Cambridge, MA: Harvard University Press, 1966), p. 5.
12. Ibid., p. 27.
13. Ibid., p. 28.
14. Ibid., p. 45.
15. Jerome S. Bruner, R. R. Olver, P. M. Greenfield, et al., *Studies in Cognitive Growth* (New York: Wiley, 1966), p. 321.
16. Jerome S. Bruner, *The Relevance of Education* (New York: Norton, 1973), p. 7.
17. Ibid., p. xi.
18. Ibid., p. xii.
19. Ibid., p. 5.
20. Ibid., p. 6.
21. Bruner, Goodnow, and Austin, *A Study of Thinking*, p. viii.
22. Ibid., p. 6.
23. Bruner, *Actual Minds, Possible Worlds*, p. 122.
24. Ibid., p. 123.
25. Bruner, *The Relevance of Education*, p. 22.
26. Bruner, *Actual Minds, Possible Worlds*, p. 131.
27. Ibid., p. 127.
28. Bruner, *Learning About Learning*, p. 119.
29. Ibid., p. 120.
30. Ibid., p. 121.
31. Bruner, *The Relevance of Education*, p. 111.

32. Ibid., p. 131.
33. Ibid., p. 115.
34. Ibid., p. 70.
35. Ibid., p. 117.
36. Bruner, *Learning About Learning*, p. 198.
37. Ibid., p. 199.
38. Bruner, *The Relevance of Education*, p. 116.
39. Bruner, *Toward a Theory of Instruction*, p. 126.
40. Ibid., p. 126.
41. Bruner, *The Process of Education*, p. 6.
42. Ibid., p. 7.
43. Bruner, *Learning About Learning*, p. 201.
44. Bruner and Anglin, *Beyond the Information Given*, p. 222.
45. Ibid., p. 224.
46. Jerome S. Bruner, "Going Beyond the Information Given," in H. Gruber et al., eds., *Contemporary Approaches to Cognition* (Cambridge, MA: Harvard University Press, 1957), p. 50.
47. Bruner and Anglin, *Beyond the Information Given*, pp. 222–223.
48. Bruner, "Going Beyond the Information Given," p. 46.
49. Ibid., p. 48.
50. Ibid., p. 52.
51. Bruner, *Toward a Theory of Instruction*, p. 44.
52. Bruner, *Learning About Learning*, p. 202.
53. Bruner, *Learning About Learning*, p. 203.
54. Ibid., p. 202.
55. Ibid., p. 200.
56. Bruner, *Toward a Theory of Instruction*, p. 50.
57. Bruner, *Learning About Learning*, p. 205.
58. Bruner and Anglin, *Beyond the Information Given*, p. 424.
59. Ibid., p. 424.
60. Bruner, *Toward a Theory of Instruction*, p. 127.
61. Bruner and Anglin, *Beyond the Information Given*, p. 409.
62. Bruner, *Learning About Learning*, p. 207.
63. Bruner, *Toward a Theory of Instruction*, p. 53.
64. Ibid., p. 53.
65. Bruner and Anglin, *Beyond the Information Given*, p. 402.
66. Ibid., p. 402.
67. Bruner, *The Relevance of Education*, p. 62.
68. Bruner, *Learning About Learning*, p. 210.
69. Ibid., p. 209.
70. Ibid., p. 209.
71. Bruner, *Toward a Theory of Instruction*, p. 51.

BIBLIOGRAPHY, CHAPTER 6

Bigge, Morris L. "The Cognitive Psychology of Jerome S. Bruner." In Wolman, Benjamin B., ed. *International Encyclopedia of Psychiatry, Psychology, Psychoanalysis, and Neurology.* New York: Aesculapius Publishers, Inc., 1977, Vol. 3, pp. 207–211. A succinct statement of Bruner's psychology.

Bruner, Jerome S., Jacqueline J. Goodnow, and George A. Austin. *A Study of Thinking*. New York: Wiley, 1956. A study based on research conducted at the Institute for Advanced Study (Princeton) and at Harvard University. Focuses on the formation and use of concepts. Technical, but an average student can read the introduction with profit.

Bruner, Jerome S. *The Process of Education*. Cambridge, MA: Harvard University Press, 1960. The chairman's report of the major themes, principal conjectures, and most striking tentative conclusions of a 1959 conference of 35 natural scientists, psychologists, and educators on teaching science and mathematics in elementary and secondary schools. The report emphasizes teaching for understanding the structure—pertinent relationships—of a subject matter rather than for mastery of facts and techniques.

Bruner, Jerome S. *On Knowing; Essays for the Left Hand*. Cambridge, MA: Harvard University Press, 1962. A series of essays derived from papers, articles, and addresses, revised to provide continuity. Part 1 is on how one comes to know; part 2 on how to teach and learn; and part 3 on how one's conception of reality influences action. Provocative and stylistically excellent.

Bruner, Jerome S. *Toward a Theory of Instruction*. Cambridge, MA: Belknap Press of Harvard University, 1966. Presents Bruner's conclusions concerning what should go into a theoretical basis for teaching procedure. Bruner writes on a theoretical level, but his ideas are highly thought-provoking.

Bruner, Jerome S., ed. *Learning About Learning: A Conference Report*. U. S. Department of Health, Education, and Welfare, Cooperative Research Monograph No. 15, 1966. Report of the working conference on research on children's learning. A major attempt to answer some important questions about the nature of the learning process. Major problems studied are (1) inducing a child to learn and sustaining the child's attention, (2) learning ideas and skills in one subject so that they will assist progress in others, and (3) promoting optimum sequences of learning materials.

Bruner, Jerome S., R. R. Olver, P. M. Greenfield, et al. *Studies in Cognitive Growth*. New York: Wiley, 1966. A study of intellectual development in children, based on the work of the Center for Cognitive Studies at Harvard. Has important implications for an understanding of child development as well as discussing how to teach meaningfully.

Bruner, Jerome S. "Some Elements of Discovery." Chapter 7 in Shulman, Lee S., and Evan R. Keislar, eds. *Learning By Discovery, A Critical Appraisal*. Chicago: Rand McNally, 1966. Treats discovery as it relates to a given culture. Bruner prefers the term *problem solving* rather than *discovery* in discussing creative learning.

Bruner, Jerome S. *The Relevance of Education*. New York: Norton, 1973. Bruner emphasizes that educational reform must begin with an understanding of how children acquire information and convert information into action. Educational strategies must expand, not constrict, the learning skills of children and youth.

Bruner, Jerome S., and Jeremy M. Anglin. *Beyond the Information Given: Studies in the Psychology of Knowing*. New York: Norton, 1973. Brings together Bruner's major contributions in his study of knowing as it relates to perception, thought, infancy, childhood, and education. Centers on the human process of knowing, experience, and achievement of insight, understanding, and competence.

Bruner, Jerome S. *Child's Talk*. New York: Norton, 1983. A study of growth in human infants and the development of human language.

Bruner, Jerome S. *In Search of Mind*. New York: Harper & Row, 1983. Bruner's professional-psychological autobiography.

Bruner, Jerome S. *Actual Minds, Possible Worlds*. Cambridge, MA: Harvard University Press, 1986. Develops two modes of thought or cognitive functioning, each having its distinctive way of ordering experience or constructing reality: (1) formal, mathematical, paradigmatic, logico-scientific and (2) literary art. Chapters 7 and 9 are highly pertinent to this chapter.

Bruner, Jerome S. and Helen Haste, eds. *Making Sense*, Methuen, 1987. A symposium on child developmental psychology.

Chapter
7

What Is Bandura's Linear-Interactionist Social Cognitive Learning Theory?

*T*his chapter centers upon Albert Bandura's linear-interactionist *social cognitive* theory of learning. Then Chapters 9 and 10 develop the *cognitive-field* interactionist position. Both social cognitive and cognitive-field theories are *cognitive-interactionist* ones. These two learning theories provide a psychological basis for both explanatory and exploratory understanding levels of teaching, described in Chapters 12 and 13.

Albert Bandura (1925-), a native of Canada, received his bachelor's degree at the University of British Columbia and his master's and doctor's degrees at the University of Iowa. Currently, he is a professor of psychology at Stanford University. He was president of the American Psychological Association in 1974. Some areas of his special interest are social learning; human aggression, especially as manifested in adolescents; and psychological modeling.[1] His psychological theory is supported by extensive research on the behavior of human beings. Bower and Hilgard have written, "In broad outline [Bandura's] social [cognitive] learning theory provides the best integrative summary of what modern learning theory has to contribute to the solution of practical problems."[2]

Some other leading contemporary psychologists who have made major contributions to the study of linear cognitive interaction are K. S. Bowers, Robert C. Bolles, Norman I. Feather, David Magnusson, Julian B. Rotter, and Bernard Weiner. Edward C. Tolman (1886–1959) and Ernest E. Bayles developed earlier forms of this position and inspired the work of contemporary interactionists.

WHAT IS COGNITIVE INTERACTION?

Cognitive interaction is the interaction of individuals with their perceived meaningful environments. It arises through the purposive relationships of persons and their perceived environments. Whereas adherents of inner motivation think that humankind is endowed with personal free will and adherents of outer motivation think that humankind's behavior is the product of mechanistic determinism, adherents of the cognitive-interactional view think that people are immanently purposive beings who exercise situational choice. People being *immanently purposive* means that they do the best they know how for the welfare of whatever they conceive themselves to be. *Situational choice* means that at any time in one's life, one may to some extent choose the way one will turn next.

There are two kinds of cognitive interactionisms—*linear* and *field*. They have much in common, but also some significant differences. The principal difference is that, whereas linear interactionists view persons' perceptions and behaviors as occurring in sequences, field interactionists concentrate on simultaneous mutual interactions of persons and their psychological environments.

Cognitive interactionists think that both behavior-outcome and stimulus-outcome expectancies depend upon inferences about the *intentions* or *purposes* that motivate behavior. However, they warn that "if expectancies are converted into global trait-like dispositions and extracted from their close interaction with situational conditions, they are likely to become just as useless as their many theoretical predecessors."[3]

In cognitive interactionism an individual is considered to be not a passive object for environmental forces to condition but an interactive, intentional subject, continuously participating in an ongoing reciprocal person- and situation-interaction process and acting on the basis of his own reasons, expectations, needs, and motives. The way in which a person, in his cognitive processes, selects situations, stimuli, and events and perceives, construes, and evaluates them is of critical importance. It is what individuals perceive that gives rise to their behavior.

Cognitive interaction, then, is purposive action. It may be either thought or a combination of thought and behavior. It is not an automatic action resulting from an impingement of a stimulus upon an organism. A person does not merely process information about the outcomes of his behavior. Instead, he/she integrates the information in order to make cognitive sense of matters involving himself and the world around him.

To cognitive interactionists, *interaction* is a relationship between a person and his psychological environment within which the person, *in purposeful fashion,* tries to give meaning to his environment so as to use objects in it in advantageous ways. "The model of the person is that of an active processor of information organizing and constructing experience into meaningful internal representations, and behaving not as an automaton but as a thoughtful, purposeful being."[4] As a person interprets and uses his environment for his purposes, both he and his environment are changed. The person's physical environment may or may not be changed in ways others may observe but its meaning is changed so that it appears different to the person interacting with it. The person also changes in the sense that through interaction he/she achieves new insights that even if only in subtle ways, literally transform him. Gone from this concept of interaction is the idea of the reaction of a passive organism to a stimulus and an ensuing chain of S-R's running back and forth from organism to environment. Rather, we now have a dynamic relation of a person and his *psychological* environment, not two mutually exclusive entities that are completely outside one another. "Environmental events, personal factors, and behavior all operate as interacting determinants of each other."[5]

WHAT ARE THE ATTRIBUTES OF BANDURA'S LINEAR INTERACTIVE SOCIAL-COGNITIVE LEARNING THEORY?

Adherents of a linear cognitive-interactionist view, in their study of human learning, emphasize that perceptions play a key role as an intervening variable between stimuli and responses, through which situational conditions influence both conscious life and actual behavior. Their linear interpretation of learning leads them to study sequential anticipations being followed by acts and the acts being followed by perceptions of their consequences.

A linear psychological situation consists of the cues perceived by an individual over a given time span. It includes both physical and social features that the perceiver associates with particular kinds of action. Therefore, it is a complex set of interacting cues acting upon an individual through a given time period. (*Cues* are the psychological meanings of situations.)

These cues determine for a person the expectancies for behavioral reinforcement sequences. They, either explicitly or implicitly, may be thoughts, ideas, or internal stimuli such as pain, pleasure, excitement, or fear. "An expectancy or insight into a behavior-reinforcement sequence is considered to be a function of an expectancy built up in the same situation over past experience . . . and generalized expectancies [arise] from relevant classes of similar situations."[6]

Not only do persons interact with situations, but they also affect the situations with which they interact. Situations are as much a function of the person concerned as the person's behavior is a function of the situation. Although our environment shapes us, we also shape our environment. "A dynamic interaction model stresses the continuously ongoing person-situation interaction process in which individuals actively seek or avoid some situations, influence and transform situations and environments by their activities, temporarily and over time, and are influenced by situational and environmental factors at different levels of generality."[7] At any moment an individual selects, interprets, and evaluates the situational information and transforms it into sources of behavior, which in the next stage of the process becomes an important part of the situational information for the individual. Simultaneously, this affects the behavior of others and thereby contributes to producing changes in situations.

The psychological significance of an environment is investigated through studying an individual's perception of the existing situation—the meaning that the individual assigns to it. The meaning or perception of a situation is an essential and influential factor that affects a person's behavior or reactions to that situation.

Within the person-situation linear interaction approach, investigators study the life courses of persons in terms of the sequences of interactions within which a person and relevant situations form an interwoven structure. The appropriate unit of analysis is a longitudinal study of person-in-situation interactions. *Personal variables* are relatively stable cognitive and emotional characteristics. *Situational variables* are psychological meanings of situations (cues) for the individual. A combination of personal and situational variables is what determines behavior. In a sense, the situation is a function of the person in that the person's cognitive schemes "filter and organize the environment in a fashion that makes it impossible ever to completely separate the environment from the person observing it."[8]

As a person enters a social situation, his person-in-situation models for thinking form the cognitive structure of, or generalization about, that situation and play a large role in determining his social behavior. His "emotional expressions and actions are a result of the meaning imposed upon the environment."[9]

Bandura's use of *social* in his social cognitive theory implies that "behavior, cognitive and other personal factors, and environmental influences all operate interactively as determinants of each other."[10] His use of *cognitive* implies that cognition is a central knowing process in learning procedures; his theory, therefore, centers upon how people gain understandings of themselves and their environments and how they act in relation to those understandings.

Bandura's learning theory consists of a blending of purposive cognitive psychology with some aspects of reinforcement theory, but he gives *reinforcement* a special meaning that contrasts sharply with that of Skinnerian radical behaviorism.[11] The consequences of one's past behaviors largely determine one's future behavior. However, this occurs primarily because of the *informative* and *incentive* values of those consequences. Reinforcement, as characterized by Bandura, works because the consequences of past behavior have created expectations or insights concerning the likelihood of similar outcomes on future similar occasions.

Social cognitive theory employs both humanistic and behavioristic terminology to explain human psychological functions in terms of a continuous reciprocal interaction between personal and environmental determinants. In the reciprocal interaction process the environment influences one's behavior, but one's behavior also partly determines one's environment, in a mutual fashion. By their very actions people play a significant part in producing the contingencies—reinforcement sequences—of which they are a part. Thus, "behavior is regulated by its contingencies, but the contingencies are partly of a person's own making."[12] Human beings do not simply respond to stimuli, they interpret them. "So-called conditional reactions are largely self-activated on the basis of learned expectations rather than automatically evoked."[13]

Although the selection of particular courses of action from available alternatives is determined by prior personal and environmental conditions, people can exert some control over the deterministic factors that govern their choices. Persons' actions are determined by prior conditions, but the conditions are partly determined by those persons' prior actions. For example, in self-control procedures, people are able to regulate their behaviors in preferred directions through arranging environmental conditions that are most likely to elicit the desired behavior and arranging self-reinforcing consequences to sustain that behavior.

WHAT, FOR BANDURA, IS THE NATURE AND MOTIVATION OF HUMANKIND?

Bandura emphasizes that the image of humankind that emerges through psychological theorizing and research depends very much upon how each of the two aspects of the reciprocal influence system—person and environment—are employed. Environmental determinists explain how environmental influences change behavior. Conversely, personal determinists (existentialist humanists) study how mentalistic behavior determines environments. Social cognitive theorists, in contrast with both, give about equal weight to both aspects of the person-environment relationship. "People are neither driven by inner forces nor automatically shaped and controlled by external stimuli."[14]

One usually changes one's behavior in situations where there is a need, adequate performance skills, and adequate incentives; but the change is facilitated by an awareness of its consequences. Therefore, "awareness is a powerful facilitative factor, but it may not be necessary and certainly is not a sufficient condition for behavioral change."[15] One's behavior is not environmentally determined, but neither does it arise through one's autonomous expression. People are neither neutral-passive organisms nor completely active persons. Instead, they are thinking beings.

Bandura's social cognitive theory involves goal setting and attainment, and it concerns how people can shape environmental conditions for their purposes. But in this purposive process, some people are more effective than others. "The greater their foresight, proficiency, and self-influence, all of which are acquirable skills, the greater the progress toward their goals."[16]

Bandura points out that "radical behaviorists" (so called by B. F. Skinner to identify his position), in their vigorous effort to adhere to environmental determinism and thereby avoid giving any credence to what they consider to be spurious inner causes, have neglected important determinants of behavior that arise through cognitive processes. Consequently, radical behaviorists provide an incomplete or inadequate, however not completely inaccurate, account of human behavior. But Bandura simultaneously warns against an existentialist humanism, within which psychologically active persons are assumed to have complete personal control of matters. For Bandura, "except for elementary reflexes, people are not equipped with inborn repertoires of behavior. They must learn them."[17] Thus, the various human response patterns must be learned.

Within the learning process, responses are acquired by either *direct* or *observational* reinforcing experiences.

Whereas behaviorists generally emphasize environmental sources of control, and existentialist humanists tend to restrict their interest to personally exercised control, social cognitive theory encompasses both sources of control, but within a reciprocal pattern. This theory entails persons' first acquiring given behaviors, then applying those behaviors in future situations. Therefore, the theory is concerned not only with how behavior is acquired but also with how behavior is activated and channeled.

Instead of considering people to be mechanical products of environmental forces, as in Skinnerian reinforcement theory, Bandura regards them as information-processing and -interpreting beings who operate on the basis of insightful expectations. Accordingly, he states, "Contrary to the mechanistic metaphors, outcomes change behavior in humans through the intervening influence of thought."[18] Human beings are thinking organisms who possess capabilities to provide themselves with some degree of self-direction.

Human thought, then, is a powerful tool for understanding, and dealing effectively with, one's environment. "Most external influences affect behavior through intermediary cognitive processes."[19] By symbolically manipulating information derived from personal and vicarious experience, people can comprehend events and generate new knowledge about them.

Human nature is characterized by a vast potential that, within biological limits, can be fashioned by direct and observational experience into a variety of forms. The unique capacity of human beings is their capability for reflective self-conscious activity. "People not only gain understanding through reflection, they evaluate and alter their own thinking."[20] Most of human behavior is regulated by purposive forethought. "People do not simply react to their immediate environment, nor are they steered by implants from their past."[21] By representing foreseeable outcomes symbolically, people can convert future consequences into current motivators and regulators of foresightful behavior.

Intention and *goal setting* play prominent roles in self-regulation of behavior. An intention is a determination to perform certain activities or to attain a certain future state of affairs. Goal setting enhances motivation through self-reactive influences. Goals specify the conditional requirements for positive self-evaluation. "Self-motivation is best maintained by explicit proximal subgoals that are instrumental in achieving larger future ones."[22]

WHAT, FOR BANDURA, IS RECIPROCAL PSYCHOLOGICAL INTERACTION?

Bandura observes that there is a consensus among contemporary psychologists that behavior, in some way, results from the interaction of persons and environmental situations and not from the action of either of the two factors alone. But he sees little professional consensus in regard to the basic question of how the two factors interact with one another in determining behavior. He accepts the actuality of determinism but challenges the idea of the deterministic process being either a one- or two-directional process. Instead, for him, person-environment interaction is a *reciprocal* process.

One-directional interaction means that persons and environmental situations are considered independent entities that combine to produce behavior. Behavior is the result of a discrete situation impinging upon a discrete organism; stimuli pass from the environment to the person that is involved, and then the organism responds.

Two-directional interaction means that persons and environmental situations are considered to be interdependent causes of a behavior, but each retains a one-directional characteristic. Within this position, behavior is considered the result of an interdependent environment and person, in turn, affecting one another. The person affects the environment and the environment affects the person; each responds to the other.

In Bandura's *reciprocal interaction,* interdependent behaviors, other personal factors, and environmental factors are interpreted to operate conjointly in mutual interaction as interlocking determinants of each other. However, the relative influences that are exerted by each of the three interdependent factors differ both in different settings and for different behaviors. "Contrary to the unilateral view, human accomplishments result from the reciprocal interaction of external circumstances with a host of personal determinants, including endowed personalities, acquired competencies, reflective thought, and a high level of self-initiative."[23] (Readers should note the similarity between Bandura's *reciprocal interaction* and cognitive-field theories' *simultaneous mutual interaction,* developed in Chapter 9, pages 181–182.)

The two concepts primarily differ only in reciprocal interaction being taken to be serially linear as contrasted with its being simultaneous. Bandura notes that radical behaviorists, within their environmental determinism, recognize that human organisms can exercise some degree of countercontrol. That is, they can rebut environments through their reactions to environmental instigating forces. But his idea of reciprocal interaction extends beyond mere countercontrol: "People activate and create environments as well as rebut them."[24]

In the process of reciprocal interactions, people learn to predict events and to make anticipating reactions to the events. "Effective psychological functioning is partly based on the capacity to anticipate the probable consequences of different courses of action."[25] However, depending upon the time, place and persons that are involved, the same behavior has different results or effects. Furthermore, within the reciprocal interaction process, one and the same event can be a stimulus, a response, or an environmental reinforcer, depending upon its place in the sequence at which an analysis begins.

Bandura observes that human operations would be quite boring and trying if solutions to problems could be achieved only by enacting possible alternative actions and suffering the consequences of each. Higher mental capacities, however, enable people to use thought as well as action in solving problems. Alternate courses of action are typically tested through symbolic exploration and, on the basis of their calculated consequences, are either retained or discarded. "By representing foreseeable outcomes [of behavior] symbolically, people convert future consequences into current motivators of behavior."[26] Through their exercise of thought giving them the capability for insightful and foresightful behavior, people can execute favored symbolic solutions of problematic situations.

Bandura considers persons to be neither autonomous agents nor mechanical conveyors of animating environmental forces. Instead, persons serve as reciprocally contributing influences to their own motivation and behavior within a system of reciprocal causation involving personal determinants, actions and environmental factors.[27] These three factors affect each other, not unidirectionally, but bidirectionally within the model of "triadic reciprocity." (This concept refers to the mutual interaction of the three cognitive causal factors—personal determinants, actions, and environmental factors.) While undergoing experiences, people are doing more than just learning the probabilistic relation between actions and outcomes. For them to predict how outcomes will affect behavior, they must know how both are cognitively processed. This requires an analysis of the reciprocally contributing influences of the cognitive factors.

WHAT IS THE NATURE OF COGNITIVE REINFORCEMENT?

Bandura recognizes the operation of reinforcement along with other human learning processes, but his learning theory is primarily a cognitive reinforcement one. Hence, he gives *reinforcement* a unique meaning. For Bandura it is a learning process within which personal cognitive factors and environmental ones are considered mutually interdependent; and a person's cognitive awareness of the implications of the learning involved plays a prominent role in his acquisition, retention, and expression of future behaviors.

Traditionally, behaviorists have assumed that behavior is automatically shaped and controlled by its consequences, that is, whatever stimuli follow it. But Bandura sees little evidence that the outcomes of behavior function as automatic regulators of human conduct. Instead of an automatic, mechanistic process prevailing, consequences determine—reinforce—behavior largely through their informative and incentive value. They affect one's future behavior through creation of insightful expectations. "Within the social cognitive perspective, social factors play an influential role in cognitive development, and the pursuit of competence is entrusted to a varied array of motivators, rather than solely to the drive of cognitive perturbations."[28]

The reinforcement process, then, is neither an environment-centered process that creates a permanent control mechanism within an organism nor a person-centered self-actualization process within which persons exercise their self-directing potentialities. Instead, the reinforcement process of learning consists of people developing self-activated, cognitively-mediated expectations through grasping the consequences of both direct and observed experience.

Learning, then, is the process of one's construing internal representations of behavior through informative feedback resulting from direct behavior, and one's observation of examples of behavior in other people, and the consequences of both. These internal representations then serve as guides to one's actions on later occasions. "After response patterns become routinized through repeated execution, they are performed without requiring intermediary visualization or thought."[29]

Although reinforcement of human behavior occasionally can be merely a direct process of mechanical forming and strengthening of conduct, in most cases it is more an informative and motivational process. That is, "so-called conditioned reactions are largely self-activated on the basis of learned expectations rather than evoked automatically."[30] Through a process of differential reinforcement, successful forms of behavior are adopted and ineffectual ones are discarded because they either have no effect or they result in punishing outcomes.

What Are the Functions of Consequences?

"Most external sources of influence affect behavior through intermediary cognitive influences."[31] That is, behavior is affected by its consequences through persons' awareness of what is being reinforced; there is conscious involvement in the learning process. Persons consider relevant information, apply cognitive operations to it, and generate possible solutions. "People do not learn much from repetitive, paired experiences unless they recognize that events are correlated."[32] Thus, the widely accepted dictum that behavior is determined by its consequences holds better for anticipated than for actual consequences.[33] By observing the outcome of their actions, people discern which responses are appropriate in a given setting and behave accordingly. In studies of both classical and instrumental conditioning, persons who discern the contingencies that govern the application of rewards and punishments typically display significant increments of performance or learning, whereas those who are unaware of those contingencies generally show few if any conditioning effects.[34]

The consequences of behaviors are active judgmental, constructive results, either direct or observed, of the behaviors. The consequences of a response or behavior serve several functions:

1. They impart information that serves as a guide for action.
2. They provide the intervening influence of thought.
3. They motivate the person through their incentive value.
4. They provide anticipatory benefits and averters of future trouble.
5. They bring remote consequences to bear through the person exercising anticipatory thoughts.
6. They give rise to examples and precepts that delineate standards of conduct, which serve as a basis for self-reinforcing actions.

What Are Conditions of Reinforcement?

The conditions of reinforcement are determined by neither the environment nor the person alone. Since these conditions are partly determined by the prior actions of the individual who is involved, the impact of prevailing conditions can be altered by either environmental stimulation or cognitive influences. When there is no awareness of what is being reinforced, consequences generally produce little change in behavior. That is, "Behavior is not much affected by its consequences without awareness of what is being reinforced."[35]

Cognitive or awareness processes play a prominent role in the acquisition, retention, and expression of behaviors. Day-by-day experiences are coded and held in symbolic form and thereby are given lasting effects in the form of memory representations. Various thoughts, achieved through cognitive processes, can enhance, distort, or negate the influence of reinforcement consequences. In turn, however, one's thoughts are partly governed by external stimuli. Thus, personal cognitive factors and environmental factors are mutually interdependent.

Human beings are not pawns of external circumstances; nor do human cognitive events occur spontaneously as autonomous causes of behavior. Instead, the nature, valence, and occurrence of cognitive events are governed by both external stimuli and conditions of reinforcement. But learning through reinforcement is still more a cognitive than a mechanistic process. "A large body of research now exists in which cognitions are activated instructionally, their presence is assessed indirectly, and their functional relationship to behavior is carefully examined."[36] For example, A. Kaufman, A. Baron, and R. E. Kopp conducted a research study of reinforcement and cognitions in regard to it. They found that *beliefs* of subjects concerning the prevailing conditions of their reinforcement outweighed the influence of the *actually experienced rewards*. Subjects regulated their levels and distributions of effort according to their cognitive expectations of reinforcement.[37]

Bandura recognizes three kinds or levels of reinforcement—direct external, self-administered, and vicarious reinforcement. All three are characterized by reciprocal cognitive interaction.

What Is Direct External Reinforcement?

In direct external reinforcement, people regulate their behavior on the basis of consequences they experience directly. In this process, behaviors can be increased, reinstated, or eliminated by alteration of the reinforcing effects that they produce. Rewards both provide information concerning the optimal responses in a situation and provide incentive motivation for certain acts because of the future rewards that, it is anticipated, will follow them. Here, even subtle variations in the pattern and frequency with which actions are reinforced can affect one's responsiveness. For example, people who have been continuously rewarded for a given behavior drop that behavior quite quickly when its reinforcement ceases. But "those who have been reinforced intermittently persist despite only occasional successes."[38]

What Is Self-Administered Reinforcement?

Self-administered reinforcement is the process of people regulating their behaviors on the basis of the consequence that they create for themselves. "In this process people adopt, through precept and example, certain standards of conduct and respond to their own behavior in self-rewarding or self-punishing ways."[39] "The development of self-reactive functions gives humans a capacity for self-direction."[40] "To ignore the influential role of covert self-reinforcement in the regulation of behavior is to disavow a unique human capacity of man."[41]

Self-reinforcing consequences are likely to be activated most strongly in those cases where the causal connection between moral behavior and its consequences is quite apparent. Also, both self-evaluative reinforcers and external consequences have their greatest effect on behavior when they are compatible with one another. But after a person develops a capacity for self-direction, a given behavior produces two sets of consequences—self-evaluative reactions and external outcomes—that often operate as opposing influences on behavior. When individuals are rewarded for behaviors that they personally disdain or are punished for behaviors that they value highly, conflict arises. How people behave in such conflict situations depends upon the relative strength of the external and personal factors.

After people adopt evaluative standards, they, on their own, improve their performances to the point of their self-satisfaction. "Skills are perfected as much, or more, to please oneself as to please the public."[42] Although innovative endeavors receive some social support, innovative individuals must provide much of their own reinforcement. Quite often early efforts of innovators bring rebuffs rather than compliments.

How Is Vicarious Reinforcement Achieved Through Modeling?

Vicarious reinforcement occurs when behavior is observationally acquired rather than directly achieved. People regulate and change their behavior based upon consequences that they see accruing to other people who, as models, manifest the behaviors in similar situations. Through the process of vicarious reinforcement, people weigh consequences of those observed to have experienced similar behavior. Once it is so evaluated and weighted, people may then profit from the vicarious experience. A person need not *ever* learn to refill his auto gas tank by being stranded out in the sticks a couple of times. It is enough to have heard a story of someone who made this thoughtless mistake to learn that cars do not run on empty.

People, then, observe the actions of others and the rewarding or punishing consequences that follow those actions. However, since a person must judge the value of observed reinforcements, the same outcome of behavior may serve as either a reward or a punishment depending upon what example of observed reinforcement is used as a basis for evaluating a situation. Also, because social cognitive theory distinguishes between the acquisition of behaviors and their performance, existing incentive and motivational processes determine whether given observationally acquired vicarious behaviors will actually be performed.

Vicarious reinforcement is achieved through modeling, which is the process within which a person observes the behaviors of others, forms an idea of the performance and results of the observed behaviors, and uses that idea as coded information to guide his future behaviors. Most of the behaviors that people display have been learned, either deliberately or unintentionally, through modeling. Modeling reduces both the burden and the hazards of direct trial-and-error learning through enabling people to learn from example what they should do even before they attempt a given behavior.

Facility in modeling is increased by one acquiring skills in selective observation, memory encoding, coordination of sensorimotor and ideomotor systems, and judging the consequence of others manifesting an observed behavior. A model's behavior is more often imitated when the model has been rewarded rather than punished. The reward-punishment variable, however, affects only a person's *performance* of imitative responses, not his *learning* them.

Modeling for vicarious learning may be either direct, synthesized, or abstract. In *direct modeling*, a person copies the behavior of a model in the form in which the person has observed it and its consequences. Direct modeling usually gives rise to socially prescribed behaviors being adopted in essentially the same form that they are portrayed.

In *synthesized modeling*, features of different model behaviors are formed into amalgams that may represent novel styles of thought and action. "By synthesizing what they see around them into new ways of doing things, observers can achieve by creative modeling novel styles of thought and conduct."[43]

Abstract modeling may be used to develop rule-governed cognitive behaviors. Through this process, observers derive principles or understandings that underlie specific performances and apply them so as to generate innovative behavior patterns that transcend anything they have either seen or heard. Based upon observationally derived rules, people alter their judgmental orientations, conceptual schemes, linguistic styles, and standards of conduct to achieve *novel* styles of operation.

Bandura observes that research conducted within the framework of social cognitive theory shows that

> In actuality, virtually all learning phenomena resulting from direct experience can occur vicariously by observing other people's behavior and its consequences for them. The capacity to learn by observation enables people to acquire rules for generating and regulating behavioral patterns without having to form them gradually by tedious trial and error.[44]

"Modeled behavior is often performed without any immediate external rewards."[45] Human behavior, however, acquired, is regulated largely by one's precepts of efficacy and the anticipated consequences of prospective actions. Hence, people will persist, for some time, in actions that go unrewarded, on the expectation that their efforts eventually will produce results.

Bandura asserts that enactive learning through direct experience is really a special case of observational learning. Whereas, in learning by modeling, people derive conceptions of behavior from observing the structure of the behavior being modeled by others, in learning by direct experience people construct conceptions of behavior from observing the effects of their own actions.

What Are the Components of Vicarious Learning?

Bandura describes four interrelated components of observational, vicarious learning—attentional, retentional, motoric reproduction, and observational reinforcement processes.

The *attentional process* regulates one's sensory input and perception of modeled actions. It involves a person observing a model's experience so as to learn from the model. It determines what is selectively observed from among a profusion of modeling influences and what is extracted from the observed matters.

Within the *retentional process*, "through coding and symbolic rehearsal, transitory experiences are transformed for memory representation into enduring performance guides."[46] To be retained in memory, a model's behavior, as a stimulus event, is verbally coded, or otherwise symbolically represented, and held over an elapse of time. In the retentional process, revival of sensory experiences, thus integrated, guide the observer's imitative behavior. In verbal coding, a person applies verbal labels to a model's behavior as it develops and thus learns its verbal description. The verbal recall of a model's behavior, then, can serve as a cue for guiding the person through imitative responses.

The *motoric reproduction process* operates through a person's ideomotor mechanism so as to govern the integration of constituent acts into a response pattern, thereby giving the person skill in a given performance. The learning of many skilled acts, such as auto driving, requires many small components to be mastered. The sequence of components may be verbally coded as a result of one's observation, but the fine motor coordination that is required in using the components correctly may be achievable only through gradual shaping of the desired skill by practice accompanied by feedback of results.

The *observational reinforcement process* consists of a person translating into action the ideas of behaviors that have been formed through observation and observing the consequences. The likelihood that an observed behavior will be imitated is influenced by the events that have followed it. But the control of behavior does not reside in mere sequential conditions. Incentive and motivational processes determine which observationally acquired responses will actually be performed. A person tends to perform, or to inhibit, a vicariously learned response to the degree that he/she thinks that he will be rewarded or punished for performance of the act. By affecting what and whom a person attends and how actively he/she codes and rehearses the modeled behavior, reinforcement also influences the level of observational learning that prevails.

HOW MAY SOCIAL COGNITIVE THEORY BE APPLIED?

"Social cognitive theory, in its broad form, is concerned with the acquisition of cognitive and behavioral skills, as well as with the knowledge of what leads to what."[47] Its adherents stress the informative and motivational functions of prospective outcomes of activities. They think that rewards enhance performance, not because they automatically reinforce prior behavior but because they motivate people anticipatorily. People anticipate the likely consequences of their prospective actions, set goals for themselves, and plan courses of action for their futures as they see them. "Through exercise of forethought people motivate themselves and guide their actions anticipatorily."[48] So, *expectancy* is given an increasingly prominent place in explanations of behavior, and people are deemed active agents in their own motivation. (*Expectancy*, as used in social cognitive theory, is quite similar to *insights* and *understandings*, as used in cognitive-field theory.)

"In the social cognitive view, outcomes change behavior in humans largely through the intervening influence of thought."[49] Cognitive skills enable people to conduct the solution of most of their problems through thought rather than through physical movement. So, human thought is a powerful agency that enables persons to understand and deal effectively with their environments as it furnishes large stores of knowledge in the form of abstract representations of experiences. Through observing outcomes of their actions, people construct conceptions of new behavior patterns accompanied by recognized circumstances in which the new patterns may appropriately be manifested.

Symbols, especially language ones that represent cognitive operations and relationships, serve as vehicles of thought. Since "most external influences affect behavior through intermediary cognitive processes,"[50] cognitive factors largely determine which environmental events will be observed, what meanings will be given them, and how the information that they portend will be organized for future use.

Bandura has stated that "psychology cannot tell people how they ought to live their lives. It can, however, provide them with the means for effecting personal and social change. And it can aid them in making value choices by assessing the consequences of alternative life-styles and institutional arrangements. As a science concerned with the social consequences of its applications, psychology must promote public understanding of psychological issues that bear on social policies to ensure that its findings are used in the service of human betterment."[51]

Improved knowledge of psychological techniques does not necessarily raise the quality of social control, nor does it grant anyone license to impose behaviors on others. Thus, psychologists should not install a system of morals; but they can provide a means for personal and social change.

Although social cognitive theory is aimed at the functions of people in general in their various social relationships, it has some definite implications for teaching procedures. Much of the teaching function actually consists of modeling. Also, "control through information, which is rooted in cognitive processes, is more pervasive and powerful than conditioning through contiguity of events."[52] The net effects of presenting reinforcers as soon as requisite responses were emitted "was a tedious shaping process that produced, at best, mediocre results in an ethically questionable manner."[53] Social cognitive theory describes how a set of social and personal competences—a personality—can evolve from the social conditions that prevail. "Whatever their orientations, people model, expound, and reinforce what they value."[54]

Bandura states that "a large body of research now exists in which cognition is activated instructionally with impressive results. People learn and retain much better by using cognitive aids that they generate than by repetitive reinforced performance."[55] Therefore, he criticizes those behavioristic theories that emphasize performance and de-emphasize awareness determinants. Yet he does not attack the concept of reinforcement; instead, he redefines it. Keep in mind, however, that he also does not condone the idea of existential-humanistic personal determinism. "In a complete account of human behavior, internal processes must eventually be tied to action."[56] Thus, for Bandura, *socially defined freedom* and reciprocal personal-social relationships should prevail over either environmental or personal determinism.

"People do not indiscriminantly absorb the influences that impinge upon them"[57] But they also do not exercise absolute freedom. Instead, "freedom is defined in terms of the number of options available to people and the right to exercise them."[58] Freedom, so defined, can be expanded by people cultivating their competencies. But anyone's attempt to exercise absolute freedom is sure to clash with the exercise of someone else's freedom.

At all levels of human relationships, because of the existence of reciprocal consequences, no one can manipulate others at will; everyone experiences some degree of powerlessness in getting others to behave in definite ways. For example, neither parents nor teachers can get children to conform to all their wishes. People resist being taken advantage of because, in some situations, compliant behavior produces unfavorable consequences. Therefore, reciprocal human relationship is one of the conditioner and the conditioned—the teacher and his students—operating as personal, behavioral, and environmental determinants of one another's behaviors.

Cognitive learning is promoted through tuition, modeling, and performance feedback. The modes of learning—modeling, enactive exploration, conditioning, and verbal instruction—represent different ways of conveying information about behavior and predictive relationships between events in the environment. Consequences serve as an unarticulated way of informing people of what they must do in order to produce certain results. By observing the differential outcomes of their actions, people eventually construct conceptions of new behavior patterns and circumstances within which it is appropriate to perform those patterns.

Since skilled activities are seldom repeated in exactly the same way, learning must be conceptually generative in nature so that it may be varied to fit different circumstances. "It is because people learn generative conceptions, rather than specific acts, that human skills have remarkable flexibility and utility."[59] After children grasp the conception of a triangle, they can draw large or small ones with either hand or foot and create triangular paths with different materials even though they have never before produced the particular new triangular constructions. "A generative conception serves two functions: It provides the rules for producing appropriate response patterns, and it provides the standard for improving performance on the basis of perceived discrepancies between conception and execution."[60]

NOTES

1. See Albert Bandura, *Social Foundations of Thought and Action: A Social Cognitive Theory* (Englewood Cliffs, NJ: Prentice Hall, 1986).
2. Gordon H. Bower and Ernest K. Hilgard, *Theories of Learning* (Englewood Cliffs, NJ: Prentice Hall, 1981), p. 472.
3. Walter Mischel, "Toward a Cognitive Social Learning Reconceptualization of Personality," in Norman S. Endler and David Magnusson, eds., *Interactional Psychology and Personality* (Washington, DC: Hemisphere, 1976), p. 192.
4. Norman T. Feather, "Introduction and Overview," in Norman T. Feather, ed., *Expectations and Actions: Expectancy-Value Models in Psychology* (Hillsdale, NJ: Erlbaum, 1982), p. 3.
5. Bandura, *Social Foundations of Thought and Action*, p. XI.
6. Julian B. Rotter, "The Psychological Situation in Social-Learning Theory." In David Magnusson ed., *Toward a Psychology of Situations: An Interactional Perspective* (Hillsdale, NJ: Erlbaum, 1981), p. 171.
7. David Magnusson, "Problems in Environmental Analysis—An Introduction." in Magnusson, ed., *Toward a Psychology of Situations*, pp. 31–32.
8. K. S. Bowers, "Situationism in Psychology: An Analysis and a Critique." In Endler and Magnusson, eds., *Interactional Psychology and Personality*, p. 154.
9. Bernard Weiner, *Theories of Motivation* (Chicago: Markham, 1972), p. 423.
10. Albert Bandura, *Social Foundations of Thought and Action*, p. 23.
11. See B. F. Skinner, *Recent Issues In the Analysis of Behavior* (Columbus, OH: Merrill Publishing Company, 1989), pp. 61–64 and 122.
12. Albert Bandura, "Social Learning Theory," in Benjamin B. Wolman, ed., *International Encyclopedia of Psychiatry, Psychology, Psychoanalysis & Neurology*, Vol. 10 (New York: Aesculapius, 1977), p. 314.
13. Albert Bandura, "Behavior Theory and the Models of Man," *American Psychologist* 29 (December 1974): 859.
14. Bandura, *Social Foundations of Thought and Action*, p. 18.
15. Albert Bandura, *Principles of Behavior Modification* (New York: Holt, Rinehart and Winston, 1969), p. 623.
16. Bandura, "Behavior Theory and the Models of Man," p. 867.
17. Bandura, "Social Learning Theory," p. 310.
18. Bandura, "Behavior Theory and the Models of Man," p. 860.
19. Bandura, *Social Foundations of Thought and Action*, p. 454.
20. Ibid., p. 21.
21. Ibid., p. 19.
22. Ibid., p. 475.

23. Ibid., p. 867.
24. Ibid., p. 867.
25. Bandura, "Social Learning Theory," p. 311.
26. Ibid., p. 311.
27. Bandura, *Social Foundations of Thought and Action*, p. 12.
28. Ibid., p. 486.
29. Bandura, "Social Learning Theory," p. 314.
30. Ibid., p. 313.
31. Bandura, "Social Learning Theory," p. 313.
32. Ibid., p. 313.
33. See Bandura, "Behavior Theory and the Models of Man," p. 860.
34. See Bandura, *Social Learning Theory*, p. 19, for a summary of research that supports this statement.
35. Bandura, "Behavior Theory and the Models of Man," p. 860.
36. Albert Bandura, *Social Learning Theory* (New York: General Learning Press, 1971), p. 10.
37. Ibid., pp. 165–166. Contains a summary of this research.
38. Ibid., p. 10.
39. Ibid., p. 312.
40. Bandura, "Behavior Theory and the Models of Man," p. 861.
41. Ibid., p. 863.
42. Ibid., p. 868.
43. Ibid., p. 310.
44. Bandura, *Social Foundations of Thought and Action*, p. 19.
45. Ibid., p. 78.
46. Bandura, "Behavior Theory and the Models of Man," p. 864.
47. Bandura, *Social Foundations of Thought and Action*, p. 413.
48. Ibid., p. 19.
49. Ibid., p. 111.
50. Ibid., p. 454.
51. Ibid., p. 213.
52. Bandura, "Behavior Theory and the Models of Man," p. 862.
53. Ibid., p. 862.
54. Bandura, *Social Learning Theory*, p. 211.
55. Bandura, "Behavior Theory and the Models of Man," p. 865.
56. Ibid., p. 865.
57. Ibid., p. 862.
58. Ibid., p. 865.
59. Ibid., p. 111.
60. Ibid., p. 111.

BIBLIOGRAPHY, CHAPTER 7

Bandura, Albert. *Principles of Behavior Modification*. New York: Holt Rinehart and Winston, 1969. Bandura's first book. Develops reciprocal interaction theory as basis for behavior modification. Develops concept of self-monitoring reinforcement.

Bandura, Albert. *Psychological Modeling: Conflicting Theories*. Chicago: Aldine-Atherton, 1971. Develops conflicting models of humankind and their consequences.

Bandura, Albert. *Social Learning Theory.* New York: General Learning Press, 1971. Bandura's most complete development of social (cognitive) learning theory with summarization of pertinent research.

Bandura, Albert. "Behavior Theory and the Models of Man." *American Psychologist* 29 (December 1974): 859–869. Presidential address to American Psychological Association. Sets his position versus both environmental determinism and existentialism.

Bandura, Albert. *Aggression: A Social Learning Analysis.* Englewood Cliffs, NJ: Prentice Hall, 1975. Treats psychology of aggression within context of social cognitive learning theory.

Bandura, Albert. "Social Learning Analysis of Aggression." In Ribes-Inesta, Emilio and Albert Bandura, eds. *Analysis of Delinquency and Aggression.* Hillsdale, NJ: Lawrence Erlbaum, 1976, pp. 203–232. Treats acquisition and instigation of aggressive behavior as processes of direct and observational learning.

Bandura, Albert. "Social Learning Theory." In Wolman, Benjamin B., ed. *International Encyclopedia of Psychiatry, Psychology, Psychoanalysis, & Neurology.* New York: Aesculapius, 1977, Vol. 10, pp. 309–314. A concise, highly readable statement of social learning (cognitive) theory.

Bandura, Albert. *Social Foundations of Thought and Action: A Social Cognitive Theory.* Englewood Cliffs, NJ: Prentice Hall, 1986. A theoretical framework for analysis of human motivation, thought, action and learning within a social-interactionist perspective.

Bower, Gordon H. and Ernest R. Hilgard. *Theories of Learning.* 5th ed. Englewood Cliffs, NJ: Prentice Hall, 1981. The authors present the high points of Bandura's social learning theory.

Popp, Jerome A. *New Goals for the Nineteen Eighties in Philosophy of Education 1980: Proceedings of the Thirty-Sixth Annual Meeting of the Philosophy of Education Society.* Normal, IL: Philosophy of Education Society, 1981, pp. 292–301. Sets Piagetian "innatism" versus Skinnerian radical behaviorism, then recommends Bandura's social learning theory as the way out of the dilemma.

Chapter
8

What Is the Cognitive-Field Interactionist Theory of Learning?

*C*ognitive-field interactionist learning theory has emerged as a current synthesis whose basic paradigm or model, life spaces, centers upon a *person's* interaction with his contemporaneous psychological environment. This learning theory has developed as an emergent synthesis, arising from active-subjective and the opposite passive-objective extremes in dealing with human motivation and learning (see page 12 for an explanation of the meaning of *emergent synthesis*). Within this psychology, learning is neither equated with unfoldment and sheer expression of inner urges nor with the result of a conditioning process that comes from the environment's impinging upon a biological organism from without. Instead, cognitive-field interactionists focus their meaning of learning upon the aspects of a situation within which a *person* and his *psychological environment* come together in a psychological field or *life space*. (Throughout this chapter and Chapter 9, the expressions *cognitive-field interactionism* and *cognitive-field psychology* are used interchangeably.)

Kurt Lewin produced the root ideas of cognitive-field psychology. He was educated in Germany and he did much of his writing in German. He moved to the United States during the Hitler regime. Here, Lewin's colleagues translated his basic ideas into English. Lewin carried the German pronounciation of his name most of his life. But shortly before his death he Americanized the pronounciation of his name.

Sometimes conventional English terminology is inadequate to explain cognitive-field interactionist psychology. Hence, it has become necessary for students of this position to develop some specialized vocabulary to communicate this position. One of your authors (Bigge) centered his doctoral dissertation on Lewin's works. So, he has been much involved in understanding and explaining cognitive-field psychology. Here, the authors have used some special words with special meanings only to the degree that they are necessary to communicate the position.

Adherents of cognitive-field interactionism recognize that this approach to learning and teaching has its specialized language which is difficult to comprehend. But, they also recognize that it is quite rewarding in its application to school situations.

HOW MAY LINEAR COGNITIVE-INTERACTIONIST LEARNING THEORY COMPLEMENT COGNITIVE-FIELD INTERACTIONIST LEARNING THEORY?

Linear cognitive-interactionist (Chapter 7) and cognitive-field interactionist (Chapters 8 and 9) learning theories have much in common. Their significant difference is that, whereas linear interactionists take person-environment interactions to be occurring serially, cognitive-field interactionists take such interactions to be occurring simultaneously. Principal similarities of the two positions are that both psychologies are purposive ones and both underpin exploratory and explanatory understanding levels of teaching and learning. Hence, they are parallel and complementary, not opposing approaches (see Chapter 13). In fact, these two cognitive approaches to teaching and learning have so much in common that a teacher who is committed to their use may well employ the concepts of both and may even strive to develop a synthesis of the two.

WHAT ARE THE SOURCES OF COGNITIVE-FIELD INTERACTIONIST LEARNING THEORY?

Cognitive-field interactionism draws most heavily from the pioneer works of Kurt Lewin (1890–1947), Edward C. Tolman, John Dewey (1859–1953), Boyd H. Bode, Donald Snygg (1904-), Ernest E. Bayles, and Maurice P. Hunt (1915–1979).

Lewin developed the principles of *topological and vector psychology*.[1] In developing his psychology, he borrowed ideas and concepts from other disciplines, the key ones being *topology* from geometry and *vector* from physics. However, in using these and related concepts, he construed them in a manner most useful to his system of psychology. (The meanings of these concepts are developed in pages 185–197.)

Tolman wrote *Purposive Behavior in Animals and Men*,[2] which centered upon human purposiveness within a behavioristic orientation. Dewey, in his *Experience and Education*,[3] presaged cognitive-field interactionism. He wrote that one's living in a world means that one lives in a series of situations (life spaces) (p. 41); that an experience is characterized as a transaction (interaction) occurring between an individual (person) and what *at the time* constitutes his environment (p. 41); and that the longitudinal and lateral aspects of experience are continuity and interaction (p. 42) within which "life space and life-durations are expanded" (p. 188).

Bode in his *How We Learn*,[4] defined *self* (person) in experiential terms. He wrote that we form concepts or constructs, then we use them as instruments with which to analyze situations (life spaces) so as to discover their possibilities, and that the concept of one's self or person is formed by the ideals or interests that one cherishes and that one's self or person is not one but many; it is constantly in the making as it expands in one direction and contracts in another (p. 112–115).

Snygg originated the concept of *cognitive-field psychology*. Bayles developed a *goal-insight* theory of purposive learning based upon works of Bode, Raymond B. Wheeler, and John Dewey. Hunt co-authored *Psychological Foundations of Education*, within which the concept of cognitive-field psychology was first developed in a textbook.[5]

A number or other psychologists have also made worthy contributions to cognitive-field interactionism, even though some have not identified themselves or their ideas with this theory as such. These include Gordon W. Allport, Adelbert Ames, Jr., Roger G. Barker, Hadley Cantril, Morton Deutsch, Norman T. Feather, Sigmund Koch, and Rollo May. More recent contributions have been made by the research and ideas of Albert Bandura (1925-), Jerome S. Bruner, Richard de Charms (1927-), Edward L. Deci (1942-), Walter Mischel, and Bernard Weiner.[6] In this chapter and Chapter 9 we draw upon the thinking and research of these people to develop an effective current psychological position and outlook.

Cognitive-field interactionist theory draws heavily from the pioneer field psychology of Kurt Lewin. However, it is not merely a restatement of Lewin's position. This German-American psychologist was interested primarily in a study of human motivation. Consequently, his field theory was developed not as a theory of learning but more as a theory of motivation and perception. However, he was concerned with the application of his theory to learning situations and did some writing in this vein.[7] Lewin's basic, comprehensive concept was *life space*. Consequently, life space has become the basic model for cognitive-field psychological thinking. It includes what one needs to know about a person in order to understand that person's concrete behavior in a specific psychological situation at a given time. Accordingly, it encompasses the *person* under consideration and the person's *psychological environment*.

One's *person*, as used here, is achieved; it includes everything that, at a given time, one is involved in taking care of. It consists of every thing, idea or principle with which one identifies one's self and to which one gives one's allegiance. Hence it is constituted of all of one's interests or involvements.

A unique *psychological environment* envelops a person and is surrounded by a nonpsychological environment, referred to as the *foreign hull*. A person's psychological environment is that which he/she makes of aspects of his psychical and social environment. It includes every thing, function, or relationship that, at a given time, surrounds the person as well as the meaning that each has for him. Hence, it is what a person makes of the aspects of his physical-social environment.

The basic thesis of cognitive-field interactionism is that each person, in keeping with his attained level of development and understanding, does the best that he/she knows how for whatever he thinks he is. In this process a person is inclined to "engage in behaviors which leads to the most valent [attractive] goals."[8]

The cognitive-field interactionist theory of learning is closely related to, and derived from, *cognitive* and *field* psychological theories.[9] The term *cognitive* is derived from the Latin verb *cognoscere*, which means "to know." The *cognitive* aspect of cognitive-field theory deals with the problem of how people gain an understanding of themselves and their environments and how, using their cognitions, they act in relation to their environments. A psychological *field* consists of the simultaneous concurrent interrelationships of a person and his psychology environment in any one situation. Hence, field theory in psychology centers on the idea that all psychological activity of a person, within a given unit of time, is a function of a totality of coexisting factors that are mutually interdependent.

An astronomer uses gravitational fields to describe the universe and predict the orbits of stars. A biologist relates the function of cells to their location in a growth field. A physicist uses electromagnetic fields in describing the structure of an atom. Similarly, a cognitive-field oriented psychologist uses *field* to mean the total psychological world in which a person lives at a given time. It includes a *psychological* past, present, and future, and also a certain concrete or imaginative level of psychological reality—all interpreted as simultaneous aspects of a current situation.

WHAT IS THE PURPOSE OF COGNITIVE-FIELD INTERACTIONIST LEARNING THEORY?

The purpose of cognitive-field interactionism is to formulate tested relationships that are predictive of the behavior of individual persons in their specific life spaces or psychological situations. In order to understand and predict such behavior, one must consider a person and the person's psychological environment as a pattern of interdependent factors and functions. *If one is to grasp the meaning of cognitive-field psychology, it is imperative that one grasp the unique meanings of the psychological terms, factors and functions used in its development and explanation.*

This psychology is an interpersonal, social one that constitutes an effective vehicle for understanding people as interacting persons. In the interactive process a person and his psychological environment are construed as *interdependent* variables. A person is neither dependent upon, nor independent of, his environment. Likewise, a person's environment is neither made by nor independent of him.

Within cognitive-field interactionism, learning, briefly defined, is a process within which a person attains new insights or cognitive structures or changes old ones. The ideas of this psychology have been developed with the hope and expectation that they will help teachers do a better job of understanding other persons, but it may also help teachers understand themselves better. Cognitive-field psychology makes no attempt to describe some absolute reality that is just there independently of our experiencing it. Instead, it develops a psychological system that is fruitful in dealing with children and youth in learning situations. It has been formulated in an attempt to construct scientific principles that are highly applicable to classroom situations. Advocates of cognitive-field psychology are convinced that in light of the present stage of scientific development, this theory is more likely than any other of which they are cognizant to lead to the most productive results in classroom procedures.

Within cognitive-field interactionism, one starts with a model or map of a person and the surrounding world as it is pertinent to that person. The purpose of the life-space model is to enhance the prediction of psychological behavior— that which is related to goals. As our knowledge of a child's or youth's life space increases, our ability to predict that person's behavior accurately also increases. Learning is the development of insights into the nature of the person's world as represented by the model. Life space—the psychological model—contains the person; the person's psychological environment; the goals that the person is seeking; the negative "goals" that the person is attempting to avoid; the barriers between the person and his goals that restrict his psychological movement toward them; and the potential and actual paths to his goals. (Psychological *paths* are ways of achieving goals. See Figure 8.1).

This theory of learning describes how a person gains understanding of himself and his universe in a situation so construed that both his self and his psychological environment compose a totality of mutually interdependent, coexisting factors. It involves the kind of generalizations about learning that may be applied to actual persons in school situations, and it is associated with the knowing and understanding functions that give meaning to situations. It is built around the purposes that underlie behavior, the goals that are involved in behavior, and persons' means and processes of understanding themselves and their environments as they function in relation to their goals. Any understandings

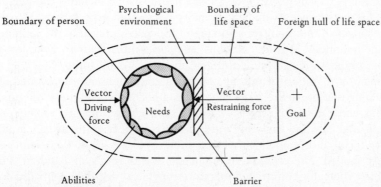

Figure 8.1 Life space of an individual.

that persons gain in regard to themselves and their worlds are generalized *insights*.

WHAT IS AN INSIGHT?

An insight, concisely defined, is a basic sense of, or feeling for, relationships; it is a meaning or discernment. A tested generalized insight is an understanding; it is a meaning or discernment that one may profitably apply to several or even many similar, but not necessarily identical, situations or processes. Although there is nothing about an insight that requires it to be right in any absolutist sense, it is a grasp of a situation that often does go deeper than words. Thus, it is a realizing sense of a matter. Insight into a situation is its meaning. The insights of a person, however, are not equated with his consciousness, awareness, or ability to describe matters verbally; instead, their essence is a sense of or feeling for pattern in a life situation. (See Chapter 9, page 206 for further explanation of insight.)

Development of insight means getting the feel of, grasping the idea of, catching on to, or seeing through a situation. One acquires an insight through either actually or symbolically doing something and seeing what happens. Although some activity is necessary, the focus of the learning is on the seeing, not, as has been assume by behaviorists, on the doing. *Seeing*, here, is broadly defined to mean catching the point or getting the idea. Any or all of the senses may be involved, and the sensory action may be pronounced, or it may be so rudimentary that the person involved may not realize it is occurring.

A person may gain an insight through experiencing a single case. However, the most valuable insights are those confirmed by enough similar cases to be generalized into an *understanding*. A tested generalized insight—an understanding—is a meaning that enables one to use a pattern of ideas and their supporting facts in a productive manner; it is an expectation or recognized rule.

A person's insights collectively constitute the cognitive structure of his life space. *Cognitive structure* means the person's perception of the psychological aspects of the personal, physical, and social *world*, which includes the person and all of his facts, concepts, beliefs, memory traces, and expectations. Consequently, changes in the cognitive structure of life spaces prevail in the learning of language, emotions, attitudes, actions, and social interrelations. Now, let us review an episode of insightful learning as observed by the author.

During World War II the author watched a group of noncommissioned officers teaching recruits to fire army rifles (the author was one of these recruits). Army rifles had a powerful recoil or kick. A soldier was supposed to squeeze the trigger gradually and smoothly until the rifle fired. Recruits usually anticipated the recoil and jumped before the shell exploded; thus, their aim was completely spoiled. The problem for a noncom was to teach his "student" not to make the anticipatory jump. Recruits were convinced that they really did not jump until after the explosion, thus, hours of pointed verbal comment had little effect. Corporal Jones helped his "student" gain an insight: He "scolded" him for jumping, with no avail. Then while his student's attention was diverted to a fellow sufferer, the corporal slipped a fired cartridge into the firing chamber. The recruit aimed, started to squeeze, and again jumped, thereby gaining an insight. He was jumping before his rifle fired and thus ruining his aim. His habit of jumping before the rifle had fired soon ceased.

HOW MIGHT WE TEACH INSIGHTFULLY?

Next, let us examine how we might teach a school subject insightfully. Our illustration is taken from the subject of arithmetic, specifically the teaching of the multiplication combinations involving the 9s. We use the 9s because these combinations generally are considered the most difficult. Furthermore, we use arithmetic because many teachers feel that, however one might teach other subjects, arithmetic must be taught by rote.

In what specific ways does this lesson in arithmetic differ from traditional procedures used in teaching the multiplication tables? The answer to this question will express the significance of cognitive-field psychology for learning and teaching. The teacher is attempting to aid students in improving their understandings or insights in regard to multiplying by 9 and is doing it in such a way as to heighten their abilities to achieve new insights independently; he/she is not giving students a gimmick. Let us assume that we are in the fourth-grade class and are ready to attack the 9s. We already have learned the 2s, 3s, 5s, 10s, and 11s and have learned them so as to have developed insight into the relationships involved in these tables. We can anticipate a dialogue between students and teacher that might go somewhat as follows.

The teacher reminds the students of the combinations they already know and has them review these until it is clear that they know them well. The review process might appear on the surface as drill in the old-fashioned sense, but there is a fundamental difference. The teacher makes certain that students understand the relationships involved—that is, relationships of the same general type as those they are about to learn in connection with the 9s. After the review, the teacher suggests that the class advance to the 9s. (Some students are likely to protest that the 9s are more difficult than any of the others.)

The teacher begins writing the 9s table on the chalkboard, at the same time asking members of the class to supply answers that they will already have learned from their earlier study of the other tables. A "side trip" may be necessary to help students grasp, or perhaps only review, the insight that the product of 9×2 is the same as that of 2×9 (the commutative property). What appears on the chalkboard is something like this.

$$9 \times 1 = 09 \qquad 9 \times 7 =$$
$$9 \times 2 = 18 \qquad 9 \times 8 =$$
$$9 \times 3 = 27 \qquad 9 \times 9 =$$

$9 \times 4 =$ $9 \times 10 = 90$

$9 \times 5 = 45$ $9 \times 11 = 99$

$9 \times 6 =$ $9 \times 12 =$

To this point, the answers supplied are based on students' prior learning of the 2s, 3s, 5s, 10s, and 11s. Let us now envisage the following dialogue:

TEACHER: How do we know the answers to 9×1, 9×2, and 9×3?
CLASS: Because we know the 1s, 2s and 3s.
TEACHER: And what about 9×5, 9×10, and 9×11?
CLASS: We know these because we know the 5s, 10s, and 11s.
TEACHER: The ones that are left are the hard ones, aren't they? What is the answer to 9×7, Jimmie? Tell me without looking at the tables in your book. (In this type of instruction procedure, when addressing Jimmie or any other pupil, the teacher anticipates that at least most members of the class are thinking along with the obvious student participant.)

Jimmie probably will say nothing but will stare at the teacher, baffled. The teacher may then ask various other members of the class the answer to 9×6, 9×8, and 9×4. After the class begins to demonstrate a certain amount of bafflement (perhaps approaching the point of mild frustration), the teacher may entice them in this manner: "Would you like to gain enough understanding of the rest of the 9s so that after today you will known the answers to all of them?" The class is likely to respond in the affirmative with considerable enthusiasm.

TEACHER: All right, let's work at this thing together. June, go to the board and write the 10s up to 10×5 right beside the 9s. (The class will now have before it the following combinations.)

$10 \times 1 = 10$ $9 \times 1 = 09$

$10 \times 2 = 20$ $9 \times 2 = 18$

$10 \times 3 = 30$ $9 \times 3 = 27$

$10 \times 4 = 40$ $9 \times 4 =$

$10 \times 5 = 50$ $9 \times 5 = 45$

TEACHER: When we compare the 9s that we have answered to the 10s, what difference do we see in the answers? What happens in the case of the 9s that did not happen in the 10s?
CLASS: Each step we move up in the 9s, one is lost.
TEACHER: How do you mean?
CLASS: 9×1 is one fewer than 10×1, 9×2 is two fewer than 10×2, and 9×3 is three fewer than 10×3. That is why we get the answers 09, 18, and 27.

Of course, finding this principle may not come so easily as the foregoing dialogue might suggest. The teacher might need to do quite a lot more "fishing" by rephrasing the question and perhaps even offering some hints. The speed with which a class comes to see for itself principles that are new to it depends much upon what atmosphere has been established and, of course, on the brightness of the students.

The teacher next helps students see that as in the 10s, the first digit goes up one each time, 09, 18, 27. By this time, the stage should be set for supplying the missing answers.

TEACHER: Now think carefully about what we have learned. Since $9 \times 2 = 18$ and $9 \times 3 = 27$, Gary, what is the answer to 9×4?

GARY: Well, if the first number increased by one for each larger table, and if we lose one in the last number of each table upward, it would have to be 36.

TEACHER: You already know the answer to 9×5. Judy, does it check with the idea that we have learned?

JUDY: Sure the first number will be one larger, and we will have lost five numbers from the second number. That makes 45.

The reader should not be misled by the foregoing hypothetical dialogue. In order to economize on space, students have been pictured as saying the right thing the first time. In an actual classroom situation there would be more hesitancy, more fumbling, more tries on the part of students and teacher. But the process would remain essentially the same.

The class is now ready to deepen its insights in relation to the multiplication process.

TEACHER: Look again at the first digit of each answer. (Teacher points to the 9s through 9×5.) Look at each of these digits in relation to the multipliers, 1, 2, 3, 4, and 5. Do you see anything interesting?

GARY: Why, the first digit of the answer is always just one number smaller than the multiplier.

TEACHER: Why do you think this is so?

GARY: Would this be caused by losing a number each time—I mean, losing a number as compared to the 10s?

The teacher has succeeded in evoking the insight (at least in Gary) that when one multiplies by 9 rather than 10, there is a loss of one at each step, including the first. The answers "never catch up," so to speak. They keep falling behind, but according to a definite and predictable pattern.

Still another relationship may be taught the class:

TEACHER: Look carefully at the answers that we have so far. (The teacher points to 09, 18, 27, 36, and 45.) Add the two digits of each answer and see what happens.

CLASS: The sum of the digits is the same in each answer. The sum is always 9.

TEACHER: Yes. $0 + 9 = 9$; $1 + 8 = 9$; $2 + 7 = 9$. Why is this so?

CLASS: $9 \times 1 = 9$, then the first digit always increases by one, and the second digit decreases by one. They kind of balance each other, so the sum remains the same.

By this time the stage has been set for teaching the remaining combinations involving the 9s. When asked the answer to 9×7, students should reason that the first digit of the answer will be 6 $(7 - 1)$ and that the second digit should be 3 $(9 - 6)$. The class should now be able to complete the combinations through 9×10 easily. At 9×11, the first digit of the answer becomes two less than the multiplier. (Why?) Furthermore, the sum of the two digits of the answer does not equal 9, as it did in each preceding step. (Again, why?) Students will know the answer is 99. The problem is, why? Answer: $9 \times 10 = 90$; at 9×11 "we start around again"; $90 + 9 = 99$. At 9×11 the first digit of the answer has lost two from the multiplier: $11 - 2 = 9$, so in 9×12 the first part of the answer is $12 - 2$ or 10. For the sum of the digits to add to 9, the last digit is 8. Thus, $12 \times 9 = 108$. This can be extended into a game.

$13 \times 9 = 117$

$14 \times 9 = 126$

$15 \times 9 = 135$

The class members are now ready to test their new insights to see whether they will work. The teacher may suggest to the better students that they put into words the insights they have learned. However, it should be borne in mind that it is not always necessary for one to put an insight into words in order to use it.

HOW DOES COGNITIVE-FIELD INTERACTIONIST LEARNING THEORY DIFFER FROM THE STIMULUS-RESPONSE CONDITIONING THEORIES?

Since cognitive-field interactionists are convinced that psychological activity depends upon energy related to psychological tension systems, stimulus-response conditioning principles do not adequately explain learning activity. They challenge forcefully the principle of adhesion, the attachment of one thing to another so that revival of the first brings forth the second. Furthermore, they think that reward and punishment do not stamp in and stamp out learnings. In contrast with the practices of behaviorists, they stress the importance of viewing the changes in the valences (attracting and repelling powers) of aspects of a person's psychological environment, and in the tension systems of the person in relation to his environment, as crucial to the description of the learning process. "So-called conditional reactions are largely self-activated on the basis of learned expectations rather than automatically evoked."[10]

Whereas behavioristic psychologies are biological-organism centered, cognitive-field psychology is psychological-person centered. *Organism* suggests a mechanism and human passivity; *person*, in contrast, suggests purposiveness and interactivity. Consequently, whereas behavioristic psychologies have emphasized overt behavior, cognitive-field interactionism has been concerned with outward behavior only insofar as it may provide clues to what is transpiring psychologically or perceptually. *Psychological*, as used here, refers to purposive personal involvement.

Cognitive-field interactionists do not deny the validity, for certain purposes, of the study of the physiological behavior of human beings, but they think that physiological and psychological study represent two different scientific dimensions, each with its own uses. Since these psychologists consider the teaching function to be most closely associated with psychological or cognitive processes, they confine their emphasis to a study of how the cognitive structures of a psychological field are achieved or changed, that is, how insight is developed. A cognitive-field interactionist teacher wants to see changed behavior as evidence of students' learning but insists that the change in overt behavior, as such, is not the learning. Whereas a behavioristic teacher desires to change the measurable behaviors of students in a planned way, a cognitive-field-oriented teacher aspires to help the students increase their understanding of themselves and their psychological worlds as well as of significant processes and problems.

Cognitive-field psychologists establish order, but they go about it differently from the way behaviorists do. They benefit from the experimentation performed under other banners, but they also develop their own unique types of scientific research. Their experimentation involves the study of such matters as the nature of cognitive processes, the recall of uncompleted tasks, the relationship of levels of achievement and levels of aspiration, psychological ecology, group dynamics, action research, concepts of self, personality rigidity, individual and social perception, and reflective teaching.

Whereas a behaviorist restricts his generalizations to those based upon the use of "objective" data, a cognitive-field interactionist knowingly uses constructs that go beyond the observable data. A *construct* is an invented idea. It is a named generalized concept that is not directly observable but formed from data that are observed. Its purpose is to correlate a broad range of data that have some basic functional similarity despite their marked superficial differences. A *need*, psychologically defined, is an example of a construct. Since it has no length, breadth, thickness, or mass, it cannot be observed. Yet it is a crucial, functional concept in studying human activity. *The meanings of all the constructs are mutually interdependent.* Each depends for its meaning upon the meanings of all the others. Thus, there are no independent, dependent, and intervening variables, as in the behaviorisms. *Instead, all the variables or constructs are interdependent.*

Some features of cognitive-field interactionism that make it distinctly different from mechanistic S-R conditioning approaches are (1) its emphasis upon psychological functions, (2) its viewing intelligent behavior as purposive, (3) its focus upon contemporaneous situations, (4) its viewing interactions of persons and their environments as being simultaneous and mutual, not alternating, and (5) its relativistic-interactional approach to understanding perception.

Why Emphasis Upon Psychological Functions?

A basic feature of cognitive-field interactionism is its emphasis upon psychological functions or events as contrasted with physical objects or movements. "It is evident that a cognitive functionalism is being developed that is every bit as precise and as scientific as behavioral functionalism."[11]

Psychological, as used here, means "in accordance with the logic of a growing mind or intelligence." Thus, to be psychological in investigating learning, one must look at the world through the eyes of the learner. To describe a situation psychologically, he/she must, to the best of his ability, describe the situation that confronts the individual under study. Such a situation is viewed as a pattern of person-environmental relationships that provides and limits opportunities. Once the personal-environmental structure is established, the problem is to use psychological constructs and methods to deal with the underlying dynamics of behavior and to do this in a scientifically sound manner.

Cognitive-field interactionists do not deny the importance of the workings of the nervous system. Furthermore, they are interested in the results of recent research in neurophysiological functions. But they do challenge the need to understand biological neurology in order to develop an adequate picture of the learning process. Hilgard and Bower have written "Both the nervous system and its behavior are complicated and neither will be understood with any completeness for a long time."[12] However, this does not mean that it is impossible to develop an adequate and harmonious conception of learning.

Why the Emphasis Upon Purposiveness of Intelligent Behavior?

The basic thesis of cognitive-field psychology is that any person, at his level of development, does the best that he/she knows how for whatever he thinks he is. Any boy or girl in any situation, at the time that he/she is doing whatever he is doing, is doing that because, in keeping with the understandings that he holds at that particular time, it is the best way that he knows to take care of himself.

A human being is born a very complex biological organism in a social environment. Throughout the waking hours, as a baby, later as a child, and then as a youth, he/she learns by trying various acts and seeing what happens. Thus, through purposive living in a human environment, an individual develops as a person or self. (Within this position, *person* and *self* are synonymous concepts and are used interchangeably.)

A normal process of development produces self-involvement with objects, people, groups, and social organizations in a physical and social environment. In a negative sense, a human organism growing up in complete isolation probably would not develop a self-concept or appear to others as a personality. It seems reasonable to assume that such a person would have no basis for distinguishing between right and wrong, no developed aesthetic sense, and no use of language or symbols; consequently, he/she would be incapable of abstract thinking.

Only by living in a human world and having a biological organism of a unique type does a biological human being emerge as a psychological person or self. "Each mature individual discriminates between self and the rest of the world; each has a sense of himself or herself as a distinct entity."[13] The form that the development of selfhood takes depends upon the learning that results from the purposive interaction of the person and his psychological environment.

This contrasts sharply with S-R conditioning theories, which either ignore goal or purpose completely or make it only peripheral and incidental.

Behaviorists have tended to consider any concept of goal-direction or pur-posiveness to be teleological—that is, deriving present behavior from a fixed future, that is supernaturally endowed with purpose and transcends the present physical world. Consequently, to them, it sounds mystical and superstitious. So they have placed emphasis upon past events as the cause of present behavior and have seemed to overlook the possibility of the "presentness" of causes of behavior. It is because cognitive-field interactionism is goal-centered that its adherents inveigh against the use of such mechanistic terms as reflex arc, connectionism, conditioning, associationism, and mechanistic reinforcement.

Within cognitive-field interactionism, *purposive* is virtually a synonym for *intelligent*: it signifies an intentionality that may or may not be conscious. A unique characteristic of human beings is their capacity to pursue long-sighted, as well as short-sighted, self-interests. Cognitive-field psychologists recognize the significance of this fact. When a child or youth is behaving purposively, he/she is pursuing his goals in light of the insights he has available; he is behaving intelligently. The goal or goals toward which the individual strives psychologically exist in his present life space. The phenomenon of goal is such that expectation—not actual realization—is its essence. Although the content of a goal may be in the future or may not occur at all, the goal as a psychological fact necessarily lies in the present life space. For example, a student's goal to become a teacher is a goal toward teaching as the student now sees it. However, this goal may be a far cry from teaching as it eventually is experienced.

The purposiveness of cognitive-field interaction theory means operating within, not beyond, the world of one's experience; it prevails in workaday life situations. Careful study of people (as well as other animate beings) in life situa-tions indicates that if they are acting at all, they are trying to do something, and it is only through our anticipating what they are trying to do that we can predict most accurately what they are going to do. So, cognitive-field purposiveness means that individuals act in such ways as to achieve their goals—satisfy their wants or desires—in the quickest and easiest ways that they sense possible un-der existing conditions; they manifest intentionality; an "intention is the most critical factor in personal causation."[14] When one is motivated toward doing something, one's purposive activity is carried forward toward a goal or away from an aversion by a process of one's constantly searching out the conditions for the next step along the way.

Cognitive-field interactionists, then, emphasize situational choice. This means that within any juncture of a person's continuous, overlapping life spaces, he/she, to some extent, may choose which way he is going to move next. Cognitive-field theorists postulate that people exercise choice, but they neither assert nor imply identification with either side of the free will vs. determinism antinomy. (*Free will* is the view that there is the power within oneself to make genuine self-determining choices, particularly in regard to moral principles—discernment of ultimate good from ultimate evil. *Deter-minism* is the view that all behavior is caused and controlled by previous chains of causes and effects.) Instead, they simply hold, to quote Dewey, that "every intelligent act involves selection of certain things [activities] as means to other things [activities] as their consequences."[15]

"The basic need for feeling competent and self-determining motivates two kinds of behavior: behavior which 'seeks' optimal challenge and behavior which 'conquers' the challenge."[16] Since people make situational choices, they can and do experience success and failures. The four principal ascribed casual elements for success or failure are ability, effort, task difficulty, and luck. Whereas ability and effort are centered in persons, task difficulty and luck are identified more with environments. Furthermore, whereas ability and task difficulty are relatively stable, effort and luck are quite variable. In predicting their future success or failure, individuals assess their levels of ability in relation to the perceived difficulty of the task at hand and estimate their intended effort and the degree of luck that is involved.[17]

Why the Focus Upon Contemporaneous Situations?

Cognitive-field interactionists do not ignore the impact of previous experience on a person's contemporary life space, but in explaining the causes of behavior they focus upon the present scene as the person experiences it. Whereas mental discipline, apperception, and behaviorism are *historical* approaches to the study of human learning and motivation, cognitive-field interactionist psychology is a *situational* or *ahistorical* approach. That is, whereas the first three psychologies study the past of individuals in order to predict their future, cognitive-field psychology studies the presents of persons in order to apprehend their presents and thereby predict their futures.

Situational Emphasis   A study always begins with a description of a current situation as a whole—the psychological field or life space—and proceeds to specific detailed analyses of various aspects of the situation. At no time are aspects of a field viewed as isolated elements. In the study of a life space with its various constructs, the idea is constantly kept to the forefront that no two constructs or concepts are mutually exclusive but that everything, to some degree and in some sense, is dependent upon everything else. Readers are cautioned that should they slip into giving the constructs independent physical or biological existence, they will be attempting to understand a relativistic psychology in a mechanistic fashion. A person's living in a world entails his living in a series of situations—the person is in the situation and the situation is in the person.

Principle of Contemporaneity   The principle of contemporaneity is the essential feature of cognitive-field interactionism that is most often misunderstood. *Contemporaneity* literally means "all at one time." A psychological field or life space is a construct of such nature that is contains everything psychological that is occurring in relation to a specific person at a given time. A unit of time may be a moment, or it may cover hours or even weeks. Whatever the expanse of time, everything is going on at once—

that is the meaning of *field*. Readers are urged neither to reject the concept of contemporaneity summarily nor to give it an oversimplified interpretation.

The principle of contemporaneity means that *psychological* events are activated by conditions that prevail at the time that behavior occurs. One cannot derive behavior from either the future or the past as such. Both behaviorists and cognitive-field psychologists see little basis for supposing a future cause of present events. However, cognitive-field psychologists differ sharply from behaviorists in their insistence that any attempts at derivation of the cause of human behavior from the past is equally metaphysical, that is beyond the realm of science. Since past psychological events do not exist now, they cannot as such have any effect on the present. Thus, influence of a future can only be anticipatory, and effects of a past can only be indirect. Nevertheless, through the continuity of life spaces, past psychological fields do have their "trace" or residue in a present field, which influences a person's behavior. *Trace* is a region or condition of a present life space that has similarity to a characteristic of earlier life spaces. In other words, trace means that there is some similarity between respective regions of succeeding life spaces. This is the psychological basis of memory. When, in solving a current problem, a person uses an insight acquired earlier, the insight is an example of trace.

An individual's views about the past, as about the rest of the physical and social world, are often incorrect; nevertheless, they constitute a significant psychological past in the individual's own life space. Furthermore, the goals of an individual as a psychological fact lie in the present, and they too constitute an essential part of the individual's current life space. The contents of the goals may lie in the future and may never occur; but the nature of an expectation is not dependent upon the event's coming to pass. If a high school student is studying chemistry so that in the future he/she is more likely to gain admittance to a medical school, whether or not he eventually is actually admitted to a medical school has no bearing upon his study of chemistry in high school. His study of chemistry is a part—a goal region—of his contemporaneous life space.

The idea of the contemporaneity of a psychological field has been developing for some time. George H. Mead has written, "We live always in a present whose past and whose future are the extension of the field within which its undertakings may be carried out."[18] Kurt Lewin, the founder of field psychology, also emphasized that behavior depends upon neither the future nor the past but upon the present field. To quote him, "Since neither the [physical] past nor the [physical] future exists at the present moment it cannot have [immediate] effects at the present.[19] In 1947 Edward C. Tolman spoke of Lewin's emphasis on the ahistorical, contemporaneous, systematic determiners of behavior as an expression of a new and tremendously fruitful intellectual insight.[20] More recently, the eminent social psychologist Gordon W. Allport has stated:

> My own position, which goes under the designation *functional autonomy of motives*, holds that motivation may be—and in healthy people usually is—autonomous of its [historical] origins. Its function is to animate and steer a life toward goals that are in keeping with *present* structure, *present* aspirations and *present* conditions.[21]

Cognitive-field interactionists grant that in order to understand a person's present personality structure, they often inquire into the individual's personal history. But such inquiry is merely a means of knowing the present structure of his life space. A person's psychological field that exists at a given time contains, as well as the environment of the present, the views of that individual about the future and past. Thus, any psychological past or future is a simultaneous part of a life space that exists at a given time. It is the contemporary meaning of events that influences our behavior in relation to them. Present situations are influenced by past or future ones only if the past or future ones, as viewed in the present, make the present appear differently from what it otherwise would. Therefore, psychologically, there is no past or future except as it enters into the present (see Figure 9.2, page 205).

Psychological behavior and *locomotion* are analogous concepts. *Behavior* describes the simultaneous functional changes within a life space of an individual. *Locomotion* refers to the relative positions of respective regions of a person's *temporally continuous* life spaces. When we concentrate study upon a person and his current environmental situation, *behavior* adequately denotes changes that occur within a life space. However, when we consider a time element, a person appears to occupy a series of overlapping life spaces. The life spaces usually manifest a continuity; they are similar but not identical. Change in subsequent life spaces is *locomotion*. Consequently, depending upon whether we are centering our study upon the person-environment interactivity or the psychological continuity of a person's life spaces, we may interpret any psychological change in terms of either behavior or locomotion.

> While behavior depends to a considerable extent on externally administered consequences for actions, everyone regulates his own behavior by self-imposed goals (standards) and self-produced consequences. Even in the absence of external constraints and social monitors, we set performance goals for ourselves and react with self-criticism or self-satisfaction to our behavior depending on how well it matches our expectations and standards.[22]

Why a Relativistic-Interactional Approach to an Understanding of Perception?

Cognitive-field interactionism represents a *relativistic*, as opposed to an absolutistic *mechanistic*, way of viewing the perceptual process. Readers are warned that should they attempt to understand this concepts mechanistically, they will not grasp this theory. Mechanists explain all the fullness and variety of a universe in terms of machinelike objects and movements; accordingly, they consider a person to be an organism that is a product of its unique history of stimulus-response patterns. Consequently, they reduce all human activities to movements, usually in terms of stimuli and responses. Just as an automobile is built by workers who assemble its respective parts, a person is educated by teachers who feed into his physiological makeup the various aspects of environment that make him what mechanistic teachers want him to be. Relativists counter that when a person perceives his world, he/she does not develop a photo-

graphic image of exactly what is "out there." Instead, he views selects, sim-
plifies, compares, completes, combines, separates, and places into context the
objects of his experience. Furthermore, it is only through viewing his patterns
of experience as a whole that he/she comes to understand, and thereby is able
to explain, what he experiences. When a person perceives a thing, it is to
some degree valent—attractive or repellant—for him or the person would not
be perceiving it at all. Furthermore, perception of an object involves not only
what one senses and feels about it but also what one is inclined to do about it.

The term *interaction* is commonly used by both behaviorists and cognitive-
field interactionists in describing the person-environment process through
which reality is perceived. But the two schools define the term in sharply
different ways. Whereas behaviorists mean the *serial alternating reaction* first
of organism, then of environment, cognitive-field interactionists consider the
interaction of a person and his psychological environment to be *simultaneous*
and *mutual*—both participate at the same time.

Behavioristic Linear Alternating Reaction   Linear alternating reaction begins with a reaction of a person or organism to a stimulus. The person is regarded as a passively waiting receiver of stimuli. When one receives a stimulus,
one responds in whatever way one must, that is, in accordance with both the
innate and the conditioned behaviors that are called into play. Then, in turn,
when one reacts, one is likely to change one's physical or social environment in
some way. Thus there is passive interaction. (The environment also is passive in
the sense that it "waits" for the organism to do something to it.) To a behaviorist,
the temporal sequence of the interactive process is stimulus-reaction-stimulus-
reaction. The chain of S-Rs may continue indefinitely. Consider an example.
A dog bites a person. The person then kicks the dog. Let us suppose the kick
conditions the dog not to bite. The dog is friendly toward the next person he
encounters, and the person reacts by patting him on the head. The dog may
then react by licking the person's hand. The person may then give the dog a
bit of hamburger.

Behaviorists tend to think of interaction as involving only physical
processes—material objects reacting to other material objects. Therefore, interaction between human beings is analogous to interaction of molecules in a
chemical compound. One molecule strikes another, which is deflected against
another, which hits another, and so on. Thus, the interactive process is regarded
as a chain of causes and effects; stimuli are causes and responses are effects.

Cognitive-Field Simultaneous Mutual Interaction   *Interaction*, when
used by cognitive-field psychologists, refers to a relationship between a person
and his psychological environment in which the person in purposeful fashion
gives meaning to his environment in order to use objects in it in advantageous
ways.

Psychologically, a human life may be considered to consist of a series of
distinguishable person-environment interactions within which neither objective physical nor objective social factors have a one-to-one psychological relation

to a person. Thus, there is no known way that a person can experience the absolute nature of things in themselves. What a person does experience is *that which he/she makes of* what he gains from his environment as he pursues his various goals; humankind "is an active, construing organism rather than a passive, mechanistic being."[23]

The basic principle of *relativistic interactionism* is that nothing is perceivable or conceivable as a thing in itself. Rather, everything is perceived or conceived in relation to other things. That is, a thing is perceived as a figure against a background, experienced from a given angle of envisionment. Furthermore, how a person perceives his environment depends upon the degree of his maturity, knowledge, and goals. Consequently, psychological reality is defined, not in "objective," physical terms, but in psychological, perceptual ones.

The field or life space that influences an individual, then, is described in the way that it exists for that person at that time. There is no attempt to explain psychological behavior in terms of the relationship of a biological organism and its physical or geographical environment. Instead, psychological behavior may be (1) an overt purposive act, (2) an attitudinal shift, (3) a change in the perceived value of an object or activity, or (4) a new relationship being established between two or more events. The psychological concept *person* is much broader than the biological concept *organism*. Gone from the cognitive-field concept of interaction is the idea of the reaction of a passive organism to a stimulus and an ensuing chain of S-Rs running back and forth between organism and environment. Instead, we have a simultaneous mutual relation of a person and the person's psychological environment, during which the two are not mutually exclusive, so we do not make a sharp distinction between them. In symbolic terms, this concept is *simultaneous mutual interaction* (SMI).

Thus, *perception*, relativistically and interactionally defined, is *a cognitive experiential process within which a person, psychologically, simultaneously reaches out to his environment, encounters some aspects of it, brings those aspects into relationship with himself, makes something of those aspects, acts in relation to what he/she makes of them, and realizes the consequences of the entire process.*

It is what occurs psychologically in a person's life space at a given unit of time that is most important to that person. Since perception is interpreted in its broadest possible sense, we cannot use consciousness as the sole criterion of what is a part of a life space. A child playing in the yard behaves differently when his mother is home than when his mother is out, yet he/she probably at no time verbalizes—is specifically aware of—her being either home or away. Children in a schoolroom with teacher A conduct themselves quite differently than when they are with teacher B. Yet they may at no time consciously formulate the two patterns of behavior.

A person interacts by relating himself, as he/she understands himself, to his interpretation of what is around him. Of course, while interacting, one may move one's body and manipulate objects in one's physical environment conspicuously to observers. But psychological interaction and physical reaction are two different processes. A person can interact within a psychological field while sitting in an armchair in front of a fireplace. Human experience as an interactive event does not necessarily require any kind of motion that an observer can detect.

See if you can get the point of the following story. What is the significance of the third umpire's "relativistic" statement? What makes a ball a ball and a strike a strike?

> The story concerns three baseball umpires who were discussing the problems of their profession. The first umpire said, "Some are balls and some are strikes and I call them as they are." The second umpire said, "Some are balls and some are strikes and I call them as I see them." While the third umpire said, "I see them coming and some are balls and some are strikes but they aren't anything till I call them."[24]

Any idea can be ridden too hard, and the reader may think of cases in which the SMI concept does not seem to fit. For example, a person who is not aware of danger may be shot in the back. It seems clear that in such a case the person has been a passive victim of a feature of the environment that was active in relation to him. However, all this example suggests is that there are situations in which a person has little control over what happens to him. Adherents of cognitive-field psychology do not deny this; instead, they emphasize that, wherever possible, a person seeks to manipulate purposefully all those aspects of the environment that at the time mean anything to him. Whether or not the attempt succeeds, the person's life space will be different as a result of it.

Examples of Perceptual Interaction   In apparently the same situation a person at different times may perceive quite different aspects of a situation and behave accordingly. Furthermore, provision of opportunity for one to perceive certain aspects of a physical or social environment in a certain way by no means guarantees that that particular perception will occur or that the perception that does occur will have anything like a one-to-one relationship to the objective environment as it appears to someone else. Adelbert Ames, E. Engel, and Hadley Cantril performed experiments at the Institute for Associated Research, Hanover, New Hampshire, that show that in perception nothing is absolutely fixed. Rather, one interprets everything in terms of the situation as a whole. What one perceives, that is, one's psychological reality, consists of what one *makes of* what seems to be oneself and one's environment. Depending upon the insights or understandings that a person brings to a particular occasion, he/she seems to give meaning and order to things in terms of his own needs, abilities, and purposes.[25] A description of an experiment performed at the Hanover Institute will give some idea of the nature and significance of these studies.

Cantril experimented with a pair of stereograms. Each stereogram was a photograph of a statue in the Louvre; one a madonna with child, the other a lovely young female nude. A typical simultaneous viewing of the pair of stereograms proceeded as follows: The subject first saw only a madonna with child, then a few seconds later exclaimed, "But now she is undressing!" She had somehow lost the baby she was holding and her robe had slipped from her shoulders. Then in a few more seconds she lost her robe completely and became the young nude. Sometimes the process is reversed. Some people never see the nude and others never see the madonna. Apparently, what a person "'sees" in a situation depends upon his needs, abilities, purposes, and insights, as well as upon what is "out there."

Since reality, relativistically defined, consists of what one gains through one's five-plus senses and one's manner of sizing it up, one's person is what one makes of oneself, and one's environment consists of what one makes of what surrounds one. In keeping with their relativistic outlook, cognitive-field psychologists shun the use of concepts implying fixed traits or rigid habits of personalities. Since they regard truth as tentative and instrumental, they shy away from making dogmatic statements about the nature of human beings and the universe. A statement is considered to be true because of its accuracy in prediction and the consensus of people competent in its area in regard to the possible consequences of acting on it—its usefulness. However, a relativistic definition of truth in no way discounts the value of truths. Rather, it defines truth in a more discerning manner.

Now, one more example of perceptual interaction. Parents and siblings usually constitute important aspects of a child's psychological environment. When a second child arrives in a family, the first child sizes up—perceives—the situation. Whether the first child feels rejected depends not upon the physical stimuli as such received from his parents and sibling but upon what the first child makes of the relationship of the parents and the second child. The important question is not "Do the parents actually favor child number two?" but, rather, "Does child number one 'see' child number two as favored over child number one himself?" In this situation the parents and the other child are key aspects of each child's and parent's psychological environment. The way child number one perceives the situation has important bearing upon the environments of child number two and the parents. Each person in a situation interacts with the others.

Experience: An Insightful Process   Cognitive-field interactionists give their conception of *experience* a major place in their learning theories, but they define experience in terms of persons purposively interacting with their respective psychological environments. This contrasts with the position of many behaviorists, led by B. F. Skinner, who espouse *radical behaviorism*, which means that they have little or no place in their learning theory for such concepts as experience, awareness, or consciousness. They may concede that thought appears to occur, but they are likely to insist that if human beings are to be studied with true scientific objectivity, mentalistic concepts must be ruled out of bonds. Professor Skinner has expressed this notion clearly:

> the private event [thought or consciousness] is at best no more than a link in a causal chain, and it is usually not even that. We may think before we act in the sense that we may behave covertly before we behave overtly, but our action is not an "expression" of the covert response [thought] or the consequence of it. The two are attributable to the same variables.[26]

Some behaviorists do use the term *experience*, but they interpret it mechanistically. Accordingly, it means the conditioning process by which a human organism either learns new responses or changes old ones as a result of stimuli impinging on its sensory organs. If a child touches a hot stove and a link is formed between the sight of the stove and a withdrawal response, then it might be said that the child has had an experience. No thought needs to have occurred and no insights need to have been developed.

Cognitive-field interactionists use the term *experience* extensively, but they define it in a way consistent with their relativistic outlook. Accordingly, they regard experience as being rooted in insightful behavior. From this point of view, experience is a psychological event that involves a person acting purposefully with anticipation of the probable or possible consequences of such action. Thus, experience is interaction of a person and the person's perceived environment. This is what Dewey meant when he said, "An experience is always what it is because of a transaction taking place between an individual and what, *at the time*, constitutes his environment."[27] "The critical element [then] for explaining and predicting behavior is the intervening personal experience. In order to produce motivated behavior one must produce the experience of arousal, commitment, and purpose."[28]

WHAT ARE THE KEY CONSTRUCTS OF COGNITIVE-FIELD PSYCHOLOGY?

We may divide the key constructs or invented ideas of cognitive-field interactionism into five pivotal concepts and a number of auxiliary ones. The pivotal concepts are *life space, topology, vector, person,* and *psychological environment*. We describe each of the pivotal concepts in some detail, after which we provide definitions of the auxiliary ones.

For one to grasp fully the ideas of cognitive-field interactionism, it is essential that its key concepts be defined precisely as they are used in this frame of reference. In studying these concepts, readers should keep in mind the essential idea of field psychology, that is, that the meanings of all its constructs are mutually interdependent. Each depends for its meaning upon the meanings of all the others. Thus, there are no independent, intervening, and dependent variables as in S-R conditioning theories; instead, all the variables or constructs of cognitive-field interactionism are interdependent.

What Is a Life Space?

A person's life space is his psychological world or contemporaneous situation. It includes the *person* and the person's *psychological environment*—that part of his physical and social environment with which he/she is psychologically engaged at a given moment's or longer time's duration, because it is relevant to the person's purposes at that time. Life space is a scientific formulation of a series of overlapping situations, each replete with its unique propensities and relationships. It is developed for the purposes of (1) expressing what is possible and impossible in the life of a person and (2) anticipating what is likely to occur. It represents the total pattern of influences that affect an individual's behavior at a certain moment or longer unit of time. Within field psychology, behavior is any change in a life space that is psychological, that is, in accordance with a growing intelligence (see page 180 for a cognitive-field definition of behavior).

Life space is a model that enables us to take into consideration the total contemporaneous life situation of an individual. The object of study, when applied to humanity, is a system that can best be described as a discerning person in interaction with his psychological environment; this is a life space. As a person develops, he/she lives through a more or less continuous and overlapping series of life spaces. Each life space, consisting of an expanse of time of a moment's duration or longer, contains a person and the person's psychological environment at that time; it is characterized by the interaction of the two.

All psychological events, such as acting, thinking. learning, hoping, and dreaming, are functions, not of isolated properties of either an individual or his environment but of the mutual relations of a totality of coexisting factors that constitute a life space.

The concept *life space* constitutes an instrument whereby one may be objective in studying human activity by being, to some degree, subjective. A teacher may conjecture, "What would I be thinking if I were a student and were acting that way?" or "If I were in his situation, why would I be acting the way he/she is?" Life space, then, is a model of psychological reality or functional relationships developed for the purpose of describing what is possible and what is impossible for the person being studied and of anticipating or predicting what he/she is likely to be thinking and doing now as well as what his subsequent thoughts and actions will be.

A life space represents not physical objects as such but functional and symbolic relationships. Hence, it includes not only presently perceived objects but also memories, language, myths, art, anticipation, and religion. A continuing series of overlapping life spaces represents the total psychological world in which a person lives. One's psychological world may include one's precepts, knowledge, and beliefs; one's forward and backward time perspective; and abstract ideas as well as concrete objects.

We should remember that a diagram of a life space is figurative. It is difficult, perhaps impossible, to show everything at once. A complete and accurate image of a life space would show all of the psychological facts and constructs in a total situation represented by a *differentiated* person and a *differentiated* psychological environment. A differentiated person or environment is one functionally divided into various aspects as perceived by the one being studied (see Figure 8.1). Some differentiated aspects of a person are friends, ambitions, self-aggrandizement, and needs and abilities to know about various matters and to carry out activities of different kinds. A differentiated psychological environment contains everything perceived by the person at the time under study.

Also, we should guard against making physical things of these psychological constructs, whose purpose is to symbolize relationships, primarily functional in nature. For example, we should at no time think of a psychological person as being synonymous with a biological organism or of a psychological and a physical environment as being the same concept.

The two principal aspects of a life space are a person and the person's psychological environment. The two are not completely separate from each other. However, they do function as subwholes of a person's psychological field or life space. Both are surrounded by a *foreign hull*. The foreign hull of a life space is the nonpsychological environment. It is composed of those aspects of a person's physical-social environment that are observable by the one who is studying the particular person but which, within the time unit under consideration, have no significance for the person being studied (see Figure 8.1, page 169).

A person, his psychological environment, and the foreign hull of his life space are represented by concentric figures. A person is within his psychological environment, and both are surrounded by a nonpsychological foreign hull. The boundaries of the respective regions of a life space are characterized by permeability. There can be movement both ways through the boundary of a person, a life space, or any of its regions. Nonpsychological factors observed by an outsider can at the next moment become psychological ones for the person being studied. For an aspect of the physical-social world to influence the intelligent behavior of a person, it must be moved from a foreign hull into life space through his interaction with it.

As succeeding nonpsychological physical and social environments or foreign hulls are outside their respective psychological environments, they can have no immediate effect upon a person's intelligent behavior. However, through a person's interaction with the environment, parts of a present foreign hull can be transformed into abilities, needs, goals, barriers, and other psychological factors of succeeding life spaces. They are then no longer a part of the foreign hull. Factors so transformed become parts—perhaps central parts—of either a psychological person or environment. Thus, what a moment before constituted only a part of the foreign hull may at a succeding moment be a central part of either the person or his psychological environment.

What Is the Topology of a Life Space?

The topology of a life space is its psychological structure. In mathematics, topology is a nonmetrical geometry, which encompasses concepts such as *inside*, *outside*, and *boundary*, but has no dealings with length, breadth, or thickness. No distances are defined. Rather, topology is concerned with the relative position of the geometric figures being considered. "Topologically there is no difference between a circle, an ellipse, a regular or irregular polygon with any number of sides.... A drop of water and the earth are, from a topological point of view, fully equivalent."[29] It is helpful to think of a topological plane figure as being made of a highly elastic sheet of rubber; we may stretch, twist, pull, and bend it at pleasure, but the relationships it represents remain the same.

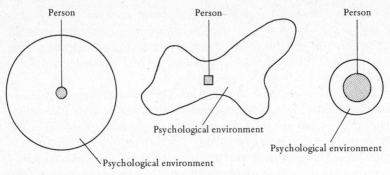

Figure 8.2 Topology of life space—three equal figures.

Two basic concepts that topological space denotes are connectedness and part-whole relationships. Topologically, things may be next to, inside, or outside one another. Size or shape has no significance in a topological figure. "Two figures are *topologically equivalent if* [and only if] one figure can be made to coincide with the other by an elastic motion."[30] The life spaces in Figure 8.2 are topologically equal. Each is a completely bounded area within a larger bounded area.

Topological concepts are used to represent the structure of a life space in such a way as to define the range of possible perceptions and actions. This is accomplished by showing the arrangement of the functional parts of a life space. The parts are shown as various regions and their boundaries. When an individual structures, that is, makes sense of, his life space, he/she divides it into regions. Boundaries of the major parts of a life space and their respective regions are either quite firm or more or less porous and permeable. Therefore, topological ideas or terms, when applied to psychology, represent the position of a person in reference to his functional goals and the barriers to their achievement. Thus, topology shows the various possibilities for psychological behavior or locomotion.

In addition to aspects of the person whose life space is being studied, regions represent operative activities such as eating, going to the movies, and making decisions; more passive incidents such as being fired or being rewarded; and social entities such as family, church, school, and gang. If the region "going to the movies" is located in a person's life space, the person is either engaging in or thinking about engaging in that activity. If "being fired" is in a person's life space, the person is perceiving that incident and its consequences. "Church" in a life space involves what one makes of what "church" means to one.[31]

How Are Vectors Used in Describing a Life Space?

Whereas topological concepts are used to illustrate structurally what is possible, vectors describe the dynamics of a situation—what is happening or is likely to happen. The concept *vector*, borrowed from mechanics, represents direction, strength, and point of application. It represents a force that is influ-

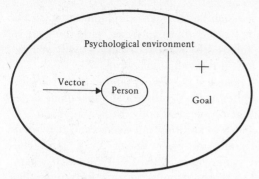

Figure 8.3 A vector.

encing psychological movement toward or away from a goal (see Figure 8.3). A goal is an aspect "region" of one's life space toward which or away from which one is psychologically drawn. Through one's learning, one's goals acquire their respective values or "valences."

A *force* is a tendency to act in a certain way or direction. A vector is equivalent to, and descriptive of, the strength and direction of a psychological force. If there is only one vector (force) there is locomotion in the direction that the vector points. However, if two or more vectors are pointing in several different ways, movement is in the direction of the resultant force.

Vectors, then, indicate the moving forces within a topological structure. They represent the *valences* of respective environmental regions or functional parts of a life space. Valences are the attracting or repelling powers of regions; they may be either positive or negative. A *positive valence* means that the environmental object or event under consideration is attractive to the person; it supports the fulfillment of a psychological need. A *negative valence* means that the object or event is repulsive to the person; it either prevents or obstructs fulfillment of a psychological need or threatens injury to the person. Goal regions have either positive or negative valences; barrier regions have only negative ones.

Each vector is drawn as an arrow that shows the respective force's direction, strength, and point of application. A vector may represent either a driving or a restraining force. A *driving force* is a tendency of a person to move either toward or away from a goal region; it is either a *drawing* or a *repelling* force. A *restraining force* is a barrier or obstacle to psychological locomotion that opposes some driving force. Both driving and restraining forces may arise from the needs and abilities of the person being studied, from the actions of another person, or from the impersonal aspects of a situation. (See page 214 for application of vectorial concepts to teaching.)

What Is the Origin and Nature of a Psychological Person?

Cognitive-field interactionists consider one's person to be central to one's psychological field. A *person* is that body or configuration of matters with which an individual becomes identified, of which he/she takes care, and to which he gives his allegiance. So defined, it is not a fixed quantity or static thing. It is achieved, as contrasted with being inherently possessed. Thus, briefly stated, a self or person consists of everything an individual takes care of.

Under no circumstances is a psychological person considered identical with a biological organism, nor is it limited either to a substantive mind alone or to a combination of a substantive mind and a physical body. Rather, a person is a purposive behaving self. It is the center of abilities and needs, and it is what a child or adolescent, and later an adult, means by saying "I" or "me." The concept *person* may be considered synonymous with *self*. Whereas teachers more often think of Billy Smith and Sally Anderson as persons, Billy and Sally, when thinking of themselves, are more likely to use the term *self*.

The content of self is taken to consist of one's cherished ideals and interests. Consequently, the kind and amount of interest actively taken in affairs is a measure of the quality of one's selfhood or personhood. To say that a child is involved or concerned is a brief way to saying that he/she is interactively engaging his person with his psychological world. Throughout his waking hours, as a baby, later as a child, and then as a youth, an individual learns by trying various acts and seeing what happens. Thus, through one purposively living in a human environment, one develops as a person or self.

The form that the development of selfhood takes depends upon the interaction of a person and his psychological environment. An organism, in a sense, is an aspect of each—person and environment. Whether a trait is primarily an aspect of the person or the environment depends, among other things, upon present needs and other factors of the inner-personal region of one's person.

Self, person, and interests, then, are names for the same psychological phenomenon. Depending upon the way individuals view matters, their persons take varying forms. There are individuals who are primarily concerned with keeping their bodies well fed, their temperatures well controlled, and the right amount of physical release as their goals in life. Other people may think that their whole person is their mind. Still others may think of themselves as beings that are neither bodies alone, nor minds alone, but combinations of physical bodies and nonphysical minds. But whatever it is that an individual is concerned with taking care of constitutes that person. Let us consider one example. A person's speech, whatever it might be, usually is a part of the person's self. Thus, any time we negatively criticize a student's speech, we are criticizing part of the student's person, not merely an organic operation or behavior. Hence, a child's self is the total configuration of all that he/she calls or thinks of as his. This can include his body, speech, thoughts, clothes, home, parents, grandparents, brothers, and sisters, as well as his reputation in various groups, his personal property, and his attitudes toward all these and the institutions for their realization.

A person is represented as a differentiated region of a life space. The field of a newborn baby is something like "one big blooming buzzing confusion." Then, as one lives one's life, although one may not think of it in these specific terms, one's total situation is structured as one's self or person and one's psychological

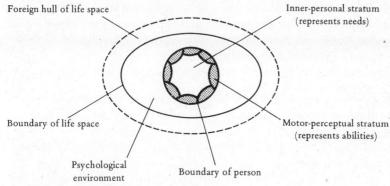

Figure 8.4 A structured person in a life space.

environment. Some aspects of experience involve the central core of a person; they are very near and dear to him. Others are of a peripheral, less vital sort.

Psychologically, a person is composed of (1) a motor-perceptual stratum or region and (2) an inner-personal stratum or region. The inner-personal region is the innermost part of a psychological person; it represents the person's needs. The motor-perceptual stratum has the position of a boundary zone between the inner-personal region and the psychological environment. It represents the cognitive and the manipulative abilities of a person. The practice of cognitive abilities entails the person using senses to know about things. Manipulative abilities involve the use of muscles and glands to do things (see Figure 8.4).

In a sense, the motor-perceptual system is the tool of the inner-personal system. Like regions of the psychological environment, it provides opportunity and limits opportunity. However, it is more closely identified with the person than with the environment. Whereas abilities are identified with the motor-perceptual system, needs are centered in the inner-personal system. A *need* is a state of a person that has a part in determining behavior toward any goal that may exist in relation to that state; it corresponds to a personal tension. Since the motor-perceptual region is *functionally* located between the inner-personal region and the environment, it performs functions of both person and environment. This means that a person acts in relation to his psychological environment and simultaneously realizes the consequences of doing so.

How Does a Child Construct His Self? A young child, to a greater extent than an adult, is a dynamic unity. When the child cries, he/she cries all over; when he is hungry, all of him is hungry; and when he is frightened, he is startled completely. Later, the child comes to perceive his self only as he/she distinguishes it from his environment and various aspects of it from one another. The rather sharp distinction between one's person and one's psychological environment is something that grows in an individual's thinking, as the "I" or "self" is gradually formed. However, one's person grows so that soon the central feature of one's social and personal motivation becomes the maintenance and furtherance of the welfare of that self. Hence, the paramount human need is for preservation and enhancement of this emergent self or person. One even owns a "loyal" dog in order to enhance and give constancy to one's psychological person.

A child's awareness of his self is manifested in at least four different ways:

1. He/she reaches certain results by his own efforts and comes to feel responsible for his acts, priding himself on his achievements and blaming himself for his failures.
2. His self, being embodied in values and goals, is realized in his transactions with other people.
3. As he/she evaluates his conduct over and against an ideal, an ideal self emerges (people often identify this ideal self with "conscience").
4. His self grows to a prominent place in his memories of a past and anticipations of a future.

How Many Selves Does an Individual Have?   Selfhood, except as it has encased itself in a shell of routine, is always in the process of its making. Moreover, any self in process is capable of including a number of more or less inconsistent selves or unharmonized dispositions. Therefore, in a sense, an individual has as many different selves as there are distinct groups for whose opinion he/she has concern. Hence, Jimmy Jones at home is one self, in school another, on a date another, and on a football field still another. Every normal human being maintains a variety of interests or values in different situations, and hence might be said to have a corresponding number of selves. However, although there is a different self in each successive life space of an individual, we can anticipate a continuity of selves of such nature that, in case of conflict, a deeper, continuous self pushes the others aside and becomes dominant. Consequently, each individual, if reasonably "normal," is a basic self or person made up of major allegiances and commitments, among which there is some degree of harmony and continuity. Usually, the psychological structure of a person is relatively constant over time, particularly as he/she advances in chronological age.

How Is Psychological Environment a Part of a Life Space?

Cognitive-field interactionists treat the meaning of environment much differently than do S-R conditioning theorists. S-R conditioning theorists maintain that a person's psychological and physical environments are identical; his environment consists of all his physical and social surroundings. Because environment is defined in objective, physicalistic terms, presumably anyone can see, hear, smell, feel, or taste the environment of anyone else.

In contrast, cognitive-field psychologists think of a person's environment as being psychological. One's psychological environment consists of every thing, function, and relationship that, at a given time, surrounds and means anything to the person as well as the meaning that it has for him. It is that part of one's physical and social environment with which one is psychologically engaged at a specific juncture of a moment's or longer period's duration, because it is relevant to one's purposes at that juncture. Such an environment is not a sum total of optical, acoustical, and tactile sensations. Instead, it consists of objects and events. A psychological environment, then, is what a person *makes of* his physical-social environment.

The meaning of *makes of* deserves our special attention. It means that some physical objects and events surround a person and that the person reaches out and makes some kind of sense of some of them as he/she brings them into relationship with himself and his goals. Whatever a person makes of that which seems to be surrounding him in his psychological environment. Thus, one's psychological environment is not merely what is "out there" in a purely physical sense. Anything that appears to be in a student's physical environment, but of which he/she is completely oblivious, is in the foreign hull of his life space. However, if the person interacts with that thing in any way, either positively or negatively, it no longer is in his foreign hull but in his life space proper.

Now, let us see what all this means. When one of the writers was teaching in a Kansas high school some years ago, he had a student (let's call him Louis Brock) who was not mad at the teacher, neither did he love him; he was just oblivious of him. Louis was usually there physically, but he seldom if ever was there psychologically. Now, what the teacher attempted to do was to get Louis to pay attention to him, so he moved Louis right up to the center of the front row under the teacher's nose. But Louis still was neither mad at nor attracted by the teacher; as far as Louis was concerned, the teacher did not exist. But, where was the teacher? He was part of the foreign hull of Louis's life space. Consequently, the only way that the teacher would ever teach Louis anything was to maneuver so that Louis would pull the teacher into his life space. Until he accomplished this, all the gyrations he performed would not teach Louis anything. This illustrates why it is so crucial that we recognize that every student's life space has a foreign hull as well as a psychological environment proper.

How Does Psychological Environment Differ from Physical-Social Environment?   The physical environment of an object or person includes everything surrounding that object or person as seen by an unbiased observer. Likewise, social environment consists of the generalized social milieu or atmosphere around a person. It includes the attitudes, values, and beliefs of the community, region, or nation. Although the physical and social environment furnishes a setting or matrix for the psychological environments of individuals in a group, it is distinctly different from the psychological environment of any member of the group. Hence, a student's psychological environment is not the same as the physical-social environment as it appears to others.

Whereas the physical environments of a group of students in a classroom are relatively the same, each of their psychological environments is unique. Let us visit Miss Smith's classroom of sixth-grade students at Carbondale Elementary School. At 10:30 Tuesday morning, what is happening in the room? Miss Smith is holding reading class. What are Alice, Frank, Helen, and John doing? Alice is so absorbed with her teacher and schoolwork that she is oblivious to everything else about her, including the other children. Frank is listening

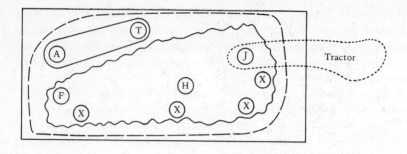

T   Miss Smith

A   Alice   ———————————— Boundary of Alice's life space

F   Frank   — — — — — — — Boundary of Frank's life space

H   Helen   ∿∿∿∿∿∿∿∿∿∿ Boundary of Helen's life space

J   John   ------------------- Boundary of John's life space

X   Other children

Figure 8.5 Life spaces involved in a classroom.

half-heartedly to the teacher but is concerned primarily with the other children in the room. Helen is a social butterfly; she wants the attention of most of the children in the classroom. She does give attention to the teacher from time to time but right now is concerned with other things. John's body is in the classroom, but "psychologically" John is riding a shiny new tractor that is being operated in the field adjoining the school.

This classroom is illustrated in Figure 8.5. Each small circle represents a person, whose initial it has on it. Each person's respective psychological environment is indicated by a larger figure that includes the person. Each person and his respective psychological environment constitute a life space. Practically everything within the four walls of the classroom, as well as much more, is included within either John's life space or his foreign hull. John's life space is significantly unique; drawn alone, it would appear as in Figure 8.6.

Since a psychological environment is a time-bound situation involving a specific person, such an environment and the person involved are constantly

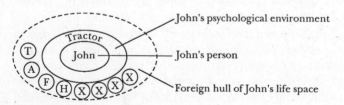

Figure 8.6 John's life space.

changing as the person actively lives in relationship to that environment. What appears to an observer to constitute John's environment may include many elements not actually in John's psychological environment, and the observed environment may exclude some elements that, for John, psychologically are in it. To understand John, the teacher must envisage John in John's *psychological* environment, not his *physical* environment as such.

Thus, to be objective in dealing with the child, the teacher must be subjective. She must see the world as John sees it. In order to predict John's behavior accurately, the teacher must understand the interactive nature of John's life space—his person and his psychological environment—and she must be able to predict (anticipate) the boy's future life spaces. Then, for Miss Smith to be able to teach John in a significant way, it is imperative that there be some intersection of John's life space with hers and with the life spaces of other children in the room.

To repeat, the principal functional parts of a life space are the person and the person's psychological environment, and a life space is always surrounded by a foreign hull. The foreign hull of a person's life space is the complex of all nonpsychological factors surrounding a life space. It is constituted of physical and social factors that, at the time, are not subject to the person's psychological interaction but that may, at some future time, become aspects of his psychological field.

Since the content of a foreign hull has physical-social but not psychological reality, its physical and social conditions limit the variety of a person's possible life spaces. Anything that appears to be in a person's physical environment, but of which the person is completely oblivious, is in the foreign hull of his life space. However, if he/she interacts with that thing in any way, either positively or negatively, it no longer is in his foreign hull but in his life space proper. Thus, a person can never experience any aspect of his own foreign hull; when he/she experiences a part of his previous foreign hull, it is no longer an aspect of his foreign hull, but it belongs to his life space proper.

As succeeding nonpsychological physical and social environments or foreign hulls are outside their respective psychological environments, they can have no immediate effect upon a person's intelligent behavior. However, through a person's interaction with the environment, parts of a present foreign hull can be transformed into goals, barriers, and other psychological factors of succeeding life spaces. They then are no longer a part of the foreign hull. Factors so transformed become parts of either psychological persons or environments. Thus, what a moment before constituted only a part of the foreign hull may at a succeeding moment be a central part of either the person or his psychological environment. The boundaries of both one's person and psychological environment and of their various regions are highly permeable.

Since each person's perceptual environment is unique, obviously two persons may appear to be in the same location in space and time and yet have very different psychological environments. Furthermore, the behaviors of two equally intelligent persons who are confronted with the same "objective facts" may differ drastically because each is different in his purposes and experien-

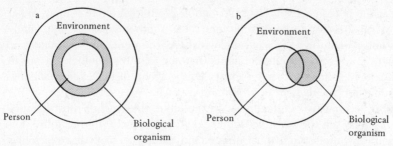

Figure 8.7 Relationship of a biological organism to a psychological person.

tial background. Whenever a person has a new experience, he/she changes his environment and will never again be able to recapture the old environment in its identical form. The cognitive-field meaning of *environment* suggests why in a particular family one son may become a minister and another turn to crime; their interpretations of their world differ radically, even though to an outsider their social and physical environments would appear quite similar. "Situations (psychological environments)... influence our behaviors by affecting such person variables as how we encode the situation, the outcomes we expect, their subjective value for us, and our ability to generate response patterns."[32]

Is an Organism Considered Person or Environment?   In a relativistic sense, an individual's biological organism is an aspect of both his person and psychological environment. A person usually closely identifies his biological organism with himself; he/she is concerned with taking care of it. But the person also sees his organism in another light as an important aspect of his environment; it is part of that with which that person must learn to live. A child's or youth's being crippled or abnormal in physical size or proportions may color everything he/she says or does. A 12-year-old girl who reaches the adolescent growth spurt early and becomes head and shoulders taller than many other students in her class may consider her physical stature a critical aspect of her psychological environment; she must live with what she "makes of" her physical stature.

We may illustrate the relation of a biological organism to a person in two different ways. The organism may be considered a boundary region of a person, which mediates between the person and his environment by providing cognitive and manipulative abilities (Figure 8.7a), or the functions of the organism may be pictured as a factor common to both a psychological person and his psychological environment (Figure 8.7b).

The basic formula of cognitive-field psychology is that psychological, as contrasted with physical, behavior is a function of a person and the person's psychological environment: $B = f(P,E)$. The pivotal concepts—life space, topology, vector, person, and psychological environment—and the constructs that are auxiliary to the basic formula are illustrated in Figure 8.1, page 169. The auxiliary concepts are defined in the following glossary.

What Are Some Key Auxiliary Concepts of Cognitive-Field Interactionist Psychology?

Foreign hull of life space   Complex of all nonpsychological facts that surround a life space. That part of a person's physical and social environment that, at a particular time, is not included in his psychological environment. Consists of physical and social raw materials. Both provides and limits behavioral possibilities.

Regions   Psychologically significant conditions, places, things, and activities defined functionally as parts of a life space. They have positive or negative valences.

Valences (environment-centered)   Positive or negative imperative environmental facts; properties that regions of a life space have when an individual is either drawn toward them or repelled away from them. A region that possesses a positive valence is one of such nature that forces correlated with the valence of that region tend psychologically to move the person in the direction of that region. A negative valence means that forces tend to move the person away from that region.

Needs (person-centered)   States of a person that, if they exist in relation to a goal, have a part in determining behavior toward that goal. Correspond to a tension system of the inner-personal region of a person. Needs develop through one's interaction with one's environment; they arise.

Abilities (person-centered)   Cognitive abilities constitute a person's capacity to know his environment. Manipulative abilities constitute a person's capacity to affect his environment.

Tension   Very closely related to, and descriptive of, psychological needs. The state of one system relative to the state of surrounding systems. Release of tension may be achieved through either reaching a goal or restructuring one's life space. The release of tension corresponds to the satisfaction of a need. When goal-directed, a tension is an *intention*.

Goal   A region of a life space toward, or away from, which a person is psychologically drawn.

Barrier   Dynamic part of an environment that resists motion through it. That which stands in the way of a person reaching a goal.

Force   Immediate determinant of the behavior and locomotions of a person. The tendency to act in a certain direction. Its properties are strength, direction, and point of application. It is represented by a vector. The strength of a force is related to, but not identical with, the strength of a valence. The combination of forces acting at the same point at a given time is a resultant force.

Cognitive structure   An environment and a person, as known by the person. Synonyms are *generalized insight* or *understanding*.

NOTES

1. Kurt Lewin, *Principles of Topological Psychology*, trans. Fritz Heider and Grace M. Heider (New York: McGraw-Hill, 1936).
2. Edward C. Tolman, Purposive Behavior in Animals and Men (New York: Appleton Century, 1931).
3. John Dewey, *Experience and Education* (New York: Macmillan, 1938).
4. Boyd H. Bode, *How We Learn* (Boston: Heath, 1940).
5. See Morris L. Bigge and Maurice D. Hunt, *Psychological Foundations of Education* (New York: Harper & Row, 3d ed. 1980).
6. We refer to the following works: Albert Bandura, *Social Learning Theory* (New York: General Learning Press, 1971); Jerome S. Bruner, *The Relevance of Education* (New York: Norton, 1975); Richard de Charms, *Enhancing Motivation: Change in the Classroom* (New York: Irvington, 1976); Edward L. Deci, *Intrinsic Motivation* (New York: Plenum Press, 1975); Bernard Weiner et al., *Achievement Motivation and Attribution Theory* (Morristown, NJ: General Learning Press, 1974); and Bernard Weiner, ed., *Cognitive Views of Human Motivation* (New York: Academic Press, 1974).
7. See Kurt Lewin, "Field Theory and Learning," in Nelson B. Henry, ed., *The Psychology of Learning*, Part 2, *The Forty-First Yearbook of the National Society for the Study of Education* (Chicago: University of Chicago Press, 1942), pp. 215–242.
8. Deci, *Intrinsic Motivation*, p. 119.
9. See Gardner Lindzey and Elliott Aronson, *Handbook of Social Psychology*, 2d ed. (Reading, MA: Addison Wesley, 1968), Chapters 5 and 6.
10. Deci, *Intrinsic Motivation*, p. 179.
11. Bernard Weiner, "Comments on the Discussion" in Bernard Weiner, ed., *Cognitive Views of Human Motivation* (New York: Academic Press, 1974), p. 100.
12. See Ernest R. Hilgard and Gordon H. Bower, *Theories of Learning*, 4th ed. (Englewood Cliffs, NJ: Prentice-Hall, 1975), Chapter 14; also see D. O. Hebb, *Textbook of Psychology*, 3d ed. (Philadelphia: Saunders, 1972), pp. 275–280.
13. Walter Mischel, "The Self as the Person: A Cognitive Social Learning View," in Abraham Wanderman et al., eds., *Humanism and Behaviorism: Dialogue and Growth* (Oxford: Pergamon, 1976), p. 145.
14. Deci, *Intrinsic Motivation*, p. 243.
15. John Dewey, *Logic: The Theory of Inquiry* (New York: Holt, Rinehart and Winston, 1938), p. 460.
16. Deci, *Intrinsic Motivation*, p. 47.
17. See Bernard Weiner, "Achievement Motivation as Conceptualized by an Attribution Theorist," in Bernard Weiner, ed., *Achievement Motivation and Attribution Theory*, pp. 3–48
18. George H. Mead, *The Philosophy of the Present* (La Salle, IL: Open Court, 1932), p. 90.
19. Kurt Lewin, *Principles of Topological Psychology* (New York: McGraw-Hill, 1936), p. 35.
20. See Alfred J. Marrow, *The Practical Theorist: The Life and Work of Kurt Lewin* (New York: Basic Books, 1969), p. 228.
21. Gordon W. Allport, *Personality and Social Encounter* (Boston: Beacon Press, 1960), p. 29.
22. Mischel, "The Self as the Person: A Cognitive Social Learning View," p. 151.
23. Weiner, *Cognitive Views of Human Motivation*, p. 100.

24. See Hadley Cantril, "Perception and Interpersonal Relations," *American Journal of Psychiatry* 114 (August 1957):126. Copyright, 1957, the American Psychiatric Association.
25. These experiments are summarized in Alfred Kuenzli, *The Phenomenological Problem* (New York: Harper & Row, 1959), Chapter 8.
26. Reprinted with permission of Macmillan Publishing Co., Inc. From B. F. Skinner, *Science and Human Behavior* (New York: Macmillan, 1953), p. 279. Copyright ©1953, Macmillan Publishing Co., Inc.
27. John Dewey, *Experience and Education* (New York: Macmillan, 1938), p. 41.
28. Richard de Charms, *Enhancing Motivation* (New York: Irvington, 1976), p. 6.
29. Kurt Lewin, *Principles of Topological Psychology*, p. 88.
30. Bradford H. Arnold, *Intuitive Concepts in Elementary Topology* (Englewood Cliffs, NJ: Prentice-Hall, 1962), p. 24.
31. See Dorwin Cartwright, "Lewinian Theory as a Contemporary Systematic Framework," in Sigmund Koch, ed., *Psychology: A Study of a Science*, Vol. 2 (New York: McGraw–Hill, 1959), p. 25.
32. Mischel, "The Self as the Person," p. 152.

Chapter
9

How Do Cognitive-Field Interactionists Use the Life Space Concept?

Cognitive-field oriented teachers use the concept *life space* to describe various situations that people find themselves in and their tendencies to behave in certain ways because of how they size up matters. The contents of a life space are inferred from watching the behavior of an individual and observing the consequences of psychological processes.

Within cognitive-field interactionism, a person's motivation develops through his differentiating his life space into regions and subregions—functional objects and activities—and simultaneously cognitively structuring the regions and subregions by grasping some of their meaningful relationships. Both a person and that person's psychological environment—the two major regions of a life space—are in some way and to some degree differentiated into subregions, each with adjacencies and boundaries. As new regions emerge, they, too, to some degree are structured cognitively—made meaningful in harmony with the person's purposes.

A person's motivation occurs not because of his past experience as such but as an aspect of the person's current psychological situation; it is more a *pulling* than a pushing process. Within a situation—life space—a person engages in those motor, verbal, and ideational activities that point toward either continuation or reestablishment of equilibrium through moderation or balance of tensions.

WHAT PSYCHOLOGICAL PROCESSES CHARACTERIZE ONE'S LIFE SPACES?

Because of the nature of human motivation and experience, cognitive-field interactionists think of four concurrent psychological processes transpiring in the life of a person. It is within the course of a combination of these processes that learning occurs. The processes are (1) interaction, within each life space, of a person and the person's psychological environment; (2) continuity of succeeding life spaces; (3) differentiation in the person's time perspective; and (4) changes in the concrete-imaginative levels of reality. Since these four processes occur simultaneously, any adequate understanding of people becomes somewhat complicated. But people are complicated, and it is doubtful that we will ever get an adequate understanding of them unless we do have a rather complicated paradigm.

What Does Interaction Within Each Life Space Mean?

Interaction is the psychological process within which one makes something of both one's person and one's psychological environment. To repeat, perceptual interaction, for cognitive-field psychologists, is a cognitive experiential process within which a person, psychologically, simultaneously reaches out to his psychological environment, encounters some aspects of it, brings those aspects into relationship with himself, makes something of those aspects, acts in relation to what he/she makes of them, and realizes the consequences of the entire process. This process is discussed in some detail on pages 181–184; we only summarize it at this point.

In a life space, a person and the person's psychological environment are in simultaneous mutual interaction (SMI) and are mutually interdependent. Each depends upon the other for its nature and functions; it is impossible to treat one adequately without also treating the other. Accordingly, one's person is definitive of one's environment, and likewise one's environment is definitive of oneself. A person's perceived reality consists of that which he/she gains through the use of his five-plus senses in the manner that he sizes things up. Hence, one's person consists of what one *makes* of oneself, and one's psychological environment consists of what one *makes* of that which seems to surround one.

What Does Continuity of Succeeding Life Spaces Mean?

Since each life space covers only a limited expanse of time, an individual lives through a continuous series of overlapping life spaces that have much in common but seldom, if ever, are identical. Thus, an individual's life spaces are characterized by continuity of both his successive persons and their psychological environments. But each life space, to some degree, is different from the one that preceded it and the one that follows. This is illustrated in Figure 9.1.

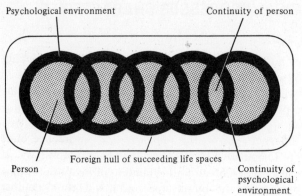

Figure 9.1 Continuity of a person's life spaces.

Since we can anticipate some degree of similarity and continuity of life spaces as the experiences of one moment shade into those of the next, for practical educational procedures (depending upon the purposes being pursued), we may assume a fixity of life spaces for longer periods than a moment—perhaps a class period, a week, or a month.

Within a series of overlapping life spaces, a person's life is a continuity of psychological tensions, locomotions, and new equilibriums. When there is an increase of tension in one part of a life space relative to the rest of the system, disequilibrium occurs. When a person finds himself in a state of disequilibrium and attempts to return to equilibrium, psychic energy is expended; the person engages in psychological behavior. Should tension throughout the system become completely equalized, output of energy would cease; the total system would come to rest. Of course, throughout a life span this absolute balance is never achieved. Since a person is intelligent and purposive, he/she constantly expands and restructures his life space to some degree. Consequently, new disequilibriums continuously emerge. This process gives a dynamic nature to human living that makes it immensely interesting and challenging.

Nonpsychological factors, observed only by an outsider, can at the next unit of time become psychological ones for the person being studied. A prime characteristic of the boundaries of a life space and its regions is their permeability. There can be movement both ways through the boundary of a person or a psychological environment or though the boundaries of any of their regions. Aspects of one's person may move into future environmental regions of one's life space or even into its foreign hull, and vice versa. Only the inner stratum of self—needs—remains relatively stable, but it too may change drastically over periods of time, as when a person changes to a different religious faith.

What Is Differentiation in a Person's Time Perspective?

The basic idea of cognitive-field psychology is that everyone lives in the present; a person cannot really live in either the physical past or future. In other words, each person lives when he/she lives, which is right now. Thus, psychologically speaking, the past is past-present, the future is future-present, and the present is present-present. The past-present consists of what we ordinarily call memories, and the future-present consists of what we ordinarily call anticipations or expectations.

During a person's development an enlargement of his time perspective occurs; a psychological past and future become more significant. A small child lives very much in the present; his time perspective includes only an immediate past and an immediate future. However, as one's age increases, one's time perspective tends to expand. Thus, anticipations of more and more remote future events and growing memories of past events come to influence one's present behavior. These time-binding events occupy such a central part of many adult life spaces that it is often assumed that a past and a future actually exist in their own right. Careful thought, however, will bring the realization that the only past that a person can deal with is what that person thinks happened in the past. Likewise, the only future that can influence a person now is his present anticipation of a future that he/she thinks may, or is going to, eventuate.

A person's present life situation contains "traces," or memories, of past incidents, but all these are in the person's present situation or life space. When a second child has appeared in a family, the important factor now, as far as the first child is concerned, is not whether his mother rejected him when the second child was born, but whether the child interpreted the past situation as one of rejection and carried the rejection into the present life space. The past can be of present significance only through the operation of factors in the present that are identified as "past." That which persists from prior experience so that it is a "past" in the present is *trace*.

Anticipation of a future also occurs in the present; it is how one envisions the future, not what will actually happen then, that counts in the present. If a child is good in school on Monday in order to get a star on Friday, whether or not the child actually received a star on Friday has nothing to do with his being good on the previous Monday. His anticipation of the star is his motivation for goodness on Monday. Recognition of the "presentness" of any psychological past and future in no way depreciates them; it merely places them in a contemporaneous frame of reference within which growth of a person's time perspective is conceived in terms of memory traces and anticipations, which are functional parts of a present life space.

What Are Changes in Concrete-Imaginative Levels of Reality?

Normal human development carries with it not only an enlargement of time perspective but also an increased differentiation of the concrete-imaginative dimensions of one's life space. As used in cognitive-field psychology, *imaginative processes* are wishing, dreaming, imagining, symbolic thinking, and kindred practices. To young children, the products of their imaginative processes are concretely real; then gradually they are distinguished more and more from actual physical reality.

A young child does not clearly distinguish imaginative objects from concrete facts, wishes from goals, or hopes from expectations. Thus, to him, Santa

Claus and Satan may be as real as any concrete object. However, when a child realizes that there "really" is no Santa Claus but still continues to talk about him, he/she is differentiating an imaginative realm from that of concrete reality. Then, as the child grows older, he/she tends to make an even sharper distinction between concrete and imaginative reality. It is true that fantasy, in the form of wishful thinking, is also common in adults. However, adults generally are better able to distinguish imaginative processes from concrete experience. Furthermore, mature adults often recognize the degree to which they are engaging in each.

How Are Concrete-Imaginative Levels Related to Time Dimensions of a Life Space?

Two salient characteristics of a life space at any given time are (1) the level of concrete-imaginative reality at which the person is operating and (2) the degree to which the individual's life space encompasses a psychological past and future. There is a direct relationship between the respective concrete-imaginative levels of reality and the degree of time binding that pervades the life space of a person at a given time. At the level of concrete facts, immediate goals, and practical expectations, a life space contains only an incipient past and future; they are just beginning to be. But as a person's life space assumes more imaginative dimensions, time-binding functions become increasingly extended and significant until, at an extremely imaginative level, one's entire life space may be centered on either a psychological past or future. But even then, the time and imaginative dimensions of a life space continue to be both contemporaneous and present.

We should not confuse the adjectives *imaginative* and *imaginary;* the two words have significantly different meanings. Whereas *imaginary* means purely fictitious or fanciful and existing only in the imagination, *imaginative* applies to that which arises through one cognitively creating concepts or plans for action. Thus, *imaginative* is a much more constructive term than is *imaginary.* In fact, being imaginative is much the same as being creative.

Imaginative levels of reality range from mere expectations and their means of fulfillment to hallucinations that give rise to extreme guilts and fears. Some levels between the two extremes, ranging from concrete reality to extremely imaginative reality, involve aspirations, wishes, imagination, symbolic thought, creativity, fancy, fantasy, dreams, and nightmares. In the psychological past these take the form of memory, pride, innocence, error, fault, sin, and guilt. In the psychological future they embrace goals, hopes, anticipations, conjectures, fabrications, visions, fears, and despair.

Figure 9.2 symbolically depicts the interrelationship of the concrete-imaginative dimension of a life space of a person and his time perspective. The figure should be interpreted to signify not merely two but numerous levels of reality, which may range from life on a purely biological level to one of complete absorption in fantasy. The figure illustrates both the concrete-imaginative and the time-binding dimensions of a life space. Think of the figure as being three-dimensional. Its lower and upper bases represent extreme

Psychological past   Psychological future

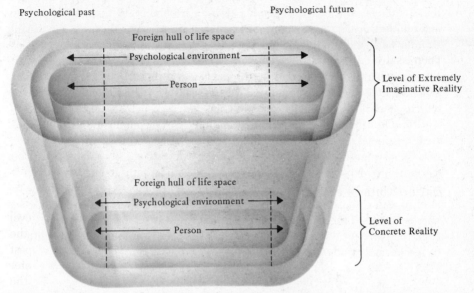

Figure 9.2 Concrete-imaginative levels of a life space as related to its psychological past and future.

levels of concrete and imaginative reality. The part of the figure to the left of the vertical left-hand dotted line represents the person's psychological past, the part to the right of the vertical right-hand dotted line represents the person's psychological future. Notice that when the person is operating on the level of concrete reality, there is very little psychological past or future in his life space. The person is little concerned with either yesterday or tomorrow; he/she simply lives each day—day by day. This type of individual, of course, is difficult to teach for the future.

As a person functions on more imaginative levels, his psychological past and future also become more salient aspects of the person's life space. Thus, whereas on the level of concrete reality a psychological past and future hold only a relatively minor significance, as a person operates on more imaginative levels the time dimension of his life space becomes more comprehensive and important.

Now, how may an adult's understanding of the concrete-imaginative levels of life spaces contribute to more effective functioning as a teacher, especially when he/she is teaching boys and girls of a social class other than his own? For one to teach a child or youth successfully, one must meet him on the level of reality where his life space is focused at the time. Recognition of this key principle is highly essential, especially if a typical "middle-class" teacher is to reach and teach a child or youth from unskilled-laboring class homes.

In working for marginal wages, the parents of those boys and girls are likely to maintain their life spaces on a low, subsistence level of concrete reality; their primary goals involve the acquisition of food, clothing, and shelter. Because of their home conditions, children of unskilled laborers are also likely to center their realities on a concrete level. However, from time to time, both parents and children leave this concrete level, and when they do, they are most likely to jump to an extremely imaginative level of reality. This imaginative level, reflected in persons' daydreams and fantasy, is focused largely on a psychological future; it is a flight from routine drudgery and boredom. An example of their swinging to a highly imaginative level of reality is their watching movies in which people dress formally, drink champagne, and drive Cadillacs.

Reserved "middle-class" people generally do not pitch their psychological realities on either of the extremes that are characteristic of unskilled laborers. Consequently, teachers, in their earlier contacts with boys and girls from the unskilled-laboring class, perhaps should deliberately focus their interest, thoughts, and teaching on extreme levels of either concrete or imaginative reality in order that their students will make the teacher's attitudes and ideas a part or region of their respective life spaces. Then, students' life spaces may be constructively reviewed and progressively improved through the joint inquiry of teacher and students.

HOW IS LEARNING A CHANGE IN INSIGHT OR COGNITIVE STRUCTURE?

According to cognitive-field interactionist psychology, a child or youth in a learning situation is neither unfolding according to nature nor being passively conditioned always to respond in a desired manner. Rather, at his level of maturity and comprehension, he/she is differentiating and restructuring himself and his psychological environment; he/she is gaining or changing his insights. Learning, then, is a dynamic process whereby, through interactive experience, insights or cognitive structures of life spaces are changed so as to become more serviceable for future guidance. *Insights* or *cognitive structures* are answers to questions concerning such matters as how something is made up, what is related to what, how one does something, of what good a thing or action is, and what one should be doing. They may be preverbal, verbal, or nonverbal; one may gain an insight before one has words to express it, one may achieve an insight and its verbalization simultaneously, or one may accomplish an insight that one does not verbalize at all. "Not only do cognitions [insights] affect internal states such as attitudes and motives, but...individuals choose what behavior to engage in on the basis of their cognitions about the outcomes of those and other behaviors."[1]

There is evidence that even nonverbal animals solve mazes by formulating a series of cognitive structures and testing them and that they solve their problems through gaining insight into their situations.[2] What occurs psychologically when by being given food, a dachshund is taught to sit up on its rear end at the command "up," and later, when he wants a toy that he sees on a table, he goes to the table, assumes his "up" position, and barks?

Insights derive from one's best interpretations of what comes to one; they may be deeply discerning or shallow. They may serve as dependable guides for action or may prove ruinous. Chica, one of Köhler's apes, attempted to reach a banana by placing a box beneath it and jumping as high as possible from the box. After several failures, she suddenly held the box as high as possible, pressed it against the wall, and attempted to climb up on it. Chica had an insight, but not a true one.[3]

It is an insightful process when a ball player gets a feel for the correct swing of his bat, when a little girl discovers how to dress herself, when a youth learns to drive an automobile, when a child gets the idea of multiplication, (perhaps through addition), or when a college student learns how to "read" Shakespeare.

A person's behavior, to a very large degree, depends upon the cognitive structure of the person's life space. Learning results in building psychological traces, which contribute to the structure and dynamics of both present and future life spaces and, thus, affect both present and future performance. Memory processes refer to cognitively structured similarities between an individual's life spaces that exist at different times. It is because of the continuity of life spaces and their cognitive structures that learning is of value to a person.

One's behavior in a relatively unstructured situation would appear exploratory, vacillating, and contradictory. An adolescent, for example, vacillates between a child's and an adult's world, neither of which to him is well structured. Newly acquired adult regions of his life space will not fit into a child's world, and some of the child's regions to which he clings will not fit into the adult world that he, at times, is attempting to enter.

Good insight into a present life space or psychological situation tends to provide excellent foresight into the cognitive structure of future life spaces. Suppose a college student wishes to understand and appreciate principles of human development and learning and prepare himself to apply them in future teaching situations. An excellent procedure would be for him to acquire a deep understanding of himself, his psychological environment, and their relationship in his current series of life spaces.

The cognitive structure of a life space encompasses a person's meaningful knowledge, with knowledge defined in the broadest sense possible. Accordingly learning is discovery of meaning. A change of cognitive structure may occur in any part of a person's life space, including the psychological past, present, or future. By defining all learning as essentially a process of developing cognitive structure or insights, we escape the hazard of forming a dichotomy or split between knowledge and motivation. This dichotomy has led to a rather sharp distinction between learning of facts and development of motives, personality, character, and attitudes. Emotional, motivational, and imaginative functions are as necessary in "factual" mathematical, scientific, and historical pursuits as they are in literature and the fine arts.

One's learning—changes in cognitive structure—includes changes in perceptual knowledge, motivation, group belongingness and ideology, and muscular control and dexterity. Whereas changes in perceptual knowledge are focused upon the topological or structural aspects of a situation, changes in motivation are focused upon its vectorial or dynamic aspects. However, since changes in motivation arise from changes in cognitive structures, for a person to change the valence—attractiveness—of a feature or activity of a life space, he/she must change the cognitive structure of his life space in regard to it.

Growing into a culture through one's change in group belongingness and ideology and one's development of muscular skills also involve primarily perceptions of oneself and the people and objects around one and one's getting the feel of performing various actions. Thus, these two types of change principally involve changes in the cognitive structure of one's life space. Consequently, in treating learning, the pivotal concept is *change in cognitive structure*. "A change in action ideology, a real acceptance of a changed set of facts and values, a change in the perceived social world—all three are but different expressions of the same process."[4]

How May the Cognitive Structures of Life Spaces Change?

A person changes the cognitive structure of his life space through *differentiation, generalization,* and *restructurization* of its respective regions or aspects. A *region* is a distinguishable, functional part of a life space. Hence, it is the psychological meaning of an object or activity.. The object or activity may be either a remembered, a contemplated, or a presently existing one. Regions of a life space may include conceptions of aspects of one's self, specific activities such as working and eating, states of being such as being frightened or feeling secure, and membership in groups and classes, as well as the personalities, objects, and events that one perceives. The cognitive structure of one's life space includes not only the arrangement and conditions of existing regions but also an understanding of what movements may occur and what may be the consequences of each. The relations between the region in which a person's activity is centered and the other regions of his life space delineate the qualities of his immediate surroundings, the kind of regions adjacent to other regions (that is, the possibilities for his next steps), and which steps mean actions toward and which ones mean actions away from goals.

What Is Cognitive or Perceptual Differentiation?

Cognitive differentiation is the process within which regions of a life space are subdivided into smaller regions; relatively vague and unstructured regions of a life space become cognitively structured and more specific. Thus, the person comes to see as different some things that he/she had previously thought to be parts of the same thing. Differentiation, then means discerning more and more specific aspects of one's environment and oneself. What once were "kitties" come to be "leopards," "tigers," "lions," and "cats." What once was "toast" comes to be "crackers," "doughnuts," and "bread." What once was "baby" comes to be "me," "my arms," or "my legs," and later "student," "member of clubs," and "ball player."

Differentiation proceeds at different rates at different times, and during crisis periods, such as adolescence, its speed rapidly fluctuates. As a child grows, he/she differentiates (1) himself or his person from his environment, (2) different aspects of his person and environment from each other, (3) a psychological past and future from the present, and (4) imaginative reality levels from the concrete reality level of his life space. (The latter two kinds of differentiation are explained on pages 202 through 206 as two of the most important features of cognitive-field psychology.)

What Is Cognitive Generalization?

Cognitive generalization is a process whereby one formulates a generalized idea or concept through discerning some common characteristics of a number of individual cases and identifying the cases as a class of ideas or objects. Thus, a person identifies similarities among aspects of himself or his environment that had previously seemed quite different. When a child learns that vegetables, flowers, bushes, and trees are plants, or a student learns that his hopes, dreams, beliefs, and anticipations are all subregions of a "future" region in a contemporaneous life space, he/she is generalizing. A student of professional education, through differentiation of various instances of learning, may develop a generalized concept *learning* to cover any learning in any situation.

Although in common usage generalization is the opposite of differentiation, psychologically they are mutually complementary. Generalization is the process whereby one groups a number of particular objects or functions under a single heading or in a single category. Thus, one generalizes when one forms a concept that includes previously differentiated aspects of oneself or one's environment. When a child learns that cats, dogs, horses, and birds are animals he/she is generalizing. Then, through a combination of differentiation and generalization, he/she may divide the physical world into vegetable, animal, and mineral classes.

What Is Cognitive Restructurization?

Cognitive restructurization of one's life space means one's making more or different sense of oneself and one's world. A person not only differentiates and generalizes his life space into new regions but simultaneously restructures his life space; he/she changes the meanings of respective regions in relationship to himself and to one another. Thus, a person discovers some significant new relationships between some aspects of his life space and some nonrelationships between others that he/she had previously considered related. Within the process of restructurization one defines or redefines directions in one's life space; one learns what actions will lead to what results. One does this through perception of significant relationships of different functional regions of one's life space. Restructurization then, consists of separating certain regions that have been connected and connecting certain regions that have been separated. (Remember that regions are defined as functionally distinguishable parts of a life space.)

When we were quite young, most of us differentiated people from their environments. Later, we differentiated people into various races, classes, and groups. Perhaps about the same time we generalized them into Republicans and Democrats, or Christians and non-Christians. As persons learn, they continue to differentiate and generalize themselves and their environments, but they also restructure the differentiated and generalized regions of their life spaces so as to give them new meanings. In this way persons become, or at least should become, increasingly better thinkers.

Restructurization includes not only extensions of time perspectives and increased differentiation of imaginative from concrete levels of reality, but also changes in motivation and group identification and in bodily coordination. A person's change in motivation arises through his seeing regions or factors of his life space in a new light. To many a 14-year-old boy, a girl, once something to be teased, becomes a thing to be wooed. A change in motivation is also closely related to changes in group identification. To a large degree it is the groups to which one belongs that are the source of one's ideology and consequently one's motivation. One's person changes as one changes one's group allegiances. An adolescent's conformity to peer group standards is a striking example of this developmental process.

HOW IS INTELLIGENCE RELATED TO LEARNING?

Cognitive-field interactionists define intelligence as the ability to respond in present situations on the basis of cogent anticipation of possible consequences and with a view to controlling those consequences that ensue. One's intelligence, so defined, consists of the number and quality of one's insights—differentiations, generalizations, and restructurizations of one's life space. Within this frame of reference, successful behavior rightfully may be called intelligent only when a person might have done otherwise and his actions were premised upon envisioning what he/she was doing and why. Learning is enhancement of one's intelligence. This means that all of its forms—development of logical organizations, social insight, appreciation, information, and skills—have a common element: They all involve a change in the experiential situation of a person that gives him a basis for greater predictability and control in relation to his behavior; they enhance his intelligence.

To a large degree a person's intelligence is dependent upon the degree of his change in motivation, bodily coordination, and time perspective, his differentiation of aspects of his person from those of his environment, and his discernment of levels of concrete and imaginative reality. As a child develops by means of these processes, he/she learns increasingly to understand and control his environment. However, teachers have no reason to fear that a student will soon acquire complete understanding and see no further need to learn. The only person who may think he/she knows everything is the one who knows practically nothing. Once a student launches a serious study of his world, his life space accelerates its rate of expansion. As one's understanding expands to encompass newly gained regions of one's life space, one's life space also grows to such a degree that one's motivation for study actually multiplies. This is illustrated graphically in Figure 9.3.

By the time John is four years old, he has some insights and understandings. However, there are still many things around him that he does not understand, but which are a part of his life space in the sense that he realizes that

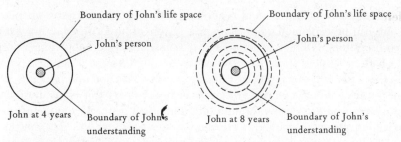

Figure 9.3 John's understanding of his life space at ages 4 and 8.

they have something to do with him. When John reaches his eighth birthday, he has expanded his world of understanding to encompass more and more of his psychological environment. But interestingly, because of the dynamic nature of human beings, John's psychological environment also expands. A teachers' job, then, is one of enhancement, enrichment, and acceleration of this psychological growth process. Teaching in its best sense, consists of promotion and enrichment of the interactive learning process, both qualitatively and quantitatively. Such teaching is a process of helping students both broaden and put greater quality into their psychological worlds.

How Does Intelligent Behavior Differ from Nonintelligent Behavior?

Cognitive-field psychologists view an intelligently behaving person as one who acts as if he/she is pursuing a purpose and has some foresights as to how it is to be achieved. "Effective psychological functioning is partly based on the capacity to anticipate the probable consequences of different courses of action.... By representing foreseeable outcomes [of behavior] symbolically, people convert future consequences into current motivations of behavior."[5] Nonintelligent behavior arises when a person is pushed or pulled about as an inert, nonliving object, just as a stone dislodged from a place of support falls to a lower lodgment. Let us picture a man straddling a pole and attempting to raise it from among a pile of similar poles. He is behaving intelligently. As the poles are moved, their position changes and suddenly a group of poles falls on the far end of the pole he is lifting; another group in the center serves as a fulcrum and the pole that he had been lifting suddenly raises him into the air. When he is moved into the air, he displays a nonintelligent behavior. He is behaving—moving—but there is no connection between this specific movement and his foresight of consequences. In intelligent behavior, an activity is carried forward to a goal through a process by which one constantly searches out the conditions for the next step all along the way. Intelligence, then, is largely a matter of foresight.

What Is Habit?

Learning is habit formation, but within cognitive-field psychology, *habit* comes to have a special definition. Habit is neither an act that is repeated automatically simply because of its frequent repetition in the past nor a fixed sequence of acts that can be explained adequately as a system of preformed pathways in the nervous system. (Of course, some sort of concomitant neural action is not denied.) Rather, habit is fluid, effective action arising through a person operating on the basis of the insights that he/she possesses. When one operates in terms of the insights or cognitive structures that one has, habit is manifested. Change in cognitive structures through differentiation, generalization, and restructurization means a change in meaning. When an event has meaning its psychological position and direction are determined; one knows what actions will lead to what results. This is the basis of habit.

Habits, then, are goal-related. In fact, a central idea of cognitive-field psychology is that all intelligent human endeavor is purposive. A *situation has meaning when it points to a course of action*. If a situation and its meaning are perceived simultaneously, then a person exhibits habit. Habit enables one to behave intelligently without thinking. Often there is not time to think; indeed, thinking then might be disastrous. What happens when your car is closely following a large truck and the truck stops abruptly?

What Is the Meaning of Cognitive-Field Psychology for Teaching Situations?

To summarize a cognitive-field theory of learning, we may say that a person learns through differentiating, generalizing, and restructuring both his person and psychological environment so as to acquire new or changed insights, understandings, or meanings concerning them, and thereby achieves changes in motivation, group belongingness, muscular skills, time perspective, and ideology. In this way, he gains greater control of himself and the world. Therefore, learning, concisely defined, is a process of one either gaining or changing one's insights, outlook, expectations, or thought patterns. Now, how is this learning theory applicable to teaching theory and practice?

Within the learning process, a constantly expanding world of understanding reaches out to encompass a constantly expanding psychological world. At birth, a child's psychological world is very small, but on his level each child is trying to understand that small world. He/she is trying to understand how to get food. Soon he/she will be seeking warmth. Later, the child will seek means of getting attention. As he/she grows, in order more adequately to influence his own destiny, he will seek insights into his world as it affects him.

A completely new situation would be cognitively unstructured; a person would have no knowledge of what would lead or point to what. Thus, at that moment the person's behavior would be completely random. (This is the position of a lower animal when it is first placed in a "problem box.") However, rarely if ever does a person function in a completely unstructured situation. More often, we find people in situations that are inadequately or inharmoniously structured. This means that they have problems and need to extend their learning, that is, to change the cognitive structures of their life spaces.

Within a cognitive-field approach to an educational situation, each teacher and each student is considered a discerning person in interaction with a psychological environment. A teacher's unique function is to implement and promote the development of serviceable insights of students so as to help students become more adequate and harmonious personalities—that is, more intelligent. To accomplish this, a teacher needs a basic understanding of the structure and dynamics of life spaces. The structure of a life space is its topology; its dynamics are its forces as represented by vectors.

The *topology* or *structure* of a life space shows the various possibilities for psychological movement or action; *vectors* or *dynamics* show the moving forces within the topological structure. To understand the behavior of a student, a teacher must determine the psychological position of the student's person in reference to the goal regions, that is, the topology, of the student's life space. This entails knowing the student's social position within and outside various groups, the student's position in relation to various ideas and activities, and the role of physical objects in the student's life space. The relationship of a student's person to the environmental regions of his life space determines the qualities of the student's immediate surroundings, which set the possibilities for the next step in the student's psychological life. The dynamics of a life space are indicated by vectors. They show what step or event means action toward and what step means action away from a person's goals. Thus, they represent psychological moving forces engendered by goals or barriers; they picture what is happening or likely to happen. The forces represented by vectors are the valences—the attracting and repelling powers—of respective regions of the student's psychological environment.

A student's life space on a given evening, topologically, may contain a television set, a book, and a movie. Vectorially, each object and activity has some degree of valence—alluring or repelling power. Should the student go to the movie, this means that the movie valence is greatest of all. When one behaves intelligently, one does what one wants to do; if one does not want to do it more than one wants to do it, one does not do it.

To analyze a psychological situation, a teacher should comprehend the structure of a person and his psychological environment and ascertain their dynamic properties—what they have to do with the student's behavior. That is, the teacher must see the relationships between the regions or parts of the student's life space, and the teacher must establish the nature of the respective factors residing within, at, and outside its boundary. Furthermore, he/she must assess the degree of permeability of the boundaries of the various regions of the student's life space. Such permeability means how susceptible the student is to change.

Factors outside the boundary of a life space, the foreign hull, are those that may be perceived by others but at the moment have no place in the perceptual world of the person being studied. Knowing these facts helps a teacher determine what is possible and what is not and what might happen and what might not. Then, to understand and accurately predict a student's behavior, a teacher, in addition to understanding the structure of the student's field—the interpositional relationships between the parts in his life space— must also ascertain the dynamic properties of the person's life space in terms of the valences of his goals and the barriers between himself and his goals.

Now what does all this mean in a school situation? Let us review the situation described on pages 193 through 196. "Alice is so absorbed with her teacher and schoolwork that she is oblivious to everything else about her, including the other children." The teacher is central in Alice's life space. Alice's schoolwork is also far within the border of her life space. The other children and everything else in the room that is not part of Alice's schoolwork are in the foreign hull of her life space. "Helen is a social butterfly; she wants the attention of most of the children in the classroom. She does give attention to the teacher from time to time, but right now she is concerned with other things." The other children are in Helen's life space; the teacher is at the margin, sometimes in and sometimes out. "John's body is in the classroom, but 'psychologically' John is riding a shiny new tractor which is being operated in the field adjoining the school." John's school environment and his psychological environment have little in common. Whereas little within the room is in his life space, the tractor is as central as it can be and its valence is very high.

For a teacher to teach a student in a significant way, it is imperative that there be an intersection of the student's life space with the teacher's and with the other life spaces in the room. Life spaces intersect when they have some regions in common. To ensure an adequate intersection of life spaces, a teacher must probe the various regions of the life spaces of the students.

Peripheral regions of a person are quite accessible in ordinary conversation. But is is more difficult to reach more central regions, that is, those that are near and dear to the person. However, a teacher who is thinking in dynamic field terms is probably more likely to see larger intrapersonal and interpersonal issues. To gain an understanding of individual students and their cognitive worlds, a teacher has to develop a sort of disciplined naiveté. In order adequately to see Helen through, the teacher must see through Helen. He/she must see Helen's person and environment as Helen sees them. When a teacher gains rapport with a student and thereby gains the student's confidence, the teacher's influence can extend to the student's central regions. The teacher now is in a position to speak of the student's needs. What a person needs depends primarily upon how he/she sizes up himself and his physical and social environment.

Teachers should bear in mind that a self or person is in the making constantly as one develops new insights, changes old ones, and forms new habits. Furthermore, a far-reaching change in the structure of a self or person can occur through one developing a significant educational insight. And finally, a student acquiring a new educational insight can be as significant and far reaching as falling in love, becoming converted, or realizing a great change in physical and social environment. "A large body of research now exists in which cognition is activated instructionally with impressive results. People learn and retain much better by using cognitive aids that they generate than by repetitive reinforced performance."[6]

Teachers who are committed to the application of cognitive-field psychology in their teaching may encourage students to memorize certain items that seem to be worth knowing verbatim, but they will strive to teach as much as possible on an *exploratory-understanding* level. At times, due to human limitations, they may drop back to an *explanatory-understanding* level. But they will guard against regressing to a memory level of teaching and learning. The levels of teaching and learning are developed in Chapters 11 through 14.

NOTES

1. Edward L. Deci, *Intrinsic Motivation* (New York: Plenum Press, 1975), p. VI.
2. See Edward C. Tolman, "Cognitive Maps in Rats and Men," *Psychological Review* 55 (July 1948):189–208.
3. See Wolfgang Köhler, *The Mentality of Apes* (New York: Vintage Books, 1959), p. 139.
4. Kurt Lewin, *Resolving Social Conflicts* (New York: Harper & Row, 1948), p. 64.
5. Albert Bandura, "Social Learning Theory," in Benjamin B. Wolman, ed., *International Encyclopedia of Psychiatry, Psychology, Psychoanalysis, and Neurology* (New York: Aesculapius, 1977). p. 311.
6. Albert Bandura, "Behavior Theory and the Models of Man," *American Psychologist* 29 (December 1974):865.

BIBLIOGRAPHY, CHAPTERS 8 AND 9

Baker, Bruce F. "Buber: Pointing Beyond the Funnel and the Pump." *Paideia* (1973); 34–37. Employs Buber's symbols of the funnel and the pump to represent autocratic and anarchic education. Then develops interaction as a desirable emergent synthesis.

Bandura, Albert. *Social Learning Theory.* New York: General Learning Press, 1971. Bandura's most complete presentation of his social learning theory.

Bandura, Albert. "Behavior Theory and the Models of Man." *American Psychologist* 29 (December 1974):859–869. Contrasts social learning theory with both environmental determination and existentialism.

Bigge, Morris L. "Dewey's Relativistic Philosophy, Lewin's Field Psychology, and Learning," in *Philosophy of Education in Cultural Perspective,* ed. James John Jelinek (Tempe, AZ: Far Western Philosophy of Education Society, 1977), pp. 399–421. A proposed harmonization of the topological and vector psychology of Lewin with the pragmatic educational philosophy of John Dewey and Boyd H. Bode. It suggests that a relativistic approach to learning is highly predictive of individual behavior.

Bolles, Robert C. *Theory of Motivation,* 2d ed. New York: Harper & Row, 1975. Good summaries of animal research on motivation and learning and critique of views on motivation.

Brown, Bob Burton. *The Experimental Mind in Education.* New York: Harper & Row, 1968. A book on general methods that applies Dewey's educational philosophy. Opens the way for using cognitive-field psychology.

Cantril, Hadley, ed. *The Morning Notes of Adelbert Ames, Jr.* New Brunswick, NJ: Rutgers University Press, 1960. Ruminations of Ames in regard to his activities and thoughts. Notes that whereas the assumptive world is a common one, a perceptual world is an individual one. Develops interdependencies of perceptions, purposes and actions.

Combs, Arthur W. *The Professional Education of Teachers*. Boston: Allyn & Bacon, 1965. Application of a perceptual view of students and teacher to effective teaching. *Perceptual* as used here is analogous to *interactive*. Shifts emphasis from a mechanistic to a personal view of teacher-student relations.

de Charms, Richard et al. *Enhancing Motivation: Change in the Classroom*. New York: Irvington, 1976. Reports study of student motivation, when students distinguish between *origins*—people who set goals for themselves—and *pawns*—people who follow the dictates of others.

Deci, Edward L. *Intrinsic Motivation*. New York: Plenum Press, 1975. "Intrinsic motivation" here has much in common with "interactive motivation" of cognitive-field theory.

Estes, William K. *Handbook of Learning and Cognitive Processes*. Vol. I, *Introduction to Concepts and Issues*. Vol. II, *Conditioning and Behavior Therapy*. Vol. III, *Approaches to Human Learning and Motivation*. Vol. IV, *Attention and Memory*. Vol. V, *Human Information Processing*. Vol. VI, *Linguistic Functions in Cognitive Theory*. Hillsdale, NJ: Lawrence Erlbaum, 1975–1978. Introduction to the major concepts, theories, and methods involved in the various facets of learning theory and cognitive psychology. Summary of research and models aimed toward development of general cognitive theory.

Gibson, James J. "The Concept of the Stimulus in Psychology." *American Psychologist* 15 (1960):694–703. Thesis: When psychologists pick the variables of physics as they appear in physics textbooks, they choose the wrong variables. Whether a potential stimulus becomes effective depends upon the individual's perception of it.

Harlow, Harry F. "The Formation of Learning Sets." *Psychological Review* 56 (January 1949):51–65. Based on research with animals, Harlow emphasizes the importance of learning how to learn—learning sets. Emphasizes problems as contrasted with trials in learning.

Kreitler, Hans, and Shulamith Kreitler. *Cognitive Orientation and Behavior*. New York: Springer, 1976. Cognitive processes and their contents are developed as major determinants of human molar behavior.

Lewin, Kurt. *Principles of Topological Psychology*. trans. Fritz Heider and Grace M. Heider. New York: McGraw-Hill, 1936. One of the two basic books written by Lewin in German and translated into English. It contains practically all of the structure of his field psychology but is more difficult to read than his later works. The later pages contain a valuable glossary of field concepts.

Lewin, Kurt. *Field Theory in Social Science*. New York: Harper & Row, 1951. A collection of Kurt Lewin's papers. The first three chapters and the last chapter develop guiding principles and constructs of field psychology. The remaining six chapters demonstrate application of field psychology principles to study of learning, development and regression, ecology, group dynamics, and social psychology.

Lindzey, Gardner, and Elliot Aronson, eds. *The Handbook of Social Psychology*, 2d ed., 1, *Historical Introduction and Systematic Positions*. Reading, MA: Addison-Wesley, 1968. In chapter 6 there is an excellent description by Morton Deutsch of field theory as it has been developed by Lewin and his students. Chapter 5 on cognitive theory and Chapter 7 on role theory contribute to understanding of the cognitive-field position.

Marrow, Alfred J. *The Practical Theorist: The Life and Work of Kurt Lewin.* New York: Basic Books, 1969. Develops the three areas of action that shaped Lewin's career: (1) his independent lifestyle, constant involvement in cooperative enterprises, and continued collaboration with former students; (2) his persistent integration of theory and practical action, exposure of theory to ingenious experimentation, and close coordination of seemingly abstruse hypotheses with affairs of everyday life; and (3) his successful combination of scientific concerns with personal and civic ones.

May, Rollo, *Psychology and the Human Dilemma.* New York: Van Nostrand Reinhold, 1967. The human dilemma results from man's capacity to experience himself as both subject and object simultaneously. Man being purely free or purely determined is not the way out.

Mischel, Walter. "The Self as the Person: A Cognitive Social Learning View." In Wandersman, Abraham, Paul J. Poppen, and David F. Ricks, eds. *Humanism and Behaviorism: Dialogue and Growth.* Oxford: Pergamon, 1976, pp. 145–156. Developed perceptual interaction within a cognitive social learning view of human activity.

Rosenthal, Ted L., and Barry J. Zimmerman. *Social Learning and Cognition.* New York: Academic Press, 1978. Application of social learning theory with emphasis on rule-governed conceptual behavior. Links human cognitive processes and observational learning. Treats language acquisition, moral and cognitive development, and modeling. Good summaries of contrasting learning and developmental theories.

Saltz, Eli. *The Cognitive Bases of Human Learning.* Homewood, IL: Dorsey Press, 1971. An examination of the cognitive process basic to learning. Centers on the nature and function of concepts.

Snygg, Donald. "Another Look at Learning Theory." *Educational Psychologist* 1, no. 1 (October 1933). Pages 9–11 present the case for cognitive-field learning theory.

Tolman, Edward C. *Collected Papers in Psychology.* Berkeley: University of California Press, 1951. Also published in 1958 under the title *Behavior and Psychological Man.* Papers reflecting Tolman's unit of psychological study as molar behavior purposively organized. Tolman's ideas bridged S-R associationism and Lewin's field theory. He accepted many field concepts, such as purpose and insight, but remained a behaviorist. He was critical of S-R connectionistic theories.

Wallace, John. *Psychology: A Social Science.* Philadelphia: Saunders, 1971. Emphasizes the study of persons in many social contexts. Develops alternative conceptions of the person, including several cognitive theories.

Weiner, Bernard. *Theories of Motivation from Mechanism to Cognition.* Chicago: Markham, 1972. Weiner's "humanistic" view parallels the view of cognitive-field theory; relates motivation and learning theory.

Weiner, Bernard, ed. *Cognitive Views of Human Motivation.* New York: Academic Press, 1974. Presents several differing cognitive views on motivation and relates the views to learning processes.

Chapter
10

How Does Learning Transfer to New Situations?

*T*ransfer *of learning* occurs when a person's learning in one situation influences that person's learning and performance in other situations. If there were no transfer at all, students would need to be taught specifically every act that they ever were to perform in any situation. Although when we think of transfer we usually consider how one learning experience *strengthens* another, there is also a negative transfer process within which one learning experience interferes with, that is, *weakens*, another. Generally speaking, what we learn in one situation tends to facilitate or help our learning in others. But the opposite effect, interference, can also occur. For example, a person's study of foreign language or philosophy can make him a slower reader of English literature, or his becoming committed to certain dogmas or absolutes can interfere with his future creative, reflective thought.

In its broadest sense, *transfer of learning is basic to the whole notion of schooling.* People who support, as well as those who conduct, our schools assume that matters being taught today will have some learning value in later times in different situations. Accordingly, the assumption that underlies our entire educational system is that knowledge gained in school not only will be available in the future but also will be applied, in some degree, to the solution of new problems as they arise in future school and life situations. For instance, we assume that today's lesson in arithmetic will help with tomorrow's problems in the same subject and that it will also help in dealing with algebra, geometry, and the physical sciences.

A predominant purpose of formal education in schools is to facilitate learning outside them. It would be difficult to justify any achievement of school learning that had no bearing upon students' future learning and life situations. Nevertheless, what is learned in school often contributes very little to children and youths solving their future problems. Thus, there appears to be much room for improvement in our teaching procedures so that transfer of formal learning to other situations will be enhanced to a much greater degree than at present.

The effectiveness of a school depends, in large measure, upon the amount and quality of transfer potential of the materials that students learn. Thus, transfer of learning is the cornerstone upon which education should ultimately rest. Unless students learn in school those matters that help them in meeting situations more effectively further along the academic sequence and later in life as well as in the present, they are wasting much of their time.

HOW IS TRANSFER A PROBLEM?

The basic problem of transfer is this: *In what way and to what extent will acquisition of skills, knowledge, understanding, behaviors, and attitudes in one subject or learning situation influence performance or learning in other subjects or situations?* Knowing the answer to this and some subordinate problems will enable us to teach for maximum, effective transfer of learning.

Some subordinate transfer problems are the following:

1. How does a person's current learning assist him in meeting future learning situations?
2. How does what students learn in school affect what they learn and do outside school?
3. Does school learning have as much effect as it should and how can it be made more effectual?

More specifically, in what manner and how much does the learning of a given material—say, memorizing the names of all the states and their capitals— aid, hinder, or have no effect upon subsequent learning, such as learning the content of a textbook? To what extent and in what way does the study of Latin enhance English vocabulary and grammar, aid in learning French or German, or contribute to knowledge of ancient history? How does a study of theories of learning contribute to one's knowledge of how to teach fourth-grade reading or high school physics? Will an individual carry over the arithmetic ability learned in a classroom to the problems actually encountered in business or in tasks about the house? Does practice in memorizing, reasoning, persevering, and willing improve the mental process in general? Can a student improve perception, retention, and imagination in all fields by practice in one?

We should guard against defining transfer too narrowly. Although it was a tremendous jump, it was an example of transfer of learning when Newton shifted the concept of falling bodies from small objects to planets. Furthermore, when we say that our central aim in education is to increase students abilities to think, we are discussing transfer.

The critical question in regard to transfer is not whether it takes place, but what conditions engender the greatest amount of it. Teaching definitely can be conducted so as to achieve transfer. Furthermore, it is highly probable that teaching can be brought to achieve a much higher degree of transfer than it now does. However, in order that we may teach for maximum transfer, we need to understand how transfer occurs. Having done this, we should help students learn how to learn so that transfer will reach a maximum level.

Everyone seems to agree that we want the maximum transfer of learning to new situations. But there is strong disagreement among both teachers and lay persons about the nature and likelihood of transfer. At one extreme, classical scholars advocate a strictly intellectual curriculum consisting of science, mathematics, classical languages, and history. At the other extreme, some educators maintain that any learning that remains completely verbal or abstract has negligible effect on learning and acting in concrete life situations. The latter group thinks of learning and transfer as being highly specific; its members believe that we should prepare students step by step for personal, civic, and vocational adulthood.[1]

Although teaching for transfer is of prime importance, it can be overemphasized to the degree that it actually impedes learning. Although we should enthusiastically promote transfer of learning, we simultaneously should recognize the possible negative consequences of an overemphasis that may contribute to a "cold storage" concept of education. We might come to think that childhood is not worthwhile in itself and that we must always be preparing for adulthood. Such thinking can have disastrous consequences; "preparation," if overworked, can have a vicious connotation.

Before embarking upon a study of the position on transfer that is held by each of the systematic learning theories, we need to consider how "generalizations" has become an important basic concept.

HOW DID GENERALIZATIONS BECOME THE KEY IDEA IN TRANSFER?

A generalization is a statement or understanding of relationships. It may also be called a principle, rule, or law. "Generalization is another name for the relating of experiences in such a way that what is gained at one point will redound to the advantage of the individual in many spheres of thought and action."[2] Early in the twentieth century, two eminent educational psychologists, Edward L. Thorndike and Charles H. Judd, carried on a running debate in regard to the nature of transfer. Whereas Professor Thorndike continued to champion his identical elements theory, Professor Judd insisted that generalizations, not identical elements, were transferred to new situations. Thus, the basic educational issue was identical elements versus generalization of experience. This issue centered upon the nature of transfer of learning, and it has persisted through the years. In its current form the issue is whether teachers should condition students with lists of specific essential serial *performances* or whether they should facilitate students' development of significant generalizations or *understandings*, which are instrumental to students' development of effectual activities or behaviors.

Judd recognized two possible kinds or levels of learning—rote memorization with little, if any, meaning and generalized knowledge with many intellectual associations. He placed very little value on the first level and a high premium upon the second. He was convinced that knowledge always should be in the form that makes generalizations possible. He even emphasized his generalizations theory when discussing the teaching of basic skills. He stated, "When new skills are cultivated by an individual, the muscles are brought into coordinated action through elaborately organized patterns developed in the nervous system"[3] "Generalizations which epitomize great numbers of experiences are the highest products of racial and individual intellectual effort."[4]

Judd's dart-throwing experiment to test the value of generalizations has become a classic. Success in hitting a target under water requires readjustment of one's ordinary habit of throwing a dart. Since the light coming from the target is refracted as it leaves the water, there is an apparent displacement of the target. Judd selected two groups of boys comparable in those variables that seemed relevant. One group, the experimental one, was instructed in the principle of—generalization in regard to—the refraction of light; the other, the control group, was not. Both groups of boys were then asked to throw darts in such a way as to hit underwater objects with them. At the beginning of the experiment, none of the boys had any skill in throwing darts.

Both groups of boys were instructed to hit targets placed 12 inches under water. The boys who had had theoretical training in the principles of refraction did as poorly at this first task as did the control group; they had to learn to throw darts before their theoretical training could help. Once this was accomplished, the target was moved to a position 4 inches under water. Immediately the experimental group showed a conspicuous superiority over the control group. Their understanding of the nature of refraction had given them cues as to where to aim the darts in order to hit underwater objects that are not where they appear to be.[5]

Since, for Judd, "the most effective use of knowledge is assured not through the acquisition of any particular item of experience but only through the establishment of associations which illuminate and expand an item of experience so that it has general value,"[6] students should be taught the advantages of generalization by every possible device.

> The preventive for the narrowness of school teaching and for lack of transfer is to be sought in the organization of instruction in such a way that the learner will constantly be made to see the broad relations of items of experience.[7]

Judd's position paralleled similar, but not identical, findings of the Gestalt psychologists. Köhler, Koffka, Wheeler, Perkins, and other Gestalt psychologists all insisted that what lower animals and human beings tend to learn in any meaningful learning situation is *relationships*. However, Gestalt psychologists imputed a purposiveness to behavior that Judd could not see. Statements of relationships also are theories, generalizations, principles, rules, or laws that, as Judd said, are "a kind of summary of many experiences. It [generalization] makes possible the proper interrelating and interpreting of a whole body of varied experiences."[8]

Current "mastery teaching" harks back to Judd's "generalizations." See Chapter 12, pages 266 through 268 for development of current mastery teaching as promoted by Benjamin S. Bloom and James H. Block.

Since accumulated experimentation has shown that attempts to base transfer on the identical elements theory leads to more problems than it solves, and since the generalization theory seems highly productive as a basis for transfer, many educational psychologists today prefer some form of the generalization theory. However, sharp differences exist among adherents of the generalization theory. The position of Judd and his followers is decidedly different from that of contemporary cognitive interactionists. This difference is epitomized by the statement that whereas Judd adhered to a mechanistic concept of transfer, cognitive interactionists see transfer of learning always in the frame of reference of purposive intellectual pursuits.

Current cognitive interactionists feel that Judd stopped short of a fully adequate statement of the conditions of transfer. It is increasingly apparent that the achievement of a generalization by a student does not in itself guarantee that transfer will take place automatically. For transfer to occur, a student must desire to use the understandings or insights that he/she has acquired. (See Chapter 7, page 150 for Bandura's treatment of this issue.)

WHAT QUESTIONS ARE BASIC TO A STUDY OF TRANSFER?

Each systematic learning theory—natural unfoldment, mental discipline, apperception, S-R bond, classical conditioning, reinforcement, and linear and cognitive-field interaction—implies a somewhat different theory of transfer. In fact, a description of the theory of transfer of a given learning theory has much in common with a description of the learning theory itself.[9] The transfer problem is so pervasive that any treatment of the position of adherents of a systematic learning theory in regard to transfer, of necessity, comprises a summary of the learning theory itself.

By its very nature, *natural unfoldment* has few, if any, positive implications for transfer. Hence, we deal with it here only briefly. Exponents of natural unfoldment regard intellectual development as something that "just naturally happens." To be consistent with their overall outlook, they would reject any kind of formal teaching for the purpose of stimulating development of intelligence. Instead, they would stress student-planned activities including highly permissive types of projects as the means for releasing or developing latent intellectual talents. In this way, contemporary existentialist humanists promote the development of autonomous, self-actualizing persons. In a laissez-faire classroom, students would exercise almost unlimited freedom.[10]

Adherents of each learning theory develop their respective positions in regard to transfer through answering some specific questions, such as:

1. How is learning best defined?
2. What exactly does transfer of learning mean?
3. How is transfer promoted most effectively?

In the remaining sections of this chapter we review the various answers that adherents of different theories provide for these questions. Although question 1 is not centered on transfer as such, we must first review each learning theory in order to establish a background for consideration of questions 2 and 3, which deal with the transfer problem proper.

HOW DOES MENTAL DISCIPLINE IMPLY GENERAL TRANSFER?

The conception of education as mental (formal) discipline seems to go far back in recorded history. Furthermore, prior to the nineteenth century, general transfer of training through mental discipline was widely accepted in educational circles of the Western world.[11] Consequently, from its beginning until the end of the nineteenth century, American formal education was dominated by the doctrine of mental discipline. During this period education was regarded as necessarily laborious. Schoolroom atmospheres were at least austere and sometimes harsh. Teachers usually were dictators—sometimes benevolent, but sometimes even contentious. Children were expected to be respectful and obedient and to accept at face value whatever teachers told them. Curriculums were relatively fixed with an almost exclusive emphasis, in elementary schools, on the fundamental skill subjects and, in secondary schools, on such "disciplinary" subjects as Latin, history, and mathematics.

The two most influential groups in the United States who continue to favor a disciplinary approach to education are some leaders in parochial education and those liberal arts professors who are under the influence of faculty psychology and the classical tradition. In addition, there are many thousands of other persons,including some public school teachers, who gravitate toward a theory of mental discipline.

How Do Mental Disciplinarians Define Learning?

The central idea in mental discipline is that the mind, envisioned as a nonphysical substance, or its constituent faculties lie dormant until they are exercised. Faculties such as memory, will, reason, and perseverance are the "muscles of the mind"; like physiological muscles, they are strengthened only through exercise, and subsequent to their adequate exercise they operate automatically. Thus, learning is a matter of strengthening, or disciplining, the faculties of the mind whose functions combine to produce intelligent behavior.

Adherents of mental discipline think that the primary value of history or any other disciplinary subject is the training effect it has on the minds of students. They are convinced that this effect will remain after the "learned" material has been forgotten. Furthermore, they consider the highest value of education to be its liberalizing effect—its development of intellectual capacities to think, reason, and judge.

How Do Mental Disciplinarians Define Transfer?

According to the mental discipline theory, germs of the various faculties are in each individual from birth, and learning is a process of one's developing these germinal, undeveloped faculties into powers or capacities. When teachers are asked about the value of studying a particular subject and they reply, "It sharpens the mind and improves the memory," or "It cultivates the reasoning faculty," they are thinking of learning as mental discipline and of that which is transferred as being generally exercised germinal capacity. Thus, the teachers think that they are building in their students a great power reservoir that will automatically go into operation in any kind of subsequent mental activity.

The various inherited faculties can be developed through training and become capable of effective performance in all areas in which they are involved. Thus, the training of the faculty of memory through memorizing anything, including nonsense syllables, presumably improves one's memory for names, for meaningful material, and in fact for anything that calls for memory. Likewise, after receiving training in reasoning through a study of geometry, a person can reason effectively in realms of philosophy, mathematics, social issues, and housekeeping. Accordingly, education is largely a matter of training or disciplining minds with vigorous mental exercise in the classics, grammar, logic, mathematics, and pure science on the assumption that such training makes a person equally effective in all areas where a given faculty is employed.

Since, within mental discipline theory, transfer is assumed to be automatic, once a faculty has developed it naturally goes into operation whenever its use is appropriate. Notice that, within mental discipline theory, *psychological processes* such as thinking, attending, remembering, and persevering became *mental faculties* such as thought, attention, memory, and perseverance.

How Do Mental Disciplinarians Promote Transfer?

Educational practice based upon mental discipline stresses the necessity for developing the "muscles of the mind" by rigorous exercise. Mental disciplinarians have little desire to make schoolwork pleasant or interesting. In fact, more discipline is engendered if the tasks are unpleasant and burdensome; the harder the exercise, the more the faculties are disciplined. Thus, the more difficult the school work, the more effective it is thought to be. Since subjects such as Latin, mathematics, and science, taught arbitrarily, seem particularly arduous, they have been enthusiastically taught in schools for their disciplinary value.

To a mental disciplinarian, the direct utility of a subject is of little consequence; exercise of the mental faculties is what is important. The material or content upon which the exercise is expended makes little difference, except that it must be of such nature as to require strenuous exertion. Certain mental powers or faculties such as tenacity and logicality, exercised and developed in the study of, say, botany, carry over automatically to all aspects of life wherein the same mental powers are required. A teacher, then, should not be an amateur psychiatrist, social worker, and baby-sitter, but a scholarly educator. Since faculties are strengthened through mental practice much as muscles are strengthened through physical exercise, the most difficult subjects are the most desirable for stretching the mind. Furthermore, long, difficult assignments develop the faculties of will power and attention.

Mental discipline as an educational doctrine was first seriously challenged by William James, who found no improvement in his ability to commit poetry to memory resulting from a month's practice in memorizing Hugo's *Satyr*. Both Thorndike and Woodworth[12] reported similar findings in regard to possible development of mental faculties through exercise. However, even in the face of James's, Thorndike's and Woodworth's research in this area, many scholars continue to endow certain subjects, particularly the more abstract ones, with immensely superior transfer power.

Students who have mastered difficult subjects usually do have above-average proficiency in whatever areas of study and thinking they happen to pursue. Although it does not necessarily follow, it is easy to assign credit for this proficiency to the nature of the specific subjects that have been studied; it often is overlooked that people who elect or survive difficult subjects perhaps had more ability when they started them. This is an example of the *post hoc ergo propter hoc*—"after this, therefore on account of it"—fallacy. Instructors and others may fallaciously reason that, after taking certain courses, youth are good students; therefore, the courses made them into good students.[13] We should recognize, however, that, even though mental disciplinarians' reasoning may be fallacious in this regard, their procedure becomes a screening device, whether or not it is an educating one. A school may "maintain high standards" through teaching for mental discipline and grading so rigorously that a high percentage of students fail and drop out. By doing so, it can raise the quality of its students; but the increased quality of students, thus gained, is no indication of improved quality of instruction.

In light of current psychological knowledge, it is difficult to justify school subjects purely in terms of improving students' minds through exercise. Evidently there is transfer of learning, but not the general transfer implied in mental discipline. Methods of solving arithmetic problems can be transferred to the solution of problems in algebra. The learning of Latin may, and often does, facilitate the learning of English grammar. However, if experimental research is to be trusted, transfer is not automatic, and it is not a matter of disciplining minds.

Herbartian apperception, S-R conditioning, and cognitive-interactionist theories of learning, while disagreeing on many points, all agree in their opposition to mental discipline. Their strongest evidence has been the results of systematic research that tests the results of different teaching and learning procedures. During the first half of the twentieth century it seemed that Thorndike, Woodworth, and James had rendered a killing blow to mental discipline and that it no longer would be seriously promulgated in our public schools. However, during recent decades many scholars in the arts and sciences and others following in their wake have seriously and vehemently advocated this theory of learning and transfer, divorced from experimental evidence and support.

As we study outlooks on transfer that have arisen to challenge mental discipline, perhaps we can formulate a point of view that is more adequate than mental discipline itself or any of the competing theories that immediately followed and challenged it.

HOW IS APPERCEPTION RELATED TO TRANSFER OF LEARNING?

There are two broad types of associationisms: (1) early mentalistic associationisms, which focus upon the association of ideas in a mind, and (2) more modern physicalistic S-R associationisms, which are concerned with formation of connections either between cells in a brain and peripheral nervous system or between organic responses and environmental stimuli.

Herbartian apperception has been the leading example of the first type of associationism. Although Herbart's associationist psychology was built on fundamentally different premises from the natural unfoldment theory of followers of Rousseau, it was equally incompatible with mental discipline. Hence, Herbartian teaching, like Rousseauean permissiveness, can be considered a counterinfluence to mental discipline. However, the formal, rigid approach of Herbartians, coupled with what seemed to be emphasis upon rote learning, made their teaching appear on the surface to be much like the kind of education practiced by the mental disciplinarians. Herbart's prescription for good teaching, as implemented by his followers, became highly mechanical. Furthermore, apperception, like mental discipline, made teachers central and dominant in the educational process.[14]

How Do Apperceptionists Define Learning?

Apperception is a process of relating new ideas or mental states to a store of old ones. A person's store of ideas constitutes his apperceptive mass. Memories stored in the subconscious and brought into the conscious mind enable one to receive and interpret current experiences. New ideas are learned through being related to what already is in an apperceptive mass. Thus, apperception consists of an idea assimilating itself with other, already acquired ideas. A student's mentality is made up of the apperceptive mass of ideas that have come to the student from without.

Learning, then, is not a matter of developing or training a mind but, rather, one of formation of an apperceptive mass. Education is a process of a teacher's causing present, specified experiences of students to combine with appropriate backgrounds. Consequently, apperceptionists emphasize implantation in the minds of students of a great mass of facts and ideas that have been organized by someone other than the learner—usually the author of a text or a teacher. The stored ideas lead to feelings and willings, and these lead to acts.

How Do Apperceptionists Explicitly Define Transfer?

According to apperception theory, a student's "subconscious mind" contains a quantity of mental states that have been accumulated during previous experiences. Any one of these elements of the apperceptive mass stands ready to spring back into consciousness when the appropriate occasion occurs; it is ready to join other mental elements with which it has an affinity.

By use of textbooks and lectures, apperceptionists "cover" their subject. Students learn the material, retain much of it in their apperceptive masses, and carry it over to meet future situations in and out of school. This information will be used whenever a situation arises in which it is needed. Appropriateness, however, is determined by the nature of the mental states or ideas, not by the person.

Mental states are stored in the form of sense impressions, copies of previous sense impressions or images, and affective elements such as pleasure or pain. Such mental states provide the total source of mental activity. Feelings and willings are secondary factors, which are derived from original mental states. Consequently, volition or willing has its roots in thought; right thinking produces right action.

How Do Apperceptionists Promote Transfer?

Apperceptionists promote transfer by building up the apperceptive masses of their students. The Herbartian principles of *association* and *frequency* are the heart of apperception theory. The *association* principle is that when a number of ideas form a mass, the combined powers of the mass determine the new ideas that will enter consciousness; this is the basis of interest. The coordinate principle of *frequency* is that the more often an idea has been brought into consciousness, the easier it is for it to return. Application of these two laws leads teachers to emphasize frequent presentation of the *proper* ideas to students. Teachers are convinced that transfer is best when a goodly supply of facts and principles are stored for later use. If people know facts and principles pertinent to a given area of learning or living, they automatically will use them as appropriate occasions occur.

Apperceptive teaching, in order to maximize transfer, continues to follow the Herbartian five steps—preparation, presentation, comparison, generalization, and application. This entails careful preparation and rigid employment of detailed lesson plans that outline and prescribe a fixed order of teaching and learning.[15]

Apperception, as a theory of transfer, has been a vital force in attacking its predecessor—mental discipline. However, the jump from the assumption that people innately are either bad and active or neutral and active to the assumption that they are inertly passive was not all to the good. In apperception theory, *transfer becomes completely a matter of mechanistic storage of ideas in a mind, which is composed only of those ideas.* As such, the theory implies that teaching is an indoctrination procedure. Thus, it throws schools out of harmony with the democratic structure of American society. Since students depend completely upon the teacher, who provides all of the leadership in learning, critical thinking is discouraged and students tend to be docile. Facts are acquired for test purposes, then rapidly forgotten; their transfer value tends to be very low. Furthermore, problem-centered teaching is largely disregarded.

We should recognize, however, that, regardless of their shortcomings, apperceptionists have told us much about experience that otherwise might escape our attention. They have realized that when a person has a new experience, there is a "reception committee" of background ideas that help him interpret it. Furthermore, they have noted that experiences, in some way, abide after being undergone and that current experiences have considerable influence in determining the nature of subsequent experiences.

Apperception was a connecting link that led the way for development of both mechanistic and purposive contemporary psychologies. We examine these next to see how they have treated the problem of transfer.

Why Did Connectionism Emphasize Identical Elements?

The S-R bond or connectionistic theory of learning was developed by Edward L. Thorndike and his followers. Its basic thesis is that through conditioning, specific response patterns come to be connected with specific stimuli. The theory of transfer that accompanies connectionism is transfer of *identical elements.*[16]

The identical elements theory of transfer means that learning is facilitated in a new situation to the extent that it contains identical factors or elements that occurred in an earlier learning situation.[17] Identical elements may take the form of like contents, procedures, facts, actions, attitudes, techniques, or principles. The identical elements theory implied that a school should list the aspects of situations that are important either out of school or in later courses and teach students to cope with each specific one. Accordingly, lists of spelling words were drawn from articles, letters, and documents written by adults. Likewise, reading vocabulary lists contained words that adults read in newspapers and magazines.

How Did Connectionists Define Learning?

Connectionism was "the doctrine that all mental processes consist of the functioning of native and acquired connections between situations and responses (Thorndike)."[18] The acquired connections are formed through random, not purposive, trial and error; they constitute learning. Since S-R bonds or connections are, in some way, the product of physiological changes in a nervous system, learning is associated with neurological changes.

Three major connectionistic laws of learning—readiness, exercise, and effect—and five minor ones—multiple response, set, prepotency of elements, response by analogy, and associative shifting—operate whenever acquired connections occur.[19] In addition to the eight laws of learning, *belongingness, impressiveness, polarity, identifiability, availability*, and *mental system* also have appeared as special learning concepts in the vocabularies of connectionists.[20] Thus, connectionists developed some 15 mechanistic laws or principles to encompass learning phenomena and pertinent research.

How Did Connectionists Define Transfer of Learning?

Connectionists regarded human activities of all sorts as responses made by human organisms to stimuli or stimulus situations. A stimulus or stimulus situation is any event that impinges upon and thereby influences an individual. A response includes all components of any unified, organic behavior. When identical elements occur in two learning situations, transfer from the first to the second is taken to be automatic. Since what one learns basically is a group of reactive responses to a complex stimulus situation, responses are the elements that are transferred to new situations. However, for transfer to occur, learning situations must be of such nature that they contain some of the same reactions. For example, transfer from a study of Latin to learning English depends upon the extent to which there are identical elements or reactions in the two subject matters or procedures.

Thorndike wrote: "A change in one function alters another only insofar as the two functions have as factors identical elements."[21] Accordingly, transfer takes place from one learning situation to another only to the extent that there are identical aspects in the two. This means that transfer takes place from playing a piano to typing to the extent that such skills as eye-finger coordination are identical in both operations. However, elements of similarity between two situations are not necessarily restricted to skills; they may take the form of information, principles, procedures, or attitudes. Furthermore, identity of elements can be in either subject matter or procedures; thus, learning is facilitated in a second situation to the extent in which it includes any factors of elements that occurred in the first.

Thorndike's colleagues and followers recognized that stimulus and response generalization were basic processes in transfer. However, they limited the generalization concept to characterization of stimuli and responses and made very little, if anything, of teaching for generalizations as such. Accordingly, they noted that if an animal learns to respond to a given stimulus, it will tend to react likewise to related stimuli. For example, when a dog learns to salivate at one tone, it will also salivate in response to similar tones. *Response generalization* occurs when a person learns to perform an act with one part of his organism and then is able to perform the same act, perhaps not so proficiently, with another segment of his organism. For example, in bilateral transfer, a skill acquired with one hand, foot, or eye is transferred to the other.

How Did Connectionists Promote Transfer of Learning?

Since, according to connectionism, each person is limited by his inborn neural structure, the most that education can do is to take advantage of what capacity a child or youth has for forming dependable S-R linkages. A person's capacity for intelligent behavior depends upon how many links can be formed and retained. Hence, the best—in fact, the only—way education can serve humanity is to condition students efficiently.

Thorndike thought that teaching specifically for transfer is the only method of teaching that is worthwhile. He was convinced that knowledge should consist of well-ordered groups of connections that are related to each other in useful ways and whose inner relationships correspond to those of the real world. Furthermore, he thought that the more clearly the crucial elements, facts, or principles in a situation are brought to the student's attention, the more readily the same elements, facts, or principles may be identified in another situation.[22]

The identical elements principle, when applied to curriculum matters, means *specific objectivism*. Schools are encouraged to decide exactly what students should be taught and to teach these directly, not through some roundabout means. Consequently, if a student is to learn English grammar, the most effective way of doing this is to learn English grammar, not to attack English grammar by way of Latin or some other foreign language. Although connectionism as such generally is no longer promoted in schools, current emphasis upon teaching specific performances has connectionist overtones.

According to the theory of identical elements, although study of Latin does not discipline either mental faculties or a generalized mind, it does contribute to transfer to the degree that there are identical elements in Latin and English vocabularies. The "port" of Latin *portare* (to carry) does transfer to the "port" of English *transport*. Consequently, in accordance with the identical elements theory, if Latin is to be taught at all, emphasis should be placed upon those of its roots or segments that are identical with those in English. However, even then the study of Latin roots of English words as they apply to English is more economical in learning English than is the study of Latin as a language.

If one bases a school program on the identical elements conception of transfer, one's only choice is to incorporate in the curriculum as many learning tasks as possible that, when reproduced outside of school, will contribute to the effectiveness of living. An entire generation of curriculum makers in the 1920s and 1930s, led by Franklin Bobbitt and W. W. Charters, did, in fact, adopt this approach. They studied American community life much as an efficiency expert would conduct time-and-motion studies in a factory. They then listed the specific verbal and motor responses that are needed in daily life and taught these, with only minor modification, in school. (The current emphasis on performance-based education has much in common with this specific objectivism of the 1920s.)

This approach to education poses many difficulties, not the least of which is that there are so many kinds of situations in life to be faced that a school cannot possibly teach them all, even in the 12 or 13 years of required attendance. Thus, curriculums tend to become cluttered with too many specific objectives, many of which conflict with one another.

What Has Skinner's Operant Conditioning Implied About Transfer of Learning?

Since B. F. Skinner was highly optimistic in regard to the application of his theory to practical schoolroom situations, we use his ideas on transfer as a contemporary representative of the S-R conditioning family. Each of the representatives of this, as well as the other psychological outlooks, has its own theory of transfer; however, there tends to be a similarity between the theories of transfer of the various members of each family of learning theory.[23]

Skinner questioned the reality of the inner qualities and faculties to which human achievements in the past have often been attributed. Hence, in his study of learning and transfer he turned from ill-defined and remote explanations of behavior to the study of observable and manipulable behavior. For Skinner, the basic object of psychological study was the probability of observable behavior, which "is accounted for by appeal to the genetic endowment of the organism and its past and present environment, described wholly in the language of physics and biology."[24] Accordingly, he thought that there is nothing to be lost by applying Newtonian mechanistic science to education and moral discourse and that any resistance to this movement is only an expression of culture lag.

How Did Skinner Define Learning?

Operant conditioning is the learning process within which a response, or operant, is both shaped and brought to be more probable or frequent through its being reinforced by a change in an organism's environment after the operant or response occurs.[25] In this process there is no necessary connection of stimuli and responses; reinforcement simply increases the probability of a response or class of responses; a reinforcing stimulus is a differentiating, not a connecting one.

In keeping with his physicalistic commitment (a physicalist is one who holds human thoughts and actions to be determined by physical laws), Professor Skinner stated, "I do not see any distinction between predicting what an individual is going to do and predicting what, let us say, a sailboat is going to do."[26] "Operant conditioning shapes behavior as the sculptor shapes a lump of clay."[27]

Through receiving reinforcement of slightly varied instances of his behavior, a child learns to raise himself, walk, grasp objects, and move them about. Later on, through the same process, he/she learns to talk, sing, dance, and play games—in short, to exhibit the enormous repertoire characteristic of a normal adult. Furthermore, in a world in which ethical training is widespread, most people are reinforced by succeeding in reinforcing others. Thus, personal gratitude is a powerful *generalized reinforcer*. (See page 98 for a discussion of schedules of reinforcement.)

A list of values is actually a list of reinforcers. "People behave in ways which, as we say, conform to ethical, governmental, or religious patterns, because they are reinforced for doing so."[28] An organism can be reinforced by (that is, it can be made to "choose") almost any given state of affairs. Literature, art, and entertainment are contrived reinforcers. Whether a person buys a book, a ticket to a performance, or a work of art depends upon whether it is reinforcing to him, and usually it is reinforcing to him if he/she had been reinforced when he previously purchased such an article.

For Skinner, any innate behavior is in the form of unlearned reflexes. A reflex has been called such on the theory that, in its operation, the disturbance caused by a stimulus passes to the central nervous system and is reflected back to the muscles or glands. Although Skinner did not give reflexes the dominant position in his behavioral theory, he definitely recognized both innate and conditioned ones. However, he noted that if we were to assemble all the behavior that falls into the pattern of the simple reflexes, we would have only a very small fraction of the total behavior of an organism.

Innate or hereditary reflexes primarily activate the internal economy of an organism, where glands and smooth muscles are operative. When dust blows into an organism's eyes, the organism reflexively washes it out with a profuse secretion of tears; when food enters the stomach, peristaltic action is stimulated. However, in addition to the internal reflexes, there are also some external innate reflexes, such as the startle reflex at the sound of a loud noise.

Skinner noted that when we study overt behavior, reflexes, particularly innate ones, are of little importance. However, he believed that responsible behavior is determined by environmental stimuli just as the reflexes are. He stated,

> We do not hold people responsible for their reflexes—for example, for coughing in church. We hold them responsible for their operant behavior—for example, for whispering in church or remaining in church while coughing. But there are variables which are responsible for whispering as well as for coughing, and they may be just as inexorable. When we recognize this, we are likely to drop the notion of responsibility altogether and with it the doctrine of free will as the inner causal agent.[29]

What Is Transfer in Operant Conditioning?

Since within operant conditioning learning is simply a change in the form and probability of a response, transfer likewise is an increased probability of responses of a certain class occurring in the future. Remember that a reinforcer is any stimulus whose presentation or removal increases the probability of a response; there are both positive and negative reinforcers.[30] Because a single instance of a response or operant may be strengthened by being followed by a reinforcing event and the effect survive for a long time even though the same consequence never recurs, operant reinforcement provides a strong theoretical basis for transfer.

Skinner thought that nearly all human behavior is the product of operant reinforcement and that most reinforcement improves the efficiency of behavior through continuously reshaping it. He wrote,

While we are awake, we act upon the environment constantly, and many of the consequences of our actions are reinforcing. Through operant conditioning the environment builds a basic repertoire with which we keep our balance, walk, play games, handle instruments and tools, talk, write, sail a boat, drive a car, or fly a plane. A change in the environment—a new car, a new friend, a new field of interest, a new job, a new location—may find us unprepared, but our behavior usually adjusts quickly as we acquire new responses and discard old.[31]

Thus, to Skinner's way of thinking, one's repertoire of conditioned operants is the basis for transfer of one's learning.

The three key concepts in understanding the meaning of transfer within operant conditioning are *conditioned reinforcement*, *stimulus* and *response induction*, and *conditioned generalized reinforcement*.

Conditioned Reinforcement   In conditioned reinforcement a new stimulus becomes a conditioned reinforcer; that is, a new reinforcer (stimulus B) is conditioned through its occurrence along with an originally adequate reinforcing stimulus (stimulus A). Stimulus B comes to reinforce an act operantly in the same way as the originally adequate reinforcing stimulus (stimulus A) would. Thus, stimulus B becomes a conditioned reinforcer.

An example of conditioned reinforcement is that if, each time we give food to a "hungry" pigeon to reinforce an act that we are teaching him, we turn on a light, the light eventually will become a conditioned reinforcer; it may be used to reinforce the act or some other operant just as food formerly was used.[32] "If we have frequently presented a dish of food to a hungry organism, the empty dish will elicit the animal's salivation. To some extent the empty dish will also reinforce an operant."[33] Thus, through conditioned reinforcement, other things may acquire the reinforcing power that food, water, and sexual contact originally had.

A characteristic of human behavior is that primary—originally adequate— reinforcers may be effective even after long delays. This presumably is only because in intervening events, other objects, such as symbols, become conditioned reinforcers. In education, techniques are deliberately designed to create appropriate conditioned reinforcers and thereby transfer is promoted. When a student performs properly, the teacher gives him a smile and an A; the A comes to be a conditioned reinforcer, it then will "reward" the student for many kinds of activity—operants.

Stimulus and Response Induction   Skinner preferred the term *induction* for what more commonly is called stimulus or response *generalization*. Thus, induction occurs in regard to both stimuli and responses; that is, there is both stimulus induction and response induction.[34]

Stimulus induction is a process through which a stimulus either acquires or loses its capacity to elicit a response, control a discriminative response, or set up an emotional "state," because of its similarity to a stimulus that has acquired or lost such a capacity through direct conditioning. If a red light is established as a discriminative stimulus, an orange (or even yellow) light may be found to share the same function, perhaps in a lesser degree.

Response induction is a process through which a response changes its probability or rate because it shares properties with another response that has changed its probability or rate through reinforcement. When a dog has been trained to roll over by being rewarded and it is "told" to "roll over," it may make a twisting motion while remaining on its feet.

For us to understand Skinner's induction theory, we must remember that reinforcement does not strengthen the response that preceded it; instead, it increases the probability of a class of responses, and the class is represented by certain specific responses that occur in the future. Furthermore, we must keep in mind that a class of responses consists of those responses that contain the same elements. Thus, Skinner's basic measure of behavior is a response element rather than a response itself. A *response element* "is a sort of behavioral atom, which may never appear by itself upon any single occasion but is the essential ingredient or component of all observed instances. The reinforcement of a response increases the probability [of occurrence] of all responses containing the same elements."[35]

A large complex of words—an idiom, a phrase, or a memorized passage—may be under the control of a single variable and thus constitute a functional unit.[36] A functional unit of behavior, however, consists of a number of basic *behavioral atoms* or elements. Behavioral atoms, as contrasted with functional units, are at least as small as separate speech sounds. We must recognize these small behavioral atoms in order to account for distorted verbal responses such as spoonerisms and other verbal slips (a spoonerism is an accidental transposition of sounds—saying "blushing crow" for "crushing blow"). These "atoms" also are evident in the stylistic devices of alliteration, rhyme, and rhythm. When we identify elements rather than responses as units of behavior, we then say "the *elements* [atoms] *are* strengthened wherever they occur." [37]

In the life of each organism, through the process of stimulus and response induction, there is constant movement from primary to generalized reinforcement. Usually, in this process, a conditioned reinforcement is being generalized.

Conditioned Generalized Reinforcement   Conditioned reinforcement and induction or generalization combine to give conditioned generalized reinforcement. A stimulus that is a conditioned reinforcer is generalized when, in the process of its becoming a conditioned reinforcer, it is paired with more than one primary reinforcer; "if a conditioned reinforcer has been paired with reinforcers appropriate to many conditions, at least one appropriate state of deprivation is more likely to prevail upon a later occasion."[38] Thus, a response is more likely to occur. For example, when we reinforce behavior with money, our subsequent control of the behavior of an individual is relatively independent of any momentary deprivation. Money becomes a conditioned, generalized reinforcer because from time to time, money occurs along with many primary reinforcers. Thus, it acquires the capacity to reinforce many behaviors.

Skinner observed that a token such as money is a conditioned generalized reinforcer distinguished by its physical specifications. He further noted that money is not the only token that is a conditioned generalized reinforcer. In education an individual behaves as he/she does, in part, because of the marks,

grades, and diplomas that he previously has received. These are not so readily exchanged for primary reinforcement as money, but the possibility of exchange is there. Educational tokens form a series in which one token may be
exchanged for the next and the commercial or prestige value of the final token,
the diploma, is usually quite clear.

How Is Transfer Promoted in Operant Conditioning?

For Skinner, "Education is the establishing of behavior which will be of advantage to the individual and to others at some future time."[39] Thus, the teacher
is the architect and builder of behaviors. Within the building process a teacher
is to supply arbitrary and sometimes spurious consequences for the sake of
feedback—reinforcement.

Skinner's criticism of many of today's teaching procedures has not been that
there are no reinforcers operating, but that the ones that do operate mostly
reinforce merely going to school and gaining a diploma or a degree. There is
a woefully inadequate number of reinforcers for learning the subject matter
elements themselves.

As stated in Chapter 5, the first task of a teacher, according to Skinner,
is to shape proper responses in children, such as pronouncing and writing
correctly. However, the principal task of the teacher is to bring these correct
behaviors under many sorts of stimulus control. Thus, in the education of a
child for future constructive behavior, four basic questions must be faced:

1. What behavior is to be set up?
2. What reinforcers are at hand?
3. What responses are available in embarking upon a program of progressive approximation that will lead to the final form of the behavior?
4. How can reinforcement be most efficiently scheduled to maintain the
   behavior in strength?

The last question states the problem of enhancement of transfer as it is understood by operant conditioning theorists.

The maintenance of behavior in strength after it has been acquired is as
much a function of reinforcement as is the original learning. After an organism
has learned how to do something, that is, after it has acquired a behavior,
further reinforcements are necessary to maintain the behavior in strength. In
this process various schedules of reinforcements are of special importance.[40]
Thus, transfer of learning is promoted by repeated reinforcement of desired
behavior and by using the most effective schedules of reinforcement.

HOW DO COGNITIVE INTERACTIONISTS VIEW TRANSFER OF LEARNING?

Cognitive interactionists represent either a linear or a cognitive-field oriented
psychological position. Whereas linear cognitive interactionism is a synthesis of purposive cognitive psychology and a uniquely defined "reinforcement"

theory, cognitive-field interactionism is a purposive cognitive psychology that is an alternate to all behavioristic-oriented psychologies. However, the two psychologies have enough in common to be treated as complementary ones that provide a psychological foundation for Chapter 13 on exploratory-understanding teaching and learning.

Since linear cognitive-interactionist and cognitive-field interactionist psychologies are purposive-cognitive psychologies, their adherents concur in their opposition to both environmental determinism and existentialist-humanistic natural unfoldment. Also, adherents of both positions think of people as being neither good- or bad-active mentalities nor neutral-passive organisms, but rather as neutral-interactive, information-interpreting persons who operate on the basis of insightful expectations and convert anticipated consequences into motivators of behavior.

For cognitive interactionists, thought is an insightful or foresightful process. Adherents of both positions emphasize reciprocal, as contrasted with either one- or two-dimensional, person-environment interaction. The serial reciprocal interaction of linear cognitive interactionism is analogous to the simultaneous mutual interaction of cognitive-field interactionism.

People interpret, not merely respond to, stimuli. At any moment a person selects, interprets and evaluates situational information and transforms it into guides for behavior. One's intentions and purposes motivate one's behavior. The consequences of intelligent behavior create insights or expectations concerning the likelihood of similar outcomes in the future.

How Do Cognitive Interactionists Define Learning?

For adherents of both cognitive-interactionist approaches, *learning* consists of the developing of self-activated, cognitive-mediated insightful expectations called cognitive structures, understandings or insights. Learning, then, in its broadest sense is insightful change in knowledge, skills, attitudes, values, and expectations, and learnings are insightful expectations acquired through self-activated interactions. So the result of learning is the capacity to anticipate the probable consequences of different courses of action. For learning to occur, one's doing must be accompanied by either actual or modeled realization of its consequences. Modeling is a key concept in Bandura's learning theory; see Chapter 7, pages 157–158.

How Do Cognitive Interactionists Treat Transfer of Learning?

Cognitive interactionists project their findings into the future in the form of anticipations or predictions. Learning that is transferred consists of existing cognitive structures being extended to future life spaces of an individual. When transfer of learning occurs, it is in the form of meanings, expectations, generalizations, concepts, or insights that are developed in one learning situation being employed in others.

For Cognitive Interactionists, How Is Transfer Promoted Most Effectively?

For cognitive interactionists, it seems as futile to expect a generalization to spring into action whenever the environment sets the stage for it as to expect such of a faculty or of an identical element. For teachers to promote transfer in a dependable way, something more than commonness of elements or appropriateness of generalizations is necessary.

Experience shows that in actual practice, transfer of a generalization will not *always* occur, even when a person understands a principle thoroughly and has applied it often. For instance, a natural scientist repeatedly can be scientific in dealing with problems of natural science and simultaneously resort to folklore and superstition in dealing with problems of the social sciences and humanities. A person either may not recognize that scientific method is applicable to the problems in the social sciences and humanities, or he/she may recognize such applicability, but have no desire to use it in the other areas of endeavor.

A person is in the best frame of mind for transfer to occur when he/she is aware of acquiring meanings and abilities that are widely applicable in learning and living. However, important as this is, it is not enough. A person must also want to solve new problems, or approach new situations, in the light of the insights gained through previous experience. For transfer to occur, individuals must generalize, that is, perceive common factors in different situations; they must comprehend the factors as applicable and appropriate to both situations and thereby understand how a generalization can be used; and they must desire to benefit by the sensed commonality. Ernest E. Bayles has stated that any insight susceptible of generalized application *"will transfer if and when— and only if and when—*(1) *opportunity offers,* (2) *a trained individual sees or senses it as an opportunity, and* (3) *he is disposed to take advantage of the opportunity."*[41]

Cognitive interactionists are committed to the proposition that transfer of learning to new tasks will be better if, in learning, the learner can discover relationships for himself and if he/she has opportunities to apply his learning to a variety of tasks. Consequently, for transfer to occur at its highest level, we must help students understand many widely useful relationships, principles, or generalizations; we must foster sensitivity to the presence of opportunities for transfer so that likelihood of recognition is high; and we must encourage students to embrace goals, attitudes, and ideals that support the conviction that progressive refinement of outlooks on life is possible and commendable.

Gertrude Hendrix's "new clue" to transfer of training is that "it is the intermediate flash of unverbalized awareness that actually counts for the transfer power. . . . "[42] She found that the way a person learns a generalization affects the probability of his recognition of an opportunity to use it. In method I (a conventional method), a generalization was first stated, then illustrated, then applied to new problems.

In method II, the generalization was not stated, but "drawn out of" the learners by asking questions; teaching was for unverbalized awareness. The instructor set the stage so that as soon as the generalization dawned on the learner, the learner would begin to apply it. Students were asked to find the sum of the first two odd numbers, the sum of the first three odd numbers, the sum of the first four odd numbers, and so on. As soon as the subjects knew the relationship between these sums and the number of odd numbers to be added, they started to gasp a little, smile, or become tense. That is, the subjects showed in some ways that something had happened to them. (The answer: The sum of the first n odd numbers is n^2.) Furthermore, they began to give succeeding answers rapidly, getting them by the learned shortcut method rather than by the laborious process of addition; by transfer behavior based upon a generalization, they revealed possession of the generalization.

In method III, students were taught as in method II, except that subjects were asked to state the rule they had discovered. Arrival at a correct verbalization (method III) took about twice as long as discovery of a generalization on an unverbalized level (method II). In every case included in two experiments, the highest transfer effects were achieved in the group taught by the unverbalized awareness procedure. The lowest transfer effects came from the group taught by the method in which the generalization was stated first, then illustrated, then applied to new problems. Groups that learned by verbalizing the discovered generalization showed up somewhere between the other two groups. Some hypotheses emerging from the data are the following:

1. For generation of transfer power, the unverbalized awareness method of learning a generalization is better than a method in which an authoritative statement of the generalization comes first.
2. Verbalizing a generalization immediately after discovery does not increase transfer power.
3. Verbalizing a generalization immediately after discovery may actually decrease transfer power.[43]

The crucial points of cognitive-interactionism in regard to transfer of learning and its promotion now may be summarized in seven points:

1. Opportunity for transfer may occur in many situations. It is not inherent in any subject but is possible from any field of knowledge.
2. Transfer is not dependent upon mental exercise with disciplinary school subjects.
3. Transfer is dependent upon methods of teaching and learning that use lifelike situations. It is facilitated by teaching for large generalizations that have transfer value.
4. Transfer is not automatic; opportunities for transfer must be recognized, and the person concerned must want to use them.
5. Transfer varies according to difficulty of generalization of subject matter and the intellectual ability of individuals.
6. Insights need not be put into words for their transfer to occur.
7. The amount of intraproblem insightful learning, not the number of trials as such, determines the amount of interproblem transfer.[44]

Chapters 11 through 14 extend our inquiry to consideration of the implications of the various outlooks on learning and transfer for methods of learning and teaching.

NOTES

1. See Percival M. Symonds, "What Education Has to Learn from Psychology, Transfer and Formal Discipline," *Teachers College Record* 61 (October 1959):30–45.
2. Charles H. Judd, *Educational Psychology* (Boston: Houghton Mifflin, 1939), p. 514.
3. Judd, *Educational Psychology*, p. 496.
4. Ibid., p. 514.
5. Ibid., pp. 507 ff.
6. Judd, *Educational Psychology*, p. 500.
7. Ibid., p. 514.
8. Judd, *Educational Psychology*, p. 509.
9. See Table 1.1, pp. 8–9.
10. See Chapter 2, pp. 31–32.
11. See Chapter 2, pp. 21–28, for a more detailed treatment of mental discipline.
12. See Chapter 2, pp. 28–29.
13. See Chapter 2, pp. 31–32.
14. See Chapter 2, pp. 35–41, for a detailed treatment of apperception.
15. See Chapter 2, p. 39, for a description of these steps.
16. See Chapter 3, pp. 47–48, for a description of connectionism.
17. See Edward L. Thorndike, *The Psychology of Learning* (New York: Teachers College Press, 1913), p. 359.
18. From Howard C. Warren, ed., *Dictionary of Psychology* (Boston: Houghton Mifflin, 1934), p. 56.
19. See Chapter 3, p. 53, for a description of Thorndike's major laws of learning.
20. For a detailed treatment of both the major and the minor laws see Nelson B. Henry, ed., *The Psychology of Learning*, part 2, *The Forty-first Yearbook of the National Society for the Study of Education* (Chicago: University of Chicago Press, 1942), pp. 111–128.
21. Thorndike, *The Psychology of Learning*, p. 358.
22. See Edward L. Thorndike and Arthur I. Gates, *Elementary Principles of Education* (New York: Macmillan, 1929), p. 104.
23. See B. F. Skinner, *Recent Issues in the Analysis of Behavior*, Chapter 11, "A New Preface to *Beyond Freedom and Dignity*," (Columbus, OH: Merrill Publishing Company, 1989) pp. 113–120.
24. B. F. Skinner, "The Design of Cultures," in Roger Ulrich, Thomas Stachnik, and John Mabry, eds., *Control of Human Behavior* (Glenview, IL: Scott, Foresman, 1966),
    p. 333.
25. Skinner, *Recent Issues in the Analysis of Behavior*, p. 50.
26. B. F. Skinner, *Cumulative Record* (New York: Appleton-Century-Crofts, 1961), p. 201.
27. Reprinted with permission of Macmillan Publishing Co., Inc. from B. F. Skinner, *Science and Human Behavior* (New York: Macmillan, 1953), p. 91. Copyright ©1953, Macmillan Publishing Co., Inc.
28. Skinner, *Cumulative Record*, p. 34.

29. Skinner, *Science and Human Behavior*, pp. 115–116.
30. See Chapter 5, p. 106.
31. Skinner, *Science and Human Behavior*, p. 66.
32. See "How to Teach Animals," in Skinner, *Cumulative Record*, pp. 412–419.
33. See B. F. Skinner, *Recent Issues In the Analysis of Behavior*, Chapter 8, "The School of the Future," pp. 85–96.
34. See B. F. Skinner, *Schedules of Reinforcement* (New York: Appleton-Century-Crofts, 1957), p. 728.
35. Skinner, *Science and Human Behavior*, p. 94.
36. Ibid., pp. 94–95.
37. Ibid., p. 94.
38. Ibid., p. 77.
39. Ibid., p. 402.
40. See Chapter 5, p. 98 for a discussion of schedules of reinforcement.
41. Ernest E. Bayles, *Democratic Educational Theory* (New York: Harper & Row, 1960), p. 58.
42. Gertrude Hendrix, "A New Clue to Transfer of Training," *Elementary School Journal* 48 (December 1947):200.
43. Ibid., p. 198.
44. See Harry F. Harlow, "Learning Sets and Error Factor Theory," in Sigmund Koch, ed., *Psychology: A Study of a Science*, Vol. 2 (New York: McGraw-Hill, 1959), p. 502.

BIBLIOGRAPHY, CHAPTER 10

Bayles, Ernest E. *The Theory and Practice of Teaching*. New York: Harper & Row, 1950. Chapter 6, "The Transfer of Training," pp. 85–98, is a historical summary of outlooks on transfer. Probably the best brief treatment of transfer available.

Bayles, Ernest E. *Democratic Educational Theory*. New York: Harper & Row, 1960. Chapter 3, "Learning and Transfer," pp. 45–62, develops a goal-insight theory of learning that is closely related to cognitive-field theory, then states four conditions necessary to transfer of learning.

Cronbach, Lee J. *Educational Psychology*, 2d ed. New York: Harcourt Brace Jovanovich, 1963. Chapter 10, "Intellectual Development as Transfer of Learning," pp. 314–348, treats transfer in terms of transfer of response. Eclectically develops conditions favorable to transfer.

Gage, N. L., ed. *Handbook of Research on Teaching*. Chicago. Rand McNally, 1963. Pages 1014–1021 review research on consequences of teaching secondary school mathematics by tell-and-do methods as compared with heuristic—discovery—methods.

Grose, Robert F., and Robert C. Birney. *Transfer of Learning*. New York: Van Nostrand Reinhold, 1963. A book of well-selected original writings on transfer of learning. Traces historical growth of the concept up to the present time.

Harlow, Harry F. "The Formation of Learning Sets." *Psychological Review* (January 1949):51–65. Based upon research with animals, Harlow emphasizes the importance of learning how to learn—learning sets. Emphasizes problems as contrasted with trials in learning.

Haslerud, George M., and Shirley Meyers. "The Transfer Value of Given and Individually Derived Principles." *Journal of Educational Psychology* 47, no. 12 (December 1958):293–298. Compares retention and transfer value of direct teaching and independent discovery and finds independent discovery method more effective.

Haslerud, George M. *Transfer, Memory, & Creativity: After-Learning as Perceptual Process.* Minneapolis: University of Minnesota Press, 1972. Summarizes historical views on learning and transfer and develops a new concept, *projecscan*, centered upon the perceptual theory of *after-learning*—the variety of behaviors subsequent to reaching a given criterion of learning, for example, memory, transfer, or projecscan.

Hilgard, Ernest R., Robert P. Irvine, and James E. Whipple. "Rote Memorization, Understanding, and Transfer: An Extension of Katona's Card-Trick Experiments." *Journal of Experimental Psychology* (October 1953):288–292. A review of Katona's card-trick experiments and findings and a report of further research to check the findings. Supports teaching for understanding as compared with rote learning, especially when transfer of learning to new problem-solving situations is involved.

Judd, Charles H. *Educational Psychology.* Boston: Houghton Mifflin, 1939. Reflects Judd's generalizations principle and its implications for learning, intelligence, and transfer.

Kneller, George F. "Automation and Learning Theory." *The School Review* (Summer 1962):220–232. Analyzes the nature of automation and its relation to learning. Points up that Skinner's teaching machines are effective only if the teacher accepts Skinner's special interpretation of behaviorism within which learning is considered to be always additive.

Skinner, B. F. *Schedules of Reinforcement.* New York: Appleton-Century-Crofts, 1957. Pages 728–730 develop Skinner's meaning of stimulus and response induction.

Skinner, B. F. *Recent Issues in the Analysis of Behavior.* Columbus, OH: Merrill Publishing Company, 1989. A collection of Skinner's most recent papers, written primarily for other psychologists; centered upon theoretical and professional issues.

Stephens, John M. "Transfer of Learning." *Encyclopedia of Educational Research.* New York: Macmillan, 1960. Pages 1535–1543 are an excellent summary of research pertinent to transfer of learning. Treats definition, characteristics, and conditions affecting the amount of transfer.

Symonds, Percival M. "What Education Has to Learn from Psychology, Transfer and Formal Discipline." *Teachers College Record* (October 1959):30–45. A good historical summary of the transfer problem and pertinent research. Emphasizes transfer through application of general principles.

Thorndike, Edward L. *The Psychology of Learning.* New York: Teachers College Press, 1913. Thorndike's early presentation of results of his psychological studies for students' use. Expands and explains his laws of learning. Chapter 2, pp. 350–433, treats transfer of learning.

Chapter
11

How Is Learning Theory Related to Teaching Practice?

*I*n earlier chapters we considered various learning theories that teachers might adopt. We now examine how the respective theories are related to teaching principles and procedures. But first, as a preface to our inquiry into the relationship of learning theory to teaching practice, let us examine the unique role of teachers in our culture.

WHAT IS THE ROLE OF TEACHERS IN MODERN AMERICA?

When we consider the role of teachers in modern America, we should study both of its aspects, namely, teachers' relationship to the preservation and improvement of the culture and their relationship to their students. A *culture* is the established way of life or social heritage of a people. It is constituted of all those socially transmitted results of human experience through which a group of people carries on its way of life. It includes language, customs, morals, tools, institutions, knowledge, ideals, and standards.

What Are the Possible Relationships of Teachers to the Preservation and Improvement of the Culture?

Most people would probably agree that one of the principal functions of teaching is to preserve, by transmitting to the young, that part of the culture that is regarded by most people as good. However, performance of this task alone makes education a highly conservative force. Teaching that does no more than merely conserve a culture is appropriate to a static culture but not to a dynamic, rapidly changing one such as ours. Hence, teaching in a fast-moving culture must operate in relationship to change with the goal of keeping cultural innovations socially beneficial. Although there is general support for this twofold

242

function of teaching, that is, cultural conservation and cultural improvement, it is difficult to get agreement on just how the two tasks are to be performed simultaneously.

Teachers may hold any one of four basically different attitudes in regard to their proper function in preserving and improving the culture. They may envision themselves as (1) ignorers of the culture, (2) cultural architects, (3) conservators of the culture, or (4) democratic leaders in developing insights pertinent to amending the culture (to amend a culture is to modify it in some way for the better). Let us explore each of these attitudes briefly.

Teachers as Ignorers of the Culture Teachers who adhere to this view consider the prevailing culture to be a necessary evil, outside nature, that should be either ignored or neutralized as far as possible. Hence, they align themselves with existentialist humanism. Within this extreme laissez-faire position, they encourage students to disregard the prevailing folkways and mores of their culture and urge each one to "do his own thing."[1] They are interested in encouraging each student's autonomous self-development and self-actualization to the point that they have little interest in either cultural conservation or improvement. In a political sense laissez-faire means anarchy.

Teachers as Cultural Architects Teachers who adopt this view see themselves as radical innovators. Thus, in their thinking they design the specifications of an ideal culture. They then teach the attitudes, values, and knowledge that will cause new generations to move in the direction of this ideal. They are likely to promote ideas toward which resistance will develop, and they are not reluctant to indoctrinate and propagandize students in order to achieve their purpose. Since teachers who see themselves as cultural architects are discontented with affairs as they are and want to introduce a new cultural design, their point of view has been called "social reconstructionism." In a political sense social reconstructionists are autocratic leaders.

Teachers as Conservators of the Culture Teachers who accept this role see themselves as preservers of traditional attitudes, beliefs, and knowledge. To the best of their ability they analyze the present culture and attempt to transmit it, intact, to new generations. They recognize that accidents of history will induce some cultural changes and that if these changes contribute to the welfare of people, they probably will be perpetuated. However, they never see themselves as active agents of cultural change. Since unorthodoxy bothers these "conservatives," they are wont to try to suppress any unconventional thinking on the part of students. In a manner very similar to that of social reconstructionists, who also have specific objectives in mind, conservative teachers often indoctrinate their students and propagandize their objectives into students' thinking and behavior.

But regardless of the degree to which teachers may be dedicated to conservation of their culture, their task is becoming impossible to perform. With the loss of the old sense of community and the accompanying decay of the cohesive and relatively consistent value pattern that accompanied it, there is no longer a harmonious structure of attitudes, values, and beliefs for teachers to promote. Confronted with a culture filled with confusion and contradictions, which elements are a conservative teacher to select and teach? Is it not reasonable that teaching today should help students examine as objectively as possible their disjointed culture in the hope that, as they live their lives, they will be able to work some integration into it? But this is a job for neither a laissez-faire "teacher," an impetuous seeker of change, nor a conservative who is frightened of deliberate change. In a political sense, conservators of the culture, like cultural architects, are autocratic leaders.

Teachers as Democratic Leaders in Developing Insights Pertinent to Amending the Culture   In contrast with either an ignorer, an architect, or a conservator position, a teacher may develop an emergent synthesis from the three positions and assume a role much like that of a head scientist in a laboratory. When the subject matter under investigation is some aspect of the culture, the primary purpose of investigation is neither solely to ignore, to change, nor to preserve it, but to appraise it and strengthen its tenability. Accordingly, an attempt is made to uncover contradictions and conflicts in a culture and to determine possible ways of resolving them, or at least preventing them from causing serious trouble. The ultimate hope of democratic teachers is that the culture will be progressively refined by a citizenry that has learned the habit of studying problems in a reflective and democratic manner. Teachers with this view should foster ideas pointed toward social change but strive to keep them constructive.

Teachers, as democratic leaders, do not discard their personal preferences. Like either social reconstructionists or conservators of culture, they too hold certain cultural goals in preference to others. However, their method of teaching, unlike that of either ignorers of culture, social reconstructionists, or conservators of culture, is the method of democracy. In a very real sense each teacher and that teacher's students, together, are gaining more adequate insights for building their culture.

Teachers who function as democratic leaders believe that, since people are cultural beings, there need not be assumed any ceiling or limit to the possibilities of human nature. When human nature is assumed neither to be tied to an autonomous natural unfoldment process nor to be static or inert, it encompasses all the institutional achievements of dynamic society. Accordingly, with sufficient application of human intelligence, a society can continue growth in the direction of more adequate and harmonious living for all individuals involved. Therefore, if teachers are to aid substantially in cultural progress, they must encourage students to study the existing cultures of their own and other societies, but always with a view toward progressive refinement of those cultures.

What Are the Possible Relationships of Teachers to Their Students?

We may visualize three broad types of relationships between respective teachers and their students: (1) authoritarian, (2) laissez-faire, and (3) democratic.

Each form of relationship produces a distinctive type of situation within a classroom, characterized by more or less predictable results and carrying with it definite implications concerning the teacher's commitment in regard to how students learn. Furthermore, a particular type of teacher-student relationship presupposes a correlative relationship of the teacher to the culture. Whereas an authoritarian teacher acts as either cultural architect or conservator, a laissez-faire teacher deliberately adheres to a policy of noninterference with students' individual freedom of choice and action, and a democratic teacher assumes the cultural role of a leader in developing insights that may contribute to the culture's amendment and refinement.

Authoritarian Teachers   Authoritarian teachers exercise firm, centralized control. They closely direct the actions of their students. They do the planning for their classes and issue the directions. Furthermore, they tell students what to think as well as what to do. In an authoritarian classroom, a teacher regards himself as the sole active agent and considers students to be passive receivers of instructions and information.

In the experiments with group climates conducted by White and Lippit,[2] it was found that boys in authoritarian groups tended to be apathetic and dependent and to demonstrate little capacity for initiating group action. When the leader left the room, they accomplished very little. Although they did not seem to resent authoritarian leadership strongly, they occasionally showed evidences of hostility, as expressed in aggressive acts toward fellow group members.

Laissez-Faire Teachers   Laissez-faire teachers go to the opposite extreme. Since they are committed to noninterference with students' choices and actions, they deliberately abstain from student direction or lesson planning, so they do not really lead at all. They are present and may answer questions, but essentially, they let students follow their own initiative. Students decide what they want to do and how they will do it.

In the White-Lippitt experiments, boys in the laissez-faire group got along together much better than those in the authoritarian group; they showed less tendency to direct resentments at fellow students. They did get some work done. However, they acted insecure; for example, they repeatedly asked for help, and after the experiment was completed, expressed dissatisfaction with its leadership.[3]

Democratic Teachers   In a democratic teaching-learning situation teachers fulfill the role of democratic group leaders. To repeat, their function is analogous to that of a head scientist in a laboratory. Their chief purpose is to lead their students in the study of significant problems in the area in which they are teaching. Such study presupposes interchange of evidence and insights, give and take, and respect for one another's ideas. In a democratic classroom the teacher's ideas are subject to both student and teacher criticism, just as are those of students. In this way both the students and the teacher learn together. Although the teacher may be, and to teach it best he/she should be, an authority on his subject, the situation is arranged so that students are encouraged to think for themselves. Accordingly, a democratic teacher is most likely to hold an outlook toward learning that emphasizes purposiveness in human experience and behavior.

In the White-Lippitt experiment, democratic groups evidenced a more friendly and confiding atmosphere than did authoritarian groups. Members seemed as able to extend mutual recognition to each other as did members of the laissez-faire groups. However, they worked on a higher level of efficiency and were much less dependent on the leader than were the laissez-faire groups. Furthermore, they showed more initiative and worked more efficiently in the absence of a leader than did the authoritarian groups.[4]

The traditional relationship between teachers and their students has been authoritarian. Until the twentieth century, teachers tended to be despots— often benevolent, but despots nevertheless. During the middle of the twentieth century, despotism in the classroom began to disappear, but when this happened, a laissez-faire attitude frequently took its place. Or, perhaps more often, teachers came to alternate between a friendly despotism and situations close to laissez-faire.

In recent years and in many places the idea of democratic schools and classrooms has fallen into ill repute. There are two basic, but unfortunate, reasons for this: (1) Laissez-faire situations often have been erroneously mistaken for democratic situations. Truly democratic teachers, however, have no enthusiasm whatsoever for laissez-faire classrooms, and they feel that it is tragic for an educator to call an uncontrolled and undirected classroom "democratic." (2) The meanings of the terms *democracy* and *democratic* have become perverted. As applied to teaching, they often have come to mean "easy," "soft," or "undisciplined." Yet, in fact, making allowances for the maturity and capabilities of students, a democratic group may work at the maximum level that health permits, and its manner of operations may be fully as rigorous as that of any scientific investigation.

There are some good reasons why consistently democratic relations could well be substituted for both autocratic and laissez-faire modes of operation. It seems unfitting for a nation that is straining itself in democratic directions to maintain in its schoolrooms nondemocratic relationships between teachers and students. Furthermore, evidence now available indicates that students probably learn more effectively in a democratic than in either an authoritarian or a highly permissive classroom.[5] Democratic learning situations seem to produce more retention and more transfer. Thus, even if there were no other reason for democratic relations between teacher and students, the general adoption of such relations would at least permit taxpayers who support education to receive more for their money.

There is a close connection between the respective types of relationships of teachers to students and the relative amount of usage of each of four different levels of teaching and learning. These levels are the subject of the remaining part of the chapter.

WHAT ARE THE LEVELS OF TEACHING AND LEARNING?

Teaching-learning situations may be characterized according to where they fall on a continuum that ranges from thoughtless to thoughtful modes of operation. But it is helpful to divide their total range into four classifications: (1) autonomous development level, (2) memory level, (3) explanatory-understanding level and (4) exploratory-understanding level consisting of either investigative or reflective processes. The autonomous development level emphasizes the importance of students' feelings and minimizes the value of hard thinking based upon empirical data. The memory level is relatively thoughtless, the explanatory-understanding level is more thoughtful, and the exploratory-understanding level is the most thoughtful of all. (See Table 11.1)

In this chapter we treat, in some detail, the nature of the autonomous development level and the memory level and introduce the two understanding levels. We then devote Chapter 12 to the explanatory-understanding level and Chapter 13 to the exploratory-understanding level of teaching and learning.

What Is the Autonomous Development Level of Teaching and Learning?

The autonomous development level of teaching and learning is based upon *existentialist humanistic* educational psychology and a *radical* (as contrasted with a *moderate*) *existentialist* educational philosophy, within which people basically are considered forwardly active selves. Hence, education aims to be completely student-centered. Each student's feelings constitute the final authority for his test of truth. Accordingly, teaching is an extreme laissez-faire process, within which the teacher promotes each student's heightened intuitive awareness of himself and the artistic expression of his self-actualization.

A *radical existentialist* stresses three basic human awarenesses; "the teacher's imperative is to arrange the learning situation in such a way as to bring home the truth of these three propositions to every individual."[6] These awarenesses are: I am a choosing agent; I am a free agent; and I am a responsible agent. My responsibility, however, is only for how I live my own life. Thus, a radical existentialist teacher or student is always searching for personal truth. In teaching, the teacher awakens awareness, freedom, and responsibility in each student. But since each person's own feelings are the final authority for the truth that is gained through this process, there is to be no analysis, prescription, or imposition of the activities of anyone by any other person, including the teacher.

Since, within autonomous development, the students as well as the teacher are considered to be autonomously proactive—forwardly active—selves, as opposed to being either passive or interactive beings, teaching proceeds in a highly permissive atmosphere, within which each individual develops largely on his own through the exercise of his feelings, and each "does his own thing."

Table 11.1 LEVELS OF THE TEACHING-LEARNING PROCESS AND THE TESTING
PROCEDURES APPROPRIATE TO EACH LEVEL

Level of Teaching Learning	Underlying Learning Theory	Attributes of the Teaching and Learning Process
1. Autonomous development (Neoprogressive education)	Natural unfoldment theory of existentialist humanism or romantic naturalism; learners are autonomously proactive—forwardly active	Promotion of intuitive awareness of each self; artistic expression of self-actualization; negative education—no coercion, prescription, or imposition, one's feelings are the final authority for truth; student-centered
2. Memory a. Verbal-factual; mentalistic	Mental discipline theories of mind substance family; leaners are active	Rote memory; training faculties of rational minds; repetitive drill, catechetical; teacher-centered
b. Behavioral; physicalistic or mechanomorphic	S-R conditioning theories of behavioristic family; learners are passive or reactive	Conditioning or behavior modification; formation of either S-R linkages or R-S reinforcements; reductionistic; teacher-centered
3. Explanatory understanding	Apperception or mastery; learners are passive	Teacher explanation and student grasp of generalizations, relationships, rules, or principles; teaching facts in relation to principles and the tool use of generalizations and their supporting facts; teacher-centered
4. Exploratory understanding; problem centered (not progressive education)	Cognitive-field and linear cognitive interaction theories; learners are situationally, perceptually interactive	Purposive involvement and perplexity, problem raising and solving, and getting an intelligent "feel" for principles, ideas, or acts; requires personal involvement, not merely interest; teacher-student centered cooperative inquiry and evaluation; goal is student perplexity just short of frustration and resultant learning

Nature of Learnings	Basis for Appropriateness of Test Items	Nature of Appropriate Tests	Method of Test Evaluation
Self-directed active unfoldments; expressed intuitive awareness; unfolded or developed natural needs or instincts and accompanying feelings		No testing; students alone evaluate their achievements according to their respective feelings	
Disciplined minds or mental faculties and retained factual materials	Recall of retained memories	Factual essay or short-answer true-false or completion	Check students' answers against list prepared at time the test is made up; teacher-centered
Either proper responses or increased probability of desired responses	Manifestation of previous conditioning or reinforcement	Sampling of desired responses	Check student responses against a prepared list; teacher-centered
Teacher-imposed understandings, insights, principles, relationships, concepts, generalizations, rules, theories, or laws	Recognition, explanation, or use of understandings, insights, principles, generalizations, rules, laws, or theories	Factual and explanatory essay or short-answer, true-false, selection, or completion	Check students' answers against prepared list, but on essay tests, credit a student for "right" answers even though he/she uses words other than the instructor's; teacher-centered
Purposely acquired exploratory understandings, insights, principles, relationships, concepts, generalizations, rules, theories, or laws plus enhanced scientific outlook and instrumental thinking	Essay questions that are real, unanswered problems for the students and pertinent to the study having been pursued; real problems involve both generalization and tool use of ideas as well as some degree of creativity	Reflective or problem-centered essay	Check students' answers on basis of criteria agreed upon prior to the test—probably pertinence and adequacy of data applied to the solution and harmony of the data, problem, and answer; teacher-student centered

Such teaching is student-centered, as contrasted with both memory- and explanatory-understanding levels, which are teacher-centered, and exploratory-understanding level, which is teacher-student centered.

Within the autonomous development level based upon existentialist humanism, the teacher's function in education is more negative than positive in the sense that there is little or no leadership, direction, coercion, prescription, or imposition of student thoughts or behaviors. Intellectual development is something that "just naturally happens." Hence, there is no need for any kind of formal teaching. Instead, student-planned, permissive types of projects are promoted for the purpose of releasing the students' latent talents. Students, as much as possible, are permitted, even encouraged, to live close to nature so that they may indulge freely their natural impulses and feelings. Inasmuch as creativity is an inherent characteristic of children and youths, it should be left to unfold in the highly permissive atmosphere of a child-centered school. Either Nature or the Creator has *enfolded* certain ideas, talents, and purposes into each child, and these should be permitted to *unfold* as a child proceeds in school. Accordingly, each student should be permitted to choose his activities throughout the school day.

Can Autonomous Development Be Tested?

Autonomous development, as an approach to teaching and learning, implies not only that students are active but that they are forwardly so or proactive. Since the desired end product of education is a completely autonomous person, teachers have little interest in imparting measurable objective knowledge about reality, truth, and goodness.

An autonomous development approach to learning betokens a negative education, within which not only is there no coercion, prescription, or imposition but there is also neither teacher leadership nor student-teacher cooperative learning and evaluation. Each student's feelings are the final authority for truth. The educative function of teachers is to promote intuitive awareness of each student's self and artistic expression of his or her self-actualization.

School learnings are in the form of naturally unfolded or developed needs and accompanying feelings being actively expressed by self-directed active persons. Hence, there can be no valid systematic, teacher-developed testing program. Students alone can evaluate their respective achievements in accordance with their individual feelings.

What Is the Memory Level of Teaching and Learning?

Memory level learning may be either a mentalistic, verbal-factual process or a physicalistic behavioral process. *Mentalistic memory* level learning is that kind of learning that embraces committing factual materials to memory and little else. It is possible for a person to memorize virtually any type of material, including that which seems quite nonsensical. But the more meaningful the material to be learned is, the easier it is to be memorized. Furthermore, the more meaningful the learned material, the longer it tends to be retained. A collection of "nonsense" syllables might conceivably be remembered for a lifetime if a person had sufficient reason for retaining it. However, when one develops a reason for retaining something, it is no longer nonsensical.

Physicalistic-behavioral memory level of teaching and learning consists of the formation in students of either S-R linkages (classical conditioning) or R-S reinforcements (instrumental conditioning). A student's learning consists of developing the proper sequence of responses and an increased probability of the proper responses. The learning process is comparable to other organic processes such as digestion and respiration.

Since behaviorists view education as a matter of behavioral engineering or technology, they think of a teacher as a designer and manager of instruction and an evaluator of specific student learnings. Hence, they view educational goals as specified behaviors that students will manifest when they have been properly processed; these are physically memorized behavioral or performance objectives. After the general performance objectives are established, they are translated into increasingly specific, lesser ones and arranged in appropriate sequences for instruction. Instruction consists of shaping, and increasing the incidence of desired behavior through presentation of appropriate stimuli at the proper time.

Behavior modification and performance-based instruction are anchored on three basic assumptions:

1. Learning of any degree of complexity, even critical thinking, can be achieved by one progressively mastering or memorizing a large number of small sequential components.
2. All attainable educational goals can be explicitly stated in terms of physicalistic behaviors.
3. Any educational objectives that are not definable in behavioral terms are either irrelevant or unattainable.

At first glance, memory level learning seems to exemplify either a mental discipline or an S-R conditioning theory of learning. Either a bad-active or neutral-active substantive mind is trained, or simple relations are formed between the stimuli and responses of a neutral-passive biological organism with no particular thought or purpose being involved. But cognitive-interactionist psychologists deny that either is the case. Instead, they insist that if anything is learned at all, insight of a sort is always present. What characterizes memory level learning, to a cognitive-interactionist, is the fact that the insights so acquired usually have no significant relationship to the material being studied. However, the learned material is still patterned by the learner during the process of learning it. Even "nonsense" syllables, when learned, are not completely unpatterned.[7]

One's capacity to memorize and retain material probably bears little positive relationship to one's capacity for intelligent behavior. Geniuses are notoriously forgetful, although not usually in their areas of major interest. Conversely, a mentally defective person may be highly proficient in memorization. For instance, Polly was a 13-year-old girl with a somewhat limited mental capacity. She had quite a brilliant memory of the "shotgun" variety. That is, she memorized indiscriminately anything she heard, and often could repeat verbatim an overheard conversation or a radio newscast. After hearing it once, she could recite faultlessly the words of every popular song being broadcast at the time. Nevertheless, Polly's "thought power" was so impaired that if asked to close an outside door of the house, she could not decide on which side of the door to stand to avoid shutting herself out.

Every experienced teacher can recall numerous students who developed a considerable capacity to memorize standard curricular materials in most or all school subjects. Such students usually make high grades. However, when placed in situations requiring reflection, they may be at a loss. If, occasionally, they take a course with a teacher who employs problem-centered teaching, they may become extremely frustrated and do very poor work. Conversely, an experienced teacher can also recall students whose grades were spotty but who achieved magnificently once they got out of school. There is a fairly good chance that in such cases poor achievement in school is a result of rebellion against required rote memorization.

Memory level teaching may, of course, contribute indirectly to intelligent behavior. If memorized facts become pertinent on an occasion when a problem requires solution, they contribute to usable background and hence to the effectiveness of problem solving. However, memorized facts usually contribute little to effective student growth. One reason is that, as already suggested, they tend to be forgotten quickly. Another is that a large proportion of the facts memorized in school are irrelevant to future thought needs. In summarizing the value of rote-memory teaching we might even say that the best way to make sure that a student will not remember many facts is to place the major emphasis upon teaching facts.

Despite all the legitimate criticisms we may make of rote memorization, it would be unrealistic to suppose that a teacher can always avoid it. In any ordinary school situation, on occasions even the most imaginative teacher will have no better approach than memory level teaching. This may occur on days when lack of time has prevented planning anything else. Or it may happen when the teacher does not know how else to handle the material to be covered.

One might ask, can the fundamental skills, such as spelling, be taught otherwise than through a process of straight memorization, using drill procedures? Generally speaking, they can be taught more efficiently through other procedures. However, much more study will be required to develop procedures for teaching all the fundamental skill subjects in ways that will free us entirely from rote memorization.

What Testing Procedures Are Appropriate to Memory Level Teaching and Learning?

Testing, like teaching, may be conducted on any one of three levels—memory, explanatory-understanding, or exploratory-understanding. Although there are many kinds of techniques and instruments that may be used for evaluating student progress, formalized testing continues to hold a very prominent position among them, especially in the minds of students. When students consider their teachers' evaluation of their achievements, they usually think first of all of tests. Thus, they tend to gauge their levels of learning to the level of testing that their teachers employ; this is where the payoff occurs. Hence, the nature of teachers' systems for evaluation of student learning has very great influence upon the quality of learning that actually develops.

Teachers' programs of evaluation not only govern their students' study habits, their manner of interaction in class, and the number and quality of their learnings, but they also greatly influence the teaching-learning level on which their learning efforts proceed. For example, even though teachers strive to teach on either an explanatory-understanding or a exploratory-understanding level, as long as they continue to give memory level tests, most of the learning that ensues will be accomplished on a memory level. Hence, teachers should give careful consideration to the nature of their testing programs and other evaluational procedures. To quote Benjamin S. Bloom, "The point to be emphasized is that the type of mental process the student *expects* to be tested will determine his method of study and preparation."[8] (See Table 11.1 for a summary of the levels of teaching and learning and the evaluation procedures that are appropriate to each level.)

In the process of appropriate mentalistic-memory level testing, either factual essay or short-answer "objective" tests are employed to check for recall of memories that have been retained in the students' minds. Questions on factual essay tests are in the form of "What are the four levels of teaching and learning?" Objective tests geared to this level take the form of "The four levels of teaching and learning are (1)———, (2)———, (3)———, and (4)———."

In behaviorism, testing, like teaching, centers upon behavioral modification or change. The desired behaviors of students are sampled so as to measure the manifestations of previous conditioning. In testing for learned physicalistic behaviors, teachers take a sampling of the behavioral modifications that had been included in a statement of behavioral objectives that was developed prior to the beginning of the course. These modifications are all in the form of observable responses. Hence, teachers who are teaching on this level would expect their students to be able to list or name the four levels of teaching and learning. Consequently, they would use test items much like those used in mentalistic-memory level testing.

WHAT IS THE MEANING OF UNDERSTANDING?

The term *understanding* has been used so ambiguously by psychologists and educators that teachers are likely to use it rather glibly without being able to define it clearly. For example, a teacher may ask students, "Are you sure you understand this?" without really knowing the meaning of the question. One may be fairly sure that the students do not know either.

An *understanding* is a generalized meaning or insight. Often it may be put into words, but not always. The understandings a person achieves in regard to driving a golf ball, running the high hurdles, casting a fly, timing a motor, or writing a sentence may lie, in part, in a "feel for the act" that would be difficult to verbalize. But most persons who have thought about such achievements are able to make statements about the probably consequences of attempting them in alternate ways. Other names for understandings are *generalizations, theories, generalized insights, general ideas, concepts, principles, rules,* and *laws.*

The *American College Dictionary* gives the following definition of the verb *understand:* "1. to perceive the meaning of; grasp the idea of; comprehend. 2. to be thoroughly familiar with; apprehend clearly the character or nature of. 3. to comprehend by knowing the meaning of the words employed, as a language. 4. to grasp clearly as a fact, or realize."[9]

A serious student of educational psychology will be dissatisfied with definitions of this kind. Although such definitions are helpful to a degree, they are not sufficiently operational. That is, they do not show what psychological action a person takes in coming to understand something. In the sections to follow, we present two key definitions of understanding, then show how they may be combined into one.

How Is Understanding Seeing Relationships?

This definition of understanding is implied in the first category of dictionary definitions; to understand is to comprehend. One meaning for comprehend is "to take in or embrace"; the Latin root is *comprehendere,* meaning "to seize." In other words, we have here the idea of reaching out and gathering in individual items. As they are pulled together, they are understood. However, the definition implies still more; it involves inclusion of a group of particulars under a single overarching idea.

Seeing solitary facts in relation to a general principle, then, is the essence of understanding implied by our first definition of the term. Although there is significantly more to understanding than this, teaching probably would be more effective than it is now if all teachers grasped even this limited definition. Too few teachers realize that any item of factual knowledge is quite meaningless unless students see how it is embraced by a general principle. A fact must be seen as either supporting or casting doubt upon some principle, or it means very little. Yet entire textbooks have been written that contain little more than "descriptive facts." Teachers often labor away a professional lifetime without trying to teach students the generalizations that would be necessary for them to "pull together" the facts that they are required to memorize.

How Is Understanding Seeing the Tool Use of a Fact?

This brings us to a second definition of understanding. We may say that a person understands any object, process, idea, or fact if he/she sees how it can be used to fulfill some purpose or goal. As soon as one sees what something is for, one, to some degree, understands it. Of course, the degree of one's understanding is always relative. If a person knows that a camera takes pictures, he/she has begun to understand a camera. But if he/she is going to use a camera successfully, he also needs to know the details of its operation and the consequences of using different types of lenses, film emulsions, lighting, and picture compositions.

It is from a person's experience that his understanding grows. Within experimental experience, a person tries first one course of action and then another, preserving only those that work best. Thus, through experience, the features of each person's environment progressively develop a "pointing quality"— dark clouds "point" to rain, Johnny's out-thrust jaw and angry squint "point" to a poke in the jaw of Freddy. This pointing quality that we give to features of our environment permits us to behave intelligently, that is, to act with foresight, because these are signposts along the way. The pointing quality of things tells us the probable consequences of using them; that is, how to use them with maximum effectiveness.

How Is Understanding Seeing Both Relationships and Tool Use?

It is important to realize that understanding, as seeing the relation between particulars and generalizations, and understanding, as seeing the tool use of things, are complementary processes. Hence, in order to have a fully adequate conception of understanding, we need to consolidate the two definitions.

Because it ignores the role of purpose, understanding as merely seeing relationships is not an adequate concept. Suppose one sees the relationship of certain specific facts to the principle of flotation, as we portray in the example of Herbartian lesson plan in Chapter 2 (page 39). A student reaction to a forced acquaintance with such relationships might simply be "So what?" and no attempt would be made to delve deeply into the implications of the principle, to remember it for future use, or to transfer it to new situations. In other words, an understanding that is confined to seeing relationships between particulars and a concept is a fragile and superficial achievement. But suppose a student is a boat hobbyist who builds boat models and operates them on a local lake. The student is involved in developing a design and needs to know how much of the boat will be submerged when it is carrying four persons whose average weight is 130 pounds. To this student the principle of flotation, and the concrete facts subsumed under it, will seem of vital importance.

Thus, what we may label "functional understanding" is much more likely to occur if a learner, in learning generalizations and the specific facts pertinent to them, sees how some purpose is served thereby. Therefore, we should not divorce the problem of teaching for understanding from that of promoting student motivation.

If understanding is best achieved when we want to use what is to be understood, it is equally true that when motivation toward understanding is present, what is understood will inevitably consist primarily of principles derived from a pattern of specific facts. At this point, we must restate an assertion made in Chapter 4 to the effect that specific insights tend to be generalized. As soon as one achieves an insight, the thought occurs, "Possibly this idea will work in other—or all—similar situations." Accordingly, the insight's general value is tested through its repeated use in similar situations. If it fails to work, it will be discarded as having extremely limited worth. If it seems always to work, it will become a valued possession that will be added to the person's intelligence. Of course, most insights are valid in varying degrees of predictability; they fall somewhere between the two extremes just suggested.

We now have pushed our analysis to the point where we can offer a third definition of understanding. *Understanding occurs when we come to see how to use productively, in ways that we care about, a pattern of general ideas and supporting facts.*

HOW DOES EXPLANATORY-UNDERSTANDING LEVEL DIFFER FROM MEMORY LEVEL TEACHING AND LEARNING?

Both memory level teaching and explanatory-understanding level teaching are teacher-centered. However, in the memory level, teachers concentrate on factual, short answers, whereas in the explanatory-understanding level, teachers describe and explain answers to students in the form of rules, relationships, or generalizations. When an explanatory-understanding level of teaching is successful, students will know, in addition to facts, some principles by which the facts are related. In contrast, memory level teaching tends either to ignore such principles or, at best, to treat them on such a superficial level that they have little meaning for students.

It is well to recognize that most behavioristic psychologists of learning, in actual practice, adhere to a combination of memory and explanatory-understanding levels of learning. Since these psychologists center upon behavior that is the result of forces exerted upon individuals, explanation for what persons do is sought in the circumstances that surround them, the stimuli that impinge upon them, and the facts and principles that they have learned. Consequently, a child or youth is something to be molded in the proper fashion. For behaviorists, a verbalized understanding is a concept characterized as a learned, common, generalized response to a number of stimuli of a given class. Teaching, then, is a matter of setting objectives for students and creating the proper environment to ensure their reaching these behavioral or performance objectives. With these purposes or goals in mind, teachers strive to transmit facts and principles in the form of memories and understandings to students through telling, showing, guiding, rewarding, punishing, and, at times, forcing and coercing them.

HOW DOES EXPLORATORY-UNDERSTANDING LEVEL DIFFER FROM EXPLANATORY-UNDERSTANDING LEVEL TEACHING AND LEARNING?

Explanatory-understanding level teaching is teaching that seeks to acquaint students with the relationships between a generalization and some particulars— between principles and solitary facts—and that develops the uses to which the principles may be applied. When teachers teach students rules governing the use of, say, subjunctives, they are instructing on an explanatory-understanding level. To the degree that they succeed, their students will be able to identify cases in which a given rule applies and then use the rules as a guide. Teachers are seeking the same kind of result when they teach rules of spelling, rules for dividing fractions, or rules for repairing a motor. They are likewise operating on the same level when they teach theories in physics, chemistry, or football. (A rule or principle, by definition, is a theoretical statement.)

Exploratory-understanding level teaching and learning also lead to acquiring understandings, but the search for understandings is pursued in a unique fashion. Instead of students being given a collection of facts and generalizations by the teacher, they are confronted with problematic—either unclear or puzzling—situations. Students' learning may be based upon the inadequacies or disharmonies of the ideas, attitudes, values, and knowledge that they bring with them. Or it may center upon some observed inadequacy, inconsistency, incompleteness, or irrelevance in the subject matter. For learning to occur, problematic situations must surface to promote students' thinking and research. In their learning process, students examine existing facts and generalizations and seek out new ones.

"In order to make a creative contribution to a field of knowledge, one must, of course, have knowledge of that field."[10] But also, within creative, insightful learning, "students need to realize that a period of ambiguity is the rule, not the exception, . . . and that they should welcome this period as a chance to hatch their ideas, rather than dread it as a time when their ideas are not fully formed."[11]

There are crucial differences between explanatory-understanding and exploratory-understanding levels of teaching. The latter requires more active student participation, more criticism of conventional thinking, and more imagination and creativeness. The classroom atmosphere associated with the two approaches differ markedly. Exploratory teaching leads to the development of a classroom atmosphere that is more alive and exciting, more critical and penetrating, and more open to fresh and original thinking. Furthermore, the type of inquiry pursued by an exploratory class tends to be more rigorous and "work-producing" than that pursued in an explanatory-understanding level learning situation.

Since exploratory teaching is problem-centered teaching, what distinguishes it from explanatory teaching and learning is the presence of genuine problems that students feel a need to solve. At the outset of a study, a real question develops for which students have no answer, or at least no adequate one. Through the study, the students and teacher, working either cooperatively or individually, develop what is for them a new or more adequate solution. Although the teacher is conscious of performing a unique function in relation to a group of students, he/she still deems himself a part of the group as its members participate in the learning process.

NOTES

1. See "laissez-faire," *Webster's Third New International Dictionary* (Springfield, MA: Merriam, 1966), p. 1265.
2. See Ralph K. White and Ronald Lippitt, *Autocracy and Democracy: An Experimental Inquiry* (New York: Harper & Row, 1960), pp. 51–55, 66–80.
3. Ibid., pp. 55–58, 61–64.
4. Ibid., pp. 58–65.
5. See Ernest E. Bayles, *Democratic Educational Theory,* Chapter 1. "Experiments with Reflective Teaching" (New York: Harper & Row, 1960).
6. See Van Cleve Morris, *Existentialism in Education* (New York: Harper & Row, 1966), p. 135.
7. See George Katona, *Organizing and Memorizing* (New York: Columbia University Press), 1940.
8. Benjamin S. Bloom, "Testing Cognitive Ability and Achievement," in N. L. Gage, ed., *Handbook of Research on Teaching* (Chicago: Rand McNally, 1963), p. 392.
9. See "understand," *The American College Dictionary* (New York: Random House, 1964), p. 1321.
10. Robert J. Sternberg and Todd I. Lubart, "Creating Creative Minds," Phi Delta Kappan, V 72, No. 8, April 1991, p. 610.
11. Ibid, p. 611.

BIBLIOGRAPHY

The bibliography for Chapters 11, 12, and 13 is at the end of Chapter 13.

Chapter
12
How May Teachers Teach for Explanatory Understanding?

*E*xplanatory-understanding level teaching seeks to give students patterns of general ideas and supporting facts in such a way that they will see the relationships between the generalizations and the particulars or facts that support them and how the generalizations may be used; it is giving students rules. (At this point readers should review the meaning of *understanding* developed in Chapter 11, pages 253–258.)

To repeat, an understanding may be gained by either of two quite distinctive processes. We may identify them as learning on an explanatory-understanding level and learning on an exploratory-understanding level. When teachers give understandings to students, the class is operating on an explanatory-understanding level. When students and the teacher cooperatively and exploratively develop understandings, the class is operating on an exploratory-understanding level. The exploratory-understanding level also is sometimes referred to as the critical thinking, investigative learning, reflective learning, or reflective inquiry level.

Most advocates of explanatory-understanding level teaching have taken for granted that a teacher begins with truths that he/she knows but that students do not. Students acquire these truths, with the teacher providing what cues are necessary along the way. Students have successfully completed their learning task when they emerge with an understanding of the preestablished truths that the teacher already knew.

WHAT LEADERS HAVE DEVELOPED EXPLANATORY UNDERSTANDING LEVEL TEACHING?

Johann F. Herbart, Charles H. Judd, Henry C. Morrison, and the contemporary educators Robert M. Gagné, Benjamin S. Bloom, James H. Block, and Jerome S. Bruner have provided the most significant leadership in the development of explanatory-understanding level teaching, based upon their respective conceptions of the nature of understanding level learning. But Bruner also has made significant contributions to exploratory-understanding teaching. Although many others have made important contributions, these stand out as perhaps the most prominent innovators in explanatory-understanding level teaching and learning.

Since Herbart's, Judd's, Gagné's, and Bruner's positions are treated in some detail in previous chapters, here we only allude to aspects of their theories that directly pertain to the explanatory-understanding level of teaching and learning. Then, later in the chapter, we treat the positions of Morrison and of Bloom and Block in more detail.

How Did Herbart's Apperception and Judd's Generalizations Theory Involve Understandings?

Johann Friedrich Herbart wrote no treatise on the meaning of understanding, yet his approach to the teaching-learning process indicated that he was aware of one aspect of understanding—that is, relating isolated facts to the general principle or rule that gives them meaning.

In Steps 3 and 4 of a Herbartian lesson plan as developed by American Herbartians (see page 39), students are asked to identify common elements in a body of factual material and to make a general statement of related facts, then to formulate the relationship into a rule, principle, or law. Then, in Step 5, students are expected to demonstrate that they clearly see the nature of the principle by applying it to novel situations. A number of school subjects today are taught with essentially the same aims. These are the courses in which the crux of the subject matter is the learning and application of principles. English grammar and mathematics are often taught this way. In contrast, foreign language, history, geography, and many other subjects are often taught primarily on a memory level. Despite the great emphasis upon students' learning about the scientific method in their science courses, many science courses continue to center upon memorization of nomenclature, principles, formulae, and concepts.

Judd's "generalizations" were statements of the understandings that were to be given to students, which translated students' anticipated experiences into rules of operation that they could use in further thoughts and actions (see pages 220–221). Teaching for generalizations relates students' experiences in such a way that what is gained at one point can be used to their advantage many times.

How Are Gagné's Higher-Order Rules Related to Explanatory Understanding?

For Gagné, intellectual skills involve organisms' knowing how to perform acts. Cognitive strategies are a special kind of intellectual skill, in the form of internally organized capabilities that learners use to guide their processes of attending, learning, remembering, and thinking. Thus, learning strategies or higher-order rules, in a sense, are understandings developed internally as concomitants of behavior.

Gagné's sixth, seventh, and eighth learning types are concept learning, rule learning, and problem solving. Concept learning is making a common response to a class of stimuli. Rule learning is forming a chain of two or more concepts so as to enable one to respond to a class of stimulus situations with a class of performances. In Gagné's problem solving, one applies previously learned rules to achieve a solution of a novel situation so as to achieve a higher-order rule. Thus, all three types involve gaining explanatory understandings through a behavioristically characterized learning process. But in no sense is the process of gaining understandings in an exploratory fashion brought into the picture.

How Does Bruner Emphasize Teaching for Understanding Through Conceptualization?

Jerome S. Bruner is a cognitive psychologist who strongly advocates a combination of explanatory- and exploratory-understanding levels of teaching and learning. However, he uses a somewhat different vocabulary and manner of describing his views than do others within the same frame of reference.

Bruner's principal concern is with how people actively select, structure, retain, and transform information and how they go beyond discrete information to achieve generalized insights or understandings. He has great interest in how people adopt models of reality from their culture and adapt them to their individual uses. His "models" are expectancies, and expectancies are insights. Bruner thinks that study of the intellectual structure of a given discipline provides the best way of teaching students to think. See page 130.

All three of Bruner's modes of representation—the enactive, iconic, and symbolic—involve, to some degree, people striving for understanding. But it is within the process of symbolic representation, centered on language, that people achieve genuine reflective thinking or exploratory understanding. Symbolic representation is an instrument for conceptualization or categorization, which is the principal product of reflective thinking and learning. It is through goal-oriented strategies that conceptualization occurs.

Bruner thinks that teachers should encourage students to discover the value and the amendability of their considered guesses and should promote students' confidence in their ability to solve problems by thinking. Education should concentrate more on the unknown and speculative, and gained knowledge should be placed in the context of action and commitment.

WHAT CHARACTERISTICS SHOULD TEACHERS HAVE FOR THEM TO TEACH ON AN EXPLANATORY UNDERSTANDING LEVEL?

Teachers, to be able to teach effectively on an explanatory-understanding level, should manifest a certain kind of attitude, values, and knowledge. Some factors involved in acquiring these desirable traits are the way in which the teachers have learned the subjects being taught, the degree to which they have learned those subjects, and their pattern of personal characteristics.

If prospective teachers have been taught on an explanatory-understanding level the subjects that they in turn plan to teach, then it is quite likely that they will need only a minimum of instruction in methodology. It is a truism that the way in which teachers have learned will be reflected in the way they teach. If a teacher has not learned the subjects by moving from instances (facts) to categories (concepts) to codes (generalizations), then he/she may need to relearn his subjects again following those steps.

Since one's ability in communicating knowledge depends largely upon one's mastery of the knowledge to be communicated, a teacher who is not a master of his subjects should take the steps necessary to ensure their mastery. For the undergraduate, this may mean studying far beyond the minimal graduation requirements. For those already teaching, it may mean returning to college for in-depth study of the subjects that they now teach or a more carefully planned program of self-study.

It is quite simple to deduce what kind of persons are most likely to be successful at explanatory-understanding level teaching. They must be fairly bright—that is, capable of exercising intelligence on a fairly high level. They must have the kind of mind-set that finds it easy to see particulars in relation to one another—the kind that leans toward conceptualization, generalization, and abstraction. Another capacity of crucial importance is patience. Teaching for understanding on either level is not something that can be hurried. The "frantic ground-covering" type of teacher is suited only for memory level teaching.

WHAT PROCEDURES ARE ESSENTIAL TO TEACHING ON AN EXPLANATORY-UNDERSTANDING LEVEL?

To teach effectually on an explanatory-understanding level, teachers must (1) keep their objectives clear, (2) utilize productive motivational techniques, (3) pace students and lessons advantageously, and (4) use lesson plans properly.

How May Teachers Keep Their Objectives Clear?

In several of his writings Bruner stresses that most students will make an effort to achieve the learning goals that a teacher announces to them. However, this does not mean that prior announcements of conclusions are desirable; such action would destroy the "discovery aspect" of learning. What should be explained to students before the learning act is the kind of learning that they are expected to achieve. Teachers are either misled or shoddy if, in making assignments, they request their students to memorize something, to spend so much time at drill, or just to "learn this by tomorrow" (which students almost always construe to mean "memorize"). Students must be taught, but not through mere memorization, the nature of a concept, a generalization, and a structured subject. This can be done by an inductive type of questioning, coupled with the study of examples showing people in the process of achieving these goals. When students not only can explain in their own words but can also invent their own examples of these processes, then they are ready for effective statements of objectives.

If students are always reminded that the object of learning is some level of conceptualization, and if no other approach works, then this is the way they will learn. Assignments will carry instructions such as: "Here we have some facts that seem unconnected. See to what extent you can categorize them" or "We have reached three generalizations concerning this topic. Try to see if you can combine them into a single, more inclusive generalization" or "After conceptualizing the known facts, we have invented a generalization. See how many presently unknown but possible facts you can deduce from the generalization."

What Is the Source of Productive Motivational Techniques?

Educators who operate within an explanatory-understanding level frame of reference assume that once a student is acquainted with a subject, told of the expected goals in learning it, and begins to experience some success, his motivation is generated rather spontaneously. Hence, they prepare students for the presentation of each unit for study by centering their activities upon making the prearranged subject matter interesting. They do so by talking about what the students already know and thereby pointing the students' interests toward what they need to know. This is not a false theory or motivation, but perhaps it is an inadequate one. It is true that some students, more often the bright and intellectually curious ones, become very much involved with a subject merely through their exposure to it. But this is the exception rather than the rule.

How May Teachers Pace Students' Lessons Advantageously?

We come now to one of the major points concerning classroom procedure. By "pace" we refer to speed of movement from one topic to another; it logically follows that the number of topics studied in a year is of great significance. The pace of learning on both levels of understanding is usually slow. It is much more analogous to the steady thrust of a glacier than to the speed of a greyhound. As we pointed out earlier in the chapter, categorizing, generalizing, and structuring cannot be rushed. This is the case even despite "intuitive leaps" (see page 141)—after all, the leaps produce only hypotheses and not firm knowledge. If a learner is to emerge with something solid, each leap must be followed by a careful series of verifying tests.

Any subject matter worth confronting students with is worth careful, penetrating, thorough study. If it is not worth this kind of study, it is not worth inclusion in the curriculum. Typically, we try to teach too many items—which remain nothing more than items—quickly to be forgotten. To achieve genuine understanding, and consequent retention and transfer, schools may have to eliminate a large part of the present curriculum. The problem of the relationship of teaching methodology to curriculum needs a great deal more study than it has received to date.

How May Teachers Use Lesson Plans Advantageously?

Historically, carefully drawn day-by-day lesson plans have been considered essential to explanatory-understanding level teaching and learning. It appears likely that until a teacher has structured the subject matter in his own thinking, he/she not only should read and think copiously but should also take notes that can be translated into lesson plans as necessary. But Herbartian lesson planning is overly rigid and leads to indoctrination. Morrison's mastery units represent an advance over Herbartian lesson plans. However, they, too, set the stage for a teacher to indoctrinate students in a rather mechanistic fashion. Bruner appears to have nothing to say on the subject of lesson plans. Possibly he assumes that a competent teacher will have his lesson plans in his head.

Throughout the United States, recent curriculum "reforms" have attempted to make teaching "accountable" and more efficient by insisting that all teachers, in all classes, in all grades, must each day follow a highly structured sequence, often beginning with preparation, then proceeding to objectives and concepts to be covered, and ending with evaluation. Such approaches, frequently tied in with state- or national-level standardized tests, have tended to eliminate both teacher individuality and creativity and in-depth exploration by students.

Our own feeling is that a beginning teacher, striving for explanatory-understanding level teaching, should have a tentative plan for each class session. For safety, the teacher should probably have an alternate plan in case the first does not work. We, however, do not recommend a rigid plan with 1-2-3 steps. Thought does not take this pattern. Plans should be informal and flexible, including reminders of factual material to be presented when needed, key questions to ask, and tentative conclusions. One manner of distinguishing explanatory-understanding from exploratory-understanding level teaching is the tendency of the former to adhere quite closely to lesson plans as drawn and to wrap up each unit in a complete package with no loose ends. This tendency has significant implications for motivation, as we will see in the next chapter on exploratory-understanding level teaching.

HOW HAVE MORRISON'S IDEAS PROMOTED EXPLANATORY-UNDERSTANDING LEVEL TEACHING?

Henry C. Morrison (1871–1945) was an influential figure in American education during the 1930s and devised a unit plan that at one time was in rather widespread use. Within an idea-centered frame of reference, Morrison described various types of learning, including conditioning, "bonding," and trial and error.[1] However, the kind of learning he felt schools should promote is none of these as such, but a special form that he referred to as *personality adaptation*. In developing his position, he borrowed freely from various schools of thought, yet to call him an eclectic would be an oversimplification. Because of his emphasis upon personality adaptation, to some degree he developed a synthesis of the then prevailing outlooks on learning.

Personality adaptation is somewhat different from biological adaptation. Biological adaptation, in its most general sense, is the structural and functional process and product that occurs whenever an organism achieves a better adjustment to the conditions of life. Personality adaptation is a psychological process of permanent personality change; it is a change in insight. It consists of revised attitudes, values, beliefs, knowledge, and other factors that constitute a psychological person.

Morrison distinguished *adaptive response* from *true adaptation*. An adaptive response is a habit learned more or less by rote that its bearer does not understand and therefore uses blindly. Morrison thought that much human behavior is on this level. But he deplored any kind of teaching that leaves students with only adaptive responses instead of with true personality adaptations.

The proper task for education, said Morrison, is the creating of true adaptation, which is a permanent change in outlook as previously indicated. Or, put in Morrison's own language, it is personality change. To him, the term personality meant a total person in its psychological and sociological sense, not those superficial aspects of a person's makeup that we sometimes signify when we say, "Jane has a nice personality." Specifically, Morrison said personality is the "sum total of what an individual has come to be by learning the cultural products of social evolution."[2]

What Was Morrison's Recommended Teaching Procedure?

Fundamental to comprehension of Morrison's teaching procedure is an understanding of his concept of *mastery*. The outcome of all teaching is mastery—not mere memorization of facts, but mastery. Mastery is reached only when planned understandings have been grasped thoroughly.

Each subject field, according to Morrison, was to be divided into units. Each unit should present a specific understanding with such thoroughness that mastery is achieved by most students. Note that Morrison did not mean by a "unit" what is commonly meant today. In contemporary parlance, a unit usually is a block of work that, to a teacher or textbook writer, comprises a logical work task. A unit, therefore, is typically conceived as simply a piece of work, based upon a certain quantity of related facts in a textbook or other source. Morrison's conception of a unit of work was psychological. To him, a unit was a generalization and its related facts, as a student should come to see them. A unit was never "covered" until all, or almost all, students thoroughly understood the generalization—its factual origins, its probable reliability, and the kinds of situations in which it could be used in the future.

Some subjects, for instance algebra, contain many units, each of which may be grasped by most students in a fairly short time. Other subjects, for instance, a foreign language, contain only one unit; the whole subject must be mastered before a student has anything worthwhile. The point is, a unit represents an insight that is relatively complete in itself. Such an insight may be relatively simple and readily grasped, or it may require years of study. Hence, a unit, as Morrison conceived it, may require anywhere from a class period to many years to be mastered. Each unit is developed according to a sequence of steps, which, although Morrison disclaimed their relationship to the famous five steps of the Herbartian method, are nevertheless reminiscent of the Herbartian steps. Morrison's contribution was a major one, and most current teaching would undoubtedly be greatly improved if Morrison's thinking were more widely understood. His notion that mere collections of descriptive facts have no meaning, provide no basis for understanding, and therefore constitute unteachable subject matter, is of especial importance.

HOW DO BLOOM AND BLOCK DEVELOP MASTERY TEACHING?

The ideas, research, and operational procedures of Benjamin S. Bloom, James H. Block, and others have developed a contemporary version of mastery teaching and learning that harks back to Morrison's position. However, this contemporary version is anchored to a behaviorism that emphasizes discrete psychomotor, cognitive, and affective objectives. Thus, it actually promotes both memory and explanatory-understanding levels of teaching and learning.

Contemporary adherents of this position think that "mastery learning offers a powerful new approach to student learning which can provide almost all students with the successful and rewarding learning experiences now allowed to only a few."[3] Adherents also think that modern educational technology now provides the means for achievement of Morrison's ambitions.

Modern mastery learning has emerged as a corollary of programmed instruction. By setting the level formerly required for a grade of A in a nonmastery class as the definition of mastery for later mastery classes, Professor Bloom and his associates have brought four-fifths of their students to reach a level of achievement that less than one-fifth of them had attained under earlier nonmastery conditions.[4] When provided with favorable learning conditions, *most students become very similar with regard to learning ability, rate of learning, and motivation for further learning.*"5 "Theoretically, almost all the students can learn to a relatively high level anything the schools have to teach."6 However, the critical question here is what level of achievement was required for an A grade in the earlier nonmastery classes.

The central thesis of Bloom and his associates is that "variations in the *Cognitive Entry Behavior* and *Affective Entry Characteristics* and the *Quality of Instruction* will determine the nature of the learning outcomes. These outcomes are the *level and type of achievement*, the *rate of learning*, and the *affective characteristics of the learner* in relation to the learning task and self."7 Variations in learning and the levels of learning of students, then, are determined by the students' learning history and the quality of instruction that they receive. Students' learning history determines their cognitive entry behavior and affective entry characteristics. Cognitive entry behaviors alone account for about 50 percent of the variation in students' achievements; affective entry characteristics alone account for 25 percent. But these two characterizations, in combination, can account for about 60 percent of the achievement variations on a new set of learning tasks.8

What Is a Mastery Learning Task?

Bloom thinks that "some of the apparent weakness of the schools may be due to lack of clear-cut objectives for education and their implementation by carefully developed instructional materials and procedures."9 Hence, attempts should be made to locate the particular kinds of learnings that are important both in their own right and for other parts of the school learning process. Then, these learnings should be organized into specific learning tasks that can be defined, their elements analyzed, and the relations among their elements made explicit. Elements of learning tasks may be either unrelated or interrelated terms, facts, and rules.10

A *learning task* is a chapter in a textbook or a topic in a course or curriculum that requires about one to ten hours for a student to master. It contains a variety of ideas, procedures, or behaviors to be learned over this relatively short period. It may include educational objectives such as analysis and application as well as knowledge or comprehension.11 A learning task provides for interaction among a learner, something to be learned, and a teacher or tutor. The learning task can be analyzed with considerable objectivity and may be evaluated on the basis of the subject material to be learned, the structural relations among its elements, and learning theory and research.

How Should Teachers Teach for Mastery?

Teaching for mastery entails the formulation of a set of instructional objectives or tasks, which all students will be expected to achieve to a particular mastery performance standard, then breaking the course into a sequence of smaller learning elements or units. The teacher follows a "cycle of group-based instruction, formative testing, and certification or prescription/correction for each student on each unit until all learning units have been completed."[12] Each student's grade is determined solely on the basis of his absolute, as opposed to relative, performance over the learning material.

Bloom advocates equality of learning outcomes rather than equality of educational opportunity; this requires *inequality* of treatment. Because of background characteristics, approximately 2 percent of the students at each extreme will not conform to the equality-of-outcomes standard. Thus, "It is the middle 95 percent of students where *equality of outcomes* is a realistic possibility for most teachers, who carefully and systematically apply appropriate instructional means to student differences."[13]

Most individuals, then, can learn the answers the school has to teach, provided they have the time and help needed. Different learners need different amounts of time to learn a given learning task, and students may commit errors in their learning process, but "a system of feedback to the teacher and students can reveal the error in learning shortly after they occur, and if appropriate corrections are introduced as they are needed, the educational system can be a *self-correcting* system. . . ."[14] "A *minimal-error* educational system should enable almost all learners to learn effectively and with considerable pleasure."[15]

The acquired knowledge and its application and relationships, however, are learned on either a memory or explanatory-understanding level. Listing specific learning objectives or tasks is not conducive to exploratory-learning procedures.

HOW IS EXPLANATORY-UNDERSTANDING LEVEL LEARNING EVALUATED?

Either factual explanatory essay tests or short-answer, true-false, selection, or completion tests are most appropriate for testing students' understandings that are learned on an explanatory-understanding level. By using these, students demonstrate how well they can either recognize, explain, or utilize the understandings or generalized insights that the teacher has expected them to acquire.

In testing on an explanatory-understanding level, just as with both types of the memory level, the teacher checks students' answers against a prepared list of answers. However, the process differs somewhat from that of memory level testing in that as long as the answers are correct, the teacher credits students for "right" answers, even though they may use wording somewhat different from that of the instructor. An appropriate explanatory understanding level essay test question would be "Describe how the four levels of teaching and learning differ from one another." An appropriate objective test item: "Select the word that completes the sentence best: When a teacher teaches on an explanatory-understanding level, he gives his students (1) advice, (2) generalizations, (3) thoughts, (4) memories." (See Table 11.1, page 250.)

NOTES

1. Henry C. Morrison, *Basic Principles in Education* (Boston: Houghton Mifflin, 1934), Chapter 4.
2. Ibid., p. 39.
3. James H. Block, ed., *Mastery Learning Theory and Practice* (New York: Holt, Rinehart and Winston, 1971), p. 3.
4. Benjamin S. Bloom, "An Introduction to Mastery Learning Theory," in James H. Block, ed., *School, Society, and Mastery Learning* (New York: Holt, Rinehart and Winston, 1974), p. 6.
5. Benjamin S. Bloom, *Human Characteristics and School Learning* (New York: McGraw-Hill, 1976), p. x.
6. Ibid., p. 213.
7. Ibid., p. 11.
8. Ibid., see p. 108.
9. Ibid., p. 213.
10. Ibid., see p. 30.
11. Ibid., see p. 22.
12. James H. Block, "A Description and Comparison of Bloom's Learning for Mastery Strategy and Keller's Personalized System of Instruction," in James H. Block, ed., *School, Society, and Mastery Learning*, p. 18.
13. Bloom, *Human Characteristics and School Learning*, pp. 215–216.
14. Ibid., p. 212.
15. Ibid., p. 16.

BIBLIOGRAPHY

The bibliography for Chapters 11, 12, and 13 is at the end of Chapter 13.

Chapter
13

How Does Exploratory-Understanding Level Teaching and Learning Proceed?

Much of the inefficiency in education that research has exposed stems from the way most school subjects are organized and presented. Subjects often remain meaningless to students, not necessarily because of students' intellectual deficiencies but because human mentalities work so that the subjects, as organized and taught, may have little meaning for students. Explanatory-understanding level teaching gives students a tool for more intelligent behavior. It equips them with generalized insights that can be applied in problematic situations both in and outside school. But explanatory-understanding level teaching, if it remains merely that, casts the students as passive agents and the teacher as an active one. The teacher tells and the students listen or the teacher stimulates and the students respond. Thus, this level of teaching is basically autocratic and authoritarian.

Teachers who are committed to the *exploratory-understanding* level of teaching and learning think that the quality and quantity of what students come to know, think, and do are inseparable from how their learning is acquired. What children and youth learn along with their learning subject matter is often as significant as the subject matter itself. In contrast with the results of authoritarian education, students may democratically and exploratorily learn both how knowledge changes, grows, and is subject to interpretation and what "good" thinking is and how difficult it is to accomplish. Within this process, they may develop intellectual habits of curiosity, inquiry, persistence, and carefulness. They may also learn to discern the difference between relevant and irrelevant information and reliable and unreliable sources of information.

When exploratory teaching and learning are successful, students emerge with (1) an enlarged stock of tested understandings and (2) an enhanced ability to develop and solve problems on their own. The latter product is as important as the former. If only the first were accomplished, no claims could be made for this level that could not also be made for explanatory-understanding level teaching. However, within genuine exploratory-understanding centered teaching, students learn the very nature and techniques of problem-solving processes. And if well taught, problem-solving approaches and procedures that are learned in school carry over to be applied to a wide range of problems both in and outside school.

Exploratory-understanding level of teaching and learning consists of both *investigative* and *reflective* processes. Whereas investigative teaching centers upon discovery-explanation processes, reflective teaching centers upon prediction-verification ones.

Investigative teaching and learning consist of students either individually or as groups, with the help of their teacher, selecting problems for their inquiry in regard to matters with which the students are truly involved. Then, they pursue inquiries into those problems to the degree that is feasible.

Reflective teaching and learning consist of problem raising and problem solving. Problem raising is the process within which students, with the help of a teacher, discover and identify some inadequacies or disharmonies in their thinking. Problem solving consists of the students' formulating hypotheses—possible answers—and their testing the hypotheses by all available pertinent data or information. For exploratory-centered teaching to prevail, it must be accompanied by exploratory-centered learning. Such teaching is implemented best by a *cognitive-interactional* psychology that draws from both *linear cognitive interaction,* described in Chapter 7, and *cognitive-field simultaneous mutual interaction,* described in Chapters 8 and 9.

The cognitive-interactionist view on learning is a generalized outlook that emphasizes the use of experimental, scientific, and reflective processes in gaining knowledge. It has emerged as a constructive *relativistic* reaction against the absolutistic thinking that has characterized much of human history. In place of centering upon correct student *behavior* and *adjustment,* cognitive interactionists emphasize students' *gaining insights* or *understandings* as they become involved in contemporaneous situations. Since cognitive interactionists test ideas by their *fruits* rather than their metaphysical *roots,* their test of any educational process is its ability to promote human intellectual growth.

Whereas S-R conditioning theorists make much of pleasure and pain, or satisfaction and annoyance, as instigators of behavior, cognitive interactionists are more likely to talk about *success* and *failure* as motivators, the former truly being the "reward" for completing the act. Success and failure are not merely achievements as such but represent the relationship between a person's ambitions and his achievements. A person who has a certain level of aspiration and is able to achieve this level feels good about it. If he/she attains success at one level or aspiration, he is likely to raise the level and to continue doing so as long as he is able to perform successfully.

Cognitive interactionism involves the kind of generalization that may be applied to actual persons in school situations. It is built around persons' purposes that underlie behavior, the goals that are involved in behavior, and the persons' means and processes of understanding themselves and their environments as they function in relation to their goals.

A cognitive-interactionist oriented teacher will be drawn toward teaching on the exploratory-understanding level to the degree that he/she can develop means to promote it in his classes. But at times, any teacher so oriented will find it necessary to fall back to an explanatory-understanding level of teaching. In doing so, the teacher will recognize that although explanatory level teaching is based upon the idea that people are neutral and passive, it can be employed by one who thinks that people are neutral and interactive. It can lead to more intelligent behavior on the part of students but does not carry the quality of experience with it that is needed to enhance the development and use of student intelligence to its fullest potential.

Cognitive interactionists strive to teach on an exploratory-understanding level. However, they recognize that it is impossible to hold all teaching to this level at all times. Hence, they often find themselves teaching on the explanatory-understanding level, but seldom do they slip back into teaching for straight memory as such. This does not mean that they do not teach facts. It does mean that they teach facts as contributors to understandings. When students acquire exploratory understandings, they make genuine discoveries. But for students to discover something, they need not necessarily invent it: they need only to explore a matter in such a way as to make further sense of it. Within exploratory learning, students continue to acquire traditional learnings, but they acquire them as verifying or substantiating data. Teachers who adhere to exploratory-centered teaching and learning in no way disparage the importance of subject matter; they merely give it a different focus.

Cognitive interactionists are convinced, by research as well as their own experience, that, when students are taught on the exploratory-understanding level, they acquire many facts as well as understandings, and when they are taught on the explanatory-understanding level, they acquire much factual information. But this does not work well in reverse. There is little about purely factual memory teaching that contributes to understanding, and there is little about explanatory-understanding level that contributes directly to students' developing their learning on an exploratory-understanding basis. However, because of the potency of certain items, teachers may at times encourage, but not require, students to memorize them verbatim. What makes inquiry-centered classroom procedures distinctly different from either memory or explanatory-understanding level teaching is a classroom atmosphere of genuine teacher-student mutual inquiry.

HOW DOES INVESTIGATIVE TEACHING PROCEED?

Investigative teaching and learning consists of students, with the teacher's help, selecting problems for inquiry in regard to matters with which they are genuinely involved and pursuing their inquiries to the point of the students' satisfying enlightenment in regard to them. An investigative approach may be employed in teaching any academic subject or block of subjects. Here we use, as an example, teaching a social studies-English block through the sixth, seventh, and eighth grades.[1]

Through their participation in investigative learning, students learn that subject matter can be used as means to ends—to define and solve problems—rather than as ends in themselves. Each student becomes involved in a real problem and, through investigative inquiry, pursues that problem to its solution. Students usually do not finish one study before they find another question that motivates them to select another. For the students, subject matter becomes a tool for development of understandings, concepts, and attitudes, not a mere atomistic possession to be hoarded. Subject matter, then, becomes a means for defining and solving problems. Although it here is centered upon social studies and English, it is not narrowly restricted to those areas.

Investigative teaching is implemented best through individualized instruction. The teacher must operate in relation to the students in such a way as to enhance their thinking-learning patterns. This requires the teacher's helping *each* student, as much as possible, to use the available instruction center, library materials, maps, and chalkboard in his achieving of understandings through investigation.

The teacher begins with a group of sixth graders and continues with them through grades seven and eight. During the first months, study units are planned jointly by the students, teacher, and parents. Then, after the students have achieved good study habits and some efficiency in independent research, each develops an individualized study based upon a problem with which he/she has become involved.

In the process of solving his problem, a student develops a study guide that contains questions for which he/she wants to find answers, literature that will extend his knowledge in relation to his problem, and words that he/she must know the meaning of and spell correctly. When a student thinks that he/she has developed at least a tentative solution to his problem that harmonizes the information in regard to it and satisfies his curiosity, he reports his findings to the entire class. Both the teacher and the students participate in continuous evaluation of each student's achievement. In the process of solving their problems, students often develop charts, maps, mobiles, time-lines, and dioramas that aid either in solution of their problems or in presentation of their solutions to the class.

In the sixth grade, group units are stressed, but by the time students reach the seventh and especially the eighth grades, they are expected to devote an increasing proportion of their time to individual problem units. During the three years, the students will have studied many group and individual problem units. Some examples of the group units are the following:

. Where and What Was the Cradle of Civilization?
. What Can We Know About Life In and On the Sea?
. How Does Our Government Function?
. How Does the Geography of Europe Contribute to Its Economy?

Some examples of individual problem units developed and presented are the following:

. Who Were the Greatest Queens of England?
. How Important Is it to Us for the United States to Explore Space?
. What Can We Do About Air and Water Pollution?
. How Is the Culture of Japanese People Different from Our Own?
. What Did Witchcraft Have to Do With Our History?
. How Did Money Originate?
. Will Plastic Credit Cards Replace Money?
. How Did Our Writing System Develop?
. Was Washington Irving Called the Father of the Short Story?

Both teacher and student participants in investigative teaching and learning grow to think of subject matter as a tool to be used rather than merely a possession to be hoarded. Subject matter, so construed, consists of understandings, concepts, attitudes, and outlooks that are usable in life's various situations. Students grow to appreciate the opportunity to investigate problems on their own, and their learning is enhanced through the general study atmosphere that prevails.

Some specific advantages of centering teaching and learning upon investigative study are as follows:

1. Because students' involvement causes them to delve into all facets of problems to find satisfactory answers for themselves, students work beyond their previously indicated ability.
2. Such study helps students satisfy their need for independence; as they work on problems designed to prepare them for adult living, they cast off some childhood patterns and restrictions of behavior.
3. Students appreciate, and benefit by, an opportunity to move about the classroom and library freely in search of a wider selection of materials. (During the adolescent period of development, a degree of physical freedom is very important.)
4. The peer group evaluation that is employed often is taken to be more important to adolescents than either parental or teacher evaluation. Hence, it is an excellent motivational device.
5. Because of his achieved superior information about his study problem, each student has an opportunity to display excellence before his peers.
6. Students learn much through listening to and discussing their peers' studies.
7. Investigative study may open the way into reflective inquiry procedures.

We now proceed to a study of the basic procedures that are involved in reflective teaching and learning.

WHAT IS THE NATURE OF REFLECTIVE-LEVEL TEACHING AND LEARNING?

Reflective-level teaching and learning involves both problem raising and problem solving techniques. Problem raising and formulation is the first aspect of reflective thinking. It is a process of persons discovering and identifying inadequacies and disharmonies in their outlooks—cognitive structures—of their life spaces. A *reflection-centered problem* is based upon conflicts of ideas. Reflective teaching and learning consists of students formulating hypotheses and testing them with all available pertinent evidence. As evidence, facts are gathered in profusion, but teachers do little to encourage fact-learning or fact-recall as such.

Practice, as a tool for gaining understandings exploratorily, has a special connotation. It is construed as experimentally trying out an idea or act in what might appear to be a repetitive process. However, there is a crucial difference between mechanical repetition and experimental practice in that within experimental practice the subject performs the act more or less differently each time and observes or experiences the consequences of the change. Only nonrepetitive practice enhances learning in the best sense. But for a learning task to be achieved, nonrepetitive practice often must be extended over time. Not only does exploratory, nonrepetitive practice improve performance; the practice of a motivated person is always superior to that done under coercion by a student who has no perceived reason to conjugate verbs or do long division.

How Does Reflective Thinking and Learning Differ from Classical-Humanistic Reasoning?

For us to understand the nature of reflective learning and thinking, we should distinguish it sharply from the mental disciplinary pure reasoning process that is characteristic of classical humanism (see pages 24–28 for an explanation of this position).

For classical humanists, people are *rational animals.* This means that they are biological organisms in the same way that lower animals are, but in addition, they are endowed with a unique rational or reasoning faculty, which is the principal characteristic of their substantive minds; no other animals have this faculty or trait. Within classical humanism, knowledge consists of a body of principles that have been either received through intuitive inspiration or reasoned out by scholars throughout time and set down in the great books. Hence, scholarship consists of an armchair rational investigation of the nature of absolute Truth, Beauty, and Goodness. Therefore, the appropriate method of acquiring true knowledge is purely rational, as contrasted with experimental thinking.

Education, for classical humanists, consists of training students' predominant faculty, reason, along with developing their subordinate faculties such as memory, perception, and imagination. An intelligent person is a highly rational individual; his faculty of reason has been well developed. An individual's reasoning faculty, when well exercised and thereby developed, qualifies its owner to reason logically and accurately in regard to any matter in most any situation. Hence, learning consists of one's emulating the great intellectuals of history in exercising, and thereby developing, the faculties of one's mind, particularly that of reason.

The current conception of the reflective thinking process, as it is implemented by cognitive-interactionist psychology, is quite different from the classical concept of rational thinking or reasoning as it has been implemented by mental discipline. Whereas contemporary reflective thinking is a process that has much in common with modern experimental science, the reasoning of classical humanism is a purely mentalistic intellectual process whose use extends back into ancient times. When one reflects, one turns one's thoughts back upon an existing idea or segment of knowledge which may have been taken to be to some degree dependable. Reflection level teaching-learning is careful, critical examination of an idea or supposed article of knowledge in light of the *empirical* or *testable* evidence that supports it and the further conclusion toward which it points. Such learning is based upon, and has much in common with, a modern scientific outlook and approach. It reflects the conviction that students study and learn best when they are seeking both the intellectual and emotional relevance of their learning to significant aspects of their lives.

An understanding of how to solve problems according to principles of scientific reflection is perhaps the most useful intellectual tool a person can possess. If the central goal of education is to foster intelligence, reflective teaching should be the basic approach used by teachers everywhere. Let us visit a social studies class being taught reflectively and see whether we can discern what is unique to reflection level teaching-learning procedures.

How May a Class Reflectively Study the Pony Express?

A fifth-grade class was reflectively studying the Pony Express.[2] The key provocative question developed was as follows: "If the Pony Express was such an exciting and successful venture, why was it suddenly discontinued after less than two years' service?"

One day a class was listening to a member giving a report on the Pony Express. This student reporter related the following to the class.

A newspaper advertisement in 1860 read:

> WANTED
> Young men not over eighteen.
> Must be expert riders,
> willing to risk death daily.
> Orphans preferred.
> Wages, $25 per week.

This notice brought a group of young men together who would carry parcels from St. Joseph, Missouri to Sacramento, California in ten days' time. The stagecoach took 25 days to complete this trip, and many businessmen and government workers in the East and West wanted important long-distance mail to travel much faster. The newspaper advertisement helped create an organization that cut fifteen days off the time needed for mail to go from coast to coast.

Pony Express stations along the way provided food and care for both riders and horses. Fresh horses were available at each station, and about every 70 or 80 miles a different rider would take over. Sometimes a rider would reach a station and find it either burned down by Indians or deserted, and he would have to go on to the next station. No matter whether it snowed or rained or whether Indians or thieves attacked, the mail was to go through. Every Pony Express rider was given a revolver to protect himself. However, his main job was not to fight, but to avoid trouble if possible and reach his next station. Obviously, the job of Pony Express riders was most exciting, and the Pony Express was highly efficient for its time. People generally were enthusiastic about the new venture and, in a way, it made heroes of the riders.

The student reporter talked at some length about the excitement and glamour of the entire affair. Then, after telling about the enthusiasm that developed for this thrilling and efficient operation, he/she said, "Having been begun in 1860, the Pony Express was discontinued in 1861 after less than two years of operation." The reporter then sat down.

The class was somewhat surprised. After finding out what a grand and successful operation the Pony Express was, they learned that it was suddenly disbanded. Why? They started asking questions. In the following report of the discussion that ensued, "Reporter" indicates the student reporter who related the history of the Pony Express. "Student" indicates anyone who responded to the reporter's particular statement. A number of students participated in the discussion.

STUDENT: Why was the Pony Express stopped?

REPORTER: Why do you think it was stopped?

STUDENT: Were all the riders killed?

REPORTER: No.

STUDENT: Did they all quit?

REPORTER: No.

STUDENT: Did people stop writing letters?

REPORTER: No.

STUDENT: Did they get faster coaches?

REPORTER: No.

STUDENT: Was a railroad built?

REPORTER: No. The railroad wasn't completed until 1869.

TEACHER: Perhaps you should tell the class how they can find the answer.

REPORTER: O.K. If you read the middle part of Chapter Ten in your book, it tells why the Pony Express stopped.

STUDENT: Wait a minute. Did they start using the telegraph?

REPORTER: Why would people send mail by telegraph? We don't send telegrams when we want to write to someone, do we? We use telegrams for emergencies, don't we?

STUDENT: I've found it! I looked in my book and it says the telegraph was just invented by Morse and so they didn't need the Pony Express to carry mail. That's why they stopped it.

REPORTER: But we don't send letters by telegraph. Telegrams are for emergencies and special occasions.

TEACHER: Boys and girls, perhaps you should all read your text and see whether you can find why the telegraph would eliminate the Pony Express, even though today we don't use the telegraph to send letters.

(Here about ten minutes of silent reading and thinking elapses.)

STUDENT: Oh. I've got it. Way back at the first you said that businessmen wanted faster time for their mail orders for shipments and things like that. Regular mail was carried on stage coaches all the time and only very important things went by Pony Express—things like you would put in a telegram. So, with the telegraph the important special messages could go that way.

TEACHER: Well, class, shall we see whether our reporter can verify that explanation?

CLASS: Yes.

The reporter then verified this explanation by rephrasing the students' questions so as to make them hypotheses and by testing the hypotheses with all available evidence. For example, the first student's question, "Were all the riders killed?" implied the hypothesis, "The riders were all killed." The reporter tested the hypothesis with information that he/she had gained from reading and rejected it. The exchange of questions and answers in this simple example illustrates the process of hypothesis formation and testing. The hypothesis concerning the telegraph almost stood the test, except for the fact that it did not make sense to send all letters by telegraph. It was only after the fact was established that most ordinary mail was carried by stagecoach and that the Pony Express was used only for messages of special business and governmental importance, that it made sense for the telegraph to have replaced the Pony Express.

The example, though simple, does show that a correct answer—the telegraph replaced the Pony Express—must still be tested and may be found less than wholly correct or convincing until other information is added to complete the picture. Notice how the notion of the telegraph sent pupils looking for what special way it served. The special way was the need by business and government for fast service for important messages.

Because of space limitation, the preceding discussion among students and between students and teacher is to some degree in outline form. In actual practice there would be more digressions, and many statements would be made that were not pertinent to the problem at hand. The latter part of the discussion particularly would be more involved and much longer than is reported.

Now, just what is there about this teacher-student and student-student reflective classroom procedure that makes it different from either memory or explanatory-understanding level teaching? Perhaps it could be summarized by describing the classroom atmosphere as one of teacher-student mutual inquiry within which genuine problems are developed and solved.

Reflective teaching, then, involves *problem raising* and *problem solving*. In problem-centered reflective classes, instruction begins with introduction of an "I don't know" or problematic situation—one in which students are faced with a question they cannot answer. The problem should be so compelling that students really want to study it, but not so overwhelming that they are prone to give up. Accordingly, it should generate an urge to analyze the possible obstacles and dilemmas in the situation, to understand them, and to devise means for resolving the difficulties. After aiding students in raising a problem, the teacher then helps them investigate it until the best possible answer is found. Problem solving consists of formulating hypotheses and testing them with all available pertinent evidence. Facts are gathered in profusion, but teachers make no attempt to encourage fact learning or fact recall as such. Problems that make for ideal classroom study involve situations that are difficult enough to be challenging, yet simple enough that most students in a class will be able to cast and test hypotheses leading to a solution.

When students acquire exploratory understandings, they make genuine discoveries. But for students to discover something, they need not necessarily invent it: They need only to explore a matter in such a way as to make sense of it. Within reflective learning, students continue to acquire traditional learnings, but they acquire them as verifying or substantiating data. Hence, teachers who adhere to exploratory teaching and learning in no way disparage the importance of subject matter.

Education that centers on reflection level teaching and learning consists of both students and teachers experimentally reconstructing their respective life spaces so as to add to their meaning and thereby to increase the involved persons' abilities, both individually and collectively, to direct the course and contents of their future life spaces.

HOW IS REFLECTIVE LEVEL LEARNING PROMOTED?

Reflective-level learning is promoted best through the application of cognitive-interactionist psychology wherein learning consists of one's either gaining new insights or understandings or changing old ones through an exploratory, experimental process. That is, each individual, when behaving intelligently, is trying cognitively to reconstruct his life space so that its various functional regions— objects and activities—can be made to serve his purposes more effectively; "people behave in ways which they expect will lead them to desired goals."[3] The predominant overarching purpose in human living is the maintenance and enhancement of one's self. This entails the progressive improvement of one's ability to structure one's psychological person and environment to serve one's purposes. Within such experimental experience, a person tries first one course of action and then another, preserving only that which works best; it is from such experimentation, within the person's perceptions, that his understandings grow.

As soon as one achieves an insight, the thought occurs that possibly this idea will work in other, or even all, similar situations. Accordingly, the general value of the insight is tested through its repeated use in similar situations. If it fails to work, it will be discarded because of its extremely limited worth. If it seems to work, it will become a valued possession that will be added to the person's intellectual makeup—the cognitive structure of the person's life space. Of course, insights are valid in differing degrees of predictability.

A person's *immanent purposes* are always involved in his exploratorily gaining understanding. The understander must have a goal, and he/she must see what he seeks to understand in relation to that goal. Moreover, he/she must see how what he is trying to understand can be made to assist in the attainment of the goal or how it can be kept from hindering such achievement. It is as important to understand things that get in our way as it is to understand those that assist our movement. A rattlesnake may well be understood as something to be avoided just as a good book may be understood as something to add savor to life.

Understanding occurs in its best form when students come to see how to use productively, in ways they care about, a pattern of verified general ideas and the facts that support them. If a person really understands a principle he/she can probably (1) state it in his own words, (2) give an example of it, (3) recognize it in various guises and circumstances, (4) discern the behaviors or lack of behaviors that may represent it, (5) see the relationships between it and other principles or generalizations, (6) see the uses to which it may be put, (7) use it in diverse situations, (8) anticipate the consequences of its application, (9) identify illustrations or examples that do not fit the principle, and (10) state a principle that is opposite to it.

We now proceed to a study of the basic procedures that are involved in reflective teaching and learning. These include both problem raising and problem solving techniques. Problem raising is a process of persons discovering and identifying inadequacies and disharmonies in their outlooks or the cognitive structures of their life spaces. Problem solving, in turn, is a process of individuals reconstructing their outlooks or cognitive structures so as to make them more adequate and harmonious. Problem raising, consisting of problem identification and problem recognition, is the first of the five aspects of reflective thinking or learning; problem solving encompasses the other four.

When Is a "Problem" a Problem?

Too many teachers who have attempted a problems approach to teaching have not adequately understood the psychology of learning as it relates to problem-centered study. Older psychologies—mental discipline, apperception, and behaviorism—have had little to say about problem-centered study. Neobehaviorists, with their more sophisticated S-R conditioning theories, also have contributed little to the understanding of reflective teaching.

Often problem-centered teaching has failed because what teachers have chosen as "problems" have not actually been problems in a psychological sense. Contributions of cognitive-interactionist psychologists enable us to understand better what happens psychologically when a person has a problem. A learning problem is not merely an objective issue to be resolved; it must involve psychological tension in a learner.

The analysis of a problem in psychological terms should help resolve a common dilemma that arises in connection with a problems approach to teaching. The dilemma is: Students have a great variety of real problems, but often the "problems" that a teacher thinks students should study arouse little tension in them. If students do feel personally some of the problems posed by a teacher, they feel some much less intensely than others. Consequently, the motivation that should accompany problem-centered study often does not develop.

Problems are either person-centered or society-centered in nature. *Person-centered* problems hold a dominant place in the life spaces of students. *Society-centered* problems represent the social needs that some adults believe exist in a community, region, or nation. They constitute part of the social matrix and, as such, are at least in the foreign hulls of the life spaces of students, but often they constitute little part of their actual life spaces.

Society-centered problems are felt personally by someone, or they never would have been identified as problems in the first place; but commonly they are perceived only by some adults, and sometimes only by experts in fields of knowledge relevant to specific questions. To students, society-centered problems often seem quite remote; the students' function of living does not bring them into play. Posed by a teacher, society-centered problems, unless students feel personally involved with them, are not real problems at all.

Are Students Motivated by "Other Persons' " Problems?

Reactions of students to the two types of problems—personal and societal—are likely to be quite different. Students can see the point of studying problems in which they are personally involved. The necessary emotional steam already exists; often all a teacher needs to do is to direct study so that it will be as mature as possible. But when students are asked to study problems that they do not accept as their own, they are likely to remain unresponsive. Since no personally felt psychological goals are involved, a personally motivated search for solutions is unlikely. Because of this detachment, relevant facts are seen not as data contributing toward a solution but only as lessons to be learned. Consequently, the quality of learning that results when students study another's problems is likely to be little different from that produced by conventional textbook-recitation teaching.

Textbook writers often include "problems" at the ends of chapters. But these more often are tasks than problems. There is little reason to suppose that, without skillful preliminary discussion led by a teacher, these "problems" as stated will induce any significant kind of psychological tensions in students. Frequently, textbook writers, authors of syllabi and courses of study, and classroom teachers themselves label as "problems" exercises that do not function as true student psychological problems at all. The following are examples of "problems" that really are tasks, not problems:

To learn about the public utility companies of your community.

To see how many articles devoted to farming and rural life appear in the local newspaper.

To measure the height of a building.

To diagram a sentence.

Since study of other people's problems results in learning that qualitatively is little different from traditional fact memorization, some writers have suggested that teachers exclude from study any problem in which students do not already feel involved and confine instruction to problems that students feel spontaneously because of their life situations. Thus, they argue that the role of a teacher is to help students define carefully problems that already exist for them and then conduct whatever research and discussion seem to be appropriate in solving these problems. Although it should not be denied that in any school there is an important place for this kind of problem study, exclusive emphasis on it is highly reminiscent of the Rousseauean natural unfoldment outlook. There is a strong flavor of "letting students do as they please." Of course, in the hands of a capable teacher, considerable freedom may be extended to students in selection of their problems and at the same time considerable rigor may be demanded in their study.

How Is a Problem a Felt Tension?

To have a problem, a person must have a goal or goals that he/she accepts as his own. "Once a person has chosen a goal, he will behave in a manner intended to achieve that goal."[4] A problem arises when the person finds it impossible to proceed quickly and directly to the goal. When a student cannot achieve his goal readily, it is either because he/she sees no open path to it or because he sees two or more competing paths, or two or more competing goals, and cannot decide which to pursue. These are the familiar "no-path" or "forked-path" situations described by John Dewey.[5]

Cognitive-interactionists provide a psychological basis for a problem-centered, exploratory understanding level of teaching and learning. Whereas behavioristic teaching required only enough tension in students to cause them to behave in ways that might be conditioned, problem-centered teaching requires the promotion of tension in students to the point that they are involved and perplexed but not frustrated.

Since teachers, in teaching reflectively, should strive to keep their students involved and perplexed to a point just short of frustration, they should be able to recognize when people are approaching the frustration point. When a student stays right in there and battles with conflicting or problematic ideas, we know that he/she is perplexed but not frustrated. However, when a student becomes unduly aggressive, perhaps impudent, in his relations with others, he is displaying "fight." Or if a student passively submits to a situation and appears either to be doing nothing at all about it or to be regressing to earlier patterns of behavior, this is a psychological "flight." Both psychological *fight* and *flight* are symptoms of frustration.

Within a cognitive-interactionist frame of reference, when a person finds himself in either a goal-barrier situation or one of three kinds of conflicting goal situations, he/she has a problem. These situations are shown in Figure 13.1. The form that a situation takes depends largely upon what the person involved *makes of* that situation. In a goal-barrier situation, there is a goal region in a

Barrier or no-path situation

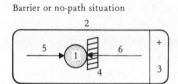

1. Person
2. Boundary of psychological environment
3. Goal; region of positive valence
4. Barrier
5. Vector of driving force toward goal
6. Vector of restraining force of barrier

Conflicting-goal situations

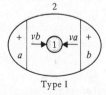

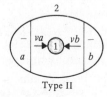

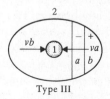

Figure 13.1 Field-conflict situations.

person's life space that has a positive valence, and a barrier exists between the person and the region of positive valence. Learning here consists of the person finding a way either to change his life space so that the barrier disappears or to surmount or detour the barrier.

In a conflicting goal situation, there are two or more conflicting goal regions toward which or away from which a person wants to make psychological movement. Conflicting goal situations lend themselves best to reflective or problem-centered teaching. In a Type I situation, a person has two conflicting goals or two psychologically opposite regions of life space, both with positive valences. (Positive goal regions being *psychologically opposite* means that both cannot be achieved at the same time.) In the illustration of Type I, vector *vb* represents a psychological force equal to the valence of region *b*, and vector *va* represents a force equal to the valence of region *a*. In a Type II situation, the person is confronted with two psychologically opposite significant regions of his life space, each having a negative valence; he/she wants to escape both, and they are of such nature that this is impossible. In a Type III situation, a region of positive valence and a region of negative valence are in the same psychological direction from the person; they are functionally similar or perhaps identical. Movement toward or away from regions is determined by the relative strength of the pertinent psychological forces at the time of movement.

Superficially, Type I and Type II situations appear much alike; however, they are crucially different. Quite often, whether a conflict situation is Type I or Type II depends largely upon what the individual *makes of* the situation. A person in a Type II situation—one with two opposite negative goals—is like a ball being pushed from opposite directions by two sticks; once it gives a little, it flies off to the side, out of the picture. A person in such a situation is trying to escape two opposite negative driving forces and is likely to become completely frustrated and, like the ball, leave the field—psychologically to flee from the scene or become irrationally aggressive, that is, to engage in either flight or fight. This means that the person suddenly moves from a relatively concrete level of life space to an extremely imaginative level (see pages 203–206). In contrast, a person in a Type I situation—one with two opposite positive goals—like a ball being pulled in opposite directions, usually will stay in the field, that is, remain engaged with the problem and try to resolve his conflict at the level of reality at which he/she meets it. He/she is attracted to two goals, both with positive valences. The goal toward which he/she moves is the one with the higher value or valence. (Should the two opposite goals be exactly equal, would the person be like the donkey who starved to death while standing exactly half-way between two stacks of hay?)

Since Type II situations (two opposite negative goals) give rise to frustrations, they should be avoided in teaching procedures. In contrast, since Type I situations (two opposite positive goals) involve and perplex but do not frustrate students, they should be sought.

A Type III conflict situation develops when a person contemplates violating one of the basic mores of his society, especially if it is for the first time. The person wants to perform the tabooed act and simultaneously wants not to do it; thus, it has both positive and negative valence. The person involved might perceive the taboo not as a negative goal but as a barrier between the person and the positive goal region. In this event the barrier would have a negative valence that would need to be counteracted by the stronger positive valence of the act, if it is to be performed.

What Level of Tension Is Best?

A characteristic of a goal-centered problematic situation is the presence of a certain amount of felt tension or discomfort. A person confronted with either a no-path or a conflicting-goal situation feels to some degree doubtful, puzzled, bewildered, and uncertain. How strongly a person feels this way depends upon at least three factors: (1) the desirability of the goal or respective goals; (2) the apparent difficulty of the obstacle; and (3) the person's own personality makeup. Whether a person finds himself between opposite positive goals that he/she is trying to achieve or opposite negative aversions that he is trying to escape often depends largely upon *how the person construes himself and his psychological environment.*

In a sense teachers must be tightrope walkers. They get the best results when they keep their students in a state of full enthusiasm. When they have students involved to the point that, during discussions, they sit on the edges of their seats, arms waving and eyes glistening and all wanting to talk at once, teachers have a potentially fine teaching situation. However, there is a fine line between this type of situation and situations in which students either become so excited that their emotions are chaotic, feel despair because the problem is too difficult, become frustrated because of too great a personal involvement, or are bored because a supposed problem is too easy.

The necessity for teachers to maintain control of learning situations cannot be overemphasized. One of the difficulties that commonly arises when a teacher attempts reflective teaching is loss of control. When youngsters are either highly excited or bored, they are difficult to manage. A teacher following the reflective approach usually learns from experience when it is time to sidetrack a discussion that is producing too much heat.

HOW DOES PROBLEM RAISING PROCEED?

Problem raising consists of both recognition and definition of a problem. For a "problem" to be a problem, a person not only needs to feel a tension in a situation but also to have some idea of the nature and cause of the tension. A problem arises in the thinking of a student whenever, by some means, he/she is induced to be either dissatisfied with, or doubtful concerning, some aspect of his present knowledge, attitudes, or values. The dissatisfaction or doubt represents either a forked-path or a no-path situation within the student's life space that is characterized by conflicting goal regions. When a student has a real problem, he/she should be asking himself questions such as "Is an existing insight, attitude, or value adequate? Is it valid? Is an alternative to it more promising? In adherence to a given pattern of thought, is there a basic contradiction? What are the real issues in regard to the ideas that I hold? What are the available alternatives in thought and action?"

Whenever two or more competing alternative ideas, attitudes, or values are at stake, there is an issue. And since, by definition, all issues are controversial, controversy is a fundamental aspect of any truly problem-centered teaching. Controversy involves either interpersonal or intrapersonal conflict. *Interpersonal conflict* arises when individuals or groups hold ideas that are sharply opposed to those of other individuals or groups. We often refer to conflicts of this type as "controversial issues." Persons on each side of an interpersonal conflict or dispute may be quite consistent, each in his own outlook, even though the outlook is in sharp disagreement with that of the opposing party. In our culture such conflict may arise among social classes, among racial, religious, ethnic, or age groups, between representatives of capital and labor, and between the sexes.

When a student becomes aware of his own incompatibilities of outlook, the resulting internal struggle may be referred to as an *intrapersonal conflict*. The content of an intrapersonal conflict may be little different from that of an interpersonal one. Yet it tends to foment greater tension in the individual. Since extreme intrapersonal tension is hazardous to an individual's personality structure, this level of intrapersonal conflict should not be deliberately promoted. Nevertheless, for a reflective learning situation to exist, issues must become felt by students in such a way that each finds himself to a significant degree in controversy with himself. Hence, each individual must be attracted to some extent by two or more competing hypotheses and feel temporarily unable to make a choice between them; otherwise, for him, no problem exists. Accordingly, if teachers are to teach reflectively, they must help students expose contradictions and inadequacies in their own thinking and action to their own critical examination.

How May Teachers Bring Students to Recognize Contradictions and Inadequacies in Their Thinking?

For teachers to accomplish much in helping students see their inconsistencies, they need a good idea of what kind of contradiction students are likely to hold. This knowledge will enable reasonably skillful teachers to pursue a line of discourse and questioning that will expose students' ideological inconsistencies and inadequacies to themselves. Some techniques for exposing contradictions and inadequacies and thereby raising problems in the thinking of students are teachers using a context switch, introducing disturbing data, permitting students to make mistakes, and helping students convert some societal problems into personal ones. The examples of these techniques that we give are hypothetical and, of course, are considerably simplified. To make the contradictions and inadequacies explicit to most students in a class, much more discussion than is herein described would be necessary.

Using a Context Switch   A context switch is accomplished when a teacher helps a class generalize—reduce to a principle—a particular idea that is expressed by a student, then demonstrates how a further thought that is held by the same student is incompatible with the generalized principle and, consequently, with the first idea. For example, a student expresses the opinion that "Government price supports for cotton are ridiculous." The teacher then seeks agreement with the principle that "The federal government should not interfere with the economy." The teacher then places the principle in a different context, that is, gives it a different subject matter with a question like "Do you favor a protective tariff on cotton?" The student, who also adheres firmly to the principle that "A high protective tariff brings prosperity to a nation," is placed in a position that makes some kinds of revision of either one or both of his contradictory opinions, should he/she attempt to extricate himself from contradiction. To achieve the desired result, the teacher must hold the student closely to the issue. If students are permitted to qualify their opinions by introducing exceptions, they may extricate themselves readily without having to do any serious thinking.

Teachers should realize that often, even when a context switch does not provoke thinking in the particular student who is trapped by it, it does motivate constructive thought in several other members of the class. The word *trapped* is used here advisedly; yet some rationale for its use is needed. A teacher who wishes to teach reflectively is probably justified in using almost any device that helps get reflection going. Some such devices may seem so teacher-centered that the whole procedure may appear to be rigged in favor of the teacher's biases. But this is only the beginning aspect of an inquiry. When it comes to casting and scrutinizing hypotheses and drawing conclusions, there should be no rigging. Although the teacher performs key functions throughout the reflective process, the relationship between the students and the teacher must be continuously centered in mutual inquiry.

It is essential that both students and teacher be committed to the use of the same criteria, the same rules of evidence, and the same inquiry procedures.

Unless the teacher also is committed to the same standards as the students, the teaching becomes indoctrination.

Introducing Disturbing Data   Another means of inducing students to feel problems is to introduce them to data from outside their life spaces that lead them to doubt some currently held item of knowledge, attitude, or value. The teacher may ask students to read a book, to watch a television program or motion picture, to go on a field trip, or to engage in some other activity that confronts them with facts contrary to those they have taken for granted. Of course, this approach, like any other, may not work. Students may refuse to admit the new facts into their life spaces. Unless they recognize the significance of the facts and truly come to doubt their existing ideas, no problem is created.

Permitting Students to Make Mistakes   Teachers usually do not let students make enough mistakes. Making mistakes often encourages students to reexamine things that they had previously regarded as true. It is much more educative to let students do something their own way, experience the consequences, and see their mistakes than to tell them the "right way," which they then follow more or less blindly. Of course, some situations preclude this. A shop teacher might achieve maximum student motivation for study of safety practices by allowing a student to cut off a finger with a power saw, but a teacher would not be morally justified in using such means to establish an efficient learning situation. However, a teacher has many opportunities to permit students to make problem-raising mistakes without unduly endangering anyone.

Converting Societal Problems into Personal Ones   One might defend the confinement of problem-centered study to problems that students already feel on the ground that it teaches them methods of problem solving that will be useful all through life. However, there are a number of significant, persistent societal problems that, for the good of themselves and their community, state, and nation, students should come to understand and appreciate. The study of those problems, about which normally only specialists or other adults are concerned, may be of great importance in preparing students for intelligent citizenship. But how can we motivate students to study, in a serious and sustained way, problems that do not seem real to them? In this question is the crux of problem-centered teaching. Failure to give it serious consideration is the reason that a problems approach so often bogs down, and after having "tried" problem-centered teaching, teachers may return to "teaching the facts straight."

In recent years teachers have tried to devise ways of involving students in problems that are not intrinsically challenging to them. "Solutions" to the enigma in which teachers find themselves have included suggestions that they explain to students just how the problems are bound to affect them eventually, that students be confronted face to face with the problems (as when we take a middle-class group to visit a slum), and that teachers use more eye-catching teaching materials (such as pictures).

But as every practicing teacher knows, these "solutions" often fail to produce real intellectual involvement. Students still do not feel the problems as their own. Of course, some students always will do whatever work a teacher assigns, and seemingly do it with enthusiasm. But what seems to be intellectual involvement and a desire to study a genuine problem is often a desire to achieve other goals such as high marks, praise, and social status.

Instead of striking out blindly and trying everything they can think of, willy-nilly, to motivate students to study seriously what does not seem to them any of their own concern, teachers may try a drastically different approach; they may view their teaching problems in light of a clear and adequate understanding of the learning process. Basic to such understanding is a knowledge of what it means for a person to experience a problem as a felt tension, and formulation, based upon this knowledge, of an approach to teaching that holds promise in many cases of effectively translating the "problems of others" into the problems of students.

There are numerous areas of adult and societal concern about which students normally have some more or less superficial attitudes, evaluations, and knowledge. These include politics and government, international affairs, economics, business, labor and employment, pure and applied science, morality, various arts, and personal relations. The ideas that students have acquired are often sketchy, disorganized, and poorly understood. Nevertheless children, and especially adolescents, do have attitudes, opinions, and some knowledge about most operations with which adults are concerned. This can be demonstrated by a reasonably free classroom discussion of any one of these subjects. Our question now is, "How may a reflective approach to learning serve to build a psychological bridge between adult-societal problems and student-personal concerns"?

When students appear in teaching-learning situations, the total knowledge, both true and untrue, that they have is usually more than teachers realize. With modern media of communication, frequent opportunities for travel, and continuously rising educational levels of parents, it seems likely that a great many youngsters have more factual knowledge than they can make much sense of. Thus, one of the major jobs of a present-day teacher is to help students both verify and make sense of the welter of information that they already have acquired.

It is a familiar observation that the amount of information stored in books, journals, magazines, computer disks, integrated chips, and videotapes has expanded prodigiously in the last decade. It is also a commonplace assertion that it is no longer profitable to teach students as if books were scarce and very costly and that the chief task of all learners was to memorize everything. Hence, students need to *process*, that is, to make sense of—understand—the mass of facts, information, opinions, beliefs, data and judgments in which most of us figuratively drown every day. This section on the classroom application of reflective teaching is designed to apply what many leaders have advocated throughout this century.

Ideas and attitudes that students hold concerning matters that are also of concern to adults constitute the psychological bridges between youth and adult involvement. If a student feels enough personal attachment to a view to care, the moment the position becomes a subject of doubt the student is likely to want to start thinking about it. At that point, if teaching is skillful, the student can be led to want to study a subject about which he/she previously felt little or no curiosity. By challenging students' existing attitudes, goals, and knowledge, teachers may arouse real concern in situations that otherwise would never have been felt by students to be in any way problematic. Consequently, in relation to areas in which students at first feel no personal goal or involvement, a learning problem can be created and, thereby, genuine student involvement can be achieved. Accordingly, students can be led to see that their problems involve the various subject matters of the social sciences, the natural sciences, and the humanities.

What Kinds of Questions Induce Problems?

The essence of a problematic situation is that there is something in it that is unknown. The unknown can be uncovered only when right questions are asked. One of the best questions is also the simplest: "Why?" "Why did you say that?" "Why do you have the opinion you have stated?" Because of the demise of several fish in the classroom aquarium, a class of fourth graders embarked upon an enthusiastic study of the biology and ecology of fish life. The students had been caring for the fish according to what they thought were "right principles." These included the assumption that fish need to eat as much in proportion to their size as do fourth graders. The teacher, whether or not by design, allowed the children to make a mistake—to overfeed the fish. She then posed the question, "Why did the fish die?" and thereby launched a reflective study.

The heart of a reflective-learning situation then, is a good, thought-provoking question—one that does not point to a highly structured answer that can be given in a neat, pat word or two. The following questions are the kind that do *not* promote reflective thinking.[6]

1. Who were the first settlers in this land?
2. Where did they go before coming to America?
3. What was the name of the boat on which they came to America?

In contrast to these nonprovocative questions, the "springboard" questions in the following list are much more likely to activate the degree of psychological dissonance or uncomfortableness that is necessary to motivate students toward their thinking reflectively. Note that we include only the "bare bones" of the questions. In actual classroom practice each question would need to be prefaced by a certain artful "buildup."

1. If the writers of our Constitution believed in equality, why did they agree to count each slave as only three-fifths of a person when determining how many representatives each state could send to Congress?
2. If warm air rises, why is it cold high in the mountains?
3. If heat cannot travel through a vacuum, how can we get heat from the sun through the vacuum of deep space?

4. Our text states that big freight trains travel 100 miles per hour. We know that trucks are limited to 55 to 60 miles an hour by law. Why do authors of our book say that trucks can deliver freight faster?
5. If Columbus discovered America, how did it happen that people were here to greet him?

The use of springboard questions does not permit a teacher to have the security of giving fixed answers of such nature that one is right and all others are wrong. Hence, in some instances, a teacher may be pressed by the class to admit some limitations to his knowledge. Consequently, even if intellectual authoritarianism should be desired, it cannot be maintained. But at the same time, teachers should be highly knowledgeable in their subject areas and should encourage students also to become the same. Psychologically, an accepting, open atmosphere is necessary to stimulate students to volunteer. But a teacher's accepting the value of the thinking of each and every student is not the same as his uncritically accepting each idea presented. Therein lies the need for a teaching art that enables a teacher to case doubt on a proposition that is offered in class without seeming to cast doubt upon the integrity of the persons who presented the proposition.

What Is the Lullaby Effect?

We suggest the use of the expression *lullaby effect* as a reminder to teachers that they should help students avoid careless and incomplete thinking, as it may be evidenced by students jumping to unwarranted conclusions, making hasty generalizations, or achieving premature closures. Generally speaking, people—adults and children alike—are so eager to reach a solution that they tend to accept a hypothesis that "sounds good" without testing it sufficiently. Better thinkers, however, avoid being lulled into false security by the first answer that seems to let their "minds go back to sleep." The soothing and lulling effect of persons accepting easy answers that only appear to be correct may be identified by calling it the "lullaby effect." The lullaby effect with its tendency to release people from further thinking should be remembered and counteracted by continuing to test all hypotheses, especially those that quickly appear to be correct.

A few questions and quick, apparent answers to them will illustrate the lullaby effect.

1. Question: Why is Eskimo life so difficult? Answer: Because the farther north one goes, the colder it is.
2. Question: Why is winter colder than summer? Answer: Because the sun is farther away.
3. Question: Why are some countries still "underdeveloped"? Answer: Because they do not have sufficient natural resources.

The answers given to these three questions all have two features in common; they "sound good" and are incorrect. Yet they are answers that will likely be accepted, if great care is not taken to avoid the lullaby effect.

How Does the Problem Raising Aspect of a Unit on Race Proceed?

We now develop the problem raising aspect of a reflective unit on the meaning of *race*. The problem described here was selected through one of the author's conversations with a number of high school students. The students had various definitions of the term *race*, they recognized that their definitions were cloudy, and they wanted to bring them into sharper focus. It was assumed that for most high school students of today the meaning of race probably constitutes a real problem. It also was assumed that this problem could emerge in a problems, social studies, history, psychology, sociology, or biology class on any one of the senior high school grade levels.

The problem and the aspects of its solution were developed by means of members of a college undergraduate class in educational psychology playing the roles of high school students. Throughout the unit the teacher is designated by "Teacher" and each of the participating students by "Student." All members of the class participated to some degree, but individual students are not identified. Only the more incisive and significant statements are recorded; limited space precludes our including every detail of the class discussion. To repeat, problem raising consists of both *recognition* and *definition* of a problem. The class discussion proceeded as follows.

TEACHER: I noticed in our reading assignment for today that the term *race* appears several times. What does that word mean to most of you?

STUDENT: Why, there are three races—white, black, and yellow.

STUDENT: I don't think it is that easy. I know some white people who are called blacks.

STUDENT: To me, *race* is a cultural word; the color of people's skin is not the real difference.

TEACHER: When you say there are three major races, are you stating the way things really are or are you merely classifying people for convenience? In other words, what is the basis for your distinction?

STUDENT: Biologists say that there are three races, maybe four.

STUDENT: That may be so, but cultural differences are also called racial features. For instance, people in the United States think of Jews as a race and in Germany Hitler talked about the Nordic race.

TEACHER: When people refer to the Jewish race, are they thinking of biological traits, social traits, or what?

STUDENT: They are thinking about the fact that Jews have been different down through history.

TEACHER: Oh! Then we identify them as a race because of their ancestors?

STUDENT: Partly because of their ancestors but also because of things they do, such as make money.

STUDENT: We are getting clear away from our discussion; one's race depends upon his genes.

TEACHER: So, you think race is purely biological. How many of you think race is purely biological? (A show of hands indicated that about one-half of the class would answer this question in the affirmative, but the other half definitely would not.)

TEACHER: So, according to biologists, there are three definite races plus a fourth that even the experts can't agree upon. Then this fourth could be almost any group, so the problem of race is wide open.

STUDENT: It is not quite that way. We can limit our definition of race to inherited physical characteristics that one group, and not others, has. It is the physical characteristics of a person and his ancestors.

TEACHER: For instance?

STUDENT: Color of skin and type of hair.

STUDENT: But, as I see it, everyone to some degree has a mixed blood.

TEACHER: Do you mean that everyone is some sort of a hybrid?

STUDENT: I think we're making too much of this. Race is simply a biological variation of *Homo sapiens*—a subdivision of the species.

STUDENT: Then, according to you, it is very easy to place each of us in a certain race.

STUDENT: I'm beginning to think that we should just quit talking about races; we should do away with the idea.

STUDENT: We can't do that. Race means something to everybody; if they didn't have the word race, they would use some other word.

STUDENT: The trouble is that *race* started as a biological word; then people have added a lot of other meanings to it.

TEACHER: Let us be more specific in regard to our problem and the issues involved. Just what are we trying to decide?

STUDENT: What a race is.

TEACHER: O.K. How many of you want to pursue this question further and attempt to arrive at an answer.? (Most of the class members favored this procedure.)

TEACHER: All right, now we may look at the meaning of the word *race* in at least two different ways. Do specific Races, each spelled with a capital letter, exist in the very nature of things, the way gravity and the planets supposedly do, or is a race merely what people call it?

STUDENT: I'm not sure I understand the first meaning, but I am more concerned with the second.

TEACHER: You may recall that a few weeks ago we developed the difference between realism and nominalism in regard to the source of large concepts. The question that I am raising is, do we want to find the real meaning of a concept *race*, which transcends or extends beyond any and all existing races, or do we want to conceive of *race* as a name for an idea that people have developed?

STUDENT: I, too, am more concerned with the second type of meaning.

TEACHER: How many prefer to concentrate upon the meaning of the named idea *race* and leave any transcendental or absolutistic definition out of our discussion? (Most students agreed with the two who had expressed more interest in the nominalistic meaning.)

TEACHER: O.K. We shall assume that a word means what it means because of the meanings people give it, not because of its being derived from some basic transcendental source. Now, we must decide one more question. Are we concerned with what the word *race* does mean, what it should mean, or both?

STUDENT: When we discussed democratic and reflective procedures, we decided that we should study both how things are and how they should be.

TEACHER: Any other reaction or ideas?

STUDENT: Just how much are we going to change things by thinking how race should be defined?

STUDENT: I get your point. But how much are we going to change things by merely studying how things are? I think we should figure out both what race means and what it should mean.

TEACHER: How many concur with this position? (About two-thirds concurred; the other third expressed the idea that their treatment would be too superficial to attempt any "oughts" in regard to the meaning of the word.)

The next step was to make a precise statement of the problem at hand through using the contributions of the students. The statement of the problem was then reworded until it was acceptable to all members of the class. The problem was "What does the term *race* mean to all kinds of people, including experts, and what should it mean to us?"

At this point, we should remind ourselves of the fact that in any fertile group inquiry, two types of discussion are always in progress—one the public discussion that an observer can hear, the other a series of private discussions within which each interested student debates the issue with himself. Most of the questions and assertions that are uttered aloud emerge from, or are influenced by, the concurrent private, silent debates. The primary aim of vocal discussion is to help each individual involved, including the teacher, push forward his private thinking. Hence, during the course of a single discussion, Mary may reach a conclusion that seems quite satisfactory to her, John may have his faith in a conclusion that he once held badly shaken, and June may merely formulate a hypothesis. In each case the student may have thought the problem through to a further degree than at any previous time. Hence, in a discussion that appears rather chaotic to an observer, members of the group involved may actually achieve a considerable amount of pointed thinking.

HOW DOES PROBLEM SOLVING PROCEED?

Helping students formulate problems is only the first of five aspects of reflective teaching. However, this aspect is highly important in that it provides the motivation and direction for the problem solving aspects of reflective inquiry.

Once doubt or uncertainty has been induced, reflective teaching and learning enter the problem solving phase.

Problem solving consists of formulating and testing hypotheses; it envelops the last four aspects of the reflective teaching-learning process. We should emphasize here that the parts of reflective thinking, teaching, and learning are *aspects,* not *steps.* They seldom are followed in a consecutive orderly fashion. They may develop in any order, or any or all of the aspects may develop concurrently. Reflective processes commonly are characterized by confusion, hesitation, and irregularity.

Formulation and testing of hypotheses should be conducted in an atmosphere that resembles as far as possible that of a scientific laboratory. The same open-minded and objective attitudes that characterize any scientific investigation should prevail. Hence, the teacher's role should be analogous to that of a head scientist in a laboratory; the teacher should help students construct hypotheses, then assist them in testing them out.

How Are Hypotheses Formulated and Their Logical Implications Deduced?

Formulation of hypotheses—considered guesses or hunches—constitutes the second aspect of reflective learning. Deducing the logical implications of the hypotheses constitutes the third. Often, the two aspects are so intermingled that it is difficult to distinguish one from the other. In reflective teaching, students are encouraged to formulate as many hypotheses as possible in regard to what might resolve the discrepancies or inadequacies in thought that have been exposed. Simultaneously, a class is urged to deduce as many of the logical implications of each hypothesis as its members can muster. Within this aspect students think, "If this hypothesis holds, what checkable consequences should result from its operation?"

In the unit on the meaning of race, hypotheses are the various alternative definitions of the concept that gave rise to the problem in the preceding dialogue. We now proceed with the second and third aspects of the unit.

TEACHER: Let us restate our problem. It is, "What does race mean to all kinds of people, including experts, and what should it mean to us?" Now, let's see how many possible answers there are to this question.

STUDENT: The use of the word *race* does a lot of harm, and no good; let's drop it.

STUDENT: But there are some racial characteristics.

TEACHER: For example?

STUDENT: Sickle cell anemia is characteristic of blacks.

TEACHER: Is this a disease?

STUDENT: Yes, and its incidence is much higher in blacks.

TEACHER: Could you say that a person who has sickle cell anemia is a black?

STUDENT: No, I couldn't do that.

TEACHER: If a person has three white grandparents and one black one, which race is he a member of? (This question opened up a great deal of discussion and disagreement.)

TEACHER: Can we say that, even though a person is much more "white" than "black," in the U.S.A. he is a "black"?

STUDENT: Are we concerned with the definition of the word in this country?

STUDENT: This should be our first concern.

STUDENT: If we even do this, we will be doing quite a lot.

STUDENT: Some minority groups think they can help their position by emphasizing their race.

STUDENT: But other racial groups have made themselves a part of the American culture. Chinatown has been pretty American.

STUDENT: A member of any minority group has things stacked against him.

TEACHER: This morning on the "Today Show" a black professor at a New York university appeared. New York public universities pay top salaries. Do you think this man still finds the cards stacked against him?

STUDENT: Yes, I do.

TEACHER: How many agree that he does? (About one-half of the class agreed.)

TEACHER: It now seems to be the time for us to "handicap" ourselves with some information. Let's all go to the library and find at least one article on the subject of race. Each of you be prepared to give us the high points of what you find out.

At the next class, students contributed the ideas that they had gained through their reading. The teacher then asked each student to write out, in one short paragraph, the very best statement on, or definition of, race that he/she could devise.

Between classes, the teacher and several class members summarized the contents of the statements. The summary in terms of the ideas stated and their frequency was as follows (ideas stated only once are not included).

1. Race primarily is a biological concept. (15 times)
2. In light of the improbability of there ever having been any pure races, the increasing miscegenation—crossbreeding—that is occurring, and the emotionality surrounding the term *race*, the concept of *race* has always been ambiguous and is now becoming archaic. (13 times)
3. The term should be either discarded or disregarded. (11 times)
4. The only term with which people should be concerned is the human race. (4 times)
5. A biological definition is inadequate. (3 times)
6. We cannot ignore the term, so we should understand it. (3 times)
7. Race should be replaced with ethnic groups. (2 times)

This summary was photocopied and distributed in the next class. The various ideas were taken as hypotheses, whose implications were to be tested through further reading and thought.

How Are Hypotheses Tested?

In the fourth aspect of reflective thinking, teaching, and learning, students are encouraged to examine the hypotheses in light of all obtainable, pertinent evidence. Provided the teacher promotes an atmosphere of mutual inquiry, problem-centered study in school may encompass a variety of evidence seeking activities. It is likely to include the use of individual and group research, home study, field trips, and guest speakers. It may also include considerable explanation and illustration on the part of the teacher. An informal lecture can be a highly useful tool for both providing data for students' consideration and instigating and promotion further reflection.

In the process of testing hypotheses, teachers do not play the role of soft-hearted baby-sitters. At times they must be quite tough-minded in their insistence that students examine and consider all pertinent available evidence. Teachers also must guard against students' making hasty generalizations, arriving at snap conclusions, achieving premature closure, or taking other liberties that either impede or pervert the reflective process.

At this point in the study of the meaning of *race*, the class reviewed the summary of hypothetical statements. The instructor next divided the areas and sources of inquiry among the students so that the investigation would be reasonably comprehensive. The entire class moved to the library during several class meetings to gather as much more pertinent information as possible in the time available. Then, the students returned to their classroom and continued their inquiry.

First, several students presented definitions that they had taken from dictionaries, encyclopedias, and other books. Next, other students presented some new ideas that they had gained from their reading. At this stage of the study, several sharp disagreements arose. Samples of student expressions are as follows:

STUDENT: Why are we talking about race at all? We are just building up more prejudice and racism.

STUDENT: Each individual has his own definition, so let's let it go at that.

STUDENT: Cultural distinctions are not racial ones.

STUDENT: William A. Boyd and Isaac Reisman, in *Races and People,* say that physical features are useless criteria of race.

STUDENT: Although a biological definition is the most ideal, it is not the most practical. A word can mean many things to people.

STUDENT: The best we can do with the word is to try to understand what it really means in relation to the evolution of human beings, to separate fact from fiction, and to pass on our knowledge to others. Then, hopefully, as people learn to live together, the word will disappear from their vocabularies.

STUDENT: Ashley Montagu, in *The Concept of Race,* says that the term race has had a long and tortuous history. Biologists see it as the subdivision of a species, and laymen have an emotionally muddled interpretation of the word. But anthropologists see the term as facts forced into predetermined categories. The major idea Montagu brings out is that the meaning of the term *race* is far from being a solved problem, and that people generally refuse to see this. The ethnic groups formed by virtue of community, language, religion, and social beliefs just add to the confusion. If race is to be a scientific term, it must have a genetic meaning; geographical, linguistic, and ethnic grouping then would be unnecessary. However, race is a trigger word, because it is loaded with prejudice and misunderstanding.

STUDENT: If we are to form an operative definition of race, we should limit it to the inherited physical characteristics that are predominant in one group of people as opposed to another group. The prejudice implied in the word *race* should be limited to noticeable anatomical features so as not to confuse Jewish "race" and black race and consider both to be races.

STUDENT: Basically, there are physical differences in people. Therefore, people need some way of explaining or understanding this. The word *race* is an attempt to do this. It describes three (or possibly more) sets of physical characteristics, each set belonging to one of the races. It should be based only on these biological aspects, because within each race there are many cultures.

STUDENT: *Race* started out as a biological term, but society has taken the term and added other meanings to it. The easiest answer would be to do away with the word, but I think that it is here to stay for a long time yet, and if we're going to find answers to our problems today, the change is going to have to come from within the people themselves. The older generations won't or can't change their feelings and ways of thinking, so it is up to the younger generations to accept changes in their society, and this takes time.

STUDENT: I think that defining race biologically is a complete waste of time and meaningless. Race does, however, imply or refer to characteristics that exist in some way or another, and quite obviously it causes much strife within our society. So, I think we can't ignore the term.

How Are Conclusions Reached?

The fifth aspect of reflective teaching-learning is drawing conclusions. This is perhaps the most difficult aspect of a teacher's endeavor to promote reflective learning through reflective teaching. However, the basic, guiding principle of reflective teaching and learning is that the teacher and students should strive to achieve at least a consensus on the conclusion, unanimity being the ideal. But even though a student may represent a minority of only one person, he/she should not be coerced in any way to swing to the conclusion of either the group consensus or the majority.

Ideally, problem-centered study should culminate in at least a tentative conclusion about how the problem might be alleviated or solved. However, in many instances a definite conclusion will not be achieved. Furthermore, when a conclusion is reached, the teacher should emphasize its tentativeness and relativity. An irrevocable conclusion is like a locked door whose only key has been thrown in the sea. Students should be taught that the door to knowledge must always be left unlocked, even ajar. Nevertheless, at the termination of an inquiry, a conclusion should be considered to be a warranted assertion; it should provide greater predictive accuracy than any alternative hypotheses that have been entertained and examined.

A conclusion may involve either reacceptance of the idea that was originally brought under question, modification of the idea, or formulation of a substitute one. The important concern is that students push their thinking further than it had gone before. They need not necessarily arrive at an answer that has been preconceived by the teacher. Teaching for reflection is *provocative* rather than *evocative*. Reaffirmation of the same idea that the teacher had earlier induced students to doubt is quite acceptable, provided that in the course of their study the students come to understand the idea better and to have a better grasp of the evidence pertinent to it.

The high school class previously discussed had completed the first four aspects of reflective inquiry. It had stated the problems in definite terms. It then had formulated some hypotheses and deduced their implications; and had gathered much pertinent data and tested the various hypotheses. The culminating task was to formulate a tentative concluding statement in regard to the hypothesis or hypotheses that seemed most tenable.

In drawing the class's conclusions, as a first step, a committee constructed a carefully formulated summary that incorporated the statements listed earlier as hypotheses. The class then discussed each clause of the summary and either made changes until a consensus would support it, or deleted it. The teacher reminded the students that their decision should rest upon what the data— pertinent information—supported, not upon personal whims. Out of a class of 30, there were from none to three dissenting votes in regard to the final form of each clause. The class's concluding statement in regard to the meaning of the term race was as follows:

> CLASS: Since we cannot ignore the concept *race* in our American cul- ture, we need an understanding of its meaning. *Race* is primarily a biological concept. But a biological definition, in itself, is in- adequate; cultural aspects also enter into its meaning. Because (1) there is an improbability of there ever having been any pure races; because (2) miscegenation is increasing; because (3) the concept *race* serves little long-range beneficial personal-social purpose; because (4) it has been and continues to be ambigu- ous; and because (5) it is emotionally loaded, the term *race* now should be either discarded or considered archaic. So, we should move toward elimination of the concept *race* as such. The only race with which enlightened people should be concerned is the human race.
>
> TEACHER: Does our conclusion imply that we should strive to build one unified culture to replace various cultures? If so, should the one

culture be a pluralistic one, that is, should it be one that reflects a unity of people but recognizes and accepts diversity within the unity? Or should people attempt to blend themselves into one generalized race? Perhaps these questions involve problems for our further study.

The teacher then urged dissenting students to develop cooperatively an alternative statement that they would support and report it to the class. These students were allotted some class time to do this as a group. The teacher also reminded the class of the many insights or understandings that they had gained during their study. These ranged from simply learning some new words—for example, *miscegenation*—to gaining a more meaningful and effective grasp of the race problem. The class then moved ahead to a new problem or area of inquiry.

Throughout the study, the teacher had made it clear that he/she preferred and expected serious thinking on the part of his students. His role had been to elicit compelling questions pertinent to the area of study and to lead the ensuing inquiry along lines of gathering pertinent evidence and doing logical thinking.

IN WHAT SUBJECT AREAS IS REFLECTIVE TEACHING APPLICABLE?

Many teachers see reflective or problem-centered teaching as a possible approach to instruction in a very limited number of courses, such as social studies, literature, industrial arts, or home economics. These teachers are unable to imagine the use of problem-centered teaching in such subjects as mathematics, physics, music, physical education, and foreign language. However, such teachers have an inadequate conception of reflective teaching procedures.

With reference to subject areas, it appears that the essential characteristics of reflective teaching have enough flexibility to be employed in all school subjects, including those that seem on the surface to be rather cut and dried. Problem-centered teaching does not require development of elaborate unit plans. It emerges whenever a teacher, through adroit questioning and use of negative evidence, induces students to doubt that which they had previously accepted and then helps them analyze critically the issue that arises. In most conventional subjects or academic blocks of subjects, opportunities regularly appear for a teacher to operate in this manner. Passages in a textbook, assertions made by students, a news story, a disconcerting experience, a motion picture or TV show—any of these may serve at times as a springboard for creation of problems. Problem-centered teaching springs into existence in those situations where minds of teacher and students engage. It grows more from a unique relationship between teacher and students than from any different nature of formal course materials.

Some courses and some types of course organization, however, do lend themselves more readily to reflective teaching than do others. A course construed broadly—that is, whose subject matter is not narrowly prescribed—is probably better for this purpose than is a more narrow course. Thus, as usually defined, general business is a better course for reflection level teaching than is shorthand; problems of democracy better than economic geography; history and philosophy of mathematics better than algebra; world literature better than freshman composition. This difference, however, is not inherent in the nature of the subject matter as such but is psychological in nature. It lies in the frame of reference within which it customarily is treated.

A course in which problem-centered teaching is used cannot be bound rigidly to a textbook. Real problems are psychological in nature; hence, data used in solving them rarely are organized in the same pattern as textbooks and courses of study. The "logical" organization of a book usually does not coincide with the psychology of thought. Hence, courses should be allowed to cut across subject matter lines whenever such deviation makes sense in terms of the particular problem being studied.

Determination of which subjects, or which topics within a subject, should be handled as problems cannot be made without reference to a specific classroom situation. In each case a teacher should reckon with the maturity and experiential backgrounds of students, community attitudes, the teacher's own preparation and skill, and anticipated consequences of having a class delve deeply into the subject.

WHAT IS UNIQUE ABOUT THE REFLECTIVE LEVEL OF EVALUATION?

Although each level of teaching and learning—the mentalistic-memory, the physicalistic-memory, and the explanatory-understanding—has its unique characteristics, the three also have a common significant trait, namely, all three are teacher-centered processes. The teacher sets the objectives for the students, and the teacher measures the relative achievement of those objectives. In some cases learners are considered to be active, but in more cases they are assumed to be either passive or intermittently active and passive. Seldom, if ever, are they considered to be perceptually interactive, as is the case in reflective teaching and learning.

If teachers assume that their students are active and if they pursue either memory or explanatory-understanding level teaching, they do so for the purpose of making sure that the students' active natures either are exercised or unfold in the proper manner. If teachers assume that their students are basically passive, and this is most often the case, they bring the proper stimuli or ideas to impinge upon the students and thereby inculcate the designed behaviors or understandings.

The seminal concept that has provided the originative power for the reflective level of teaching and learning has been *perceptual interaction*. To repeat, perceptual interaction, that is, simultaneous mutual interaction (SMI), is a cognitive experiential process within which a person, psychologically, simultaneously reaches out to his psychological environment, encounters some aspects of it, brings those aspects into relationship with himself, makes something of those aspects, acts in relation to *what he/she makes of them,* and realizes the consequences of the entire process. Perceptual interaction, so defined, is supported and amplified best by a cognitive-interactionist psychology of learning.

The results of reflective level teaching and learning, as is the case with the explanatory-understanding level, include understandings, principles, rules, or laws, but not these alone. The reflective level implies that these results are *purposively acquired.* Consequently, reflective level learning enhances students' scientific outlook and experiential-instrumental thinking and thereby points them toward doing further creative thinking on their own.

Since reflective teaching entails problem-centered, exploratory personal involvement, evaluation that is compatible with it will likewise be centered on genuine problems. When one is teaching on a reflective level, one should be trying, in testing as well as in all other evaluational procedures, to ascertain whether each student is able to apply adequate information to the solution of a problem so as to harmonize the problem, all available pertinent data or facts, and the answer. The most practicable instruments for the accomplishment of this purpose are problem-centered essay tests. A reflection level essay test usually consists of four, three, or even fewer carefully constructed questions. Each question should be pertinent to the study that the students have been pursuing and should constitute a real problem for them. A sample reflection level test question is: "How is the listing of the behavioral objectives of a course related to the course being taught reflectively?"

The best type of reflective-level question is one to which there is possibly more than one true answer. Thus, answers cannot be written out at the time the test is constructed. Each answer must be evaluated on its own merits. In an adequate answer, many facts will be used, but the number of facts listed as such will not be the basic for evaluation. Instead, answers will be evaluated on the basis of some criteria or measuring sticks that the teacher and students have agreed upon prior to the time of the test. These criteria probably will be *pertinence* and *adequacy* of the data that are applied to the solution of the problem, *harmony* of the problem, data, and answer, and perhaps one or two others.

Teachers who are committed to reflective teaching would neither test their students on a memory level nor use so-called true-false tests. Instead, they would prefer to use essay tests and strive to make their questions truly reflective. At times the teachers might use selection tests, but they would realize that in doing so they would be drawing their students away from reflective thinking (see Table 11.1, pages 248–249).

In concluding, we should remind ourselves that regardless of the level of learning pursued, students need information in order to understand anything. Furthermore, they need both facts and understandings in order to learn reflectively. However, teachers need not be reluctant to experiment with both explanatory-understanding level and reflective-level teaching and evaluation for fear that their students will not learn a sufficient number of facts. When students are taught and evaluated on the reflective level, they acquire many facts as well as understandings, and likewise when they are taught and tested on the explanatory-understanding level they acquire much information. However, this process does not work in reverse; there is little about factual learning as such that contributes to understanding, and little about teaching for understanding in a nonreflective way that contributes to a student's reflective powers and habits.

NOTES

1. These investigative teaching procedures were developed and implemented at Emporia State University by Jeanette Bigge, Professor of Education.
2. This teaching-learning unit was developed, implemented, and recorded by Dr. William B. Lieurance, using an actual class in a school situation, as a part of the Tri-University Project in Elementary Education at New York University in 1968.
3. Edward L. Deci, *Intrinsic Motivation* (New York: Plenum Press, 1975), p. 119.
4. Ibid., p. 97.
5. See John Dewey, *How We Think*, 2nd ed., Boston: Heath, 1933, p. 107.
6. See Grant Bateman, William B. Lieurance, Agnes Manney, and Curtis Osburn, *Helping Children Think*, Tri-University Project in Elementary Education (New York: New York University Press, 1968), pp. 2–8.

BIBLIOGRAPHY, CHAPTERS 11, 12, AND 13

Aschner, Mary Jane, and Charles E. Bish, eds. *Productive Thinking in Education.* Washington, DC: The National Education Association and the Carnegie Corporation of New York, 1968. A report on two conferences on productive thinking. Part 4, "Education for Productive Thinking," and Chapter 12, "Summary and Interpretation," are especially pertinent to these three chapters.

Bassler, Otto C., and John R. Kolb. *Learning to Teach Secondary School Mathematics.* Scranton, PA: Intext Educational Publishers, 1971. A systematic behavioristic approach to teaching secondary school mathematics. Adheres to the tenets of scientific realism as well as behaviorism.

Bateman, Grant, William B. Lieurance, Agnes Manney, and Curtis Osburn. *Helping Children Think.* Tri-University Project in Elementary Education. New York: New York University Press, 1968. Pages 6–8, 19–21, 26–31, and 49–79 describe approaches to, and units in, teaching reflectively in the various elementary grades. Pages 81–97 contain "springboard" questions that may be used to initiate reflective learning. This book is probably the best source for elementary school teachers.

Bayles, Ernest E. *Pragmatism in Education.* New York: Harper & Row, 1966. Pages 109–127 depict elementary school units for teaching spelling, arithmetic, art, nature study, and grammar reflectively. Pages 127–140 describe secondary units in literature, American history, and natural science.

Bigge, Morris L. *Educational Philosophies For Teachers,* Columbus, OH: Charles E. Merrill Publishing Company, 1982. Develops the positions of eight different educational philosophies in regard to the nature of learning.

Block, James H., ed. *Schools, Society, and Mastery Learning.* New York: Holt, Rinehart and Winston, 1974.

Bloom, Benjamin S., et al. *Taxonomy of Educational Objectives: Handbook I: Cognitive Domain.* London: Longmans, Green, 1956. Develops six general areas of educational objectives and test exercises, namely, knowledge, comprehension, application, analysis, synthesis, and evaluation.

Bloom, Benjamin S. *Human Characteristics and School Learning.* New York: McGraw-Hill, 1976. A theory of school learning that accounts for mastery learning under a variety of conditions. Centers on ways to alter historical determinism.

Brophy, Jere E., and Thomas L. Good. *Teacher-Student Relationships: Causes and Consequences.* New York: Holt, Rinehart, and Winston, 1974. Behavioristic-oriented summaries of research on student differences that affect teacher expectations and attitudes. The effect of the latter on teacher-student alternating interaction patterns and student performance.

Bruner, Jerome S. *The Process of Education.* Cambridge, MA: Harvard University Press, 1960. The chairman's report of the major themes, principal conjectures, and most striking tentative conclusions of a 1959 conference of 35 natural scientists, psychologists, and educators on teaching science and mathematics in elementary and secondary schools. The report emphasizes teaching for understanding the structure—pertinent relationships—of a subject matter rather than for mastery of facts and techniques.

Bruner, Jerome S. *Toward a Theory of Instruction.* Cambridge, MA: Harvard University Press, 1966. Presents Bruner's conclusions concerning what should go into a theoretical basis for teaching procedure. Highly recommended to be read in connection with the section of Chapter 13 entitled "How Is Reflection Level Learning Promoted?" Bruner writes on a theoretical level, but his ideas are highly thought-provoking.

Cartwright, Dorwin, and Alvin Zander, eds. *Group Dynamics,* 3d ed. New York: Harper & Row, 1968. A collection of readings, all of which are relevant to classroom procedures. Readers will detect a strong Lewinian influence. A very useful reference.

Combs, Arthur W., Robert A. Blume, Arthur J. Newman, and Hannelore L. Wass. *The Professional Education of Teachers: A Humanistic Approach to Teacher Preparation,* 2d ed. Boston: Allyn & Bacon, 1974. An application of modern "perceptual-humanistic" psychology to problems of teacher education. Teaching is described as a "helping" relationship.

Coulson, John E., ed. *Programmed Learning and Computer-Based Instruction.* New York: Wiley, 1962. Proceedings of the Conference on Application of Digital to Automated Instruction. The last half of the book, on linking computers to teaching devices to provide a more sophisticated kind of feedback, is interesting.

Ebel, Robert L., ed. *Encyclopedia of Educational Research,* 4th ed. New York: Macmillan, 1969. Benjamin S. Bloom, "Higher Mental Processes," pages 594–601, treats theories of learning, schools of psychology as related to teaching and learning, analysis of problem-solving processes, and education for improvement of thinking abilities. Margaret Ammons, "Objectives and Outcomes," pages 908–912, summarizes historical approaches to educational objectives and their evaluation and discusses meaning of "behavioral objectives."

Eisner, Elliot W. "Educational Objectives: Help or Hindrance." *School Review* 75 (1967): 250–282. Reviews history of specific objective movement back through 1918. Develops case for and against the use of specific educational objectives.

Fenton, Edwin. *The New Social Studies*. New York: Holt, Rinehart and Winston, 1967. Emphasizes an inductive approach to teaching to teach the concepts that make up the structure of social science. Makes much of teaching strategies.

Fraenkel, Jack R. *Helping Students Think and Value*. Englewood Cliffs, NJ: Prentice Hall, 1973. A well-organized presentation of strategies for teaching social studies on an explanatory understanding level. Presents strategies for developing thinking with little place for reflective thinking.

Gage, N. L., ed. *Handbook of Research on Teaching*. Chicago: Rand McNally, 1963. See Chapter 17, "Research on Teaching the Social Studies," by Laurence E. Metcalf. Pages 941–943 present two reflective units, one on who discovered America by Ernest E. Bayles and one on the election of 1800 by Alan F. Griffin.

Gage, N. L., ed. *The Psychology of Teaching Methods*. Chicago: The National Society for the Study of Education, 1976. Summarization of current teaching procedures and psychologies that underpin them.

Gage, N. L. *The Scientific Basis of the Art of Teaching*. New York: Teachers College Press, 1978. An analysis of the teaching art—teachers behaving so as to change students' behaviors.

Glasser, William. *Control Theory In the Classroom*. New York: Harper & Row, 1986. Presents an alternative to S-R behavioristic psychology. Psychological needs—love, power, freedom, and fun—overshadow survival needs.

Hunt, Maurice P., and Lawrence E. Metcalf. *Teaching High School Social Studies*, 2d ed. New York: Harper & Row, 1968. Part 1 contains a general treatment of reflective teaching that applies equally to all subjects and grade levels.

Jourard, Sidney M. *Healthy Personality: An Approach from the Viewpoint of Humanistic Psychology*. New York: Macmillan, 1974. One of the best presentations of existentialist humanism. Human beings are taken to be free, good, and active.

Judd, Charles H. *Educational Psychology*. Boston: Houghton Mifflin, 1939. A comprehensive educational psychology text that emphasizes the learning of generalizations as opposed to atomistic learning. Readers will be impressed by the richness of content.

Klausmeier, Herbert J., Elizabeth Schwenn Ghatala, and Dorothy A. Frayer. *Conceptual Learning and Development*. New York: Academic Press, 1974. A cognitive view of concepts within a behavioristic orientation. Model of conceptual learning and development to serve as a guide to research. Attributes of public concepts are various degrees of learnability, usability, validity, generality, power, structure, instance perceptibility, and instance numerousness.

Kolesnik, Walter B. *Humanism and/or Behaviorism in Education*. Boston: Allyn & Bacon, 1975. Treats humanism and behaviorism as the two dominant psychological theories in contemporary education. An attempted synthesis of the two conflicting positions.

Lewin, Kurt. *Resolving Social Conflicts*. New York: Harper & Row, 1948. A fundamental reference. Lewin's experimental work paved the way for much that is now known about the dynamics of groups.

Meyer, Agnes E. *Education for a New Morality*. New York: Macmillan, 1957. A provocative little book with profound implications for what and how we teach. It suggests a philosophy of education that might close the gap in our thinking between science and humanism.

Morris, Van Cleve, and Young Pai. *Philosophy and the American School*, 2d ed. Boston: Houghton Mifflin, 1976. Introduces students to the problems of teaching and learning through the medium of philosophy. Develops philosophical models of teaching and learning.

Raths, Louis E., Arthur Jonas, Arnold Rothstein, and Selma Wassermann. *Teaching for Thinking*. Columbus, OH: Merrill, 1967. Perhaps one of the best methods books on teaching reflectively. See especially the introduction and Chapter 1.

Rogers, Carl R. *Freedom to Learn*. Columbus, OH: Merrill, 1969. A plan for self-directed procedures in education. Emphasizes openness, spontaneity, and learning how to learn. A contemporary presentation of autonomous development and existentialist humanism.

Saucier, Weems A., Robert L. Wendel, and Richard G. Mueller. *Toward Humanistic Teaching in High School*. Lexington, MA: Heath, 1975. Psychological and sociological basis for moderate humanistic teaching of various high school subject areas. Humanistic teaching of specific high school subjects. Cognitive-field oriented.

Severin, Frank T. *Discovering Man in Psychology: A Humanistic Approach*. New York: McGraw-Hill, 1973. A symposium of articles by authors of both psychedelic and scientific humanistic bents.

Taber, Julian I., Robert Glaser, and Halmuth M. Schaeffer. *Learning and Programmed Instruction*. Reading, MA: Addison-Wesley, 1965. Probably one of the best written and most scholarly expositions of Skinner's linear programming. Includes a concise theoretical treatment of Skinner's concept of operant conditioning.

Torshen, Kay P. *The Mastery Approach to Competency-Based Education*. New York: Academic Press, 1977. Relates the mastery model of teaching to competency-based education.

Travers, Robert M. W., ed. *Second Handbook of Research on Teaching*. Chicago: Rand McNally, 1973. Perhaps the best comprehensive source of information concerning contemporary research on teaching.

Walker, Marshall. *The Nature of Scientific Thought*. Englewood Cliffs, NJ: Prentice Hall, 1963. Written by a physical scientist for general readers. Basic purpose of science is prediction; basic procedures are use of conceptual models.

Willoughby, Stephen S. *Contemporary Teaching of Secondary School Mathematics*. New York: Wiley, 1967. Presents an approach to teaching high school mathematics that harmonizes with cognitive-field psychology and reflective teaching. Does not use all of the language of reflective teaching but emphasizes teaching for genuine discovery.

Wynne, John P. *Theories of Education*. New York: Harper & Row, 1963. A philosophical-historical treatment of educational theories. Describes principles, psychological approaches, methods, and practices implicit in each theory. Excellent background material for this book.

Chapter
14

How Are Teaching-Learning Theories Related to Computer Education?

*I*n this chapter, we first briefly describe computers and their functions. We then center upon how computers are, and may be, used in education. Next, we briefly review the psychological underpinnings of computer-centered education. Lastly, we develop the levels of teaching as they relate to computer-centered learning.

WHAT ARE COMPUTERS AND HOW DO THEY FUNCTION?

A computer is simply a machine that is capable of storing, processing, and retrieving a great deal of data almost instantly. In Europe and the United States, computers have been used so widely since World War II that most of us are not aware of just how pervasive they are. Industry, government, the military, and school offices employ computers routinely; they can schedule passengers on hundreds of flights a day, provide information on thousands of class schedules and credit ratings, design jet airplanes and automobiles, and much more. The primary interest of this chapter, however, is in the learning theories involved in using computers as aids to teaching and learning in schools.

The most prominent fact about computers today is their decreasing size and the increasing amount of data that can be stored by them. The first computer, called ENIAC, came into being in the mid-1940s and took up an entire floor. When transistors replaced vacuum tubes in the mid-1950s, the size of computers shrank almost immediately. The next invention that decreased computer size was the integrated circuit, or microchip. Smaller than a fingernail, a most recent microminiature integrated chip can handle millions of "bits" of information in a second, moving them throughout the computer via electronic pathways. Not only has the size decreased and the storage capacity increased, but also the range of computer functions has multiplied considerably. In most educational settings, microcomputers, usually called personal computers (PCs for short), have tended to replace terminals (keyboards with television monitors) which are connected to central computers called mainframes. Personal computers can be used even by preschoolers and school children, who are usually much more comfortable than are adults when they are first confronted with using a computer.

The bulk of personal computers are either made by or are similar to products of the Apple and IBM corporations. Computers which are similar to IBM PCs are called "clones." The Macintosh ("Mac" for short) is a highly successful line of Apple computer; another Apple product is the IIe.

What Are the Components of a Computer?

While both microcomputers and mainframes look fiendishly complicated when one views their insides, in fact the basic components are not especially difficult to understand. There is a *central processing unit (CPU)*, which receives the information from yet other parts of the computer, works on it, and relays it to yet other parts of the computer. There is a *keyboard*, looking very much like a traditional typewriter keyboard, which is used to feed information to the CPU. A computer can store information temporarily in *memory* or permanently on small, removable *floppy disks* or larger, built-in *hard disks*. A *monitor*, essentially a television screen, enables a person to view processed information. There is usually a *printer*, which is used to produce a paper record, known as a *printout* or *hard copy*, from the processed information. Computers employed to replace what used to be done routinely by typewriters are known as *word processors*. Many other *peripherals* are available that provide different ways either to put information in, to store it, or to get it back out. Although each of the foregoing sentences can be amplified to book length, this is essentially all there is to a computer. These components are known as the computer's *hardware*.

How Do Computers Process Information?

Computers have the capacity to store and retrieve, in digital form, information that can be updated, exposed to formal logic, transferred from one storage location to another, and used in many textual, numeric, and graphic modes. Computers have two kinds of memory—*read-only* memory (ROM) and *random access* read-write memory (RAM). The contents of read-only memory are built-in; *they cannot be changed* and they are preserved when the computer is switched off. The contents of random access memory may be altered and are lost when the computer is switched off unless they have been stored on a disk or tape. The chips inside an IBM PC can store up to 640,000 characters; hard disks can store millions of characters.

A computer works by following carefully written sets of instructions called *programs*, which are stored in the computer's memory in the same way as any other information that the computer is to handle. These programs are known as *software*, because they can be changed more easily than can the hardware. When a person turns a computer on, it retrieves from its ROM a program that causes it to get the next program from a disk and start that program, and so on. This is called "booting" the computer, because it brings itself up "by its bootstraps."

Since present-day computers hold and manipulate information in only binary form, they deal exclusively in either-or's and with an "excluded middle." The basic unit of information, the *bit* (binary digit), has only two alternatives — 1 or 0, yes or no, open or closed, on or off, true or false, or right or wrong.

A *word* is a group of adjacent binary digits that a computer processes as a unit. The most common combination of digits, a *byte*, consists of eight bits, giving 256 possible arrangements. With larger unit words consisting of twelve to sixty bits, depending on the machine and the program, the number of possible arrangements can be astronomical.

Optical computers of the 1990s are getting to be very much faster than purely electronic ones, but they still are digital in basic pattern.

How Are Computers Used in Education?

The ultimate objectives of computer-based learning programs extend from the knowledge directly imparted by initial computer activity to more general strategic planning, testing, and revision ("debugging") skills. These processes can place a great range of new tools for learning in students' hands. Furthermore, students' success at mastering challenging material may increase their self-assessment as learners and their interest in subject matter.

WHAT ARE THE PSYCHOLOGICAL UNDERPINNINGS OF COMPUTER-CENTERED EDUCATION?

In a psychological sense, we may think of *all* people being psychologically — in relation to their environments — either active, passive, or interactive. People being *active* means that their driving forces come from within each of them; their motives are inner-directed. They are either rational animals whose minds are developed through being exercised (the classical, mental disciplinarian tradition), or they are self-actualizing persons (the existentialist-humanistic position). People being *passive* means that their characteristics are largely the result of their original biological heredity plus their environmental influences; they are environmentally determined biological organisms. This is the behavioristic tradition in psychology.

People being psychologically *interactive* means that their psychological characteristics result from their making sense of, and dealing with, their physical and social environment. Each person's psychological reality consists of what he/she makes of what is being gained through his unique experience. This position is identified as either linear or cognitive-field interactionist psychology.

Generally, both mental disciplinarians and self-actualization theorists have little enthusiasm for the use of computers in mainstream education. Hence, the crux issue in the use of computers is between behavioristic, conditioning theorists, who assume people to be neutral-passive, and the interactionist theorists, who assume people to be either linearly or simultaneously interactive. (Microcomputer enthusiasts such as Seymour Papert speak of people interacting with their environment, including computers. But they mean that a student first does something to the computer, then the computer does something to the student, and so on; students are passively interactive.)

HOW DO MENTAL DISCIPLINE AND TWENTIETH-CENTURY CLASSICAL HUMANISM RELATE TO COMPUTER EDUCATION?

A review of Chapter 2, pages 21 to 27 will suggest two enduring learning theories—mental discipline and its cognate, classical humanism—which have pervaded Western thinking about education for two and a half millennia. Mental discipline is based upon the assumption that an entity called "mind" exists, and that this entity is separate and distinct from a "body." However, mind is similar to body in that both can be developed by their exercise. An important axiom of mental discipline theory is that of automatic transfer. This means that when one has developed or disciplined a particular component of mind, say, logic, through the study of mathematics, logical skills so developed will then be applied to logical problems outside the field of mathematics.

By and large, classical humanists have rejected most forms of educational technology, seeing them as inherently inhumane, destructive of values, and unworthy of the efforts of an educated person. For them, an education can come only from reading and meditating upon a body of knowledge. In the twentieth century, the body of knowledge is thought to reside in "great" books, that is, the writings of inspired authors who have tapped into certain eternal truths. Hence, there is no substitute for a concentrated, intensive study of the liberal arts.

To be sure, certain professors in the liberal arts have made use of some aspects of computer technology, such as computer-compiled dictionaries, bibliographies, and *concordances*—indexes that list all of the occurrences, in context, of each of the words in a particular text. Recently historians and political scientists have begun to make use of databases—lists—of authors, articles, and topics, which are located in extensive computer programs with such names as THOR, (The On-line Resource) and ERIC (Educational Resource Information

Center). But this use is concerned with the computer as a source of data for research. As far as the authors know, there is no widespread use of computer programs for the teaching of liberal arts subjects at the college or university level comparable to those developed after several decades of computer use in teaching science and technology subjects.

The conclusion is that those fields which are generally based upon the assumptions of mental disciplinary theory and its contemporary manifestation, classical humanism, do not perceive a relevance of computers in classical humanistic education and generally regard them with distaste.

There are, of course, some exceptions to this attitude. Thus, some colleges and universities contain "language labs," in which computer programs have begun to replace audio tapes. These labs, however, are designed to teach pronunciation, syntax, vocabulary, and so forth to beginning language learners. They provide basic drill in a foreign language but do not deal with the teaching of literary skills, the development of appreciation, discrimination in literary style, or literary criticism. Also, in some writing or reading clinics, computer programs teach students study skills, developmental reading, and the vagaries of written grammar, spelling, and punctuation. While some of these labs or clinics are located in departments of English, they are just as likely to be located within student assistance programs under the direction of administrators such as the dean of students. That is, departments of English ordinarily do not define their mission in terms of the acquisition of basic skills but rather the cultivation of refined appreciations. Whether these attitudes will change in the near future cannot be known. However, for the present, classical humanists are unlikely to turn to computer programmers for assistance in doing what, for them, only trained human beings and traditional depositories of humane knowledge can provide.

HOW DOES THE BEHAVIORISTIC TRADITION RELATE TO COMPUTER EDUCATION?

Behavioristic teaching consists of either promoting the proper responses in students or increasing the probability of their proper responses. Computer enthusiasts usually assume that the human mentality is machinelike in nature. Hence, it can work best within machine-like instruction. In a sense, then, computers serve to make people more machine-like and machines more people-like. Most currently functioning computer-based instruction, then, is based upon Skinnerian programming, which in turn is based on the assumption that people are psychologically passive in nature. True, computer enthusiasts speak of computers being actively operated. But this merely means that students do something to a computer, then the computer does something to them; the best feedback comes linearly immediately after the event.

For behaviorists, computers are super teaching machines. Hence, they are the ultimate tool for teaching and learning. Computer teaching begins with the answers already in the chips or tapes. Students learn by finding the right answers, often in the right sequence. Within computer teaching, in itself, students do not go beyond the data and answers that are given. They do not form for what is for them a new hypothesis and check it out. A computer can produce a large number of alternate hypotheses, but it cannot produce considered, weighted ones.

The psychological leaders of mainstream computer education appear to be B. F. Skinner, now deceased, and Robert M. Gagné. Skinner's R-S reinforcement is central to computerized learning, especially in drill and practice and tutorial learning. Here students' behaviors are reinforced by their either getting the right answer or being permitted to proceed to the next frame or contingency of reinforcement. Gagné's types of learning underlie the different ways that organisms react to their stimuli. To the degree that computer theory reflects a psychological position, it is a combination of behavioristic reinforcement theory of learning and Gagné's types of behavioristic learning, within either of which people are taken to be psychologically passive. Gagné categorizes learning into four levels—association, discrimination, rule, and principle. But he tends to ignore the level of greatest personal-social significance—the exploratory-understanding, reflective level. For Gagné, in problem solving, a student develops a combination of previously learned rules that apply to a problem that is given by a textbook or the instructor. So, "rules are the stuff of thinking."[1]

Computer enthusiasts make much of the cognitive thinking process, but usually in the mechanistic pattern of traditional mathematics and Newtonian physics. Papert and other computer enthusiasts make much of the interactive process in learning, but by this they mean alternating reactions—first a student does something to the computer, then the computer does something to the student.[2] Exploratory-understanding, reflective level learning, in contrast, is careful critical examination of an idea or supposed article of knowledge in light of the empirical, testable evidence that supports it and the further conclusions toward which it points. Education that centers on the reflective level consists of persons experimentally reconstructing their experience or life spaces so as to add to their meaning and thereby increase their abilities to direct the course and content of their future experiences or life spaces. In contrast, Gagné's problem solving is a process of combining old rules into new ones, not one of cooperative student-teacher problem development and problem solution as championed by teachers who think that students are neutral and interactive.

Most computer use, then, reflects a behaviorist position. A simple analog is useful: computers have largely been used as were workbooks. Since their inception, workbooks have drilled students in the learning of concepts, facts, spelling, grammatical usage, and formulae. A computer program, a set of written binary—yes/no, right/wrong, on/off—instructions, can be stored on a disk. A program takes a student through a unit, which is broken down into many smaller subunits or component parts.

The most common pattern of computer use in schools today involves either teaching students about computers or having students go through an established drill or practice sequence for a skill such as doing long division or using a scientific instrument such as a spectrophotometer. This use identifies "the computer as tutor." Programs used to tutor learners are designed around rules or established procedures known as *algorithms*. This is perhaps why the predominant use of computers has been in science and technology, which, many educators tend to believe, require routine learning of knowledge and skills or a body of concepts and generalizations. However, some writers believe that this approach to computer use is rapidly waning, and that while it is still common at the elementary level, it is being replaced at the secondary and post-secondary levels with simulations, tutorials, and tool practice.[3]

Whereas computer programmers may not be aware of the details of either classical or instrumental conditioning, contingencies of reinforcement, and other concepts within behaviorism, many programs appear to reflect the notion of learning as conditioning. It is assumed that a student learns much as does a lower animal when it is placed in a circumstance in which correct responses are rewarded in confidence that the favored response will be made more frequently in the future. That is, a student is provided some information and then asked to do a task or answer a question. The right response by the student will usually elicit a message on the screen, from a simple "ok" to a hearty "You got that one right. Good for you!" But because the sequence of questions, tasks, information, explanations and corrections are organized as separate and unrelated parts of a whole, there is little likelihood that the student will develop insights, which, in any event, are irrelevant to behaviorist learning theory. The computer program is seen as a means of changing verbal behaviors. The changed verbal behavior is inculcated by the programmer, who tells, directs, guides, arranges, manipulates and rewards students for saying the right things at the right times. (See Chapter 5, pages 110–111.)

These "tutorials," "simulations," and "drill-and-practice exercises" have dominated computer use in the recent decades. However, some authors may "criticize the routinized drill-and-practice orientation of most software actually used in schools today."[4] It is probably that drill-and-practice simply continues a tradition that extends back many years. In short, computers are used in ways that support both what teachers have done in most classrooms and what behaviorist psychologists assert is the way organisms actually learn.

WHAT IS COMPUTER-CENTERED TEACHING FOR EXPLANATORY UNDERSTANDING?

The explanatory-understanding level of teaching consists of teacher explanation and student grasp of generalizations, relationships, rules, principles, or theories, and their tool uses. Such teaching seeks to acquaint students with the relationships between generalizations and their supporting facts. A review of Chapter 12, "How May Teachers Teach for Explanatory Understanding," will reveal that there are variations of the learning theory that are designated "explanatory understanding." However, these various strands share a number of points in common. First, the position we have traced from Herbart through Judd, Morrison, Gagné, Bloom, Ausubel, and Bruner departs in a basic manner from behaviorism. It diverges from a mechanistic approach to understanding human nature and does not define learning in terms of a correct response to a particular stimulus. Second, at least in the hands of its twentieth-century exponents, explanatory understanding is generalization- or rule-driven. That is, the emphasis is upon acquiring a body of generalizations, rules, principles, and axioms from which students are then expected to draw and to apply to novel situations. Hence, learning and thinking are seen as matters of acquiring and learning how to use laws, principles, rules, and axioms. Third, the emphasis is upon insight into the formation of generalizations or models. In the hands of perhaps the best known expositor of this position, Jerome Bruner, the best source of models of rigorous thought come from the intellectual disciplines — fields of study such as science, literature, the social sciences, and mathematics. With this brief summary in mind, let us look at a few examples of explanatory-understanding teaching in computer use.

A recently developed use of computers is known as "the computer as tutee." Instead of learning *about* computers or learning *from* computers, students in effect *teach* the computer to perform a series of prearranged steps. They are asked to program a computer, using the older BASIC or the more recently invented Logo programming language designed for student use. The objective is not simply to teach students to program for its own sake. Instead, it is to teach students the processes that skilled computer programmers employ in the hope that the students may then apply these to a wide variety of novel circumstances and situations. It is also designed to teach what proponents of this position call "structured thinking."

"Currently, the most cognitively demanding classroom use of the computer is probably for learning to program."[5] For example, Logo, by Seymour Papert, is a well-designed symbol system for student programming that embodies a *mechanized* version of thinking. Papert emphasizes that children learn best by teaching. In "teaching" a computer or a tutee to do a particular thing, students learn more about their own thinking. They construct their own programs and control a small robot, the turtle, to draw physical shapes.

A child sits at a keyboard with a screen and types instructions to the "turtle" using Logo language to make a circle, a bird, or some other figure. The student tells the turtle what to draw and, within its binary limits, the turtle draws as directed. In explicitly telling a computer to draw something, the student is learning "without curriculum." This is Piagetian knowledge acquisition through self-guided problem solving experiences.

Logo makes computers entertaining as a means of introducing children to powerful ideas. For example, a student has a computer draw a circle by having it draw a series of alternating short straight lines and angular turns. The student ends up with a series of short chords, but is expected to think "circle." Papert's Logo involves a programmed, mechanized version of thinking within which 7- to 12-year-olds learn like most 12- to 15-year-olds. The assumption behind Logo teaching is that a child of 7 to 12 can develop the rational thinking necessary for programming and at the same time develop a feeling for geometric and logical relationships by actually creating them.

Another approach that reflects computer teaching for explanatory understanding involves what many computer programmers and teachers call "discovery." One such program involves the use of computers to teach students how to use the rules of mathematics by manipulating geometric figures on the screen.[6] A student is "given" a problem and told to manipulate the lines of a square in different ways. The student, through means of a submenu (a list of computer options arranged as is a conventional restaurant menu—vertically, with titles and perhaps descriptions), allows the user to draw segments, circles, and parallel and perpendicular lines, and to bisect angles. Other menus allow the student to erase, extend, rescale, or in other ways modify the lines. Its creator insists that this program, called SUPPOSER, allows the student to think mathematically and not simply follow directions in a familiar "cookbook" pattern.

Computers are also being used in institutions of higher education to provide models that students can use for acquiring research skills. Hence, one graduate institution, Claremont Institute for Antiquity and Christianity, is using a program called Ibycus to analyze ancient Greek, Coptic, and Hebrew texts.[7] Students in statistics classes are sometimes required to learn, not a mass of particular formulae, but rather, how to use programs called "statistical packages" that can perform such operations as stepwise multiple regression, discriminant function, and canonical correlation, whose underlying principles they are expected to learn and to apply to real-life statistics problems, typically the kinds that are used in empirical research.[8] In one Texas school district, students are "exploring the principles of chemistry and physics with a mix of traditional laboratory activities and an interactive videodisk-and-computer system."[9] Students use what is known as a "touch screen" technique, in which they simply press their fingers on the screen of a large television monitor equipped with sensors that tell the computer where the touch occurs. The computer then presents the students with concepts, generalizations, and principles from physics and chemistry. At regular intervals students are asked what they have learned, by means of "practice exercises and simulations." Students can also see physico-chemical interactions take place—something that could not be done in a regular classroom—by means of a mixture of graphics, stop-motion photography, and animations.

In another computer use, students are taken through a simulated archaeological "dig" wherein they are first presented with "general archaeological techniques, including the need to keep accurate and careful records, the nature of archaeological finds, and their analysis and significance."[10] They are then presented with a simulation of a real archaeological excavation in which, for instance, students discover, interpret, and analyze the artifacts they see at different soil strata. Students are expected to "appreciate the methods of excavation, recording, and subsequent analysis which help the archaeologists understand the past." The goal of this particular program is to develop "analytical and decision-making skills," a simplified but realistic approximation of how archaeologists inquire.[11] Other simulation programs provide students with an opportunity to manipulate a variety of options in order to discover uniformities and patterns.

There are real problems in the way different researchers on computers discuss the field, and therefore, it is not always clear that different writers are describing the same program, computer use, or educational objective.[12] The computer uses just described would appear to fit into the theoretical frame of reference of those whom we call advocates of explanatory understanding. In describing how one program teaches problem solving, its author summarizes as follows:

> The would-be problem-solver poses a question to the expert system, in much the same way as to a human expert, but limited, however, by the capabilities of the computer interface (normally by keying in a standard name for the problem type.) The system then asks for further specific data to be provided, and eventually, formulates a problem solution which it presents to the user.[13]

In this quotation, the "would-be problem-solver" is a student. The "expert system" is the program, which imitates a human expert. The problem is chosen from a list of problem categories. Note that the program "formulates a problem solution which it presents to the user." In short, the computer program contains the source and definition of the "problem," and the student's role is limited to posing questions in a format that has been selected by the programmer. The program then proposes a solution based upon the "problem" that has been provided. This description parallels almost precisely the characteristics of explanatory understanding. It is granted that such a computer use is considerably more sophisticated than "traditional rote learning orientation" and includes other aspects of learning, such as the development of higher-order thinking and planning skills, that may result from interaction with the technology and effects of situational factors that are involved.

HOW IS TEACHING FOR EXPLORATORY UNDERSTANDING RELATED TO COMPUTER TEACHING?

Exploratory-understanding-level teaching promotes purposive involvement and perplexity in students. It consists of problem raising and problem solution within a process of teacher-student cooperative inquiry and evaluation.

A computer-centered dilemma lies in the following: Whereas social democratic and scientific outlooks point education toward teaching for an exploratory-understanding level, computer teaching, to date, has centered upon memory and explanatory-understanding levels, within which the ultimate teaching machine for operant conditions is a computer. In light of the meaning of exploratory-understanding level of teaching and learning, is there any reason to think that computers may be able to lend themselves to this level of teaching? Yes; though it is not easy, computers can be employed in teaching for exploratory understanding.

There is nothing inherent in a given tool that requires that it be used in a mechanistic, reductionist, or atomistic fashion. Mathematics teachers who confine the use of hand-held calculators to drill in the basic arithmetical operations are simply using a machine to save time. The same hand-held calculator, however, can be used as a *tool* or *instrument* to solve complex problems that an individual originates in a purposive manner. By the same token, there are a number of experiments and investigations that imply the assumptions of exploratory-understanding level teaching.

A quite recent and as yet largely undeveloped computer strategy is known as "hypertext" (also called "multimedia interaction"). Hypertext involves the selection of literally hundreds of different kinds of data on a CD ROM, which, as its name suggests, is permanent, read-only storage of data on the same kind of compact disc as is used for audio records. A history teacher, for instance, can use a disk programmed with maps, charts, graphs, diary excerpts, photographs, newspaper articles, memoranda, letters, and even animations, music, sound, and moving pictures. By pressing the right command keys, a user can instantly retrieve whatever information has been stored that relates in some way to the information that the user has already retrieved. With many different kinds of data and with help, a student can learn to do what only historians in the past have been able to do: identify a historical problem, locate a variety of different kinds of data, and interpret primary sources and secondary works. Although hypertext programs are commercially available, their use is presently quite limited. Hypertext, however, provides an emergent illustration of innovations in computer use that depart from the traditional use of computers.

Why could one argue that *this* organization of content might reflect an exploratory-understanding view of learning? Here is an informative quotation from an entire issue devoted to hypertext:

> The essence of hypertext is the dynamic linking of concepts, allowing the reader to follow preferences instantaneously and to be in control. The scope of a topic is no longer defined by editor or author and is limited only by the initiative of the reader.... The referenced material could be a paragraph or an article or an entire book.[14]

There is no assumption about rules, procedures, or algorithms. There is no presentation of a topic labeled as a problem. There is no premise that there is a component of mind that, once developed, will transfer to another set of circumstances. The assumption appears to be that, under certain circumstances, students will be able to generate their own problems and questions and that access to a large amount and variety of different references will provide both data and the origin of subsequent problems.

Another similar use of hypermedia relates to a study of literature. A given hypertext file may be programmed with all of the published and unpublished works of a given poet. It may also include extensive biographies of the author, as well as a selected reference list. It may be programmed to include readings of poems by prominent actors, critical analyses, diaries, newspaper clippings, journal articles, and maps indicating geographical areas relevant to the poet. A discerning teacher may use hypermedia to encourage students to compare different texts or perhaps to compare conflicting interpretations or criticisms of a given poem. The teacher may use a concordance to assist student in examining patterns of word usage. A map may even be used to *raise* a problem. For example, how could one account for the disproportionately large number of poets and writers from certain counties in Ireland? Students being encouraged simply to "scroll" through a hypermedia program could well construct and identify their own problems simply by being encouraged to be alert to the unexpected, to that which does not make sense, or to strange or unusual uses of rhyme, rhythm, alliteration, hyperbole, scansion, or other literary devices.

One of the authors (Shermis) has deliberately attempted to devise computer uses that reflect exploratory-understanding level learning involving undergraduate and graduate students in education who have been asked to generate problems and prepare research papers. The usual experience is that most teachers who ask for any extended written treatment usually discover that many, if not most, students are unable to organize ideas or to support arguments. For example, introductions are missing, conclusions are tossed in haphazardly, value judgments are made but are unsupported, the same ideas or observations are repeated three or four times, concepts are undeveloped, and the writing abounds in *non sequiturs* and breathless logical leaps.

The author has employed a technique involving a student who believes he/she has located a problem and who is then asked to sit with the instructor before a computer used as a word processor. (Many recent printers can, if switched to "draft mode," print as many as 300 characters per second. This permits an entire page to be printed in 10-15 seconds.) The student is asked to list ideas, concepts, principles, generalizations, conclusions, or questions concerning his chosen topic, in no order whatsoever. A "hard copy" or "printout" is then made, and the student is asked to examine and think about it for a few minutes.

The next stage requires the student to play with the concepts, principles, and observations by trying to discover pertinent relationships. Could a certain phrase be used as a title? Are these two ideas related? Is there some affinity or connection between *this* question and *that* concept? Then the next stage requires the student, using the capacity of the computer to erase information, to move it up and down, or to join two sentences, to reorganize the concepts so that they form something that—to the student—"makes sense." The ideas are then reorganized as the second draft of what is now shaping up as an outline. The student then is asked to take this draft home and think about it some more.

The next stage involves both the student and the instructor, again in front of the computer, this time for the purpose of seeing which ideas can be grouped as major subheadings, what might function as an introduction, and what might be a conclusion. The outline is then reworked to include the newly reorganized information, and the student is assisted in asking some analytic questions of the newly revised outline; for example,

What ideas will require additional support?

What might be missing?

Can you identify an assumption that is implicit that perhaps ought to be made explicit?

Where might a summary—if this is necessary—be placed?

What can be done to create a conclusion through use of subquestions?

Subquestions, in turn, include the following: If *this* proposition is accepted, what consequences flow from it? What implications follow from what has been said? Given certain statements made in the article, what might be predicted or anticipated? What new ideas, only raised so far, might be useful as questions to be asked later? Similarly, if there are some problems that have not yet been identified, what are they? What interpretation would you, the writer, like to make? Is there a final, definitive statement that might effectively conclude the paper?

There is nothing especially novel about this strategy. It simply allows a rapid visual inspection of a large mass of ideas. Precisely the same thing could be done with a typewriter, paper, and a pair of scissors. The unique characteristics of the computer, however, permit rapid reorganizing and reordering of a good many complex concepts, with the student being allowed to move something from here to there, combine it, eliminate it, or expand upon it. In fact, once this preliminary organization is accomplished—which most students have indicated is both useful and stimulating—the actual writing of the paper is much less time-consuming and tedious.

It is readily granted that a plethora of such data may not add up to any sort of exploratory understanding. Indeed, it is also granted that this use of computers is so new that any argument concerning it is debatable. It is entirely likely that teachers habituated to thinking in terms other than exploratory understanding can subvert hypertext, the technique described above, and any other computer use. Indeed, teachers have often assimilated most other "reforms" and "innovative strategies" into traditional content-covering processes.

Some authors cite reasons to believe that the critical factor is not really the computer but rather the knowledge, skill, and willingness of a teacher to allow students to identify and pursue their own intellectual goals. Some even believe that what is being measured in thousands of experiments on computers is not what the computer is capable of doing but more the *novelty* effect of the computer, which perhaps can be described as the striking capacity of the computer to retrieve information in a split second, to display catchy graphics, to do precisely what someone tells it to do, and not to lose patience with a fumbling student; and to the fact that computer mastery in our society yields status, much the same as skill in riding horses or shooting rifles accurately did in our agrarian frontier past.

TENTATIVE CONCLUSIONS

People generally have used computers to do much more quickly those things that they have done all along. But they are not utilizing the computer's potential; they are limited in their vision to doing what they have always done, but doing it more quickly.

The future of computers as a unique species of technology in classrooms cannot be accurately predicted. Although computers have certainly been assimilated into many of the nation's classrooms, in fact, most classrooms do not have computers. Although only a limited number of teachers are on record as opposing the educational use of computers, many teachers do not in fact have computer skills, many have no burning incentive to acquire them, and some are simply anxious and apprehensive when they get near a computer. It would seem, however, that industrial advertising, administrative bandwagon effects, and pressures of the community are likely to increase, not decrease, computer use in schools.[15] Also, the preponderance of computer use in schools is concerned, not with exploration or reflective problem solving (at least not in the exploratory sense of this concept), but with drill, practice, and rote-memory acquisition of low-level concepts.

Whereas, within the last decade, there are a good many claims that computer use does enhance cognitive skills and problem solving, the hard evidence that this is the case indeed is either lacking or unpersuasive.

However, technology often appears to take on a life of its own and to create its own agenda and purposes. It is also true that technology is always a two-edged sword. For example, television can be used to provide mindless "sitcoms," professional wrestling, and unending commercials as well as thought-provoking, stimulating in-depth treatment of a wide number of issues and concerns. There is no inherent reason why the technology of computers cannot be adopted to thoughtful ends.

It is certainly conceivable that the spreading use of hypertext will require teachers to change their roles from information providers to facilitators of research. It may also be imagined that having become familiar with computers and having learned to experiment and play with new ideas, teachers will invent their own uses that will allow students to employ computers as tools to their own self-chosen ends. For example, a colleague of an author living in New Zealand is carrying on an experiment with the use of databases by high school students to frame their own questions, gather pertinent data, and employ statistical analysis. There is also another recent program, *Hometown*, which encourages students to create a questionnaire, interview a population sample, input the data into a program, and analyze the results.

The uses cited above, however, may be little more than straws in the wind; or they may signal a momentous change in the use of the computer to alter the role of teachers.

NOTES

1. Robert M. Gagné, *The Conditions of Learning*, 2nd ed. (New York: Holt, Rinehart and Winston, 1970), p. 216.
2. See Seymour Papert, *Mindstorms: Children, Computers, and Powerful Ideas* (New York: Basic Books, 1980).
3. Personal communication with Dr. Terry Northup, Dean, College of Education, McMurry State University, McMurry, TX, December 1990.
4. See Kathy A. Krendl and Debra A. Lieberman, "Computers and Learning: A Review of Recent Research," *Journal of Educational Computing Research* 4 (1988): 370.

5. Joanne S. Smith and Marcia C. Linn, "Capitalizing on Computer-Based Interactive Feedback," in Milton Chen and William Paisley, *Children and Microcomputers* (Beverly Hills, CA: Sage Foundation, 1985), p. 214.

6. Judah L. Schwartz, "Intellectual Mirrors: A Step in the Direction of Making Schools Knowledge-Making Places," *Harvard Educational Review* 59 (February, 1989): 51.

7. David Eli Drew, "Why Don't All Professors Use Computers?" *Academic Computing* (October, 1989): 13.

8. Ibid., p. 12.

9. Christopher O'Malley, "The Revolution Is Yet To Come," *Personal Computing* (October, 1989): 119.

10. Greg Stragnell, "DIG—An Archaeological Simulation: Investigate, Analyze and Interpret," *New York Times Education Supplement* 3728 (December 11 and 12, 1987): 36.

11. Ibid., p. 36.

12. Described well by A. J. Romiszowski, "Artificial Intelligence and Expert System in Education: Potential Promise or Threat to Teachers?" *Educational Media International* 24 (June, 1987): 96–104. Here the author deals with problems in defining such standard computer terminology as "computer," "artificial," and "intelligence."

13. Ibid., p. 96.

14. Ann F. Bevilacqua, "Hypertext: Behind the Hype," *American Libraries* 20 (February, 1989): 158. A useful source of information on this topic is an entire issue devoted to hypertext, *Educational Technology*, 28 (March, 1988), containing articles with titles such as "Designing Structured Hypertext and Structuring Access to Hypertext," "Hypermedia in Instruction and Training: The Power and the Promise," "Authoring Considerations for Hypertext."

15. For a review of literature that is skeptical about computer claims and critical of present computer use, see Michael Apple, "Hidden Effects of Computers on Teachers and Students," *Educational Digest* 53 (October, 1987): 2–6; C. A. Bowers, *Cultural Dimensions of Educational Computing: Understanding the Non-Neutrality of Technology*, New York: Teachers College Press, 1988; C. A. Bowers, "Teaching a Nineteenth-century Mode of Thinking Through a Twentieth-century Machine," *Educational Theory* 38 (Winter, 1988): 41–46; John W. Murphy and John T. Pardeck, "The Technological World-View and the Responsible Use of Computers in the Classroom," *Boston University Journal of Education* 167 (February, 1985): 98–107; and Douglas Sloan, ed., *The Computer In Education: A Critical Perspective*.

BIBLIOGRAPHY, CHAPTER 14

Apple, Michael. "Hidden Effects of Computers on Teachers and Students." *Educational Digest* 53 (October 1987): 2–6. A negative appraisal of the effects of computer use in education.

Bevilacqua, Ann F. "Hypertext: Behind the Hype." *American Libraries* 20 (February, 1989): 158. Develops a computer-simulated archeological "dig." An entire issue is devoted to an explanation of "hypertext."

Bowers, C. A. *Cultural Dimensions of Educational Computing: Understanding the Non-Neutrality of Technology*. New York: Teachers College Press, 1988. Exposes the generally mechanistic commitment of computer education enthusiasts.

Bowers, C. A. "Teaching a Nineteenth-century Mode of Thinking through a Twentieth-century Machine." *Educational Theory* 38 (Winter, 1988). A negative appraisal of current computer teaching.

Chen, Milton and William Paisley, eds. *Children and Microcomputers*. Beverly Hills, CA: Sage Publications, 1985. A symposium on computer technology, teaching, educational effects, and future prospects. Chapter 1 is an excellent introduction to computer teaching.

Culbertson, Jack A. and Luverne L. Cunningham, eds. *Microcomputers and Education*. Chicago: University of Chicago Press, 1986. A symposium on computer education programs and the application of computer technology in education. Chapter 6, pp. 109–131, by Jack Culbertson, is especially pertinent.

Drew, David Eli. "Why Don't All Professors Use Computers?" *Academic Computing* (October 1989). Shows how one graduate institution is using a program called *Ibycus* to analyze ancient Greek, Coptic, and Hebrew texts.

Kinzer, Charles K., Robert D. Sherwood and John Bransford. *Computer Strategies for Education: Foundations and the Content Area Application*. Columbus, OH: Merrill Publishing Company, 1986. Develops slightly dated history and status of computer education.

Krendl, Kathy A. and Debra A. Lieberman. "Computers and Learning: A Review of Recent Research." *Journal of Educational Computing Research* 4 (1988). The authors review recent research and show how tutorial simulations and drill-and-practice exercises have, to date, dominated computer use in education.

Murphy, John W. and John T. Pardeck. "The Technological World View and the Responsible Use of Computers in the Classroom." *Boston University Journal of Education* 167 (2, 1985): 98–107. Develops relations of world views and classroom computer uses.

O'Malley, Christopher: "The Revolution Is Yet to Come." *Personal Computing* (October 1989). Texas school district students explore chemistry and physics with a mix of traditional laboratory procedures and use of a videodisc computer system.

Papert, Seymour. *Mindstorms: Children, Computers, and Powerful Ideas*. New York: Basic Books, 1980. A "Logo" approach to learning, underpinned by Piaget's "genetic epistemology," is developed especially for teaching mathematics and science.

Romiszowski, A. J. "Artificial Intelligence and Expert System in Education: Potential Promise or Threat To Teachers?" *Educational Media International* 24 (June 1987): 96–104. Explains the goals of an archeological "dig" to develop analytical and decision making skills. Describes how one computer program teaches problem solving.

Schwartz, Judah L. "Intellectual Mirrors: A Step in the Direction of Making Schools Knowledge-Making Places," *Harvard Educational Review* 59 (February 1981). Develops "discovery method" of teaching for explanatory understanding illustrated by teaching rules of mathematics by manipulating geometric figures on a screen.

Sloan, Douglas, ed. *The Computer In Education: A Critical Perspective*. New York: Teachers College Press, 1985. A critical appraisal of the use of computers in schools. See "Putting Computers in Their Proper Place," pp. 40–63.

Stragnell, Greg. "DIG—an Archeological Simulation: Investigate, Analyze, and Interpret." *New York Times Education Supplement* 3728 (December 11 and 12, 1987). A description of how students follow a study of general archeological techniques, first with a simplified "dig" and then a simulation of a real archeological excavation.

Index